SALESMANSHIP:

PERSONAL COMMUNICATIONS
AND PERSUASION
IN MARKETING

**FIG. 1.  A salesman for DuPont explosives and the quarry superintendent view spectacular blast at Cherokee Dam in Tennessee.**

# SALESMANSHIP:
# PERSONAL COMMUNICATIONS
# AND PERSUASION
# IN MARKETING

by

THOMAS F. STROH
*Florida Atlantic University*

1966
RICHARD D. IRWIN, INC.
Homewood, Illinois

Library of Congress Catalog Card No. 66–24616

Printed in the United States of America

# PREFACE

The author has a firm commitment to the marketing concept of customer orientation for greater long term profits to the supplier and the role of selling in the American economy. However, if one wishes to learn some useful generalities about marketing a product—specifically about the personal selling of an item or service—he is faced with a dichotomy of existing literature. Either it is inspirational with little regard for knowledge and truth; or it is textual, relying on a single discipline.

This work is directed to college students interested in communication and persuasion basically as they apply in business. It is further intended to give some insight into oneself for a more realistic and mature viewpoint as well as a better understanding of others.

The approach is to provide findings which will enable the salesman to perform his role more effectively and to predict within an ever decreasing margin of error the effects of his decisions and actions. This should be more in keeping with the graduate school of business orientation. By almost any definition, sales—or personal communication and persuasion in marketing—is related to human activity and should include a large proportion of applied behavioral science. We must borrow the findings, methods, and insights of other disciplines but maintain the organization of business education in marketing. We are dealing with many senior citizens in business who have earned their positions of decision and command. Immediate feedback is available if one is bold enough to apply his classroom theory and experiments to the cold, hard reality of the business world.

On the other hand, preparing young people for a future sales job can be dangerous in that some of them get so wrapped up in the future that they cannot see the present. At the college level, many students do not know what career they want to pursue in life. Even experienced salesmen often have self-doubts about their choice of professions. No one can know what the future really holds for him because opportunities will appear that he could not have foreseen.

At the college level, a course in a business subject should do more than teach a vocational technique. It should attempt to broaden the students' outlook on all of life and hopefully it should provide the basis for a greater understanding of people. This has been the guiding philosophy throughout this endeavor.

Most business subjects are founded on economic theory, often with a second discipline superimposed for increased meaning. But new insights, productive hypotheses, and useful increments to knowledge have come from many quarters. None need be neglected in order to bolster another. This particular work is a multi-discipline approach which attempts to draw applicable material from many sources in the spirit of the liberal arts tradition. The serious student will be able to identify elements of business administration, marketing, economics, psychology, sociology, anthropology, law, political science, history, logic, ethics, and rhetoric. It is not an attempt to teach any one of these areas but only to excerpt minute portions which seem to be appropriate to the discussion. Therefore, it is hoped this work can serve both as a culmination for such subjects indicating one practical application of pure theory as well as an interesting guide of self development for the beginning student.

Instructors might be interested to know that for the traditionalist, the fundamentals of salesmanship have been preserved. Indeed, this work was used for several such courses at the Community College level. For those who wish such a course to be broader and more meaningful, for example to college students who are not marketing majors, there is a multi-discipline approach and organization which enables each instructor and each student to pursue his interest in greater depth. This material was used for college seniors with rewarding results. Finally, for those who would pursue the "why" of behavior more than the "how to" of technique, there is considerable material for individual direction. This material is being used effectively as the basis for training college graduates in industry for various functions of marketing.

To the cynic who would doubt the validity of learning theory for improving a skill such as persuasion in business, one can only say that it is not necessary for a student to repeat the same mistakes which we in marketing have made for twenty years before he recognizes patterns and generalizations which are more effective. Vicarious learning can shorten the trial and error period considerably. On the other hand, it is very true that such a skill is developed and perfected by actual practice in one's daily life. Knowledge, in this sense, must be put to use and become habitual behavior before it can be classified as a skill. Hence, while knowledge of communication and persuasion must precede the skill of selling, its value to oneself and to humanity is the skillful use of such knowledge. With this aid to personal development and growth, many of life's frustrations and irritations can be reduced. Knowing how to change or at least modify the behavior of others is the fundamental message of this text. Such knowledge can be rewarding to the individual and to society only through the proper use in one's daily life.

Such a broad approach could not be undertaken by one mind -limited in knowledge, experience and time. The author is indebted to many specialists in the various disciplines for analysis and application of theory to this subject matter. He is particularly indebted to Abraham Shuchman and Alfred R. Oxenfeldt, both of Columbia University Graduate School of Business and to Walter H. MacGinitie of the Psychology Department and Mary Ellen Oliverio of the Business Education Department, both of Teachers College. While they will hardly agree with everything in the text, they will surely recognize their pervasive influences.

The author is grateful for the constructive help of Harry E. Cohen of the Marketing Department of the Bernard Baruch School of Business of C.C.N.Y. as well as Albert Haas of the Business Administration Department of the University of the State of New York at Farmingdale. Their encouragement and constructive criticism of the use of this material in a number of classes helped to enlighten the author. Of course, the college students themselves contributed immeasurably as have graduates using this material in business training for industrial marketing. In this last context, James M. Dysart of the N.S.S.T.E. has been most helpful.

Finally, the author assumes full responsibility for the synthesis and of course all errors of both logic and content. It is hoped this will serve as a beginning or rough guide for others so that future multi-discipline endeavors will be more exact and meaningful to all students.

THOMAS F. STROH

West Babylon, N.Y.
*August, 1966*

# TABLE OF CONTENTS

## PART I. THE FIELD OF SELLING

## PART II. THE PSYCHOLOGY OF COMMUNICATIONS AND PERSUASION IN PERSONAL SELLING

## PART III. SALES STRATEGY: PLANNING
## A SALES PRESENTATION

## PART IV. TECHNIQUES OF PRACTICAL SELLING

# PART I

# The Field of Selling

# 1

# The Role of Personal Selling in Marketing

In the twentieth century, marketing began as a descriptive study of what happened between the end of the production line and the ultimate user of the product. It detailed the wholesale and retail distribution institutions as an economic activity and described such events as the development of the modern chain stores and discount houses. Marketing was viewed basically as an economic function.

## THE MARKETING CONCEPT

The new marketing concept was popularized during the late 1940s and early 1950s and emphasized five basic ideas. *First*, a business should be customer oriented and not product oriented. In the past, experts such as engineers designed and developed a good substantive product which was highly functional but they had little concern or regard for customer reaction. The masses might not have liked the product. The sales problem then was to find the market which the product fit and to promote the functional superiority of the product. In the new marketing concept business is oriented to the customer. Business studies the consumer's needs and desires so that it can adapt to him and give him a product close to what he wants at a price which permits profitable operations.

*Second*, the new marketing concept champions the doctrine that a business should seek profit rather than sheer dollar volume. Cost studies had often proven that increased volume frequently increased costs disproportionately. Machines could not run at peak efficiency beyond certain designed ranges. Overtime labor costs more than offset the economies of volume purchasing of raw materials. Extra production, beyond a calculable point, actually reduced profits.

The *third* emphasis was on the idea that rapid change in marketing

3

conditions should not only be expected by a firm but that business itself should contribute to change and lead innovation by research and development of new products to replace present products. Much has been written about the public reaction against innovation in some industries which has simply been planned obsolescence without substantive product improvement. The original concept was to improve the consumers' standard of living.

The *fourth* emphasis is on planning, particularly long-range planning, as a vital element for success. Business is encouraged to think through changes that might take place in the future and how it will be able to adapt to such changes. For example, the market for a given product might be expected to drop 15 percent in the next five years and profit would also drop unless a firm added new product features, reduced selling costs, or planned some offsetting action.

Finally, the *fifth* doctrine of the new marketing concept is that of organization. All activities that a business engages in which relate to the customer should be under a single executive and not operated under autonomous or independent branches of a firm. The modern marketing executive should control market research, product planning, product features, customer services to be rendered, distribution channels, advertising, sales promotions, personal selling, and pricing. This executive is all-powerful and has the potential for becoming the company president when he attains and proves his competence in these highly divergent areas.

Thus one can see that behavioral science was brought into marketing to help determine what people are like and to indicate what businessmen might do to change consumer buying habits or to suggest how products and services should be changed to meet the consumers' fixed habits. Market research was brought into marketing to obtain the benefits of quantitative and statistical sciences. Hence, marketing today is more than simply a branch of economics: it is a multiple discipline including economic theory and the applied behavioral sciences of psychology, sociology, anthropology, and history as well as quantitative and statistical science.

## ELEMENTS INCLUDED IN MARKETING

Today, marketing includes market research and motivational research to segment and select specific groups of customer targets. First, the marketing executive must analyze those things at which his company excels, such as mass production or skill at selling to chain stores. Then he must inspect the various customer classifications, searching for uncovered market segments whose interests are either neglected or poorly served. He must determine or select those segments which are compatible with each other and with his company's strong points. He must design products which will appeal to these segments and develop appeals to cultivate those particular segments. In allocating the various resources of his firm, the marketing executive must combine at least seven elements in a "marketing mix" in such a way that the combination will yield the largest number of sales at the lowest cost. These elements include: product quality; price; advertising; personal selling; customer services; nonproduct substantive services, and distribution.

## The Four Ps of Marketing

Traditionally the elements in the marketing mix have been taught as the four Ps: product, price, place, and promotion.

*Product.* The product includes not only the physical product and necessary accessories but also a study of how much quality to put into a product. No product, not even one such as a U.S. outer space vehicle, is so good that it cannot be improved. The problem concerns how much quality is required in a product. Giving a customer what he says he wants can be quite disastrous unless profit is the paramount goal. Surveys of customer wants too often indicate either no opinion or contradictory wants. The customer often is found to be unwilling to pay for the extra he said he wanted. Customers are not loyal to a product or manufacturer for long periods of time. They often fail to recognize a better product, easy to understand when one considers that recognition of superiority is difficult even by trained testing specialists who have all the elaborate testing facilities at their disposal. Often customers do not compare different products in use. They simply purchase one or two brands that serve their needs and shop no further. For product quality, then, manufacturers often invest in demonstrable features for higher immediate profits, since the public often cannot recognize a better product. Even though the past has proven a particular product superior, the consumer often doubts the continued superiority of any single brand.

*Price.* Price is another 'iceberg' type of consideration in that most of the problem is hidden, with very little apparent on the surface. Pricing a new product can be based upon expected production and distribution costs; it can be based upon supply and demand schedules, with the objective of getting as much as the traffic will bear for a desired production level. Prices can be based upon recovering all developmental costs within a limited time period such as three years. However arrived at, price should also include consideration of all the parties involved. This would include, at least, the people within one's firm, such as production and finance personnel; customers and prospective customers; competitors and prospective competitors entering into what appears to be a new and profitable field; suppliers of labor, capital, and raw materials and the prices which they might charge according to how much profit appeared to be within the product; and finally, the government because of its interest in discriminatory practices and limiting of competition.[1]

*Place.* Determination of the place of operation includes not only the decision on the channels of distribution through which a product must travel before reaching the ultimate consumer, such as brokers, distributors, wholesalers, and retailers but also decisions concerning the markets into which a product shall be introduced—both geographically and according to the desired population segments in any given area. Each channel level is expected to perform a service for the manufacturer and, in return, these channel levels demand a profit for their effort. One can easily see how each decision in this composite mix is interrelated with every other decision.

*Promotion.* Having the right product in the right place at the right price is of little value if the consumer does not know about it. Promotion is the fourth P. It includes advertising, promotional literature and point-of-purchase selling aids, and personal selling. It is currently popular to refer to all promotional activities as the "communications mix" because these activities inform the consumer about the product. Unfortunately this is oversimplifying and misleading. Other elements in the marketing mix also communicate. For example, product quality such as "a mirror chrome finish" communicates an image of the superiority of the product or for which market segment it is intended. Modern packaging methods used in the cosmetic industry, for example, have communicated quality messages very successfully to consumers. Customer services such as credit, delivery, or professional aid in the selection of applicable items within a product line and similar services communicate what selective market segment is being sought. They often equally obviously communicate what other segments are incompatible. A drop in price can communicate to some consumers a comparable drop in product quality or the idea that the product is being dumped as a poor selling item. The very place a product is offered (such as an exclusive department store) can communicate quality and

---

[1] For a clear and concise description of the interrelated elements in pricing see Alfred R. Oxenfeldt, *Pricing for Marketing Executives* (San Francisco: Wadsworth Publishing Co., Inc., 1961).

service, product acceptance, or a form of high style endorsement by the intermediary between the manufacturer and the consumer. Similarly, a guarantee communicates a message regarding the expected life of a product.

Advertising, sales promotional literature, and point-of-purchase aids are all forms of nonpersonal influence upon the consuming public. Personal selling is a direct, face-to-face, seller to buyer influence which can communicate the facts necessary for making a buying decision; or it can utilize the psychology of persuasion to encourage the formation of a buying decision.

## WHY PERSONAL SELLING?

Within the realm of promotion, what can personal selling do better than the other elements of the marketing mix? Personal selling is *flexible* in that a message can be adapted or tailored instantaneously to the reaction of each individual buyer. Because of this flexibility, personal selling is *more effective* with each specific prospect than nonpersonal influences would be. It is *less expensive*, for the end results, than other forms of promotion because per dollar return on investment is greater. Industrial selling, for example, might run as high as $65 per call, including supporting people in the home office; however, this is still less expensive than advertising or other nonpersonal selling activities. Business spends approximately $2 billion on outside salesmen annually; this is more than double the expenditure for advertising.[2]

Personal selling is effective whenever demonstration is required for a buyer to understand the offering, due either to product complication, application, or usage. Obviously, personal selling increases in importance directly with the size of the order. Million-dollar machines are not sold through advertising or mail order and it would be equally foolish to sell toothpaste or cigarettes directly to consumers through personal salesmen. Personal selling is more effective under conditions where there are relatively fewer prospects than in mass consumer markets and where the few prospects can be identified. Such prospects tend to be localized or concentrated geographically. Personal selling is mandatory when items are rarely purchased, as in the case of a yacht, or as in the purchase of a new automobile when appraisal of the old car and credit terms must be nego-

---

[2] Indeed, Bursk, Clark, and Hidy state personal selling accounts for three to four times advertising of the sales dollar. (Edward C. Bursk, Donald T. Clark, and Ralph W. Hidy (eds.), *The World of Business*, Vol. I [New York: Simon & Schuster, 1962], p. 514.)

tiated. Personal selling is indicated when personal service, such as training or instruction in product use, is expected by the buyer.

If individual leaders of public opinion are known, personal selling is indicated. Interpersonal groups often include opinion leaders, pioneers, originators, or pacemakers who must be sold before the group will follow. This is often seen with regard to farm products, medical products, and products and services for banking institutions.

Under the conditions cited above, personal selling is more effective because it is adaptable or tailored to meet the specific objections of a single buyer at a time; it permits experimentation and constant improvement of the message; it enables the salesman to demonstrate a product to make the user benefits clear and understandable; it permits a personal relationship to be established between the buyer and the salesman. There is an immediate and personal reward for the buyer because the salesman will like him— and it is human nature to want to be liked. Complicated products are easily understood by a buyer because the salesman can determine what is critical and important for the particular buyer. Because of the personal element and the time permitted, personal selling is more effective than mass media in changing peoples' opinions, which, in marketing at least, must precede changing behavior.

Personal selling expenditures are usually more stable than advertising expenditures because the sales force is less flexible—one rarely fires half his salesmen—and management has more confidence in salesmen who can be evaluated individually on a cost basis. The results of a greater effort by a larger sales force can be more readily predicted than can the results of an increased advertising budget. Consumer goods require a higher advertising budget than that for personal selling, particularly in promoting brand names where the public is sold through strong emotional appeals which are heavily advertised. On the other hand, products which require dealer cultivation at the retail level have relatively higher personal selling costs than advertising costs. Products which move in both consumer and industrial markets, such as typewriters, paint, and hardware supplies, have higher personal selling costs in the industrial portion of the market and higher advertising costs when in the mass consumer market. Industrial products have personal selling costs substantially higher than advertising costs due to the need for many calls and service. Private label brands do little or no advertising and therefore have a high personal selling cost. Finally, promotion costs may vary for each of several products made by one company, with advertising costs heavy on a few items to promote the brand image which then is expected to carry all the products in the line.

Personal selling effort would then be required to gain the dealer's coopera-tion at the retail level to carry and promote the full line of products.

## PERSPECTIVE OF SELLING

The selling job, it can be seen, is more than simply the arrangement for the transfer of goods in exchange for money or other form of value. It is the direct personal influence or the persuading of others to buy or increase the size of their order. When a person enters a store to buy some cigarettes, normally there is no personal selling involved, as indeed vending machines have proven. When a man who had never thought of doing so is persuaded to buy a safe to protect his records, personal selling is involved. Salesman-ship is the persuasive behavior of an individual who uses symbol manipu-lation to produce buying action in others. His symbols are words, pictures, samples, manner, appearance, and the like, and his skill in using these tools determines the buying action. Selling is persuading others to buy. Personal selling is done directly by an individual as distinguished, for example, from mail-order selling or persuasion through advertising, both of which are nonpersonal buying influences.

## CLASSIFICATION OF PERSONAL SELLING

Sales and salesmen can be classified in a number of ways. They can be classified by product, for example, an auto salesman or a life insurance salesman; by level of selling, such as a manufacturer's representative or a wholesale salesman; and so forth. Some of the more popular groupings are
By market or who is doing the buying:
1. Consumers (retail buying in stores or in homes).
2. Retailers (store owners ordering their stock for the shelves).
3. Wholesalers (distributors who buy from producers in carload lots).
4. Manufacturers (processors ordering raw materials).
By nature of the selling operation:
1. Door-to-door selling to the private home.
2. Inside selling within a store or showroom.
3. Outside selling in the customer's office or place of business.
By objective or purpose of the sales call:
1. To produce awareness—as the missionary salesman or detail man in the drug industry who introduces new products to doctors, knowing that it is the patient who will do the actual buying

2. To provide consulting service—as the sales engineer who aids in determining product application to solve a problem—typical of the raw chemical industry
3. To maintain inventory—an order taker who checks stock and advises the store owner to reorder merchandise to a predetermined level
4. To deliver merchandise—as the beer and soda truck sales routeman and the dry cleaning routeman
5. To generate new business—as the creative salesman of commodities or services. He moves merchandise that cannot be moved in equal quantity without him, selling to both old and new accounts. An office machine salesman or a construction material salesman would be typical.

There is much overlapping in classification of sales types. The manner and type of persuasion required in sales varies with the purpose intended. Even within one field, there is much variation in successful sales behavior, which throws suspicion on "typing" salesmen.

## SCOPE

For simplicity, this book is directed toward a study of the efforts of the creative salesman as he attempts to persuade American businessmen. The businessman might be an individual consumer himself, needing an electric typewriter, for example. He might be a store owner or retailer who needs lighting fixtures or additional lines of merchandise to resell or he might be a wholesaler or a manufacturer. He could be a purchasing agent, office manager, an engineer, a plant foreman, or other employee of a large corporation who would influence buying. He might even be the chairman of the board of directors of a corporation.

In past decades it was felt that people could be manipulated with honeyed words, false promises, emotional appeals, flattery, unfounded threats, and irrelevant testimonials, but today's businessman most often sees through such methods of persuasion, and such irrational selling approaches are increasingly self-defeating. Many of the studies and theories covered herein are applicable to most selling forms. Indeed, a true understanding of the various aspects of persuasion and selling psychologies are applicable to many other phases of life—whenever one deals with people. For simplicity, the scope of this book is necessarily narrow and specific; it concentrates on the logical decision-making process of an intelligent businessman who tries to weigh available factors before committing his capital. There is no need, on the other hand, to rule out other types of selling, as the modern emphasis on consumer reports and the like have set the American trend toward more rational buying.

## SUBJECTIVITY OF SALES LITERATURE

Reading through a considerable number of sales books, magazines, articles, and sales manuals, one is struck by the myriad of so-called primary factors in a selling situation which seem to defy grouping and classification. Sales, accordingly, seems something of an art and certainly a far cry from the sciences. Referring to successful sales stories, men in the sales field often state, "Don't argue with success," or they may say, "I know it sounds crazy but it works for him. How can you argue that he is wrong?" Sales experts continue to write articles expounding theories based upon their own personal experience. It works for them and since they are successful, they gain a certain authenticity in the eyes of their audience. Unfortunately, their reports are highly subjective; they are usually based upon one man's experience and his own interpretations which cannot be easily duplicated by other salesmen. Generally they are written honestly enough in view of the understanding of the selling process and how it has worked for that author in a specific field. The message conveyed seems to be, "Develop success by developing good personality habits."

In reality, good and bad personality habits are learned in the same way. An experiment in the psychology of learning illustrates this quite clearly.[3] A group of hungry pigeons was placed in cages constructed so that they received food from swinging hoppers at regular intervals of 15 seconds. Six of eight birds used as the experimental subjects developed extraordinary behavior. One acquired a habit of turning counterclockwise about the cage, making two or three turns between feedings; another developed a tossing response, as if repeatedly lifting up an invisible bar with its head. Two birds showed a pendular swinging of the head and body and the other responses were equally bizarre. The learning process had an obvious source. Each bird happened to be making some movement just before the first food was given. The rewarded response was repeated immediately and the reinforcing additional food came at such short intervals that other behavior did not have time to occur and interfere with the response before it was rewarded again.

The experimental behavior of the pigeons is analogous to superstitions

---

[3] B. F. Skinner, "Superstition in the Pigeon," *Journal of Experimental Psychology*, Vol. 38, 1948, pp. 168–72.

seen in people who perform certain rituals. It is also like the repetitious behavior of some successful salesmen, whose responses, however irrelevant, have been reinforced by the reduction of their anxiety. If a man wore a bright red necktie one day and coincidentally got a large order that day, he might very well testify that his success was due to the red tie. If he repeated the act successfully, as the pigeons did, and reinforced this false impression, it would become, for this salesman, his primary factor for successful selling. Such sales behavior has been written into books and magazines as the accepted procedure for beginners to imitate. Without reason, other than the fact that the author may have made many dollars, trainees are continually urged to emulate such pigeonlike behavior. "Get ready for the food; jump quicker than your competitor for the prize; pull every trick in the book to fool the buyer; but get that sale!" This could be the well-trained pigeon but, unfortunately, it sounds like a poor sales manager instructing the fledgling salesman. At this level, the methods of sales can never gain scientific status.

Successful salesmen do many things scientifically and with insight. Regrettably, much of this behavior is not glamourous and entertaining to tell and therefore it is neglected or glossed over in their career biographies. Many salesmen are successful in spite of their false ideas, not because of them. Those who successfully gain insight often leave it up to their protégés to pick out the scientific selling approaches from the glamourous trivia. Much of what we read from the successful salesman therefore is invalid and untrustworthy because it is so highly subjective and it cannot be duplicated by the would-be learner.

## SUBJECTIVITY OF SALES TRAINING

Assume a likable young man applies for a sales job. Through interviews, references, and aptitude tests it is determined that he is honest, sufficiently intelligent for the particular market, stable, and can work independently. He is ambitious and has adequate education for the job. He is hired as a sales trainee. Then what?

Most companies have a formal training program which stresses knowledge of the product and its various applications. The trainee memorizes several formal talks or presentations to the satisfaction of the sales manager and is then assigned to follow and observe a man who had similar training years ago but now, due to longevity, is a senior salesman. Through mimicry, the trainee is expected eventually to gain the necessary knowledge of technique to be able to sell successfully in his own area. After a relatively brief period (more often dictated by the company's need to fill an area than by the trainee's progress) the trainee is assigned to his own territory and is expected to function with independent success. He is considered a well-prepared salesman!

If the salesman earns $7,000 a year and his company averages 10 percent profit over costs, then the salesman must bring in orders for $70,000 for the company to break even on his efforts. If this new man can carry his own costs for the first year, many industrial companies consider him a promising young man with a bright future and are thus pleased with their training program. If the newcomer should be sufficiently fortunate to bring in a few outstanding orders, both the man and the training program are considered superior. But is this really effective preparation for a sales career? Hogwash! One must consider that if a man sells this early in his career, it is frequently because his past life experience has taught him some of the art of salesmanship. The company has taught him only product facts and nothing of the science of persuasion and sales.

## OBJECTIVE APPROACH TO COMMUNICATIONS AND PERSUASION

The successful salesman, even before recorded history, was the man who could persuade another to exchange some material or other form of value for something that was felt to be of more value to the buyer. How he accomplished this persuasion has not materially changed since early civilization. The task of historically tracing sales techniques, investigating current psychological, sociological, economic, and business administration theories is one of analysis and not creation. It is urgently required by modern sales research. The more one learns of the social sciences, the more obvious becomes the conclusion that successful salesmen practice a science, not an art, even if they are not aware of it!

Research from experiments in social psychology has now accumulated sufficient data to permit a fresh appraisal of sales psychology. Scientific analyses show why certain selling efforts have failed while others have succeeded. New theories of selling can now be formulated on a more scientific foundation with much greater accuracy than in the past.

## QUESTIONS TO BE ANSWERED

In most instances, the junior salesman makes many calls and eventually he will become exposed to a potential buyer who is aware of a need but has no existing source of supply. If three competing new salesmen call on this buyer, only one, obviously, will get the order. *For what reason does this buyer accept one valid argument while rejecting the other equally valid arguments?* Each reader will have an opinion on this; each sales magazine will suggest its novel idea and present the unique case histories illustrating the particular success of a salesman in solving his individual problem. Can this be considered scientific analysis? Again, hogwash! All the subjective opinions available only serve to illustrate the art of sales. There is, however, objective data which can be obtained from controlled experiments that can be readily reproduced which indicate the value of the scientific approach to the techniques of sales.

*Why does a businessman listen attentively to one interesting presentation but not to another equally interesting presentation?* The subjective data here again are voluminous and point only to the art of sales. Each illustration is unique and applies to one specific product in a given situation. Is there any objective data on the subject of human attention maintenance which can be used to formulate the fundamental principles that underlie these subjective theories? Yes. Research in the science of psychology has provided one sound basis for making professional salesmanship a science.

*Why does an intelligent businessman twist what is said by most would-be persuaders?* Is human nature so fickle? Is the attention span so brief or is it something else? Each sales manager could contribute a serious explanation of this observed phenomenon based upon his own concrete experience. One can read literally hundreds of plausible reasons and very few will be alike. As long as this concrete and valuable experience is left in an isolated subjective form, sales will remain solely an art. It is possible to find objective data, formulate and test a hypothesis, and emerge with a proven theory. Thanks to the objective data of social psychological research, sales can now move outward to become a behavioral science.

*Within one company, why does one executive encourage a given argument while another will simultaneously discourage the same argument?* Most salesmen and sales managers can exchange stories all night about a "big deal" gained or lost due to several executives being involved in the buying decision. Is it possible to use this subjective experience, collect this isolated data, and put professional salesmanship on a scientific footing? There is a danger in taking these stories at face value, of course, but the social sciences can safely guide the study to a sound foundation.

*Why does a businessman, reasonably satisfied with one supplier and under relatively stable conditions, switch partially or completely to another supplier?* Here again sales literature abounds in subjective experiences which are, for the most part, alike only in their illustration of creative thinking in the novel situation where there are proven psychological principles which might apply. This study will later illustrate how they apply.

## DIRECTION

The early chapters of this synthesis are an attempt to communicate to the reader those psychological theories and social psychological experiments which seem to apply to persuading men in business. Later chapters are devoted to a discussion of the major strategies or approaches to sales, from canned or planned talk through so-called depth selling and team selling. Criticism of each strategy is meant to be constructive in the light of known social science factors previously cited. The hope is to make the salesman aware of what basic approach he is now using, why it works when it does, and, more importantly, why it so often does not succeed. In this instance the hope is that new knowledge will become a powerful force toward inducing self-improvement.

Even in legend, one will not meet a man who can sell all businessmen, nor does one ever expect to meet him. No one individual can possibly be an expert in all fields. This is not to say one cannot improve. Modern sales training must improve to be effective. Given some insight into his blind spots and some general quide lines into the science of persuasion, each salesman should improve. Whether or not he makes the effort to improve determines whether he will become the professional salesman or will merely remain the reflexing pigeon.

## SUMMARY

Personal selling is the direct, face-to-face, persuasion of others to buy. Sales can be classified in many ways. The most popular classifications are (1) by market, (2) by the nature of the selling job, and (3) by the objective or purpose of the salesman. For simplicity and clarity, this book directs its attention to the salesman who is attempting to persuade American businessmen in their own places of business. While this may seem a narrow and specific approach, there is no need to rule out other types of selling since many of the studies and theories used can apply to most other types of selling as well.

Much sales literature today is invalid or untrustworthy because it is highly subjective and individual reports of successful sales cannot be duplicated by others. Sales training in business today generally consists of emphasis on product knowledge and a highly subjective tutorial system. There is little or no focus on the scientific aspects of persuasion. A study of the data contained in research papers submitted by social psychologists can provide foundation for an objective approach and for the scientific basis for future sales theory and training. In this book, the discussion will evaluate some of the known major aspects of persuasion and apply them to the five recognizable psychological approaches to selling.

◆    ◆    ◆

## THE MARKETS*

The challenge to sales today is a far cry from the one traditionally characterizing selling in the past. The press of competition and the outpouring of Twentieth Century technology have shattered sales concepts once held to be immutable.

In earlier centuries, the fundamental materials used by man were few; their uses followed traditional lines. While there were variations, differences were more in degree than in kind. Competing salesmen offered the same products to the same customers for substantially the same end uses. The salesman's "personal following" was his chief asset, firmly cultivated.

Time has not dimmed the importance of personal relationships in selling, but it has drastically altered the functions of the salesman. It has presented him with a new range of markets and with responsibilities his predecessors never anticipated.

Research and technology have blurred the boundary lines that once separated nature's materials and the uses to which they were put. Coal's prominence as a fuel was challenged by oil; oil's by gas. Coal is no longer merely a fuel; it has become a raw material for the synthesis of hundreds of products which have no counterpart in nature. Furniture can be made of plastic or metal, as well as of wood. Wood, in turn, has become an ingredient of rayon and cellophane.

Interchangeability has become the distinguishing sales characteristic of the century. Just as the concept of interchangeable parts shaped the progress of industry through the Nineteenth Century, so interchangeable products shape the Twentieth. Where once a salesman with an exclusive "key ingredient" was in an invincible position, today he is just another competitor. Du Pont cellophane salesmen not only face stiff competition from two other cellophane makers, but they must sell against glassine, wax paper, metal foil, kraft paper, and a host of other wrapping materials. Similarly, a building materials salesman can take little comfort from the fact that his price on brick betters competi-

---

* The above is reprinted with the kind permission of E. I. du Pont de Nemours & Company, Inc., Wilmington, Delaware, from "The Salesman Story," 1955.

tion's. The buyer may well forget brick entirely, and sheath his building in aluminum, glass, wood, composition shingles, or plastic-coated steel panels.

This new competition is the driving force for new product research and increased production efficiency. To hold his own in a market of interchangeable products, a salesman must produce better ways to help his customers. In essence, he must help create products with maximum consumer appeal.

To give sales forces the best possible tools for creative selling, more and more companies have diversified their products across a broad spectrum. In a vigorously competitive climate, new products often make old ones obsolete at astonishing speed; to stifle research is to invite disaster. (Du Pont's records show that over one-half of the company's sales today are in products stemming from Du Pont research, and introduced within the past 25 years.) With history likely to repeat itself, many modern manufacturers choose to keep many eggs in many baskets, and depend upon their agile sales forces to stay at least one step ahead of customers' swift-growing needs.

America's history has been marked by a growing sales effort to keep that economy progressing. The challenges of the future, though, and the potential gains it holds for consumers, far exceed those of the past.

By 1976, assuming only a straightforward projection of present trends, with no economic daydreams added, a typical worker's annual income, now about $4000, is expected to jump to $5900 per year, with a shorter work week. Americans may be buying two million new houses a year instead of one million, ten million cars instead of seven million, and twice as many home furnishings and appliances. Overall, individual living standards are expected to climb 46 per cent.

The future is bright, but to make it a fact an enormous creative selling effort will be required. If this potential is realized, the consumer, as always, will be the principal beneficiary.

# 2

# What It Takes to Be an
# Effective Salesman

Recruiting and training good salesmen is widely recognized as one of American industry's most pressing problems. However, there is little agreement among executives or educators as to what makes a good salesman. There is such disagreement because industry searches for traits or attributes which will objectively identify the "ideal salesman" who is equipped to cope effectively with any problem in any organization. Industry thus searches for those innate traits or characteristics to identify what good salesmen are rather than what good salesmen do.

## THE PROBLEM OF GETTING THE RIGHT JOB

Qualified salesmen and interested applicants are in short supply today for several reasons.

1. A selling career currently doesn't have the prestige and glamour that are attached to other professions.

2. The generally high level of business activity enables educated people to get and switch jobs easier and, as a result, selling is competing with many alternative vocational opportunities.

3. The dip in the population age curve caused by the low birth rate of the 1930s has also had a limiting effect on the current supply of salesmen. In the 1960s there are fewer men in the 25 to 35 age bracket from which salesmen are drawn than there will be after 1970.

Young applicants for a sales job are in the position of being able to demand enough information about the job to determine their chances of being satisfied and successful.[1] If they select the right job they will find

---

[1] For a note on this reversal of job interviewing roles, see Philip Salisbury, "Notes from the Editor's Side Pocket. Questions without Answers," *Sales Management*, May 7, 1965, p. 90.

training easier and later they will have less supervision. The work itself will be stimulating and they will be highly productive. Once established, good salesmen find the work progressively easier. Long tenure in a territory can help a salesman to build goodwill. He becomes familiar with the customers' needs, problems, and desires and they place their confidence in him. Finally, the need to get the right job for the right man at the beginning is particularly important to the applicant who wishes to develop into a future sales executive.

One of the reasons a selling career does not have the prestige that is attached to other professions is that sales managers tend to overrate the qualifications needed to fill the job. This results in greatly increasing the chances of salesmen being bored, dissatisfied, and eventually leaving because the position offers no challenge. While management may lose its investment in recruitment and training, which incidently in 1963 averaged about $8,300 per trainee, the dissatisfied man who leaves has lost something even more precious.[2] He has wasted part of his life at the most important time of his business career. Getting the right start is essential to young educated people. If sales management does not analyze the job and draw up realistic qualifications, then the applicant should. With the continued shortage of good salesmen, an intelligent applicant can literally call the tune.

## STANDARDS OF SUCCESS

The standards of success used by one firm are not necessarily valid for others even in the same industry. Companies handling the exact same items such as brand name appliances may require different qualities in their salesmen because of differences in objectives or methods. For example, a manufacturer that is interested in high sales volume, fast inventory turnover, and low margin on each unit sale will require different characteristics in its salesmen from those required by the company whose objective is high unit margin with extensive customer services.

The various types of sales work require different characteristics. Qualifications differ for a consumer route salesman selling such products as milk, bread, laundry, and other repeat items from the qualifications required for a business specialty salesman selling business machines, advertising, insurance, air conditioning, or accounting services. The traits found in successful sales engineers will not be the same as those held by the successful sales

---

[2] These figures are based upon periodic surveys by Sales and Marketing Executives International, New York, as quoted by Leon Morse in "The Sound of a Different Drummer," *Dun's Review and Modern Industry*, August, 1963.

people in consumer specialties such as selling vacuum cleaners or brushes by the door-to-door method.

Even within a given firm salesmen who have done only an average job in one territory have become very successful after a transfer to another area. Often social and ethnic factors are the key to success in one geographic area but become an obstacle somewhere else. The man who dresses in the latest high style and sincerely behaves accordingly might not do well selling to garages and service stations yet he might be very successful selling the same products and services to top executives in their corporate offices. There are many cases of men who became a huge success with one company after being average or less in an earlier sales job.

Standards of success should vary with the type of selling involved, the individual company, the individual territory, and the individual qualifications of the applicant. One anonymous company is said to have made a detailed study of the past history of its data-processing machine salesmen to determine what characteristics a good salesman should have. They checked for sensitivity to people, intelligence, motivation, social poise, independence, and the like. The traits common to the top 200 salesmen showed:

1. A strong desire for early recognition. They had dominant fathers who emphasized the son's need to succeed, with heavy emphasis on material success.
2. Boundless energy.
3. Boundless confidence in themselves. Less successful salesmen were from families in which the son fought the father and tried to outdo him. Least successful were those who had a background of a happy family life.
4. A chronic hunger for money with an almost abnormal desire to show off themselves and their material possessions.
5. A habit of industry to the extreme extent of being physically uncomfortable when not busy.
6. A tendency to regard every obstacle and threat as a challenge and to exhibit a basic need to put something over on a buyer.

One can only hope this company gets the rewards it so justly deserves if it pursues such qualifications in recruiting and hiring.

## COMMON QUALIFICATIONS REQUIRED BY SALES MANAGERS

The qualities considered essential for success in a selling career read almost identically to those for any successful career. Basic character qualities include such things as honesty and trustworthiness; stability, firmness, and resolution; courage and fearlessness; initiative, or enterprise to pursue and exploit; industry to make a diligent effort to act and exert oneself; thoroughness in absolute and complete mastery of a job; ambition, or a zeal and eagerness to reach high goals; and finally, self-discipline, or control through willpower.

Human qualities considered essential for success include such things as a liking for people; an understanding of people; tact and consideration; loyalty and allegiance; sincerity and directness; enthusiasm and an ability to stimulate the emotions; cheerfulness in disposition; cooperativeness in teamwork; and a constructive outlook or positive approach to life.

Mental qualities essential for sales success include teachability, flexibility, judgment, observation, analytical ability, foresight, business sense, knowledge, imagination, and resourcefulness.

Impressionistic criteria used to judge successful salesmen include health, energy, dress, neatness, poise and self-confidence, stature and bearing, voice and speech. Finally, successful salesmen are judged by their degree of maturity, which includes the ability to assume responsibility; the ability to take criticism and praise gracefully; a well-developed social instinct, or the appreciation and understanding of the rights of others and the realization of one's social and civic obligations; selflessness, or the ability to think in terms of the interests of the whole rather than of narrow, personal ends.

While no individual can be perfect in every item on this selected list, successful salesmen generally are above average in intelligence, have a high level of verbal facility, a broadly based interest pattern, and are especially interested in persuasive activities. They usually exhibit a high degree of objectivity in interpersonal relations, and are highly agreeable and very cooperative. They possess a good character and are above average in maturity, with an abundance of attractive human qualities.

The problem of judging such qualifications is that there is no way to measure or test these characteristics or to evaluate the degree or amount of each necessary for success. How much imagination must a salesman have to be a success and how much does a high degree of industry offset a minimum of thoroughness?

## WHAT MAKES AN EFFECTIVE SALESMAN DIFFERENT FROM EFFECTIVE PEOPLE IN OTHER FIELDS?

### A Salesman Is the Company

To customers individually and to society in general, the salesman represents his company. Whatever the salesman does or says, the impression

*Courtesy: E. I. du Pont de Nemours Co., Wilmington, Del.*

**FIG. 2. A salesman calls on one of his retail accounts.**

he makes on people becomes the basis for opinions of his firm. This applies whether he is at work or at play, and he must constantly be on his guard in his contacts with the public. The individual salesman builds a firm's goodwill in his area through his behavior in business and private life. People in other fields who are not in contact with the public in their capacity with the company do not have to be on their guard as constantly as do the salesmen. Frequently a poor job done in another occupation within the same firm is never noticed by the customer or the public. However, a salesman is constantly on display and a poor job can do tremendous damage.

## Responsibility

The salesman in the field represents his company independently of immediate supervision. It is his responsibility to establish facts, interpret information, and act upon situations in accord with company policy. The average worker in the home office or factory has constant, immediate, and direct supervision over his activities. The salesman is on his own and when he visits a customer exactly what transpires usually remains unknown to his manager.

## Drive

Most factory and office workers produce steadily without special motivation. The work flow must be processed and any bottleneck is easily noticed and quickly corrected. The salesman in the field is in a position to produce in spurts and loaf in spurts if he so desires, and he must frequently be highly stimulated to do his job properly. The inner drive for a successful salesman must be such that the need for material success is at least equaled if not exceeded by the need to personally succeed. His self-image improves sharply with each successful sale and diminishes with each failure. This personal need causes him to work hard, be persistent, and show great initiative.

## Travel and Time Away from Home

Many sales jobs geographically encompass several states, which requires the men to do considerable traveling and to spend a great amount of time away from home and family. The salesman's wife and children may require him to be home nights or at least not to be away from home for more than a few days at a time. Family sickness often requires a decision to change a call route or time schedule. This is in sharp contrast with other occupations where it is possible simply to phone the office and have someone else handle the work for that day.

Traveling can be physically exhausting once the novelty wears off. Eating in a different restaurant three times a day for many days on end can become annoying, particularly with the highly different styles of cooking and service. It is not easy to be sleeping in a different bed each night and puzzling out different bathing facilities. A salesman under these conditions must be in good health to begin with and maintain constant habits of clean living. Riding in an auto, train, or plane for many hours every day can also be physically demanding. Very often this traveling is done at the end of a busy selling day so as not to cut into precious selling time.

## Use of Company Funds

Most salesmen are authorized to make expenditures for the company and for their own expenses. The salesman is often the sole judge of whom to entertain, how often, and how extensively. He decides where to eat and sleep, where to have his auto serviced, where to take a taxi, and where to take a bus. The proper and wise use of company funds, a responsibility usually reserved for the top few corporate officers, is extended to most salesmen. This responsibility rarely touches successful people in other jobs for the same firm.

## Social Intelligence

Many sales jobs require mixing socially or even entertaining various prospects and customers who may vary considerably in their status within their own social groups. The salesman must be able to deal comfortably with a very high social level as a completely separate and distinct part of his job. His diplomacy and social poise must be far superior to that of other employees of his own firm who are successful but whose jobs do not require after-office-hours contact with the firm's customers.

## Feedback

In marketing today, customer wants, needs, opinions, and desires are eagerly sought by top management of the production companies. This information is required to determine product features, pricing, and many phases of the marketing mix. This information can be effectively obtained by the salesman in the field and fed back to top management. In addition, he is usually the first one aware of competitive actions and campaigns and the customer's reaction to such efforts. Quick reporting of the proper information can be an important element in top management's decisions.

## Emotional Stability

Because of the nature of all selling, the successful salesman will fail to sell more often than he will succeed. Since failure tends to diminish his self-image, his mental toughness cannot be so uncertain that the poor self-image continues for too long a time. The failure must act as a trigger which drives the salesman to greater effort to succeed and again improve his self-image. He must be able to take adverse developments without letting them affect his morale or determination. Most prospects will say no and at times they can be highly sarcastic and even abusive. The salesman must be realistic and highly self-confident.

## The Lone Wolf

Unlike most employees in an office or factory, the salesman operates alone and is rarely observed by anyone from his own company. He travels alone and spends his time in the presence of strangers who are different on each sales call, each meal, and each hotel he stops at. Frequently the salesman sees other salesmen from his own company only at an annual convention. It is virtually impossible under such conditions to receive direct recognition for work habits or self-improvement efforts which the successful salesman develops.

## Skills Required To Be an Effective Salesman

Since there is little agreement as to what identifies the "ideal salesman" perhaps a more useful approach would be to find out what effective salesmen do. What kinds of skills do they exhibit in carrying out their jobs effectively? *"Skill is an ability which can be developed, is not necessarily inborn, and is shown or exhibited in performance, not merely potential."*[3]

There are three basic skills which appear fundamental to successful salesmen. They are technical skill, human skill, and conceptual skill, and although they are definitely interrelated, one must examine and develop them one at a time, independently.

Technical skill is most familiar because it is required of most salesmen and is easily seen. Technical skill is an understanding of and proficiency in a specific kind of activity, particularly one involving methods, processes, procedures, or techniques. One is familiar with the technical skill of a musician, an engineer, an accountant, or an actor. All of these work primarily with things, as does the successful salesman. In the salesman's

---

[3] Performance depends on fundamental skills rather than personality traits. (Robert L. Katz, "Skills of an Effective Administrator," *Harvard Business Review*, January–February, 1955.) An article based on a study prepared under a grant from the Alfred P. Sloan Foundation.

case, we refer to his tools as locating and qualifying prospects, giving an effective sales presentation, demonstrating his product, overcoming objections, and obtaining buying decisions. This involves sales knowledge, analytical ability within the specialty of sales problems, and finally, it involves a facility in the use of tools and techniques of salesmanship.

Human skill includes the salesman's ability to work effectively as a group member of his own company and to build cooperative effort within his customers and prospects. This skill is demonstrated in the way the individual perceives or sees and understands his superiors, equals, and subordinates and in the way he behaves subsequently.

He is aware of his own attitudes, biases, beliefs, and assumptions regarding other people—both individuals and groups—and can see the usefulness and limitations of these feelings. He can accept the existence of viewpoints which are different from his own and is skillful in communicating to others in their own contexts and language what he means by his behavior. He is sensitive to the needs and motivations of others so that he can judge the possible reactions to, and outcomes of, various courses of action he may undertake. He is willing and able to act in a way which takes these understandings by others into account. Human skill is demonstrated through understanding oneself and others, motivating others, leading others, and inspiring others.

Conceptual skill involves the ability to see the company as a whole, recognizing how the various functions of the organization depend on one another and how changes in any one part affect all the others. It includes visualizing the relationship of the individual business to the industry, the community, and the political, social, and economic forces of the nation as a whole. Recognizing and understanding the significant elements in any situation, the successful salesman is then able to act in a way which advances the overall welfare of his own company and of his customer's organization.

This three-skill approach emphasizes that good salesmen are not necessarily born; they may be developed. It eliminates the need to identify traits to find the "ideal salesman." Once one isolates those skills most needed at various levels of a particular job, it should prove useful in the training of salesmen.

## Job Analysis

A job analysis is the actual practice or task of determining what constitutes a given sales job. From the analysis, a job description—a document which sets forth in writing the findings—is drawn up. The job description includes the job title, which indicates the type of job such as driver-salesman, missionary salesman, engineering consultant, or whatever. It includes management's relation to the salesman, spelling out in detail whom he reports to, the compensation agreement, criteria for promotions and pay increases, the path of advancement, and the like. Most important, the job description spells out in great detail the duties related to the specific job. These should include:

1. Planning. This covers routing, determining the time required for various functions, the time and methods for new prospecting, and analyzing market potential.

2. Actual selling activities. This would include the number and type of calls to be made, specific buying influentials to be contacted, presentation, and demonstrations to be given.

3. Servicing customers. Depending upon the specific job, this might include such things as training dealers' salesmen, maintaining inventory records for dealers, advising dealers for more effective local advertisements, or some other management service.

4. Clerical and routine duties. Most sales jobs require filling out and promptly turning in various reports and courteously handling customer correspondence.

5. Self-management. This would spell out exactly how much time is spent on which activities including improving himself in selling ability, knowledge of existing and new company products, understanding of customers, their industries, territory conditions, and the like.

## Job Qualifications

Once a specific job in a given company has been analyzed, hiring specifications can be drawn which list the several specific personal qualifications and characteristics applicants should have in order to be selected for the given job. Normally the sales manager must determine which traits must be possessed and the degree or range of acceptability. Many degrees exist within the extremes of how persuasive, how self-confident, and how ambitious a candidate must be. Most skills can be taught. However, any applicant should have high ambition, resourcefulness, and industry.

The major categories included in *job qualifications for each type* of sales position for each firm hiring new men would be:

1. Mental—including technical and conceptual skills.
2. Physical—including health, appearance, and verbal abilities.

3. Environmental—including social intelligence, marital status, race, religion, family, and social background.
4. Experience—including education and business background.
5. Human skill and personality factors—ambition, industry, resourcefulness, and enthusiasm.

The job description might call for many calls per day with an average of 15 minutes spent on each call. The job qualifications then might require a concise talker who is quick and spontaneous with his sales presentation. If the job description includes making adjustments for damaged goods or customer claims, the job qualifications might require a man who was logical, firm, and tactful. If the job description calls for considerable written contact with customers, then the job qualifications should specify high ability in English usage. If the job description includes carrying heavy samples, then the job qualifications must include high physical energy, strength, and stamina.

## Sales Training

Beginners as well as experienced salesmen can be trained to become more successful in four major areas. These are knowledge, skills, attitudes, and work habits. While interrelated, each area of subject matter should be considered separately.

## Knowledge

Product knowledge is basic to any form of selling. However to increase success, training should cover user benefits and those related product qualities which substantiate claims. Knowledge of company policies and procedures helps to answer customer questions and to gain the salesman's cooperation. If the salesman knows why the policy was established, in relation to his own selling job, he can more effectively implement it in the field. If he knows what alternatives were considered and why this one was selected, he will realize it was not established to hurt customers or to limit his earnings. For example, required call reports are normally intended to supply feedback of useful information to the salesman to aid him in solving problems in the field or to further his self-development. A knowledge of company history, its reputation, and its objectives, as well as the specific sales job in relation to all other jobs of the same firm, enables the lone salesman off on his own to act in agreement with the overall purposes of the firm. Finally, a knowledge of the market conditions enables the salesman to locate likely customers by teaching him where to find them, how to contact them, how to get around competitors, and how to handle typical objections.

2. Training in skills would include some psychology of persuasion and communication as it applies to the skill of selling. This would be applied to the salesman's specific product or service and cover his basic sales presentation, dramatization, and closing techniques. Skill might be required in servicing customer problems of legitimate adjustments and complaints in which situation the salesman might act as the customer's agent with the selling company. Another skill commonly taught is that of operating the product or accessory equipment, both for demonstration purposes and for installing the product, as well as teaching the new user how to get the best results from his purchase.

3. Attitudes are not normally taught independently of knowledge and skills but are woven into that training. Attitudes desired include proper motivation to work steadily and productively without putting undue pressure on prospects and customers, as well as responsibility to the salesman's own company, his factory workers, to stockholders, and to customers and the public in general. When the salesman realizes his steady production provides many factory and office workers with steady employment, he sees his responsibility as appropriate to his own desires for success.

4. Work habits are taught to increase the efficiency and effectiveness of men in the field in such things as desired number of calls per day, optimum length of each call, routing of calls, buying customer lunches, and meeting entertainment responsibilities, as well as reporting, letter writing, and handling intracompany inquiries.

## Evaluating the Sales Personality

Much has been written about the salesmen with little technical ability who have been outstanding producers and salesmen who were technical experts but who just couldn't sell. Good human relations or a "natural" salesman's ability to handle people are claimed to be the difference.

Good human relations are *not* natural. They are learned procedures. The skill of good human relations is putting the learned procedures into practice. A baby is selfish and demanding of those around him. He is the center of his entire world. When he does not get his way he cries, has temper tantrums, and sulks. The youngster threatens to stop loving his mother. The teenager is often insubordinate and gives his elders back talk and other displays of temper. It is the mature person who is capable of seeing what the other person wants and who is able to sense how the other person feels. Understanding the customer's point of view and feelings is essential to the salesman's success. This does not mean the salesman is sympathetic or in agreement with his customer's opinions but it does mean he can understand what the customer feels he wants. The successful salesman senses the reactions of the customer and is able to adjust to these reactions. He is not simply bound by a prepared sales presentation, but he functions in terms of the real interaction between himself and the customer. Sensing what the customer is feeling, he is able to change pace, double back, or make whatever creative modifications might be necessary to close the sale. The successful salesman has learned to trigger a friendly interaction with his customer so that both the buyer and the seller enjoy being together.

The proof of skill in human relations of a successful sales personality is the putting into practice of the learned knowledge. The successful salesman has learned to put himself in the prospect's shoes and feel as the prospect feels; he has learned to put this knowledge to use in persuading the prospect to buy.

## Who Can Become an Effective Salesman?

One recent study of 7,000 men with diverse educational backgrounds and employment and nonemployment showed that as many as one man in ten is capable of becoming a top producing salesman and another two men are capable of becoming effective salesmen with good chances of becoming top producers.[4]

But selling is plain hard work with long hours, and those who would choose this profession must be prepared for the task. Many of the things listed earlier as being job differences are the exact reasons men like selling. They do not want to be chained to a desk indoors for eight hours a day. There are many individuals who thrive on being independent and free of close supervision. Also there are men who like to travel and enjoy meeting old customers again and continually facing new prospects. As pointed out, above all, there are men who need the constant challenge of proving their own self-image. They must feel that they are accomplishing something of importance and something tangible. Their monthly sales total is concrete evidence of their superiority by their standards and they know that through

---

[4] The one man in ten is high on test scores of ego drive and empathy. See David Mayer and Herbert M. Greenberg, "What Makes A Good Salesman," *Harvard Business Review*, July–August, 1964, pp. 119–25.

their efforts many office and factory workers have steady jobs while their customers increase their standard of living.

Finally, an effective salesman is very well paid and is eagerly sought by other companies. Not only can the effective salesman have many of the material comforts of life, he also has the confidence of job security no matter what the future economic conditions may be. While the salesman may be the highest paid person in his company, it is usually top management people in the home office who lose their jobs when business conditions warrant a drastic change in policy.

◆ ◆ ◆

## A NEW KIND OF SALESMAN*

Selling a new product today often means selling a new technology. Convincing customers of a product's excellence is only part of the job; the salesman must also help customers adapt the product to production and market conditions. Particularly in the chemical industry, this calls for extraordinary versatility. Sometimes a salesman must be part scientist, sometimes part economist, sometimes part market- or product-development specialist. At times his work calls for all four skills.

In Du Pont, there are a number of avenues to developing such versatility. Many salesmen have scientific or technical degrees. Others hold degrees in business administration, marketing, or economics. Still others acquired their knowledge through experience and self-education. Among Du Pont's sales executives, and its top management, all three types of background are represented.

Whatever the route into selling, to succeed today a salesman must know not only his own products, but also his customers' products, and the techniques of making and selling them.

---

* The above is reprinted with the kind permission of E. I. du Pont de Nemours & Company, Inc., Wilmington, Delaware, from "The Salesman Story," 1955.

# 3

# How to Sell Yourself

Many people have been conditioned over the years to expect the worst in any selling situation. When they are aware of a need, have the financial means and the desire to purchase a product or service, they are highly suspicious and often reluctant to take any action. They are reluctant to have any contact with salesmen.

Anthropologists trace this fear of strangers back to man's early beginnings of living together in groups.[1] When a single stranger approached the cave home of any one group of people, the group learned to expect danger and prepared to protect itself. If the stranger appeared markedly different from the group, as in height, shape, skin color, or amount of body hair, then the stranger was feared more than if he were quite similar. This natural fear of strangers persists today even in well-developed and sophisticated societies.

After the newcomer became a regular and familiar sight, the fear gave way to suspicion. The stranger could be tolerated as long as he gave no sign of hurting the group or stealing its possessions. Eventually the newcomer might be allowed to join the group but he would not be trusted by most tribe members. This distrust would last until the newcomer proved himself a contributing member to the group welfare by catching food or helping to fight off an enemy. There would still be considerable doubt about the depth of his sincerity. Perhaps he was simply ingratiating himself with the group or its leaders in order to gain a position of trust so that he might eventually steal from or otherwise harm the group. After many seasons or even years of proving himself, the newcomer would still seem untrustworthy to some members. There would always persist some doubt about his character.

---

[1] For excellent background material see Loren Eiseley, "Introduction," *Epic of Man*, by ed. of Time, Life, Inc. (New York: Time, Inc., 1961), p. 308.

## COMMON REACTIONS TO SALESMEN

People today are not as intellectual and sophisticated in their behavior as one would like to believe. Unfortunately, it is still very natural for a man to fear strangers. Many people instinctively resist salesmen and set up some form of defense. They have been conditioned not to trust salesmen. Being unfamiliar with a new salesman or his company, people are wary of becoming involved with him. Most people are skeptical about any new or unknown product, particularly if some claims seem exaggerated. Often it is the inability to measure the quality or value of a product which causes suspicion. If a large expenditure is involved, people tend to vacillate between spending and not spending and worry about what is the right thing to do. Unfortunately, overeager salesmen utilize high pressure tactics, attempting to force a prospect to buy before he has decided that it is in his best interest to do so. Another common reaction to a salesman is a sense of irritation at being disturbed or taken away from other activities, particularly if the salesman has used subterfuge to gain admittance.

## WHY PROSPECTS WISH TO AVOID SALESMEN

All organisms tend to maintain the constancy of the internal conditions essential to their well-being, such as body temperature at 98.6 degrees, various foods, water, and rest. Once the balance is disturbed, automatic functions give rise to drives that stimulate the person to restore the needed constancy. This has also been found to apply to the broad external relationships between a person and his social environment. When a danger or a need is drawn to an individual's attention, a state of tension or restlessness will arise and persist until satisfied or merged into another state such as action.

In selling, the prospect should be approached with the realization that he is happy with the *status quo* and is likely to resist change. The selective processes in resisting persuasion all normally serve to protect the prospect from salesmen who wish to disturb his self-satisfied sense of well-being.

When a situation involving conflict arises, people have three basic courses of action: to move against people, or fight back; to move away from people, or withdraw; to move toward people, or join them. Once the prospect is confronted with a situation created by a salesman, he can no longer remain psychologically at rest and must act to restore his inner balance. The salesman encourages him to change his behavior but this usually means the prospect must give up familiar and satisfying relationships, comfortable and habitual behavior, for the uncertain results of new behavior. This sets up psychological conflict, tension, and fear, and causes anxiety. If he does not move toward the salesman and buy, he has only two remaining alternatives—to move away and escape, or to move against and argue with the salesman.[2]

Insofar as the predisposed attitudes, ideas, and beliefs of the prospect are protected by mental defenses, the salesman comes on the scene as a disturber of the peace and the prospect regards the salesman's purpose as a menace. One can have at his disposal only a limited number of possible means of defense. At particular periods in life and according to his own specific structure, the individual selects now one defense method and now another. If we know how a particular prospect seeks to defend himself, the nature of his habitual resistances, we can form an idea of his probable attitude toward our unwelcome effects.

Bodily attitudes such as stiffness and rigidity, personal peculiarities such as fixed smile, contemptuous, ironical, and arrogant behavior—all these are residues of very vigorous defensive processes in the past, which have become dissociated from their original situations or conflicts and have developed into permanent character traits known as the armor plating of character. This abnormal or neurotic prospect is not flexible; he is driven to comply, to fight, to be aloof, regardless of whether or not the move is appropriate in the particular circumstances, and he is thrown into a panic if he must behave otherwise.

On the other hand, the normal prospect has all three defenses and he is capable of giving in to others, of fighting, and of keeping to himself. The basic defenses can complement each other and make for a harmonious whole. If one defense predominates, it merely indicates an overdevelopment along one line. To protect their self-image and maintain their sense of mental equilibrium, normal people prefer to avoid frustration and conflict. They erect elaborate behavior patterns of escape and defense to restore their balance. In sales, the persuader must learn enough about the prospect to predict how he will interpret what is said and what emotional overtones the prospect will infer. Once the persistent tendency to behave in a given manner becomes evident, the salesman can plan his presentation accordingly.

---

[2] For those interested in depth in this field, see Anna Freud, *The Ego and the Mechanisms of Defense*, trans. Cecil Baines (New York: International Universities Press, Inc., 1946).

## HOW PROSPECTS JUDGE SALESMEN

The natural fear of strangers and the suspicion of anything new causes prospects to look for the ulterior motives of the salesman. Each prospect is interested in himself and believes the salesman is equally interested in his commissions. The question immediately raised in the prospect's mind is, "Who benefits if I purchase this proposition?"

Beyond the physical appearance and mannerisms of the salesman, the buyer judges the salesman on his apparent knowledge in his specific field. The salesman must be thought of as an authority in his area. Building a prospect's confidence in the salesman includes the creation of a feeling of trust through intelligent suggestions and genuinely useful advice freely given in a friendly and pleasant manner. Building a good personal reputation with a trade and working for a reputable concern increase the prospect's confidence over months or years. Prospects buy primarily to help themselves and not because a salesman wishes to sell goods and services. Since the prospect is interested in his own benefit first, the salesman must learn to communicate his message in terms the prospect will understand.

## PRODUCT VS. BENEFITS

In general terms, the product is the total offering of the physical product and accessories needed as well as normal services of guarantee, delivery, installation, and related elements. Service, on the other hand, is everything of value given to the customer beyond the product offering.[3] Service includes, but is not necessarily limited to:

1. Product performance-enhancing services such as aid in the selection; adjustments to work properly, altering or tailoring to fit the need; instruction in optimum usage.
2. Prolonging the product life by stocking of spare parts over long periods.
3. Risk reduction of purchasing through return privileges and warranty.
4. Reduction of purchase effort through telephone and mail-order privileges, parking facilities, and a nursery for children.
5. Reduction of capital required through credit; through carrying local inventory for resellers; through financing of showroom models, furniture, and fixtures.
6. Efficiency-increasing services whereby the manufacturer does account-

---

[3] Alfred R. Oxenfeldt, *Executive Action in Marketing* (San Francisco: Wadsworth Publishing Co., Inc. forthcoming 1966–67).

ing for the distributor; the retailer provides restaurant facilities for the
shoppers' timesaving convenience.
7. Sales-increasing services for the reseller, such as training his salesmen;
   specialists' advice in advertising locally; floor traffic control through layout; and the like.
8. Meeting the customers' intangible need to feel important by such means
   as courtesy, attention, prompt handling of complaints, and the like.

Customer service and product offering are often difficult to separate, as
the service is merely an extension of the product. A customer buys a
washing machine from a department store for the benefits she expects,
such as to get clothes clean and to have more free time, but not to possess
so many nuts, bolts, electric motor, and metal pieces. She expects all the
accessories needed, delivery, installation, and guarantee of trouble-free
operation. She might also expect some instruction in the actual use of the
working machine in her home as well as many of the services enumerated
above applicable to the consumer.

The same consumer might order a telephone, not for the sake of having
the physical instrument, but for the benefits expected. She expects to be
able to talk to friends, to conduct business, to reduce traveling, to gain
information, to have emergency contact with fire and police if needed, to
hear from members of her family during lonely hours, and probably many
more benefits. She expects such customer services as aid in the selection of
the proper model and color, adjustment for ring and tone volume desired,
and possibly instructions for teaching her children how to handle the
instrument effectively. She expects complete repair and maintenance not
only of her telephone instrument but also all telephone lines everywhere
and the necessary central office equipment. She expects monthly credit
without interest charges. Her husband might expect special training for his
employees in telephone selling techniques and consultants to survey his
business telephone usage.

Whether buying a washing machine from a department store or ordering a Princess telephone, the consumer expects her intangible needs to be
met. These would include courtesy, attention, friendliness in handling
complaints, and similar intangibles that make her feel important.

While the salesman must know his product and its applications, he
must talk in terms of customer benefits if he is to be effective. Does the
salesman talk simply to impress the prospect with his knowledge and self-
importance or does he converse to enlighten the prospect? Built into a true
meeting of minds is the concept of two-way communications. The prospect
must be allowed to talk, to express himself, his needs, wants, and desires.

Courtesy: E. I. du Pont de Nemours Co., Wilmington, Del.

**FIG. 3. An industrial account salesman talks to a buyer for a large industry.**

The salesman who is courteous will listen but the salesman who is also intelligent will listen to gain an understanding of a prospect's needs or problems and to learn the particular words the prospect uses to express himself. In order to communicate, the effective salesman must know how the prospect uses words and phrases—what meaning the prospect is apt to read into the salesman's message.

Once a prospect feels that the salesman understands him, he will listen to what the salesman says. If the salesman avoids extreme claims and honestly offers sound advice, the prospect will tend to accept what the salesman says. If the salesman recognizes a need which his proposition will best satisfy, it is then his task to enlighten the prospect with words, pictures, and actions which the prospect will understand. The salesman must communicate his message so that it will be not only heard but understood and internalized by the prospect. If the salesman is effective, the buyer will realize this proposition is the best solution to his problem— the best way to satisfy his needs or desires if he acts now.

## HOW TO MAKE A GOOD IMPRESSION ON A PROSPECT

Besides the other parts of the marketing mix, what the salesman says and does definitely affects the prospect's decision to buy. We have come a long way from the backslapping, cigar-handing, storytelling canvasser of the past. Today's salesman is neat, informed, able, ambitious, versatile, and tactful. He serves the prospect's need by telling him what is new, what is better, and what will best fill his requirements.

### Look and Act the Part of a Friendly Authority

The salesman should dress conservatively and be well groomed. In business a receptionist screens salesmen to save her boss some time and she often volunteers her opinion to the prospect before the salesman gets a chance to give his. The prospect is also going to judge the salesman's character and habits partially from how he looks and what he wears. Loud clothes and too much jewelry are often interpreted as an attempt to influence but they may work against the salesman as well as for him. Too expensive clothes and jewelry may give the prospect the feeling that this salesman can well afford to lose an order.

However friendly a salesman may feel toward the prospect, being overly friendly on the first visit is uncalled for because the salesman is still a stranger. Since it is ill-timed it may not be accepted as cordially as it was intended. Let the prospect take the initiative on such things as a handshake, smoking, telling jokes, and other trivial matters.

If the salesman calls on a person who is a logical prospect for what he has to sell and the product would really benefit the prospect, then the salesman can show certainty about his true mission. He is rendering the prospect a service by calling and showing him what he has to sell and how it will fill the prospect's needs. There is no reason to be humble, servile, or apologetic. Prospects would rather feel that the salesman has some backbone and a full share of human dignity and pride.

The salesman's objective is to convince the prospect that what he has to

sell will prove beneficial to the prospect. The effective salesman knows his
business, the buyer's business, and what he is talking about. The effective
salesman talks business simply and quietly, without big words and clichés,
without blasphemous or profane words, and without emotional or highly
personal innuendos.

## Search and Develop Areas of Similarity to Prospects

In realistic sales interviews, one can often observe a prospect and a
salesman hitting it off spontaneously. They seem alike and understand
each other instinctively. Psychologists describe this behavior as a psychological fit because the two personalities seem predisposed in the same
direction. They have the same way of looking at things and tend to
reinforce each other's attitudes, ideas, opinions, and beliefs.

The effective salesman learns to recognize such similarities quickly and
to make the prospect aware of any personality traits or predisposed ideas
and attitudes they may have in common. In industrial selling, where the
salesman calls repeatedly over long periods of time, this similarity to the
perceiver is intentionally developed and cultivated as much as sincerity will
permit. In the type of selling which requires attempting to close the sale on
the first call, the effective salesman builds up the prospect's confidence in
him as an expert and authority and often almost intuitively will exploit one
or more personality traits they have in common.

Intuitive sales behavior is currently being studied at several universities.
However, little has been concluded to date. It would seem there are really
two types of intuitive behavior. First is the seeking of a self-image. The
salesman looks for physical or psychological traits in his prospect that he
thinks are admirable and that he himself possesses. Thus a salesman
intuitively likes the prospect who conducts his business in the same way as
the salesman thinks he would do it. He also likes a businessman who, for
example, treats his employees in the same stern manner that the salesman
thinks he would treat them. The second and more probable explanation
for intuitive sales behavior is the lifetime learning—observing, recognizing,
and categorizing—of minute signs and symbols and instantly deducing
fundamental attitudes in the buyer. Often a simple, apparently irrelevant
question will serve to confirm the salesman's tentative conclusions. Something in the makeup of the prospect, for instance, may give the salesman
the hunch that the prospect is a hunter. During a lull in the conversation,
the salesman might then ask, "By the way, do you by any chance own a
Springer Spaniel?" Some minute observation and the instant deduction is

done so habitually from early childhood through years of selling experience that the mental process becomes automatic and the salesman himself is not aware of its method of functioning, but he is aware of its results.

Both the buyer and the seller engage in this intuitive type of behavior and are delighted when further facts and knowledge confirm their instinctive guesses. People will often question information which does not conform to their first impressions, because they want their hunches to be correct, and this doubt about nonconforming information may linger for some time after the first meeting. There is something about the stranger that reminds them of someone else and they will continue to search for confirmation. Since the salesman is normally the visitor, he has the advantage of seeing the prospect on his home grounds such as in his office and with his fellow employees, or perhaps in the consumer's home and with his family and furnishings. These factors supply additional clues to guide the salesman's deductions. The prospect, on the other hand, usually sees only the individual salesman and not his associates and can observe only how the salesman behaves when first meeting strangers. The effective salesman will become aware of such clues to similarity.

Intuitive behavior differs from the psychological fit in the degree of compatibility of attitudes. While an intuitive salesman may on occasion correctly guess how to treat a prospect, he need not particularly hold the same attitudes and beliefs nor even like such attitudes as would be typical of a psychological fit. Being insincere and giving lip service to a prospect's biases and prejudices can be dangerous, as it is often seen through. But by politely avoiding possible areas of conflict, the salesman can discuss other social and business subjects without making the prospect hostile. While salesmen differ widely in their perceptive and deductive abilities, the various sales situations often dictate that no intuitive action is possible or would play any part in the selling situation. This is not to deny that some salesmen do succeed with hunches or intuitive behavior well beyond the odds of mathematical probability.

## Become an Uncritical Listener

All human behavior is basically goal directed, not random, and serves to satisfy needs and wants of the individual.[4] One need not judge whether another's behavior is rational, conscious, practical, or moral when he seeks to determine specifically what is wanted by the individual. It is not what

[4] For an excellent viewpoint of human behavior, see Harold J. Leavitt, *Managerial Psychology* (1st Phoenix ed.; Chicago: University of Chicago Press, 1962), p. 12.

an observer thinks the individual should want or need that is important but what the individual himself feels.

In order to learn what the prospect wants for himself, the salesman must create a permissive atmosphere, allowing the prospect to talk of anything he wishes. While he need not agree with the prospect's viewpoint, he must understand that viewpoint and how it serves some need of the prospect. The effective salesman may even provide examples which illustrate the prospect's point of view but he does so under specific conditions and limitations. This supportive feedback proves to the prospect that the salesman is listening attentively and is a nice person who agrees with him. This uncritical listening will neutralize hostile feelings which the prospect may have as well as establish a meeting of minds. When the salesman discovers what the individual prospect feels is important, what the prospect wants, what the prospect will infer from the seller's communication, then he will be in a position to be heard and understood.

The effective salesman gives the prospect every opportunity to express his own views. One of these views may give him the reason why the prospect should buy. What the prospect says may well add fuel to the salesman's motivating talk. At the very least, it provides the prospect with an opportunity to get something off his chest and clear his mind to receive the salesman's message. By being uncritical, the salesman neither approves nor disapproves of the prospect's attitude but simply illustrates that he does understand it. This paves the way for mutual understanding and a reasonable hearing of the salesman's proposition.

## Put Yourself in the Prospect's Position

An effective salesman has the ability to feel as the other fellow does. This does not necessarily mean being sympathetic; one can know what the other fellow feels without agreeing with that feeling. But the effective salesman has the invaluable and irreplaceable ability to get powerful feedback from his prospect. As noted earlier, the greatest value of personal selling in the marketing mix is the effective salesman's ability to adjust instantly to the prospect's thinking. He senses the reactions of the prospect and is able to adjust his presentation to these reactions. He is not simply bound by a prepared sales talk or planned program of presentation but functions in terms of the real interaction between himself and the prospect. Sensing what the prospect is feeling, he is able to change pace, repeat certain effective selling points, and make whatever creative modifications might be necessary to close the sale.

It is this ability to put oneself in the prospect's position, to truly feel as the prospect does, which enables the effective salesman to understand people and what things he might say to close the sale. Without this feeling a salesman may bulldoze his way through to some orders but he will miss most and hurt his employer through his lack of understanding people. When the salesman truly understands what the prospect wants and what his problems are, he can then help the prospect gain satisfaction by seeing his problems in a different way or seeing additional alternative solutions to them. The salesman feels the unspoken fears and doubts of the prospect and can reassure him so that he will be willing to attempt change.

This skill in dealing with people is often exhibited when an adult attempts to persuade a child to do something which is for the child's benefit. The novice salesman who studies human behavior and practices feeling with another in order to understand the other's viewpoint will, as his actions becomes habitual, become a skillful and effective salesman.

## Analyze Prospect's Needs

The effective salesman knows the complete name of his prospect, the exact nature of the prospect's business, the goods he can logically use, and the information which the prospect should have. He takes the time and effort to investigate the situation of a particular prospect and studies the prospect's individual needs and desires. He is in a position to develop various solutions to the prospect's problem and suggest new or different methods of accomplishing the prospect's objectives. The effective salesman who understands how his prospect feels is in a position to make him unhappy or dissatisfied with his existing situation, and to help him realize there are other ways to achieve his desires. The salesman helps the prospect project the probable results of each alternative course of action and makes it easier for the prospect to see how only one course of action will achieve his wants, needs, or whatever his goal is.

When a salesman knows everything he can about what he is selling and knows about the prospect's needs and feelings, he can supply the prospect with information about the industry he represents. If the prospect doesn't buy from him this time, he will remember the salesman as the man he wants to buy from someday because this man's visits have always been worth his time. Well-informed salesmen are a constant source of his general knowledge. This is particularly applicable in industrial selling. However, in all types of selling the point is to avoid a "cold" call, one which lacks human warmth and reveals little knowledge of the prospect's needs. If the salesman indicates he has not looked into a particular prospect's situation, that he has not taken any trouble to dig for facts and analyze them, the prospect naturally feels he is simply another statistic to the salesman who honestly couldn't care less if he in particular were served as long as someone gives the salesman an order that day. In retail selling, an effective salesman will ask the customer several questions concerning the expected use of the product and the desired life of the product. Even a few brief questions communicate to the prospect that the salesman is interested in this particular person and his satisfactory use of an intended purchase.

The nature and extent of investigation and analyzing of a prospect's need will vary with the product or service being offered. However, even in the simplest of selling situations, the salesman can make a good impression on a prospect by showing his interest in the prospect's ultimate welfare. Sincere advice and helpful suggestions from an authority in a given field are normally appreciated and the salesman who keeps this in mind is thought of as being considerate of the prospect's interest.

◆    ◆    ◆

## PORTFOLIO OF A TOP SALESMAN*

During 1964 a quiet, soft-spoken S & H field representative in Mobile, Alabama, made quite a noise stacking up sales records. He signed 148½ contracts. (The one-half is a result of working with another salesman to sign an account.) That was tops among all field representatives. He also increased his field managed sales by more than $57,000 during the year.

The man who registered this amazing record is Don Risser, who patrols the Gulf Coast of Alabama and Mississippi for S & H. He has a crew cut and looks younger than his 36 years. But he's had years of sales experience—six with S & H—and he sells like the most seasoned veteran.

What's his formula for success? "Basically, it's like Walter Whitnack (executive vice president) says," said Mr. Risser. "Success is a four letter word—work." To fulfill this requirement Mr. Risser starts his day at 8:00 A.M. and usually makes calls until 6:00 P.M. or later. Paperwork is saved for Friday mornings and weekends.

---

* The following is reprinted with the kind permission of the *Sperry and Hutchinson Company Magazine*, New York, N.Y., June–July, 1965:

## Have Fun Selling

"But there's more to it than just work," explained Mr. Risser. "I feel that to be successful one must enjoy what he's doing. To be a good truck driver one must enjoy it. To be a good salesman one must enjoy selling. I have fun selling."

Another important ingredient in Mr. Risser's success recipe is what he calls the personal touch. He constantly looks for ways to take a more active interest in an account's business and, in many cases, in the people he works with. "You can often find mutual interests with these people," pointed out Mr. Risser. "This makes the work more enjoyable for all concerned."

The 36-year-old field representative started with S & H in 1959, but he was in sales long before that. Prior to joining S & H he sold for A. B. Dick Company (office machines) for three years. He started his sales career as a part-time clerk for Sears, Roebuck Company while he was a student at the University of Toledo (Ohio).

The native Ohioan has worked out of the Mobile office since starting with S & H. During this six-year-period S & H sales for the area have quadrupled. Almost 70 percent of his business is in Mobile. According to him this has both advantages and disadvantages.

"It points up our family of merchants concept," he said. "If a dry cleaning operator can stand in front of his building and see a service station, grocery store, and other merchants in his neighborhood that are giving S & H Green Stamps, it's going to impress him. It makes the job of providing service for an account more difficult, however, for you have the problem of traffic, parking, and a large metropolitan area to cover."

"There are many things that make a man sell," declares Mr. Risser. "Confidence is one of the most important. The best way to build confidence is to learn all you can about your company, your product, and your competitors. If you know this, confidence in yourself comes naturally."

Mr. Risser constantly reads about the trading stamp industry—material both pro and con—and always examines literature about the company. "I do my best to keep up with all the happenings in the industry and in our company. This gives me an additional something to talk about with accounts and prospects."

## Team with an Account

Mr. Risser works under the theory that as a field repesentative you are working as part of a team with an account. "I constantly keep in mind that my responsibility is to help an account's business. When I make a call on an account I always try to have something special to talk with them about such as new signs, or a group savings project, or special S & H promotions. Happy accounts are a must in cultivating new accounts."

This theory carries into calling on prospects, too. Mr. Risser's main requirement for making a call on a prospect: Will S & H's service increase his business? "If our service won't help him, I'm wasting my time and his," declares Mr. Risser.

Mr. Risser thinks in broad areas when making a prospect list. He has signed such varying types of business as a savings and loan association, a garden nursery, a lumberyard, dry cleaners, a slaughterhouse and meat locker service, beauty salons, a fence company, and an upholstery shop.

"I take a close look at a business before I make a call. This gives an idea of the operation. You can usually tell a lot about a business just by looking. A prospect must be a sound business led by an aggressive businessman. S & H's service can make a good business much better. However, not even S & H Green Stamps—and for that matter no single promotional tool—can make a poorly run business a success."

The serious-minded Mr. Risser is a positive thinker and is always optimistic. "It may seem a little corny," says Mr. Risser, "but at the start of each day I tell myself that I am going to do the best I can. That I'm going to help the accounts I call on and I'm going to find some new accounts for S & H."

This approach has worked for Mr. Risser. He's continuing his selling ways. Through the first four months of 1965 he signed 62 accounts and was seventh in the overall standings among all S & H field representatives. (On the basis of a five point rating system used to rank all field representatives.)

"S & H's strength in the Gulf Coast area," Mr. Risser said, "is one of the main reasons I've been able to sell. We were the first stamp plan in the area (Spring, 1957) and we're firmly entrenched. Our only competition is from some small local stamp companies and they just don't have the prestige and organization that S & H has. Merchants and consumers both recognize this. Kwik Chek Supermarkets, a division of Winn-Dixie, gives S & H Green Stamps as does National Food, a division of National Tea. Both are good, aggressive merchants. That helps build S & H savers."

What makes his sales presentation so effective? "I don't have a tailored sales presentation," pointed out Mr. Risser. "Each business is individual and I vary my sales points accordingly. This keeps my presentation fresh and also puts the prospect's personal interest into it."

There are, however, basic planks that Mr. Risser includes in his sales presentation. He points out that S & H Green Stamps are saved in more than 48 million households. He also stresses the advertising benefits that an account receives, including national promotions, signs, point-of-sale material, and window displays.

Another good way to get their interest is to tell a success story. "Everyone loves to hear about success," exclaims the enthusiastic Mr. Risser. "I like to tell prospects about the Calametti brothers. They were the second business in Mobile to give S & H Green Stamps. That was in 1957, and they had one service station. Next month they're opening their third station—and it, as the others, will give S & H Green Stamps."

Mr. Risser tells a prospect that Frank Calametti, senior partner in the operation, points out that "S & H Green Stamps cost money—but they make money. And you can't make money without spending money!"

He also often recounts the story of the first account he signed for S & H—a tire and fishing supply company, "This retailer increased his business by more than 30 percent during the first year with S & H," recalls Mr. Risser. "In 1962 he decided to try a marketing program that didn't include S & H Green Stamps. After 30 days without stamps his business was down considerably. He started giving stamps again and regained his losses. He hasn't mentioned dropping stamps again!

"But the most important thing that you must show a prospect," according to Mr. Risser, "is how S & H's service will increase his business. And if I've done my homework on his business and competition I can show him this." Mr. Risser's homework includes listing the other types of retailers in the shopping area giving S & H Green Stamps, an analysis of the prospect's competitors, and a look at the prospect's business.

## Watch a Business Grow

"After accounts are signed," stressed Mr. Risser, "the job has just started. It's up to me to help in any way I can to increase their business. I work with them on signs, special promotions, or any other way that I feel I can help them. It's always fun to watch an account's business increase after starting with S & H."

This is when the personal relationships for Mr. Risser start, too. "After working with an account for some time," he pointed out, "you often find you have many things in common. For example one of my good accounts is an avid camper—and so am I. We have fun swapping stories and are even planning an outing together."

Mr. Risser has plenty of company when he camps. His wife Joanne, and their four children, ages 13, 11, 7, and 4, are enthusiastic about the sport, too.

In S & H's Lucky 13 contest Mr. Risser placed 10th and won more than 600 books of S & H Green Stamps. Some of the books went for an Apache camper, six sleeping bags, and other camping gear.

Church work is an important part of Mr. Risser's life. He's an active member of the Dauphin Way Methodist Church where he sings in the choir and is a counselor for the Methodist Youth Fellowship. "Working with young people I especially enjoy," explained Mr. Risser. "After all, I have four children of my own and participating as a counselor helps me understand them."

Mr. Risser is also a member of the Kiwanis Club and the Chamber of Commerce.

For his sales success, Mr. Risser gives credit to his superiors. "Ray Meyers, my zone manager, and Bob Kuhnhein, my district manager, have been most helpful. They've taught me a lot about selling—and their ability is shown in their records." (Mr. Kuhnhein's district was tops in 1964 and Mr. Meyers' zone was the second best of all among S & H last year.)

Mr. Meyers has some plaudits of his own to pass out about Don Risser. "An outstanding man. He knows how to pick his prospects, he knows how to sell them, and he knows how to keep them. He's a good salesman . . . and a good S & H man."

## BIRTH OF A SALESMAN†

*Formal training, broad experience mark the professionals of today*

Contrary to the old maxim about a person being "a born salesman," salesmen are made, not born. Personal attributes are as important in selling as in any career, but today special knowledge and training are essential as well.

The modern industrial salesman is a professional. Glad-handing and back-slapping are not his basic attributes. Glibness cannot compensate for lack of knowledge, training, and experience. The newcomer to sales is not given a sample kit, a list of prospects and a quota, and sent on his way the day he starts to work. Rather, the industrial salesman is the product of a long and thorough sales education. He is mature, in experience and know-how, before he tries to sell.

Du Pont's 10 industrial departments use a broad spectrum of sales training techniques. Some employ formal courses in classrooms; others use on-the-job training. Recruits for sales training may come from research or production. Sometimes they come directly from college, and such candidates usually are given production or laboratory experience before they move into selling. In all cases, sales directors seek men with experience as broad as possible, and they make sure that candidates have substantial knowledge before they call on a single customer.

Du Pont today has over 2000 salesmen calling on some 75,000 customers across the country. They sell more than 1200 product lines, ranging from anti-freeze to sulfuric acid, from household cement to synthetic rubber. Each of these men has been specifically trained, not only in sales techniques, but also in the potentialities of his products, the fields in which they are sold, and the specific needs and demands of his customers.

---

† The above is reprinted with the kind permission of E. I. du Pont de Nemours & Company, Inc., Wilmington, Delaware.

# 4

# Converting Knowledge of the Sales Proposition into Prospects' Language

In this chapter the phrase "sales proposition" denotes the physical product and its features, the normal accessories and services, the entire sales agreement, the extra customer services designed for the selected target market, and the knowledge of the manufacturer or supplier as well as the market. An effective salesman can never know too much about his industry, his company, and his entire sales proposition but he can *use* too much information when attempting to sell some prospects. It is not possible to know a sales proposition too well, but trouble may come from how the information is used. Good salesmen can talk for hours about their sales propositions; however, few prospects will spare enough time to hear the entire story.

## REASONS FOR STUDYING THE ENTIRE SALES PROPOSITION AND ITS LANGUAGE

The primary reason for understanding the sales proposition is simply to communicate with the prospect. One must know all the facts so that he can make an adequate sales presentation in language easily understood by each individual prospect. The message itself can then be adapted to each prospect's specific needs or problems and positive statements of facts can be made instead of meaningless generalizations. The effective salesman can give accurate answers to questions and he will understand the prospect's objections and satisfy them fully. From a thorough knowledge of his proposition, the salesman will gain the self-confidence which is necessary for him to look and act the part of a friendly authority. Finally, an effective salesman in the new marketing concept acts as an intelligence agent for his company, bringing back marketing information to improve the product, services, or market position.

48

## COMMUNICATIONS

One does not use the Chinese language or any other foreign language to communicate with an American who understands only his native tongue. A father does not use polysyllabic words when teaching his four-year-old son to ride a new bicycle. A technician, scientist, or engineer often uses simplified models and examples to illustrate his theories and designs when asking nontechnical men for their financial backing. In the same vein, an effective salesman who knows his industry, his company, his product, his proposition, and his customers does not use technical language. An accounting desk may be known to the salesman as a No. 4042 stock number but to a prospect the number by itself means absolutely nothing and the title, accounting desk, does not communicate much more. The effective salesman will paint a word picture so descriptive that his prospect will easily visualize the desk in operation in his own office.

While a person often thinks in numbers and symbols, a form of mental shorthand, he cannot speak that way and expect to communicate his message to anyone who does not use the same symbols. The product knowledge of the salesman must be converted into language which prospects will easily understand, visualize, and internalize or mentally accept before they can agree with the salesman and take his suggestions to act or purchase.

## ADEQUATE SALES PRESENTATION

Clearly, to make a complete sales presentation, one must know the entire story. In many industries, sales trainees memorize, word for word, a two-hour sales presentation and are taught to give the entire talk even if interrupted or temporarily sidetracked. In other industries, sales trainees are taught to solve problems and present only those salient or pertinent facts which apply to the individual situation. In either case, whether the sales presentation is complete or not, the objective is to make the presentation adequate for a specific prospect. To be adequate or effective, the message must be in language which is easily understood by the individual prospect and it must be complete in those areas which are important— important not to the salesman but to the prospect. The salesman must have a wealth of knowledge to permit the necessary flexibility in choosing the appropriate information to include in his sales presentation. If he knows only a few facts, his choice is limited to those few facts. An effective salesman knows literally thousands of facts and can selectively utilize them

*Courtesy: International Business Machines Corp., Armonk, N.Y.*

FIG. 4. Problems of transportation industry are studied by a sales
representative for business machines.

in a given situation to cover adequately the areas of interest to the prospect
in language the prospect can understand.

## ADAPT TO INDIVIDUAL PROSPECT'S SPECIFIC NEEDS

An effective salesman is an expert in his field and he knows more about
his proposition and products and the problems they will solve than any
other person. The salesman is a consultant to his customers where they
have technical problems. A junior salesman with only a few months of
training knows infinitely more about his product and its applications than
does the prospect who suddenly finds himself with a problem related to
this product. If the salesman were not available, the customer would have
to hire the same technical assistance elsewhere. Even in retail selling the

customer depends upn the retailer to convey information about the product features—of a camera, for example—to aid his selection. When a woman buys a dress she is often guided by the sales explanation of the fiber it contains and the correct cleaning process necessary to preserve its effective life. Eliminating the salesman does not necessarily lower costs and might even increase them since the customer might not be able to obtain such technical assistance at a lower price elsewhere. What is a good buy for one prospect might be totally inadequate for another prospect and the knowledgeable salesman is the one person best qualified to offer sincere advice and useful suggestions. This is particularly true of new products or in areas which are new to the prospect. As a product grows more technical or complicated, the more valuable product knowledge and sincere advice become. Prospects seek different information to aid in their selection of products and the effective salesman has enough information to adapt his message to each prospect's specific needs.

## SPECIFICS RATHER THAN MEANINGLESS GENERALITIES

Prospects are primarily interested in their own problems, needs, or desires and not what most Americans or the average person does. When a salesman knows his entire proposition and its language, he can make positive statements of fact instead of loose or meaningless generalizations. If one wants a high fidelity stereo record player he is probably interested in what the sound will be like in his home. It is his home that is important to the buyer, not the fact that a certain model outsells all others. Where he physically places the console within his living room might easily make the difference between choice of models. One set with detachable speakers might be more practical than another set without such a feature. Only after the selection is narrowed down to a few models will the prospect consider why different brands sell as well or poorly as they do, but this is secondary.

In business offices the same problems arise. Prospects for office furniture or business machines are primarily interested in solving their own specific problems of production, work flow, space, time, costs, or the like. The knowledgeable salesman attempts to solve the customer's problems with specific recommendations rather than with glib and useless generalizations. As the product grows more complicated, the need to state facts simply and clearly becomes more important. Complete knowledge of the sales proposition enables the effective salesman to look and act the part of a friendly authority.

## ANSWERING QUESTIONS AND OBJECTIONS

Even worse than the meaningless generalization is the misleading state-ment of fact or the wrong facts. A prospect may be led to buy on the basis of a false statement; however, he will eventually discover the error and probably react bitterly. Making the sale but losing the customer is the sales manager's nightmare. Not only are future sales lost to this particular buyer, but too often the word spreads in the trade to many other potential customers. In door-to-door selling, a salesman may mislead to get an order, knowing full well he will never pass this way again. Such practices have seriously hurt the reputation of professional salesmen and their companies as well. Many large door-to-door selling organizations have million-dollar advertising campaigns designed specifically to build goodwill with consum-ers to overcome the malpractices of a small percentage of salesmen.

Any salesman who hopes for either repeat business or referrals to additional prospects must accurately answer all questions asked by his prospect. Any company that expects to stay in business and attempt to sell in the same areas in the future must build a reputation which appeals to prospects, not repels them. To answer questions accurately and to meet customer objections, the effective salesman has a solid understanding of his proposition, including the limitations of the product, and can speak with authority on his subject.

## BUILDING SELF-CONFIDENCE

Whenever one is faced with an entirely new situation, he normally feels uneasy. It is only after he understands the situation and knows what problems or dangers face him that he begins to feel at ease. When he knows how to handle the problems correctly, he gains self-confidence. In selling, complete knowledge of the entire sales proposition in the broadest sense is the foundation for building self-confidence. An inexperienced salesman who has been taught his product, his company, his industry, and the customer's needs is much more of an authority in his specialty field than most of the prospects upon which he will call.

Experienced buyers enjoy meeting young salesmen because of their enthusiastic attitude, their courage and energy, and buyers often feel an urge to support the young man. This does not imply favoritism, for the claims the young salesman makes will be scrutinized as thoroughly as, possibly more thoroughly than, the older salesman's claims. Experienced buyers are often more tolerant and cooperative with young salesmen and sincerely envy their youth. Such men can, and often do, complete the education of the sales trainee. They go out of their way, take extra time and effort, to help the young salesman become more effective.[1]

Self-confidence is built on knowledge and developed through real practice in the field. It is the application of knowledge in trying situations that increases the salesman's self-image and enables him to face new prospects and new problems. Gradually he learns to look and act the part of a friendly authority. The more he learns about his field of specialty the more expert he becomes as a salesman.

When prospects believe that the salesman is an authority in his field, they will respect his opinions and suggestions and more readily believe what he tells them. Being an authority denotes a degree of mellowness, experience, knowledge, and mature judgment. These give the buyer confidence in the salesman, a situation which normally precedes a sale.

## FEEDBACK

In modern marketing, the emphasis is on the consumers' desires and the salesman has a responsibility to act as an intelligence agent and feed back vital information to his own company. The salesman must be the company's consultant on product, packaging, pricing, advertising, channels of distribution, customer services, and problems relating to customer needs and motivations. This includes competitive action and the attitudes and reactions of the various middlemen between the manufacturer and the consumer. Such information is vital to the decision-making process of the marketing manager and it is an essential function performed largely by salesmen.

New products are often test marketed, or introduced in a limited area, and the competitive salesmen in the area know of it before the general market is aware of its existence. This information, together with the attitudes of the various middlemen and consumer targets, can be very important to the salesmen's company regarding its own product. Information on trends in style is essential in many garment industries to enable them to produce the right items in the right quantities early in the season. Often the package is the key to success in consumer goods purchased in self-service supermarkets because the package design gains the customer's attention. Competitive experiments in test markets can be generalized to

---

[1] One of the most popular expressions by an experienced purchasing agent is Joseph Gentile, *Some Do's and Don'ts of Selling As One Buyer Sees Them* (New York: Dun and Bradstreet, Inc., 1955), p. 27.

apply to other companies particularly if the details and results are known early.

Pricing may seem obvious at the consumer level. However, when a company is dealing with the various middlemen price policy becomes complicated with advertising allowances, free promotion materials, extra discounts for exclusive dealers, and the like. To earn and maintain a strong marketing position, the salesman quickly discovers competitive price practices and reports them to his management.

Advertising is the major nonpersonal influence upon prospects but its effect is generally unknown until the personal salesman visits his prospects. Long before sales are written, the effective salesman realizes the impact the advertising makes on his prospects. Since advertising is relatively expensive, quick reporting of prospects' reactions can make the advertising dollars more effective. The same is true, of course, of competitive advertising's effect on prospects, and if this is reported early, countermeasures may be taken.

In America's huge and complex society, the salesman in the field has become the intelligence agent for his company and is responsible for feeding back vital marketing information quickly to his management so that it may make decisions more accurately and more quickly. Knowing his entire selling proposition enables the salesman to recognize important developments in the market and to report their urgency as required.

## WHAT INFORMATION IS IMPORTANT TO THE PROSPECT?

Buyers frequently state, "I want the best product at the lowest possible price." The reader should be aware that product, as stated earlier, really includes the product features, guarantee, delivery, installation, and other customer services such as aid in the proper selection of a specific item, maintenance of spare parts for long periods, credit accommodations, prompt and courteous service, and many nonproduct customer services cited in the previous chapter. What is best for this prospect? What is best for one prospect is dependent upon what he will do with the product. Thus, the salesman must determine who will use the product, how the product will be used, where it will be used, how long the customer expects the product to be of service, how soon he wants it, and many other questions regarding the expected use and expected benefits.

Individuals will place different emphasis on the various elements of the product and either assume or ignore other elements. These variations in emphasis indicate which condition of product usage will be important to each individual. The lowest possible price is also dependent upon a number of conditions. Clearly the expected benefits of the product must be of a value equal to or greater than the selling price. But the selling price is rarely the total cost of a product. Other factors in total cost include but are by no means limited to delivery charges, installation costs, the normal cost of operating or using the product, the cost of cleaning or repairing the product over its life usage, the cost of lost time when the product is waiting for service, the value of trade-in at the end of usage, the cost of storage when not in use, and possibly the cost of space required for its optimum use. Lowest possible price might also be a relative term meaning in relation to similar product which will permit the buyer to achieve the benefits which he desires. A careful analysis of what the buyer expects is necessary to determine which similar products are really offering the benefits which are important to him.

Thus the simple statement, "I want the best product at the lowest possible price" really breaks down into three major categories, each with many subdivisions. What does the prospect mean by product? What does he mean by best? What does he mean by lowest possible price? For each prospect at any given instant, the combination of variables can be very different and only one combination will adequately satisfy his needs. The same prospect at another time might easily require a different combination of the same variables. To be effective, the salesman should know what combination of factors is important to the individual prospect and the relative value he places on the individual conditions. In order to be adequately prepared to supply information required by the prospect, the salesman needs knowledge of many facts in at least four major areas—the product, the company, the industry, and the market.

## THE PRODUCT

Buyers are interested in product performance and want to know what the product can do for them. When a woman buys a dress she wants more than protection from the weather. Among other things the dress is expected to enhance her appearance and help her to feel better. In a more technical sense, the buyer of industrial products wants to know what quality is needed for his intended use; what is the most economical way to purchase and ship the product; what sources can be considered as alternates in the event of strikes, fires, or some other forced shutdown by his major supplier. For every product there are certain advantages and disadvantages because no product is so superior that it cannot be improved.

Any product substantially above the quality of competitive offerings is bound to be imitated within a relatively short period of time and in the interim competitors are likely to lower their prices to hold their share of the market. Since many products in a given field are approximately equal in quality and price, buyers are often confused in attempting to narrow their choice and select only one.

Product features are the distinguishing characteristics which make the product unique and they are usually designed to appeal to a particular segment of the market. It is these distinctive characteristics which can be converted into the prospect's language to indicate what they will do for him that enable the salesman to build his presentation. If modern design, expensive chrome trim, and other appearance factors are the product features, then the salesman normally will make the most of the pride and sense of satisfaction that comes from owning such a product. A competitive salesman may point up the practical utilitarian value of his product which does not have expensive trimmings. The salesman for a manufacturer of 5,000 items plays up the convenience in time savings and the possible volume discount in ordering from a single source instead of doing business with many different salesmen. The salesman for the specialty company stresses the advantages of buying from a small house that excels in its field and can give personal attention to every customer order. Products are often appealing because they are members of a well-advertised and promoted family or group of products all carrying the same brand name with its implied standard of quality, the producer's reputation extending to the individual item. Other products are proudly advertised as being superior because the producer concentrates all his efforts on the single item.

Product performance is the most universal of all buying interests, from the inexpensive house dress to the most complicated piece of earthmoving mining equipment. It is the salesman's job to find out what the buyer's specific needs or interests may be and then to supply the appropriate information so the buyer can see how easily he can satisfy these needs. An inexpensive product for temporary use might be a much wiser purchase than a higher quality product which is expected to last ten times longer. Conversely, a cheap product that breaks down sooner than the expected life might be very expensive.

After the salesman has learned the product's technical aspects, he must learn how they may be applied to the customer's problems in the field. If the salesman is calling upon only one type of customer, he will need to learn only the product-use problems in that industry. However, to become effective he will always be on the alert to learn about any new product uses that come to his attention. In checking new uses, the salesman should make certain that the product is used correctly to assure proper utilization and optimum benefits for the customer. Products are designed and manufactured for specific purposes and the claims of performance as well as the guarantee are generally limited to normal use.

While salesmen are frequently taught to give a complete sales presentation, including the common features of most products in the field as well as their own exclusive or distinctive features, the purpose is not to overwhelm the prospect but simply to make the prospect familiar with all the basic desirable features of the product and the benefits of owning and using the product. Clearly, it is the prospect's knowledge or lack of knowledge that determines how much information should be presented. A few well-thought-out questions regarding the prospect's areas of interest and knowledge, interwoven with the sales message, can work wonders in saving time and making the presentation much more effective.

## COMPANY

"Whom do you represent?" This is another common question asked by prospects and many salesmen reply by simply naming their company and moving directly into their sales presentation. They should stop a moment and consider the buyer's quesion again. Inherent in this loaded question are many unspoken questions:

Is the concern reliable?

Will delivery be prompt,

Is the concern physically and financially able to handle my orders,

Is the concern really interested in my type of small (or large) orders?

Will my competitors buy at the same price quoted to me?

Will this concern be around or still in this line of business in a few years to supply necessary replacement parts?

Are they known to provide extra services?

Do they constantly strive to improve their products?

Will they make good on complaints?

These and many other unspoken doubts, if left unanswered, will tend to distract from the sales message and hinder or possibly prevent persuasion.

Knowing the company's history and objectives will provide answers to most questions cited above and will enable the interested salesman to understand why current policy and procedures exist as they do. If the firm is catering to a highly select market that demands a great deal of free service, then the price of the products must cover these extra costs. Attempting to sell this product in a market area where buyers are primarily concerned with low purchase price would seem at best to involve a handicap if not to be outright foolish.

In today's complex and ever expanding business world, a company tends to become an unseen and unknown, cold and distant object. Prospects generally prefer to know with whom they are dealing and tend to like a company image. The effective salesman can breathe life into his sales message by building a company personality which involves specific people in his home office and their personal involvement in processing each order for prompt and accurate fulfillment.

Building a company's reputation for quality and service aids persuasion because it increases the buyer's confidence in the people behind the product. Many products require an expert to judge their quality and the consumer is not qualified to evaluate accurately. Refrigerator-freezers, for example, often have a hidden and completely sealed mechanism. Most often the buyer puts his trust in the reputation of the manufacturer. If a firm is new to the market, an extra effort should be made to familiarize the prospect with pertinent facts about the owners or principals which will reassure him of their reliability and experience.

Company loyalty is basic to all salesmen who have self-respect and pride in their jobs, and whenever possible they praise their company and justify its position. Prospects respect this attitude for their own assurance of reliability and because loyalty is an expression of good manners. People admire loyalty and will often go out of their way to reward it.

## Company Services to Customers

Many manufacturers extend services to their customers beyond the regular product offering and guarantee. Mentioned earlier were instructions in product use to gain optimum benefits; proper maintenance instructions to prolong the product life of satisfactory service; testing and laboratory facilities to help solve customer problems in related or unrelated areas; training of customer's salesmen; expert aid on sales promotion and advertising as well as management functions of accounting, personnel management, stocking, inventory control, and the like. In most industries the service concept and customer-oriented marketing policy is dominant.

It would be an error in basic selling tactics to assume that a legitimate prospect is familiar with all of the desirable services available to him. The salesman should point out all the services his company offers even though he knows every other quality supplier offers similar services. This does not distract in any way from his honest offer to help the buyer. It might be a wise technique to cover all the services that are normally offered in lower-priced lines first and then go on to show that, in addition to these areas, his extra services are available in a number of other strategic areas of importance to this particular prospect.

## Industry Knowledge

An effective salesman has a good grasp of the general business conditions in his industry and understands how the industry came into being and what needs it serves. He is well aware of national economic and social developments that affect his industry such as population growth, location, and movement and trends in income for such groups. Government actions affect most industries through controls and other direct intervention; however, government spending and financing often have an indirect effect to which the alert salesman is sensitive and which he is quick to apply in his daily selling activities.

Knowing the size of an industry is necessary to understand its importance in the national economy and how this in turn relates to customer actions. Knowing the size of one's own company in relation to the industry can be important to reassure prospects of ability to handle their orders properly. A small company can boast of special services and rapid growth which will encourage prospects to do business with the underdog.

An effective salesman is aware of the leading companies in his industry and the top executive personnel because what they are saying and doing can be indicative of changes in policy and procedures which will benefit his customers. Often information and sales aids are available from company leaders and trade associations which enable the salesman to present his proposition in a much more favorable and interesting manner.

Industrial trends toward new features or improvements in product lines can be used effectively to persuade prospects, particularly when they are concerned with being modern and up to date in their purchasing. New applications of old products often open completely new markets to alert salesmen. Many industrial trends, such as new services, color, styles, sizes or miniaturization can be used effectively in selling; price trends due to inflation also are used to promote sales.

Related complementary lines are often a leading indicator of industry trend and the alert salesman can quickly utilize such information. For example, when related lines of merchandise incorporate ideas, styles, or concepts which his company has been promoting, it tends to be more convincing to the prospect as the salesman's claims seem more apt to be true. Related lines will vary depending upon the product; however, they are obvious in such areas as women's wear, which would include dresses, hats, gloves, shoes, handbags, and lingerie. Products are often related only in their marketplace, such as the variety of offerings found in a supermarket, and packaging trends of related products might be an important selling factor. Related or complementary lines are often indicative of price or promotional trends and this knowledge can be important to the salesman and his customers.

In some industries, the actions of suppliers to the manufacturer can foreshadow future events. Suppliers in this context include not only suppliers of raw materials but also suppliers of tools, labor, and suppliers of the capital to finance an operation. An alert salesman can often advise his customers about the effect suppliers' actions will have on future costs to the consumer.

Prospects and customers have many problems and needs which demand their attention and they will often rely on trusted salesmen to alert them to industrial occurrences which will affect their interests. They cannot possibly watch all things in all fields and welcome this legitimate service rendered by respected salesmen.

## MARKET KNOWLEDGE

By doing a little brainwork a salesman can save a lot of legwork, particularly in the area of market knowledge. Each salesman should know to what customer targets he is supposed to be directing his attention. Why should his company seek this group instead of that group? Most often a company will pick its market on the basis of its special ability to serve a customer need better than the competitors. This may be due to the location of the plant, its unique type of production, its product features, distribution channels, market outlets, or its strength in promotion. The area in which the producer and its personnel excel will normally determine the company market objective. Since each company even in the same field is slightly different, each company will have a different view of its customer targets. The informed salesman knows his objectives and why his company is in an advantageous position to serve that particular market.

After identifying the type of customer desired, the salesman must then find out where to locate such prospects geographically and how big the market is in each area. This information is required in order to divide the time and effort of the individual salesmen for the optimum sales coverage.

The marketplace includes many competitors offering products or services that claim to serve the same purpose for the buyer. Competition may be direct, such as between two airlines, or it may be indirect, such as between an airline and a railroad to the same terminals. An effective salesman should know what his competitors are best able to do for specific customer targets and what typical points they are apt to make which he must counter. Often knowledge of competitive products and practices in pricing, distributing, and selling will enable the alert salesman to eliminate some objections in his presentation. It will enable him to prepare to handle other points which might come up in the prospect's mind during his sales presentation. Such knowledge not only builds the salesman's self-confidence but also increases his value to the buyer since sincere advice which comes from an authority will be most convincing.

◆    ◆    ◆

## THERE ARE ALL KINDS OF SALES*

To most shoppers in the American marketplace, the sales world is covered by the retail trade. The nation's 42 million families currently are spending $260 billion a year for goods and services and over 70 per cent of what they buy comes through stores, door-to-door sales, mail-order houses, or other retail channels. Overall, there are more than nine million people in the retail trade, and they ring up more than $170 billion sales annually.

What the shopper does not see is the sales that precede his purchase. A pair of nylons, for example, can involve 10 intermediate sales before reaching a store; a man's suit, 18 sales.

Compounding these sales, manufacturers buy technical assistance, machine shop supplies, telephone and other services. Each is essential to the primary job —efficient production. Each represents a different kind of sale. The manufacturer, in turn, sells to other industries, to wholesalers and jobbers or to retail outlets. Again, each sale is a different type.

Du Pont, for example, sells most of its chemicals to other companies who use them to make consumer products. Only about five per cent of Du Pont's annual sales (for the past five years, sales have averaged $1.6 billion a year) are in products that go direct to the ultimate consumers.

As there are innumerable types of sales, so there are all kinds of salespeople. The drug store clerk, the locomotive salesman, the travel agent—diverse as their

* The above is reprinted with the kind permission of E. I. du Pont de Nemours & Company, Inc., Wilmington, Delaware.

jobs may be, they are all engaged in a vast sales effort that employs, directly or indirectly, perhaps 15 million men and women.

One thing all have in common: Ultimately, their efforts contribute something to the production and distribution process so that the consumer gets a better buy for his dollar. Their cumulative success is written in the U.S. living standard.

## SELLING *THE WALL STREET JOURNAL*†

Successful salesmanship, is built on your own experience of what works best for you and you are not required to follow any particular approach in selling the Dow Jones publications. The purpose of the enclosed material is to make available to you Dow Jones' experience, sifted by trial and error over the past 15 years, to act as a general guide towards successful selling.

*OPENING:* "This is Mr. Smith calling for *The Wall Street Journal.* I wanted to check with you to see if you are reading a copy of *The Wall Street Journal.*"

*THE BASIC SALES APPEAL:* "*The Wall Street Journal* finds that a lot of businessmen don't have time to read . . . is that true in your case, Mr. Wilson?" (Pause for response.) "Well, sir, *The Wall Street Journal* has found a solution to the problem."

"For example, every day in the *What's News* column you receive all the important business and world-wide news in capsule form, with a Bold Headline for a quick check. If you see an important business development, and you want more details, you'll find the WHOLE story on the inside pages."

"Another popular feature many businessmen find valuable, is in column five. Each day they check the special report. Starting with the *Outlook* on Monday you receive the *Labor Letter, Tax Report, Business Bulletin* and *Washington Wire* on successive days of the week."

"To round out the front page, every day in columns one, four and six *The Wall Street Journal* News Staff surveys some phase of the business, political or international scene . . . fifteen different stories each week to keep you well informed on important matters that are liable to affect your business or personal income."

*CLOSE:* "There are many more TIME SAVING features to *The Journal,* of course, but that gives you an idea how it solves the busy man's reading problem."

"I'd like you to try *The Journal* as your personal paper so you can form your own judgment with a little experience."

"The cost of the service will make you smile . . . only . . . 50¢ a week and delivery can be made to your home or office. *Which* location would be best for you?"

---

† The above is reprinted with the kind permission of Dow Jones & Company, Inc., Community Sales Program, Circulation Field & Phone Sales Division, Princeton, N.J.

# PART II

# The Psychology of Communications and Persuasion in Personal Selling

# 5

# Why Customers in General Buy—Theories of Customer Choice

In order to prepare a marketing program, a supplier must learn why and how people buy his products. Once the marketing target is identified and understood, then appeals can be designed which will interest the intended consumers. These appeals to groups of people are woven into most standard sales presentations in a natural conversational manner and are intended to create or increase the consumers' desire for buying the product. To understand the theory and practices of salesmanship, it is necessary to be aware of why customers buy. There are at least eight theories which attempt to explain customer choice from the buyers' standpoint. The divergent theories are divided into two main categories, rational and non-rational, each with four opinions or theories concerning what goes on in the mind of the buyer. Each theory helps to explain some group of buyers and therefore is of value in understanding prospects.

## CUSTOMER IS AN ECONOMIC MAN

In this theory, man is fundamentally oriented to material needs and as an intelligent being he is able to learn all about merchandise which is offered to him. Before making a choice, man knows all about the various products offered to him that claim to fill his needs. He knows about each product's applications and its relative utility value, price, service, and quality, and he is able to make his decision on the basis of cold logic. It is a mental exercise in simple economic reasoning. In practice professional purchasing agents for business and industry attempt to buy in this manner.[1] Some companies offer this professional buying service for specialized

---

[1] For a thorough presentation of the professional buyer's attitude see "Value Analysis," *Purchasing*, May 18, 1964.

groups such as religious institutions, hospitals, or schools. Many consumers enjoy shopping to find a bargain and literally do behave as an "economic man." When purchasing, most people want true value for their money.

Unfortunately this theory applies to a rather limited number of consumers and does not explain what motivates many other buyers. Granted that some people attempt to decide in this manner, too often they cannot know with any certainty which product really is best for their purpose. Elaborate testing laboratories with highly trained specialists have tremendous difficulties trying to choose between a number of similar products.

## CUSTOMER IS A PROBLEM SOLVER

In this theory, man is an intelligent and rational being who identifies his various needs and problems and gives them mental priority. He then seeks a reasonable number of solutions or alternatives but does not attempt to make an exhaustive search of every field. From the limited number of alternatives, man then selects the most reasonable choice that solves his problem or satisfies his known needs. He behaves as a problem solver who reasons out his needs and each step in his choice of products. The focus of his attention is limited to a reasonable number of alternate product offerings.

This theory is broader than the economic man opinion; however, it suffers from the same disadvantages. Many people buy products with little or no awareness of their true needs and very often without any effort to shop or compare their choice with other possible alternatives.

## CUSTOMER IS A LEARNER

According to this theory, consumers make their first choice or buy a product on the basis of solving a problem. They identify their needs, seek a reasonable number of solutions, and select the product that appears to satisfy their needs. Through the actual purchase experience and use of the product over long periods of time, the consumer, through trial and error, gains greater knowledge of available products. If his initial ideas, attitudes, and beliefs become reinforced by pleasant or satisfying experiences with a product, the consumer will repeat again and again. Each time he buys the same product he will make fewer and fewer comparisons and the decision time is shortened with each experience. Finally, the purchasing process becomes habitual and there is no conscious thought process in his choice.

While this theory has considerable merit, like the two previous theories it also is based upon the assumption that all buyers have knowledge of and weigh the relative value of each of their choices. In reality there are many people who make their choice between products in several other ways.

## CUSTOMER IS A RISK TAKER

This theory of customer choice also begins with the customer as a problem solver. He identifies his needs, seeks a reasonable number of alternatives, and selects the most promising to satisfy his needs. The theory then goes on to include the concept that the buyer is psychologically concerned over the annoyance of being stuck with a bad product or fear of being overcharged. In this view, the consumer buys national brands when aware of risk and he buys nonnational brands when he feels no risk.

Clearly this theory covers a larger group of customer choices because it admits the element of awareness. In this case the awareness is of risk or of feeling no risk. Unfortunately, the emphasis is entirely negative—annoyance, bad product, fear, overcharge—and buying becomes an exercise in reducing the unpleasant elements. In the market there are probably an equal number of customers without any feelings of risk who select a product based upon expected feelings of pleasure, happiness, or anticipated satisfaction. And, of course, there are some consumers who literally enjoy buying for the sake of buying, with little or no idea of when or how they may use the product.

## NONRATIONAL OR SOCIAL BEHAVIOR-ORIENTED THEORIES

### Customer Is an Impulsive Buyer

This view of the consumer rules out conscious mental reasoning on the buyer's part and has him make his product choice on a spontaneous basis without any critical appraisal or other evaluations. This theory attempts to explain studies of female consumer behavior in supermarkets where 30 to 60 percent of the items purchased were not on the shopper's list when she entered the store.[2] If the consumer had planned to buy beef but found the butcher talking about lamb, she impulsively chose lamb and then changed the other items on her shopping list to complement a lamb dinner.

---

[2] Gilbert Burck, "What Makes Women Buy?" *Fortune*, August, 1956. The author makes the point that any such figures must be qualified by the fact that women use the systematic displays of supermarkets as a substitute for a shopping list.

A recent survey of consumer attitudes toward food products showed that on one item 53 percent of the purchasers reported no brand preference, and of those with a brand preference, seven out of ten stated if their favorite brand were not on the supermarket shelves they would immediately buy another brand. Convenience was reported to be the biggest consideration in customer choice.[3]

While applicable to some buying situations, this theory of customer choice is limited by its condition of noncritical evaluation. The study cited above also showed that 6 out of 10 consumers checked advertised specials before they went shopping. Clearly, the relative size and importance of a particular purchase would influence many customers to screen all information very critically before making a choice. On the other hand, it should be acknowledged that some people under some conditions will ask themselves "Why not?" in a light offhand manner rather than "Why should I?" with a serious, critical attitude.[4]

## Customer Is a Creature of Society

This theory of customer choice explains buying behavior in terms of the power of reference groups, or group behavior which is considered normal and to which all the members of the group conform. Thus one sees businessmen wearing jackets and ties in the hot summer and women buying pointed shoes to keep up with the styles regardless of the amount of personal discomfort. Much has been written about conspicuous and ostentatious consumption which is based upon this theory of customer choice. Many people choose a product or brand name more to show off their status in society than for personal pleasure.

This theory introduces the new and valid element of the effects of socialization on customer choice. Unfortunately, it is too narrow to apply universally to many customer choices. If a person bought a particular expensive automobile as a status symbol, would he buy all other products for the same reason? An individual may have different buying motives under different circumstances and what is true for the individual is also true for the mass.

---

[3] For a detailed study of the changes in purchasing habits, personal fashion preferences, and opinions on public issues see Elihu Katz and Paul F. Lazarsfeld, *Personal Influence: The Part Played by People in the Flow of Mass Communications.* (Glencoe, Illinois: The Free Press, 1955.)

[4] See Margaret Edin, "Portrait of the Woman Shopper: The New "Professional Consumer," *Merchandising Week,* April 19, 1965, p. 36. A study of appliance buying by women, conducted by Dr. Eva Mueller, indicated that one-quarter of the group surveyed bought appliances on the spur of the moment, without deliberating on brand, model, or price.

## Customer Choice Is Pure Chance

This view of customer behavior sees the customer with no important pulls or pressures to select one brand over another and states it could not matter less to the individual which product he chooses. Each customer choice is pure mathematical chance and, in effect, no theory can explain customer behavior. A lucky salesman, calling in the right place, at the right time, with the right product, at the right price might be successful purely by chance. At least this "no theory" tends to neutralize the overemphasis of any other single theory.

It has been used to explain surveys which depicted prospects entering a store intending to buy one brand but quickly and easily switching and actually purchasing a different brand. In some cases pure chance does play a part in customer choice; however, in most cases there are other influences which do affect the final selection. One television manufacturer found a high percentage of customers entering stores in one part of the country had a preference for his brand, yet a very low percent of these same people actually purchased his set. Investigation disclosed the retailers were downgrading that brand because of forceful and unfair practices used by the manufacturer's wholesaler in that area.[5] When prospects switch brand preference it is normally due to a specific cause and rarely due to pure chance.

## Customer Choice as Viewed by the Psychoanalyst

The trend in marketing today is toward behavioral studies, and motivation research is currently in high style. Many psychoanalysts and psychiatrists view the customer as having three distinct parts: The id which emphasizes man as an animal with blind instinctive reactions, driven by his needs and seeking pleasure. The ego which is the deliberative part of a man that retains contact with reality and manages or controls his instincts for the benefit of the total individual. The superego, or conscience, which is the internalization of parents' words and views without thought—what the individual has been taught as being right and wrong regardless of his own feelings.

The base man, the id, says, "I want that," but the conscience or superego answers, "Momma wouldn't like that." From such motivation re-

---

[5] This occurrence was discovered as part of a detailed study of the entire television industry by Alfred R. Oxenfeldt, *Marketing Practices in the TV Set Industry* (New York: Columbia University Press, 1964).

search, marketers attempt to build appeals which take advantage of the basic man's desires and neutralize the internal controls which prevent his acting.

This Freudian view of the customer emphasizes the irrational, destructive, instinctive, and childlike behavior of the individual and is of interest. However this theory is now in disfavor with many leading authorities in this field. A substantial portion of the next chapter deals with current psychoanalytical views of the individual consumer. The reason the psychoanalytical approach to understanding customer choice is grossly undervalued is because it is a complicated and highly subjective evaluation which most marketing men admit they are not qualified to handle. For the individual salesman in the field the theory has little practical value at this time.

## CHARACTERISTICS OF COMMON BUYING MOTIVES

Theories of customer choice indicate there are many buying motives and a complete list would not be possible. Even if such a list could be prepared, the danger is that each motive would be pictured as separate from the others. In reality, there are usually several motives at work in any customer choice and the total combinations possible is infinite. General buying motives are classified as rational and emotional and both categories are often present in a single customer choice. Fortunately, most selling companies have found through experience that their products and services appeal more strongly to a few particular common motives. The sales presentation is then constructed around these five or six motives. Each company and each salesman should adapt his sales message to the particular needs of the individual prospect.

Common emotional appeals are directed to pride and ambition, love and affection, securing social approval and imitating, self-preservation and alleviating fear, acquisitiveness and gaining an advantage, dominating others, and pleasure and recreation.

### Pride and Ambition

The most common or universal of buying motives are the strong emotions of pride and ambition, either in self or in the business to which the buyer belongs. The young student works to improve himself through personal pride. Businessmen of all ages often buy their clothes to indicate their success. New autos and home improvements are often purchased not because they are needed but to reflect family prosperity. Contributions to charity are often caused or motivated by personal pride.

Manufacturers use this motive to sell to retailers when they state their line is being offered only to the better stores. Purchasing agents and professional buyers are influenced by pride in doing an outstanding job for their employers. They are often quite anxious to learn from the salesmen of new products or methods to increase efficiency or to cut costs. If the salesman's idea helps the buyer to look better or show off his efficiency, it will be hard for the buyer to resist. Appeals to the customer's pride in his company—to show off their facilities, for example—are often used by salesmen to get into plant areas that would not otherwise be accessible. Advertising and public relation expenses are often the result of management's desire to show their company in a favorable light. Office equipment is frequently sold on an appeal to businessman's pride in the appearance of his surroundings. Most high-priced products or services include an appeal to pride in their sales presentation.

### Love and Affection

It is universal to all normal people to want to be liked, understood, and appreciated. This includes the desire to be attractive as well as the desire to be accepted in family relations and business relations. Beyond the obvious increased spending for luxury gifts for loved ones this emotion motivates people to expend considerable energy to avoid being hurt emotionally or ignored. A company president will permit expenditures to please some of his employees when he values their opinion of him. If he must refuse their requests, he will often take great pains to be sure the employees understand why and appreciate his position. The same is true in more personal situations between father and children or man and wife. Alert salesmen quickly recognize such situations and are able to capitalize on this strong emotion.

### Securing Social Approval

The pressures of group norms often motivate people to maintain a standard of living beyond their economic needs. Clothing is often purchased by both men and women to keep in style and that clothing which is out of style is considered old, however valuable from a utilitarian standpoint. The length or style of a teenager's haircut is dictated more by his peers or the group norm than it is by his personal desire. Many products and services are purchased because opinion leaders have already purchased them. Recognized business leaders, outstanding medical authorities, large corporations, and leading colleges are often cited as using a particular product or service in an attempt to motivate the mass of smaller or less known people who want to follow the practices of the group leaders.

### Self-Preservation and Alleviation of Fear

A certain amount of fear is a normal and healthy emotion because it serves to protect an individual from many dangers. Every normal person avoids getting hurt or being placed in a painful situation. People try to protect their health, life, and limb, and appeals to this emotion are used to sell safety devices, fencing, good lighting, medical products, and many others.

Beyond the obvious self-preservation is the uncomfortable feeling of not knowing what will happen in a given situation. This uncertainty often causes fear and is generalized to include not only the individual but his family safety, his job, his company, his industry, the national economy, and even international or world conditions. Any product or service which will help eliminate or alleviate fear and uncertainty will have an emotional appeal and motivate the individual who is overly concerned in that area.

Fear of losing their physical appeal often motivates men and women to buy products which reduce the aging process—to maintain proper weight, proper diet, and proper rest. Cosmetics, hairpieces, and similar items are often purchased to maintain a youthful appearance. Ailing people desire to restore health and are frequently motivated to try any product which promises relief or cure.

Many products utilize the reduction of fear as their prime appeal, for example, emphasizing safety glass, safety tires, padded dashboards, and other safety features in autos. Fancy wrought-iron grillwork around a porch and steps may be attractive, but it also reduces fear of children falling off and getting hurt. Industry spends millions of dollars to reduce plant accidents and eliminate hazards. In marketing today, very expensive market research projects are started because of fear of the uncertain future.

### Acquisitiveness and Gaining an Advantage

Americans have been culturally taught that it is admirable to acquire many possessions and collections are evidence, in and of themselves, of something admirable about the owner. Books may be purchased to fill library shelves and paintings to decorate walls. However, the owner may never look at either. Renting equipment or housing is not as admirable or satisfying in our society as owning the same things even though renting may be economically more desirable. Mere ownership of many products gives people a feeling of pleasure. It is tangible evidence of a degree of success.

Americans are also taught it is admirable to increase their incomes and their wealth and to reduce outgo or expenses. The desire to acquire dollars is a common trait in Americans and appeals to this trait will tend to motivate the individual to buy. Economy and efficiency are designed to reduce outgo while investing for capital growth; earning interest and buying inventory, plant, and equipment low and selling high are all designed to increase income and wealth. Often speed and timesaving features are designed to appeal to this emotional motive of acquisitiveness.

Very similar to acquisitiveness is the emotional desire to gain an advantage or to get a bargain or something for nothing. People often like to show others that they are smart and shrewd buyers and will purchase merchandise more for the emotional satisfaction of putting something over on the seller than for the use of the product. Price specials are designed to appeal to this emotion. While it rarely builds customer loyalty, it at least moves merchandise that might not be purchased otherwise.

## Dominating Others

Many people have an inner compulsion to prove themselves superior to others in one or more areas and to dominate or "lord it over" others. American culture has taught its people that it is normal to compete with others and the one who excels is to be admired. The grading system in schools, Little League baseball, and other athletic events instill the desire to excel early in life. Our capitalistic business life and democratic political life both point up the American way of life that encourages anyone to build his own business or to become President. Professional athletes command enormous salaries and are highly admired by most Americans. Salesmen earn large commissions yet still strive to be named top man on the sales force.

## Pleasure and Recreation

People often work at jobs which they find distasteful and live for the time they have to enjoy life away from their jobs. Others, who enjoy their vocational activities, desire a different kind of activity off the job so they may return to their jobs refreshed or with a new outlook. In either case, evenings, weekends, and annual vacation times are used to gain pleasure and recreation. Some people enjoy physical exercise, many friends, and outdoor activities while others enjoy quiet hobbies, physical comfort, and being alone. Recreation and entertainment account for many large industries and many products can be used by some people for relaxing. For example, a carpenter's tools might be purchased by a business executive for his hobby workshop. With imagination, a creative salesman can often motivate his prospect by appealling to this emotional desire for pleasure.

Common rational motives, or those which the customer consciously considers and reasonably judges, include gain or the opportunity for profit, economy, convenience, utility, and dependability.

## PROFIT

Profit is the normally accepted reason for business in a free enterprise system and all products or services offered to a business are judged rationally and objectively with regard to their possible effect on profits. Original equipment manufacturers closely regulate their purchasing of raw materials, parts, and production equipment in relation to the expected selling price of their products in order to maintain profitable operations. Most merchandise is offered to resellers on the basis of their making a profit. The faster the items sell, the more inventory turns over and the higher the total profit. Buyers are often tempted to buy more than current needs dictate if a price concession is involved. Businessmen often purchase items for future use with the expectation that costs will be higher in the future. Such inventory speculation can be a dangerous practice, particularly if the businessman is a specialist in a field other than prognosticating the future of the commodity. Business failures because of inventory speculation are not unknown. This illustrates how strong the profit motive is in many rational individuals. Used legitimately, this common motive can be highly persuasive in selling.

Individual consumers have the same strong desire for profit or gain and they seek reasonable opportunities to increase their earning power. People will purchase products which will enhance their appearance if they can see that doing so will increase their job opportunities or promotions. They will buy many self-improvement products and services when they understand how these things can help them gain their objectives.

## ECONOMY

Economy is the optimum utilization of resources for a long term and the concept includes among many possible costs the initial purchase cost, operating costs, length of life, and in some cases the trade-in value. One product may be more expensive to purchase than another; however, it may permit a steady flow of uninterrupted production and hence be a more economical purchase.

For the retailer, economy may mean better utilization of floor space to increase sales; greater sales per clerk; quicker service and therefore ability to handle more customers per clerk; reduced inventory with little chance of being out of stock in the particular item, size, style, or color that the customer asks for; greater traffic producing window displays or more effective local advertisements to tie in with national promotions.

The individual consumer frequently considers economy of operation and maintenance when he purchases an automobile, clothing, fabrics, home furnishings, and many other products. Once he decides which item will give him the lowest operating and maintenance costs, he may then shop for prices on the exact brand and identical model which is carried by several stores, seeking the lowest initial cost.

## CONVENIENCE

Many consumers are fully aware of being motivated to buy because of the convenience features of a product or service. Consumers frequently make a mental note to buy certain items the next time they are at a certain store or the next time a salesman calls. At a later date it may appear to an observer that they are behaving on impulse. However, the reasoning had been done prior to the buying situation. Consumers consciously reason the value of convenience features before making a choice. This may include laborsaving features common to home appliances, ease of operation for accessories such as a self-starter on a power lawn mower, one-stop banking services, and the packaging of consumer goods which make six packs or other multiple purchasing and carrying more convenient for the buyer.

## UTILITY

Perhaps the strongest rational buying motive for most people is the use to which the product will be put. An after-shave lotion which emotionally

appeals to men to make themselves more attractive to women is often purchased with the conscious and rational thought that one brand has a
more pleasant odor than another and does not sting the skin. Even when
the buyer suspects his motives may not be socially acceptable, he is
conscious of what he wants the product to accomplish, no matter how he
may disguise his feelings to others. The point is that product usage is
primary and clearly reasoned by most buyers. They choose a product because they expect to realize certain satisfactions.

Utility may take the form of flexibility if the product or service has a
number of applications or can be adjusted or adapted to do more than one
thing for the user. Business machines, shop tools and equipment, printed
forms, and many other products are designed with features that permit
several uses. For the reseller, utility may be bulk packaging for storage or
packaging that folds into a floor display and container. Some items can be
easily marketed in several types of stores or different departments within
one store. This flexibility means the product has an additional utility value
to the buyer.

## DEPENDABILITY

Closely allied to utility is a separate factor termed dependability. The
buyer expects to realize certain benefits or satisfactions from his purchase
but in addition he expects these benefits to last a minimum length of time
and his selection is strongly influenced by appeals which stress trouble-free
dependability.

It is to assure the buyer of dependability that most guarantees and
warranties are issued. This is particularly important in mechanized or
motorized equipment and electrical equipment. The Underwriters Laboratories' label on a product is meant to assure the buyer that the product has
been well tested and found satisfactory. In consumer goods, the addition of
the Good Housekeeping seal of approval has appeal in the same manner.

By eliminating breakdowns or reducing the frequency of repair manufacturers appeal to this common buying motive of dependability. When
the manufacturer builds a reputation for dependability, he normally includes the concept of maintaining stock parts for repair and prolonging the
life of the product. Although automobile models change annually, the
manufacturers produce enough extra parts to enable the buyer to service
and repair his model for many years beyond the production run. This
supply of stock parts represents a considerable investment for the manufacturer and to some buyers is a very important influence on their choice.

One facet of dependability is uniformity of output or the production of products which are uniform in quality, size, color, and/or packaging. If parts must intermember in the future, this can be an important influence on the buyer's choice. In automated production, it should be apparent that quality control of the raw materials being fed into production is essential to maintain a steady flow of goods. In the garment industry, color control and size control are essential to maintain customers who will repeat their purchases. Office equipment is also purchased on the basis of uniformity for the sake of appearance and to prevent personnel conflicts.

## THE DISTINCTION BETWEEN BUYING MOTIVES AND THE BASIS FOR MAKING A SELECTION

If one were to analyze the motivations which caused a particular group of people to buy electric light bulbs, he might list six or seven motives which were common to most purchases. These motives might include safety, comfort, convenience, health, pride, profit, love and affection of family, and recognition. But notice, these motives would be applicable to any brand of electric light bulb. If a sales message were based on buying motivations alone, perhaps it would help sell a lot of light bulbs and be great for that industry, but it would not help any one company to increase its share of the market.

One must move from the abstract of common buying motives down to the specific sales problem. For example, why do some people buy GE light bulbs and not Westinghouse, Sylvania, or some other make? What is the basis for making a particular brand selection? If one were to list the company's strong points or sales advantages, he should be able to match each point with a benefit to the consumer which will influence the basis for making a selection or choice of brands.

| Company | Consumer Benefit |
|---|---|
| Old, established company | Indicates satisfactory service for years. |
| Excellent reputation and credit rating | Reliable and good company to do business with. |
| Position in industry | Continuity of supply; stands behind products. |
| Research by company | Products well accepted; safe buy. |
| Location of warehouse | Availability; speed of delivery. |
| Policy: "Progress is our most important product." | Assurance of correct buy; best available. |
| Nationwide price policy | Assurance buyer is not paying more than others; offers printed on bulk packages. |

| Company | Consumer Benefit |
|---|---|
| Range of line | One reliable source for all requirements in light bulbs; 6-watt to big spots. |
| Breadth of distribution | Convenience to buyer; select this brand and buy it most anywhere. |
| Color bulbs and "how to" booklets | Interior decoration and creating mood effects with lighting. |

Clearly every competitor can make a strong sales presentation exactly the same way and point up its unique advantages. If the purchase is large enough to warrant shopping as an industrial buyer might when he buys electric light bulbs in quantity for the entire plant, then the sales message becomes important. After the prospect hears several sales presentations, he will select the proposition which he feels will best satisfy his needs. The message that emphasizes the benefits which seem most important to the buyer is the one most likely to succeed.

## Product Features vs. Customer Benefits

Occasionally a prospect narrows his focus or attention down to a single feature of competing products. If a sales presentation has not covered this feature to his satisfaction, the prospect may ask questions about it. The salesman should be prepared to describe the product feature in detail but to be effective he must include all the benefits which will accrue to the buyer when he uses the product. For example, large users of file cabinets are often concerned with the one basic moving part, the slide. This may be a heavy duty cadmium plated roller bearing slide which supports the file drawer and permits the drawer to roll completely out of the file case or housing. If the salesman merely describes the physical attributes of the file slide, he has only half told his story. He should include the resulting user benefits which in this case might include the following: this will enable the file drawer to roll with a minimum of effort, which saves the operator's energy. This in turn will reduce filing errors, which are frequently caused by fatigue. As a result there will be quicker service from the file department and a considerable savings in personnel time and expense. These are the benefits the buyer desires and can easily understand. The salesman is now talking the buyer's language and is communicating.

A young college graduate may apply for a sales job and attempt to sell himself to the prospective employer. He might list his strong points as follows: intelligent, healthy, strong, understanding, sophisticated, educated, and ambitious. It would be a mistake in sales tactics simply to list these points and assume the prospective employer understood how they would benefit the company. To eliminate any doubt the sales presentation should list both the features and the resultant benefits that the user, or in this illustration the employer, will realize.

| | |
|---|---|
| Intelligent | Ability to gain and hold a high status job. |
| Healthy | Trouble free and reliable. |
| Strong | Ability to do a good day's work accurately. |
| Understanding | Sympathetic and easy to get along with. |
| Sophisticated | Interesting, fun to be with, socially acceptable. |
| Educated | Ability to learn and to do complicated jobs. |
| Ambitious | Willing to work hard for future rewards. |

Each college graduate could make a similar list but since people are different each list would vary slightly from the rest. In reality even graduates who were marketing majors in school rarely present this type of sales message when applying for a job. When the message is well planned for a particular company and it is delivered in a natural conversational manner, it has tremendous impact. Perhaps seven out of ten men will fill out an application form and go into an interview blind or without a sales message. Of the three who do prepare to sell themselves, the one who has studied the company and is able to relate his strong points to their needs or desires will most likely succeed.

Effective salesmen are aware of the buying motives which are common to most prospects in their line of business and use these motives to encourage the prospect to buy. Once the prospect has decided to buy, then the attention is shifted to the basis for making a selection and product features or strong points are put into the language which prospects want to hear and can easily understand. The product features enable a salesman to tell his prospect what makes it possible to produce the desired results from using the product. These features indicate that the product has the power to support the claimed benefits, making them believable.

# 6

# Why an Individual Buys—Prospect's Predisposition

Before a salesman makes his first call, consider what he would like to know about a specific prospect. The hundreds of bits of information he might want can be categorized into four groups as follows:

1. Predictable behavior. Does the prospect like to bargain. Does he like cold facts? What ideas, attitudes, and beliefs does he have fixed in his mind?
2. Right appeals. What does this individual prospect need, want, and like?
3. Right information. What information will be necessary to translate product knowledge into that which meets his needs?
4. Right language. What words and phrases should be used to communicate so the buyer will understand the message?

Marketing intelligence about consumers is assembled from four main sources: demographic and economic information, sociological information, and psycholgical information. Selective parts of this data are put together to form an understanding of small marketing segments or groups of targets. Each of these elements contribute to an individual's existing attitudes, interests, and typical buying behavior.

## INFLUENCES OF IMMEDIATE NEED AND ECONOMIC REALITY

Deomographic and economic information is used fundamentally to enable a business to determine who the prospective buyers may be and where they are located. The manufacturer of surfboards, for example, would not want to locate his plant in the middle of the United States because transportation charges to his market would be prohibitive. Distribution channels—such as selling directly to consumers, selling through wholesalers, or to a certain type of retail outlet—are decided in part upon knowing the market. For example, pesticides normally sold in drug and variety stores would not sell well in southern states where such items are normally purchased in food stores. Often the product itself must be altered to suit a particular market. The soap companies, for example, add hard water detergents to their formulas for certain geographic areas and common pancake syrup is varied in its viscosity to suit a special market by being thicker for the Pennsylvania Dutch.

Some areas of the country will readily accept products in aerosol spray cans while other areas will not. This variation of acceptability also occurs in packaging cream, liquid, or paste waxes in relation to the area these waxes will be marketed. Suburban populations shift like the sand and one area may grow rapidly while another almost imperceptibly recedes. This could be of value to any salesman covering a large area by indicating where greater time and effort should be spent regardless of the previous sales history of his territory.

Economic data includes information about the buyer's purchases, expenditures, income, assets, and liabilities. The U.S. Census Bureau has evolved a series of Standard Metropolitan Statistical Areas of the United States and reports regularly on these. Dun and Bradstreet reports this information on individual commercial firms and they include the Standard Industrial Classification code numbers for all business upon which they report. Various trade associations also compile and publish selected economic data for their members. *Sales Management* magazine reports annually its "Survey of Buying Power," which is an index of consumer buying power compiled by county population, effective buying income, and retail sales recorded for different consumer products.

## INFLUENCES OF A SOCIOLOGICAL NATURE OR GROUP PRESSURES

Sociological data include information about the buyer's relations with other people who influence him, such as social class, family, clique, voluntary associations, caste, age, sex, religion, neighborhood, and so forth. This information is normally obtained by direct survey of an entire area or by using various sampling techniques. Social stratification or ranking status in the American society can be done by type of income, type of occupation, type of neighborhood, and type of spend-saving aspirations, to cite a few examples. This type of information often provides excellent insight into group motivations and effective appeals.

This way of looking at the predisposition of the buyer is through social classes and spending behavior. A study has been conducted in a city of 10,000 to 25,000 population and later duplicated in the city of Chicago showing there is a very clear relationship between spend-saving hopes and expectations and the factors of mobility-stability. There studies started as sociological investigations of the broad patterns of living, moral codes, occupational status, and the like and were later successfully applied in marketing studies of the individual's economic behavior. They conclude that income is a poor basis for forecasting economic behavior while class membership and social mobility, together with spend-saving expectations, yield significantly reliable data for group projections in marketing.[1]

On the one hand, the values and beliefs of most Americans are pulled toward the accumulation of money by increasing the amount of money income and reducing its outgo. On the other hand, American values emphasize the accumulation of objects and products for display and consumption. The self-regard and self-esteem of a person and his family, as well as the public esteem and respect of a valued social world around the accumulator, are increased by such symbols of accumulation and consumption. These two sets of values, the accumulation of product symbols and the accumulation of money, may be, and usually are, in opposition. New varieties of objects, product symbols, are most readily accepted by the accumulators and most often opposed by the savers. Social class levels are occupied by people some of whom are upward mobile by intent and in fact, while others are nonmobile by intent and in fact. The stable individual would emphasize saving and security while the mobile individual is characterized by spending for various symbols of upward movement. Stable people overwhelmingly prefer insurance, the symbol of security, while the mobile people at all levels prefer stocks, which are risk-taking, perfectly willing to gamble on themselves as a sure bet to succeed, completely able to handle the world.

The light-blue-collar workers have the income for more ostentatious living than the average factory worker but lack the personal skills or desire for high status by social mobility. This man sees his home as his castle, his anchor to the world, and he loads it down with hardware, solid heavy appliances—as his symbols of security. The average factory worker is far less interested in his castle, and is more likely to spend his income for

---

[1] The original study was conducted and reported by W. Lloyd Warner and Paul Lunt, *The Social Life of a Modern Community* (New Haven: Yale University Press, 1950). The second study was by Pierre Martineau, "Social Classes and Spending Behavior," *Journal of Marketing*, October, 1958.

flashy clothes or an automobile. He is less property minded and he has less feeling about buying and maintaining a home. The newly rich or upper middle class of people are highly mobile and preoccupied with status symbols.

Another set of behavioral distinctions related to social class position was revealed in the spend-save aspiration study. The higher the individual's class position, the more likely he is to express some saving aspirations and the lower his class position, the more likely he is to think of spending only. Of those who would save, the lower status group preferred tangible investments such as real estate or a solid business while the upper status group preferred insurance and stocks and bonds.

A salesman's knowledge of a particular businessman should include some idea of his social class position and his mobility-stability dimensions in order to appeal to what the businessman wants for himself. A prestige symbol might appeal to one man who was highly mobile while another man who was stable and content would rationalize his purchases in terms of cost and economy, the ultimate savings he would gain by buying now.

One of the more popular discourses on the social predisposition of a businessman is expounded by Vance Packard.[2] He lists seven layers of status or occupations by prestige as reported by sociologists. As incomes go up, class differences intensify. Homes, automobiles, and fashionable addresses are some of the preferred status symbols and private schools and prestige-giving clubs are traditional vehicles for social climbing. Businessmen in modern city offices are subjected to this pressure in the form of desk size and type, the number of windows in a private office, and carpeting on the floor.

## INFLUENCES OF A PSYCHOLOGICAL NATURE

Psychological data include information about the ideas, attitudes, and beliefs of individuals and how they will react to specific appeals. Depth interviews are generally used to obtain this type of information. However, many social-psychological studies have been conducted which can be used in marketing decisions as well as individual selling or persuasion attempts. Market research specialists can separate the population into segments or groups of customer targets but they do not suggest that all in the group are identical. One approach[3] suggests four questions with reference to person-

---

[2] Vance Packard, *The Status Seekers* (New York: David McKay Co., Inc., 1959).

[3] This approach is adapted with permission from an article by Ernest Dichter, "How to Tailor Your Selling to the Individual Prospect," *American Salesman*, January, 1959, p. 36.

ality types and development in attempting to understand a particular businessman. Oversimplified, they are: How old does he feel? How does he accept and look upon his family status? How does he look upon his job status, his associates, and society's standards? What is his self-image, his psychological notion of his own richness?

While the bulk of this chapter deals with the psychology of the individual buyer, one should first appreciate how the various bits of information are used in business. Most often a selling organization will use a combination of information of the type mentioned, plus their own historical sales data, their knowledge of customers and competition, and the insight gained from feedback of information from their own sales representatives. By combining selected bits of information in an imaginative manner, market research people often discover sharp patterns and easily distinguish market segments. Consider the value of the following information to an East Coast manufacturer of lightweight luggage designed to appeal to people flying to Europe.

## MARKET INFORMATION

| | DEMOGRAPHIC | | ECONOMIC | SOCIOLOGICAL |
|---|---|---|---|---|
| RANK | Pop. rank # 1960 (millions) | | State income as % U.S. total | U.S. passports issued to state residents (RANK) |
| 1. | N.Y. | 16.7 | 11.6 | 1 |
| 2. | Calif. | 15.7 | 11.2 | 2 |
| 3. | Pa. | 11.3 | 6.1 | 6 |
| 4. | Ill. | 10.1 | 6.6 | 3 |
| 5. | Ohio | 9.7 | 5.5 | 9 |
| 6. | Texas | 9.5 | 4.6 | 8 |
| 7. | Mich. | 7.8 | 4.4 | 7 |
| 8. | N.J. | 6.1 | 4.1 | — |
| 9. | Mass. | 5.1 | 3.3 | 4 |
| 10. | Fla. | 4.9 | 2.5 | 5 |
| 11. | Ind. | 4.6 | 2.5 | — |
| 12. | N.C. | 4.1 | 1.9 | — |
| | | | Percent of total   50% | 17% |

Thus it can be seen that four states account for 50 percent of all U.S. travelers to Europe and a total of nine states account for two-thirds of the total market. Surprisingly, Massachusetts and Florida which are ranked ninth and tenth in population statistics and ninth and tenth in income as a percent of the U.S. total, are fourth and fifth in the number of passports issued to state residents. Pennsylvania, which ranks third demographically and third economically falls back to sixth on the sociological scale.

Within these nine states that account for two-thirds of all European travelers from the United States, who makes up the market? Sociological surveys have shown that predominantly middle-class people evidence ambitions to spend on recreation, self-education, and travel. These people are generally mobile by intent and in fact and they think in terms of symbols of upward movement. European travel would be such a symbol to them. This conclusion seemed to be validated when the airlines lowered their transatlantic fares in 1964 and achieved a tremendous increase in passenger traffic, indicating the mass market is substantially middle class.

Assume the luggage manufacturer's salesman was attempting to promote his line of lightweight luggage for air travelers to a department store in Boston, New York, or Philadelphia. Would the store buyer take on this additional line of merchandise based upon this general marketing information? If competitive salesmen shared this same marketing data, which one would get the order? Clearly the successful salesman must know much more than is provided by the general market research information. He should know the character of the individual department store, which includes the type of customers the store is trying to cultivate and he should know the particular person who makes the buying decision in his field. He should know the psychology of persuading this individual buyer.

A buyer might be predisposed to like a soft-spoken, intelligent salesman who used pure logic in his presentation. Obviously such a representative would have a better chance of persuading this buyer than a salesman who was boisterous and flashy and who depended solely upon showmanship to sell. The businessman might be predisposed to act favorably when a salesman talked of helping to make this department store the largest in the city. The buyer's behavior would be triggered by certain words which clearly pictured this desired result.

A successful farmer knows his soil and climate and he knows which seeds to plant at what time of the year. He knows how much effort he will have to exert in cultivating his plants and how much of certain fertilizers will be required. The successful farmer can predict his crop yield within reasonable limits. In the same way, the effective salesman knows his prospect individually, the business climate of the prospect, and which ideas to plant with the prospect at a given time. He knows how long to be patient and when to add sales aids to persuasion. The successful salesman can reliably predict the size of his order within reasonable limits.

If a businessman's reactions to the salesman's manner and message are predictable before the salesman makes his first contact, the salesman can be prepared with the right types of sales information—that which is interesting and congenial for this particular businessman and which will harmonize with his existing attitudes, beliefs, and needs—and the right type of sales approach to gain a receptive hearing. The chances of persuading this particular businessman increase in direct ratio to the accuracy of the predictions of his behavior.

## PREDISPOSITION AND PERSONALITY DEFINED

Predisposition is the collection of attitudes, opinions, beliefs, interests, and psychological needs of a person—the mental set of a person—before he is exposed to any persuasive message. It is the prior inclination, tendency, or susceptibility of a person to act or become receptive before being stimulated. Just as fatigue will predispose a man to a cold, so will an extremely egotistical personality predispose a man to the effects of flattery. Predisposition is influenced by physical and economic needs as well as by social or group pressures but the attitudes and opinions of an individual are based primarily upon his personality. The kind of person he is will most often determine how he will appraise a given situation and form his opinions.

Psychologists have defined personality as the persistent tendencies of an individual to make certain kinds of judgments or appraisals and to make certain kinds of adjustments to stimuli.[4] Most people are familiar with the idea of a particular person's character being indicative of how he will behave in a given situation and they readily prejudge another person's character.

A simple psychological experiment illustrates how common this readiness to prejudge really is. It shows how a reader almost automatically pictures an author and ascribes certain characteristics to the author. From a local daily newspaper, a topical but nonpersonal letter to the editor is read to a group. The members of the audience are then instructed to write their various impressions of the author of the letter and the results are tabulated. The types of impressions recorded are reliable in that they can be repeated with different groups. These impressions include the physical looks and age, the religious and psychological makeup, the educational experience, and even the specific family situations of the various letter writers. For example, the judgments of an audience reading a letter on juvenile delinquency might describe the author as a big dumb cop, probably Irish and Roman Catholic, with six children, a man who uses his belt to beat the children for any minor infractions of his rules. All of these impressions are gained from reading a single nonpersonal letter to an

---

[4] Laurance F. Shaffer and Edward J. Shoben, Jr., *The Psychology of Adjustment* (2d ed.; Boston: Houghton Mifflin Company, 1956), p. 310.

editor. The impressions are reliable in that they do show up repeatedly in subsequent tests but clearly they are not necessarily valid or true.

Imagine how easily a salesman will prejudge or appraise a prospect after a single interview. Even though the conversation may have stayed strictly to business, every salesman will come away with certain ideas regarding the race, religion, temperament, education, and many other attributes of the prospect. Obviously many of these impressions will be vague and some will be completely unconscious but many of them become fixed in the salesman's mind. Clearly many of these impressions will be invalid or wrong but nevertheless people do readily make such assumptions. At the same time, the buyer will make certain judgments or form certain opinions about each salesman he sees. This characteristic of human nature is reliable but not necessarily valid. These assumptions can be, and often are, quite wrong.

In a sales situation, a buyer's predisposition is his collection of attitudes, opinions, beliefs, interests, and needs as they relate to the product, the company, and the sales representative before the buyer is exposed to any persuasive communication. For example, one buyer may be predisposed to listen to a message suggesting economy while another buyer may be predisposed to listen to a message suggesting expensive, prestige-building products. Underlying his predisposition, one particular buyer's personality, for example, would lead to his persistent tendency to judge all salesmen as fast talkers who are basically interested only in themselves. Therefore, this buyer is skeptical of the claims any salesman may make. He persistently judges sales talks in a certain way and adjusts to the sales situation in a certain way.

## PERSONALITY TYPES AND THEIR BUILT-IN FALLACIES[5]

Since the differentiation of personalities involves the identification of what kind of person an individual is, a very natural tendency is to classify all mankind into various types. But every individual does not fit exactly into one of a limited series of classes. If a man is classified as a type without consideration of his other characteristics, it tends to blind the observer and conceal significant facts, which hinders a real understanding of the person. If one is given to "either-or" thinking, he is likely to regard people as good

---

[5] This section is adapted with the kind permission of Dr. Laurance F. Shaffer (Coauthor with Dr. Edward J. Schoben) *The Psychology of Adjustment* (2d ed.; Boston: Houghton Mifflin Company, 1956).

or bad, bright or stupid, and tall or short. Actually such qualities really exist on a continuous gradation from one extreme to the other without any abrupt separation into groups, classes, or types. When we have a clear and precise measurement such as a person's height, we can most easily accept the idea of a continuum rather than of separate types. In the field of personality, where accurate measurements have been slow in developing, the misleading habit of dividing people into types is as old as it is persistent.

One of the oldest concepts of personality types was that of the four temperaments ascribed to Hippocrates (circa 400 B.C.) and developed by other early writers. This doctrine of temperaments was accepted without question during the Middle Ages and well into the modern period. The four temperaments were attributed to an excess of one or another of the bodily fluids which were blood, yellow bile, black bile, and phlegm. The sanguine temperament was described as active and quick but lacking in strength and permanence. The choleric was easily aroused and strong but irascible. The melancholic was slow and pessimistic, and the phlegmatic was slow and weak and without emotion.

In recent times so many ways of classifying personality types have been proposed that it is impractical to list them all. There is little or no agreement among experts in the classification of personality types. One to which reference is often made in the social sciences is William James' classification of the rationalist and the empiricist.[6] The rationalist, or tender-minded person, is guided by principles and abstract ideas and tends to be idealistic and religious. An empiricist is a tough-minded, practical person, influenced most by facts and expediency. In this either-or classification, most American businessmen by implication are opportunists and are to be treated as empiricists. Obviously such an oversimplification is of no value in selling.

The characteristic behavior of persons who suffer mental disorders has been the basis of a number of types of classifications, such as schizophrenia or manic-depressive psychosis. The schizoid type of person is described as shy, uncommunicative, given to fantasy, having few external interests, and not mixing well with people. The cycloid personality, in contrast, is outgoing, talkative, overemotional and given to unstable fluctuations of mood. In extreme cases this type of theory has some validity but modern psychologists object to the either-or tendency when applying such formulas to a

---

[6] William James, *Pragmatism* (New York: Longmans, Green, 1907).

given case because most behavior shows some evidence of more than one category.[7]

The classification of types which has aroused much interest and controversy is the one proposed by Carl G. Jung. His best known distinction is between the two general attitude types—extrovert and introvert.[8] An extrovert is one who is dominated by external and social values while an introvert takes a subjective view and is governed by the relationship of things to himself. An extrovert is a man of action while an introvert is a man of deliberation. Here again is the either-or type of thinking.

Jung's complete picture of personality types is not quite so simple and the usual condensations are unjust to his entire theory. In addition to the two general attitude types, Jung also distinguishes four special function types based on the chief varieties of human expression which he observed. These he listed as thinking, feeling, sensation, and intuition. According to Jung, one of these four processes is especially well developed in a given individual and plays a dominant role in his adaptation to life. Since the extrovert-introvert classification overlaps the four special types, eight principle classifications of personality now appear. The extroverted thinker is concerned with facts and their classification while the introverted thinker is concerned with theories and their application to himself. An intuitive type is dominated by indirect judgments or hunches and can also be either introverted or extroverted. Jung's doctrine is further complicated by his assertion that more than one of the four main functions may be important and that an individual may be extroverted in one function but introverted in another. Also, if the conscious attitude is extroverted in any one line, the unconscious attitude is introverted, and vice versa. Jung's complete theory goes far beyond the excessive simplicity of the extrovert and introvert primary classifications but does so by delving into numerous subclassifications which serve more to confuse than to clarify.

A major fault of all theories of personality types is the assumption, direct or implied, that every person fits exactly into one of a limited series of classes. This rigid classification is not in keeping with some widely observed facts. Tallness, noted earlier, varies continuously from one extreme to another and this concept of a continuum rather than separate types should also apply to the various facets of personality. Another valid

[7] Carney Landis and M. Marjorie Bolles, *Textbook of Abnormal Psychology* (New York: MacMillan Co., 1947), particularly chaps. i–vi.

[8] For Jung's complete theory see Carl G. Jung, *Psychological Types* (New York: Harcourt Brace, 1923).

criticism of a type theory, and more pertinent to salesmen, is that it leads to a partial and one-sided view of personalities. Even an extreme introvert, for example, might be bright or stupid, ambitious or lazy, altruistic or self-seeking; hence merely to label him an introvert without consideration of his other characteristics conceals significant facts and hinders a real understanding of him.

The only valid justification for a doctrine of types lies in its application to a very small minority of persons who have acquired fixed habits of adjusting by one or another of the major mechanisms.[9] If some aspect of such an individual's personality has become so extreme as to be conspicuous to all trained observers and so important to him that it persistently influences all of his adjustments, then there is some reason for describing him as belonging to a certain type. The effective salesman knows enough about these extreme cases to recognize them when confronted with them and can adapt his presentation accordingly. The extreme egotist must be constantly flattered to maintain his interest in the sales message but this does not mean that a businessman who is justly proud of his achievements should be typed as an "egotist" and all other phases of his personality ignored.

## PERSONALITY DEVELOPMENT AS A LEARNING PROCESS

There is some evidence that personality is formed partially through structural factors, physiological factors, and hereditary factors, but basically personality is developed through the learning process. If a man persistently withdraws from many situations that demand adjustment, it is not because he belongs to a type but because his past learning has reinforced that kind of response.

The learning of personality, like all other learning, is determined by several factors. The first consists of the general principles of learning which apply to all mankind. One teaches a pet dog to sit up and beg or to be house-clean through reward and punishment. This is reinforcement and it applies in the selling situation when the salesman actually does perform as he promised. The buyer learns to appreciate the salesman through reinforcement. The second way people learn is called generalization. When daddy takes his four-year-old daughter out in his T-Bird and they go to the dealer for service, she finds out that T-Bird is made by Ford. From her playmates she later finds out that Chevrolet and Chrysler are similar and

---

[9] For a modern viewpoint see Dr. Karen Horney, *Our Inner Conflicts* (New York: W. W. Norton & Co., 1945).

the whole group is called autos. Later she finds out the same companies make trucks and buses and the whole group is called motor vehicles. Buyers also learn by generalization when they accept the leading product such as Pepsi-Cola, for example, and then group Teem and Diet Cola into the same general category.

The third way people learn is through inhibition. If a college student looks back on his early childhood and schooling—from kindergarten, grade school, junior and senior high school—he will tend to remember the fun. The experience didn't hurt or scare him enough to keep him away from higher education. Listen to old army buddies reminisce about their service experiences. They remember the fun but tend to forget the monotonous routine and uncomfortable events. This blocking of unpleasant memories or quickly forgetting wrongdoings is due to inhibition. In the selling situation, a loyal customer looking back over the years of associating with a supplier tends to remember the extra service he received and to forget the occasional errors or problems.

The fourth general way people learn is called reappraising. This is a form of trial and error behavior, as in teen-age dating experiences. After a few bad or unsuccessful experiences, one looks back to judge what went wrong and, hopefully, to increase his chances for a higher percentage of good experiences in the future. In selling, as a buyer gets to know a salesman better he is inclined to forgive his mistakes and suggest ways which they can work together better in the future. This is reasoning based upon past experiences. These four general principles provide tools for understanding the effects of events in the lives of specific persons.

Thus, one can realize, a young businessman who gets headaches that prevent his taking some action is probably a person whose adjustment by illness has been reinforced through prior experiences in which it removed him from fearful or anxiety-creating situations. Since the strength of an adjustment is a function of its past reinforcements, one can suspect that the young businessman grew up under conditions where getting sick permitted him to escape trying responsibilities. Perhaps his mother protected him when he was sick, babied him, excused him from obligations, and appeared to enjoy having him home to care for. The general principles of learning, such as reinforcement and generalization, help us to understand personality development.

The second factor in the learning of personality is the particular conditions of learning which govern what a specific person learns at a certain time. Personality is learned primarily from experiences with other human beings. Each person belongs to a number of social groups and each group may affect his behavior in significant ways. Members of the American culture speak English, have certain tastes in food and entertainment, tend to put a high value on material success and personal ambition. Many European, African, and Asiatic cultures have quite different norms and customs. In the same light, membership in a regional group, a church, a school, and the corner gang shape adjustment and influence the contours of personality through the contact such membership provides with other people and with their ideas of how one ought to behave. In short, personality is, in large measure, a product of social learning.[10]

Some social learnings are crucial to a person's happiness and effectiveness—those which involve conflict or freedom from conflict. Adjustments that help make a person at ease with himself and effective among others require in each case a response that is clearly either seeking or avoiding without the contrary impulse being present in undue strength. Conversely, adjustments that create inner tension occur when social learnings basic to personality have inculcated responses which are both seeking and avoiding of the same essential life experiences. Can the American businessman eat, achieve, enjoy, and love without simultaneously feeling guilty? Can he forego a satisfaction when circumstances require without having strong pangs of regret?

Some learnings that breed conflicts are fear or a strong anxiety in connection with one's usual roles or strivings, such as the desire to be a strong, authoritarian father who is also permissive with his children. When fear is strongly reinforced by punishment it tends to generalize to situations beyond the original learning and therefore to render the person ambivalent and conflicted in many spheres of activity. If a young boy chips a tooth while playing football and is severely punished by his parents, he may withdraw from all sports that involve body contact or he may generalize his fear and wish to withdraw from all competitive sports. He may in fact generalize his fear further and wish to withdraw from all competitive activity.

Another commonly learned nonintegrative attitude is hostility, or the expectation that other persons are unfriendly and must be combated. This seems to be at the root of many teen-age gang wars as well as most bigotry in adults. In getting to know a specific American businessman, special attention must be paid to the origin and degree of strength of several

---

[10] For the social influences in learning personality see F. J. Shaw and R. S. Ort, *Personal Adjustment in the American Culture* (New York: Harper & Bros., 1953); J. W. M. Whiting and I. L. Child, *Child Training and Personality* (New Haven: Yale University Press, 1953).

factors and their integrative opposites—confidence versus fear, self-regard versus anxiety, cooperation versus hostility, and freedom versus dependence.

While all people learn by certain general principles noted above, each one is individually subjected to specific conditions at a given time. The opposite of the young businessman with headaches cited earlier might be a man who believes that sickness is caused by some disapproved or unlawful act committed by the sick person himself. This self-condemning attitude implies that sickness is a retribution for wrongdoing. Still another theory of disease ascribes it to disobedience or neglect of duty. This concept shows the dependence some people place on the protection of parents and other authority figures. When one fails to please them, he feels uneasy and insecure. The unique experience of each individual and its effect on his particular learning can be illustrated by the following story. Assume three prospects were once from the same neighborhood in New York City, were of the same nationality, attended the same church, and were members of the same corner gang. As boys they were all unprepared for an approaching examination and became slightly ill. In one case, the mother liked to have her son home to baby him and fuss over him. He learned that being sick can be a pleasant experience through which he avoids facing an upsetting situation. Now he gets slight headaches to avoid facing business problems. The second boy, also home sick, had an unpleasant experience because his mother nagged him and forced him to do extra homework as punishment. He learned being sick and staying home is worse than facing an unpleasant issue. As an adult he now goes to work even when he shouldn't and he looks down on sick people as being weak and inferior. The third boy complained to his mother about feeling sick and she blamed his sickness on his being a bad boy who would not eat properly and therefore deserved to be sick. It was a form of retribution for his wrongdoing. She gave him little or no sympathy. This boy learned to feel guilty whenever he was faced with an upsetting or unusual situation. Now, when the boss calls him in, he becomes uneasy and wonders what he has done wrong.

Personality is alive and continues to change with experience from birth to death. It is never so completely determined as to be unalterable. Children have the most to learn and are more docile, less critical learners, and therefore acquire many long-enduring behavior patterns. Later learning proceeds against a background of older adjustments that are strong because of effective and frequent reinforcements. Much of the later learning involves a modification of adjustment patterns rather than the acquisition of new ones. For this reason adult education courses are much more involved than the same courses given to children in the lower grades. It is the entire cluster of learned attitudes of the personality which predispose a businessman to behave in a fixed or limited manner when faced with a situation involving conflict.

As noted in Chapter 3, in sales the prospect should be *approached* with the realization that he is happy with the *status quo* and is likely to resist change. The selective processes in resisting persuasion all normally serve to protect the prospect from salesmen who threaten his sense of well-being.

## DEFENSES OR PROTECTIVE UMBRELLA OVER PREDISPOSITION

The process of resisting persuasion includes selective exposure, selective perception, selective retention, and selective recall, each of which will be examined in detail in subsequent chapters. These selective processes are forms of escape, or defense mechanisms, all of which form a protective umbrella over the predisposition of an individual. Due to the principle of homeostasis, a person will go to extreme lengths to shield off attempts at changing his behavior and will generally resist in a predictable behavior pattern.[11] The prospect has already made certain decisions. He has decided to buy or not to buy. He may already buy from certain suppliers and he realizes certain satisfactions out of doing business with certain salesmen and with their products. Any new salesman, any new product, any change or new method of doing business is looked upon with suspicion and distrust by the businessman and he will not readily reexamine his habitual ways of maintaining his mental peace. Without realizing it he may look for the phony, the misleading statements, the lack of salesman's knowledge, the errors, the sloppiness of the salesman, or anything else that he does not like about people. He does this because the new salesman represents a threat to his inner balance.

Assume a prospect is the treasurer of his firm and the salesman learns the prospect is happily married, the father of two young happy boys, lives in suburbia, drives a new Oldsmobile, votes straight Republican, attends church occasionally, drinks moderately, smokes a pipe, and is pleasant to meet. One could learn a lot more about this treasurer such as his ambitions, sincerity, loyalty, and other character factors. One major piece of

---

[11] The originator of this word, *homeostasis*, was W. B. Cannon as he applied the principle to physiological processes. See *The Wisdom of the Body* (rev. ed.; New York: W. W. Norton & Co., 1939). This concept was later broadened to include the mind. See R. Stagner, "Homeostasis as a Unifying Concept in Personality Theory," *Psychological Review*, Vol. 58, 1951. pp. 5–17.

information in his predisposition would still be lacking. What is the company image which he tries to portray? If the corporate policy is economy at a given moment, does he interpret this to mean saving all income and spending only for production or does he interpret this as a policy of buying laborsaving materials to get the best use out of the company facilities? Clearly, before the salesman sees this treasurer, this predisposing factor would exist as a very important part of his makeup.

Another factor in predisposition is the immediate circumstances or situation preceding the sales call. A given businessman is subject to all the human frailties that other normal people are. A family argument the night before, sickness in the family, personal physical ailments or irritations, or character faults recently exposed at work, such as impatience, can influence a businessman's immediate behavior. If his day has been full of minor frustrations, the businessman will probably be short of temper. If the receptionist, whose job is to screen visitors, announces the salesman with any particular inflection in her voice, it may easily trigger certain responses in the businessman before he sees the salesman. The receptionist acts in behalf of the businessman to protect him from persuasion through selective exposure. His personal life experiences help maintain his self-image by predisposing him to hear and understand only that which is comfortable and compatible with the existing ideas he holds. He will tend to learn and remember only that message which agrees with his predisposed attitudes and interests and will fight in a predictable manner anything that attempts to change his behavior.

All personalities will vary quantitatively with respect to various intensities of stress and also qualitatively with respect to particular areas of adjustment. A businessman will react to certain ideas, people, words, and things according to what his individual experience has taught him. These predetermined behavior patterns are conscious and unconscious, sometimes rational and sometimes irrational, sometimes premeditated and sometimes impulsive, and they are predictable.

Predisposition seems to be a tremendous block to any salesman. However, it can operate in favor of an intelligent salesman who is willing to work. Before making the first call the salesman should learn as much as possible about his prospect and about the business and industry. He should do as much as is consistent with the size of the account before deciding on his approach and his general presentation. There are literally thousands of articles and books by successful salesmen about planning the call and its importance. Psychologically, the predisposition of a given businessman is the key to planning a sales call. But after all the intelligent planning in the world, the salesman must make a personal call. Studies of persuasion show that direct personal contact is the most effective means of communication.[12] This is due to feedback. The spoken objection or the unspoken expression on the face of the listener, the tone of his voice, his gestures, his general demeanor, or any combination of them constitutes feedback. The prospect's reaction may be mild, intensive, passive, or aggressive and the salesman must be skillful at observing it and evaluating it. He should adapt his presentation with a view to maintaining the prospect's interest throughout. Finally, the businessman must decide a proposition is in his own best interests before he will act favorably toward the salesman. Sincerity is paramount in any attempt at persuasion. The soft sell, without pressure or underhanded subconscious manipulation is the successful theme in effective selling today.

## SUMMARY

Reliable predicitions of a businessman's behavior enable the salesman to prepare his sales message so the prospect will understand and so that the message will contain those particular motives which will more easily persuade. The businessman has certain attitudes, opinions, and beliefs and he is predisposed to act in a given manner. This tendency to buy or not is influenced by physical and economic needs as well as social or group pressures but the repetitive behavior of an individual is based primarily upon his personality.

Typing people by rigid classifications can be misleading and confusing, as it often blinds the observer to the many subtle differences in individuals. People are primarily products of the learning process: the result of their individual life experiences and contacts with other groups of people. Due to the principle of homeostasis, people tend to maintain the *status quo* and avoid conflict and frustrations even though they have material, social, and psychological wants which are often contradictory. The mechanisms of defense are quite common and people generally do have a persistent tendency to behave in a fixed or limited manner when faced with conflict. Predisposition, as it applies in a selling situation, includes both the personal needs of a businessman and his organizational role. The processes involved in resistance to persuasion are forms of escape, or defense mechanisms, and they form a protective umbrella over the individual's predisposition.

---

[12] Elihu Katz and Paul F. Lazarsfeld, *Personal Influence: The Part Played by People in the Flow of Mass Communications* (Glencoe, Illinois: The Free Press, 1955).

A salesman must learn enough about an individual prospect to know what meaning the prospect is apt to apply to the sales message and what emotional overtones he will infer. The salesman can then become the authority to help the prospect solve both organization and personal problems that the prospect recognizes. By sincere and honest means, the salesman attempts to reeducate the businessman in how to look at a problem and how to get around obstacles and achieve his needs or goals.

# 7

# The Prospect's Selective Exposure or Willingness to See Certain Salesmen

Why does the normal businessman limit his exposure to a few select salesmen? Beyond the obvious physical limitations on his time and space or facilities, there is the universal trait of human nature—self-interest. Whether or not the salesman has fully investigated a particular businessman, he should be aware that the buyer is predisposed to behave in a particular manner. The salesman should examine the approach to the first call to see how it will effect subsequent visits. Selective exposure is the process of protecting the predisposition of an individual by selectively choosing communications that promise to agree with, confirm, and be compatible with existing attitudes and beliefs.

Studies have shown that a man will follow his own beliefs. For example, most people who are Republican in political outlook will read predominately Republican newspapers, follow Republican news broadcasters, and watch Republican-sponsored television programs. They will have social contact with other Republicans and, generally speaking, will tend to reinforce opinions they have previously held, often adopted from their parents. This reinforcement may or may not be conscious and rational but in either case it clearly illustrates the general principle of selective exposure. This tendency of people to expose themselves to communications in accord with their existing opinions and interests and to avoid unsympathetic material has been widely demonstrated. One study[1] showed the political exposure of voters in Erie County followed the pattern indicated above. Another study[2] reported similar findings in World War II in tests made by the U.S.

[1] Paul F. Lazarsfeld, Bernard Berelson, and Hazel Gaudet, *The People's Choice* (New York: Columbia University Press, 1948).

[2] Dorwin Cartwright, "Some Principles of Mass Persuasion: Selected Findings of Research of the Sale of United States War Bonds," *Human Relations*, Vol. II, 1949, pp. 253–67.

Treasury Department in Bridgeport, Connecticut, where only 5 percent of the adult population attended a well-publicized film designed to heighten citizen identification with such home front activities as bond purchasing and donating blood. The audience later was found to consist, for the most part, of already more active citizens.

A more recent study was of a media campaign designed to increase information about the United Nations and to improve attitudes toward it.[3] The results were similar to the previous studies. Those who attended most widely were persons whose interest in and opinion of the United Nations organization were high to begin with. Still more recently, a study revealed that articles on health, including those dealing with the possible relationship between lung cancer and smoking, were consistently read by 60 percent of the nonsmoking males among a probability sample of adults but by only 32 percent of the male smokers.[4]

Some time ago there was an educational radio program which showed in different installments how all the nationalities in this country have contributed to American culture. The programming was designed to teach tolerance of other nationalities. Results showed, however, that the audience for each program consisted mainly of the national group which was currently being praised. There was little chance for the program to teach tolerance because the self-selection of each audience produced a body of listeners who heard only about the contributions of the country which each already approved. Clearly, the problem for the nationality out of favor is to get its message to an audience that ordinarily will not select it.[5] In marketing this can be seen in ads run by newspapers and magazines themselves to gain advertisers and to show various percentages of selective audience or readers. Trade magazines, professional journals, and industrial publications attempt to gain admittance to a highly selective audience, those who will selectively expose themselves to an advertiser's message.

---

[3] Shirley A. Star and Helen McGill Hughes, "Report of an Educational Campaign: The Cincinnati Plan for the United Nations," *American Journal of Sociology*, Vol. LV, 1950, pp. 389–400.

[4] Charles F. Cannell and James C. MacDonald, "The Impact of Health News on Attitudes and Behavior," *Journalism Quarterly*, Vol. XXXIII, 1956, pp. 315–23. And for an updated study, see Karl H. Stein, "Disease and Cigarettes—A Consumer Opinion Study," *Business and Society*, Autumn, 1964, pp. 32–37 (A telephone survey taken four months after publication of *Smoking and Health*, The Surgeon General's Report).

[5] Paul Lazarsfeld, "The Effects of Radio on Public Opinion," in Douglas Waples, (ed.), *Print, Radio and Film in a Democracy* (Chicago: University of Chicago Press, 1942).

## COMPATIBILITY OF MESSAGE WITH PREDISPOSITION

When applying this selective exposure principle to businessmen who have the opportunity to see more salesmen than their time will permit, which salesmen will they see? More specifically, why will they give some time to one salesman but not to another? Basically, a businessman will give time to the salesman who he expects will confirm his existing beliefs and his buying actions and to the one who will talk about ideas that are comfortable to him and compatible with his predisposition.

If the businessman most often buys name brand or nationally advertised items and his surroundings indicate he is predominantly concerned with symbols of quality and prestige, he is most apt to allot time to a salesman representing a name brand, for example, International Business Machines or General Electric. The brand names which the prospect considers to be top quality will usually trigger acceptance within a given industry insofar as permitting exposure. This businessman is not likely to give some of his precious time to the salesman who is representing a brand name that the prospect perceives as inferior, regardless of the true quality of the product represented. In other words, the selective exposure in this instance works to the advantage of the brand name salesman whose product the prospect believes to be the best in his industry.

On the other hand, a businessman who is primarily concerned with the initial purchase price of an article if he can be reasonably sure the quality is comparable will not devote much of his time to the brand name company that insists on its nationally published prices. This businessman will give more of his precious time to the lesser known company, particularly if the request to see him includes a teaser indicating a price bargain. While this illustrates the extremes of either-or, in practice the majority of businessmen are between these two extremes and are on a continuum of buying philosophies. This illustrates why the salesman should know as much as possible— as much as is consistent with his purposes—about the businessman's predisposition to act in a predictable manner. Even brand name companies have their cost reduction appeals and the lesser known sales company has its prestige items and prestige users. If the small company representative requests to see a particular businessman about a reduction in the cost of certain items which he normally buys, the appeal may be interesting enough for the businessman to devote some time to listen.

To gain selective exposure a salesman must convincingly promise the businessman satisfaction for the time he takes and he should appeal to the known predisposition of the individual in his personal needs and in his business role. If tricks or lies are used, the salesman may gain an audience but more quickly lose a prospect. The appeal must be genuine and sincere to be effective in making possible a repeat call.

## PERSUASION AND CONFIDENCE

If there is a single key to persuasion, it is confidence. The prospect must learn to trust what the salesman says before he will place any confidence in his proposition or take any action the salesman recommends. The effectiveness of various techniques of persuasion appear to be contingent on the presumed character of the message source. Studies have shown that sources which the audience holds in low esteem appear to constitute at least a temporary handicap.[6] What constitutes such esteem? Studies have shown that audiences respond particularly well to specific sources because they consider them of high prestige, highly credible, expert, trustworthy, close to themselves, or just plain likable. The Yale Communication Research Program has extensively investigated this influence of sources and their effect on persuasion.[7] Its findings have been confirmed by other researchers.

If the businessman, for reasons of his own, gives some of his precious time to a salesman and hears a memorized talk that he has little or no interest in, he cannot develop much confidence in the salesman and will be less apt to see him on his next visit. If the businessman hears a salesman using the formula method and follows him in the steps from attention to the desired portion of this planned talk but then without apparent reason he loses interest, he may think more of this man than the first but still be far from having confidence in the salesman. The salesman using questions to learn of the buyer's wants and needs will prove more interesting because the buyer is encouraged to participate in the conversation. Too often this salesman will jump to conclusions and this may overwhelm the prospect, particularly so if the salesman is successful in hitting the key emotional need on his first call. This can be a frightening experience which the buyer will not wish to repeat. No one wants to be manipulated by others and particularly not by a salesman who is a total stranger. Rather than build confidence, this approach often works negatively and creates suspicion and

---

[6] Carl I. Hovland and W. Weiss, "The Influence of Source Credibility on Communication Effectiveness," *Public Opinion Quarterly*, Vol. XV, 1951, pp. 635–50.

[7] Carl I. Hovland, Irving L. Janis, and Harold H. Kelly, *Communication and Persuasion* (New Haven: Yale University Press, 1953). See also Frederic A. Powell, "Open- and Closed-Mindedness and the Ability to Differentiate Source and Message," *Journal of Abnormal and Social Psychology*, July, 1962, pp. 61–64.

doubt. The salesman using an honest problem-solving approach is completely sincere and builds confidence by his very manner. He is truly interested in the businessman, his firm, and what he has to say. This begets interest because an individual normally likes people who like him. This salesman may not even talk of his own product and herein lies the danger. The buyer may not associate this salesman with any product or company and hence not even think of him in the future when he does have a need in this area. The most effective impression will be created by the salesman using the combined approach. He utilizes the effective features of the other techniques in a soft friendly manner and leaves the buyer with the impression that this salesman not only knows what he is talking about but also is a very likable person who can listen. The buyer will be predisposed to see this salesman again. Each subsequent exposure should reinforce his confidence in this salesman, eventually in what he proposes, and ultimately he will be persuaded by his own changing predisposition to act upon this salesman's recommendations.

## EXPOSURE DUE TO IMMEDIATE INTEREST OR KNOWN NEED

Almost everyone knows some lucky salesmen. They make fewer calls than average but sell more; they talk to a businessman about a small order and suddenly get a big order. However, the very fact that this happens again and again should make one suspicious of their so-called luck.

Many salesmen use sheer numbers to offset their poor luck and make 100 calls, applying the law of averages, in the expectation of finding ten prospects and ultimately getting one order. The lucky salesman makes 20 calls, develops ten or more prospects and closes five to ten orders. Luck? Sales managers constantly nag at salesmen to make more calls and to increase the chances for exposure to their product or to go out and find that small percentage of the market that needs their product. In private, sales managers admit they would love to hire a dozen more "lucky" salesmen instead of all the plodders they now employ.

The lucky salesman in reality is well on his way to being an effective salesman and he stands out head and shoulders above the crowd of amateurs. Although he may not realize it, he makes fewer calls because he has done the brainwork before he attempts the legwork. Given a list of 100 names, the effective salesman will sit down and analyze their possibilities for an honest use of his product and will investigate the industry and a number of companies in particular. He narrows the list down to 20 and ranks these as to probability. The true professional will now start with the smallest possible buyer, in terms of potential order, and use him as a trial case, or dry run, for his theory on approach and sales presentation. In this process, he learns the common objections, the normal applications, the points the buyer considers of interest. After this call, this salesman revises his approach and presentation and calls on the nineteenth company on his list and learns more. Long before he calls on the company ranked tenth on his list, he will have developed a more thorough knowledge of the situation than all of the unlucky salesmen competing against him and many of the buyers he contacts.

The effective salesman becomes something of an expert in this area and is well versed in the honest applications of his product and the honest objections to it. Depending upon how quickly he can perceive the important points and adjust his selling techniques to them, some of the number 20 to 11 companies on his list will become prospects. From the tenth rank on down to number one, he will have the necessary confidence that comes with knowledge and his closing average or number of orders will shoot up effectively. By the time he reaches the company with the largest potential, he is confident of his approach under various conditions and will have learned much about this particular buyer. To gain selective exposure, he will appeal to the area in which the buyer is known to be most interested. He will often have a recent sale and be able to incorporate the results of the application into his final presentation.

Compare this technique to that of the unlucky plodding salesman who gets the same list of 100 names and rushes out hoping to make 100 quick calls and find the 10 who may listen to his story. Even if his stamina holds out, the discouragement of being told no by 90 intelligent businessmen is hard for anyone to hide. Even if ten men tell him they are interested, this salesman is 50 percent behind the effective salesman in sheer numbers of prospects and he cannot begin to compare as an expert who has knowledge of application, objections, and methods of presentation. One need not wonder why one man is successful and the other is not.

## EXPOSURE DUE TO A KNOWN PROBLEM

When a businessman is aware of a problem he will often seek help. For most salesmen this is the most desirable situation. The buyer is predisposed to listen and will selectively expose himself to those companies or salesmen who he expects can help him solve the problem. If the salesman has this lead or inquiry, regardless of what sales technique he uses, his closing average should be high. If his product honestly solves the problem, the salesman using a memorized talk can quickly and concisely present the many facts necessary for the buyer to make his decision. If his sales technique follows a set mental formula such as attention, interest, desire, conviction, and action, the salesman that gets the lead is already 40 percent ahead of a cold call because he has two of his five steps achieved before he begins his presentation. If he is adept at analyzing and thinking on his feet, he has the advantage over the first salesman in that he can create—on the spot—a talk that will fit this particular application and be more personal.

A third salesman might use the question and answer, or want-satisfaction, method of selling. He will encourage the businessman to do most of the talking while he listens for the needs, or wants, both personal and organizational. If the salesman is accurate in his understanding of the true wants, which may vary from the spoken obvious to the hidden motive, he will hit the magic emotional button and quickly get the order that either of the first two men would have missed. If the selling technique is problem solving, the salesman will sincerely put himslef in the buyer's shoes and analyze the total situation, its immediate alternate solutions, and their long-range effects. He may recommend his own product, his competitor's product, or possibly that no purchase be made at this time. This has tremendous impact upon a businessman when done sincerely. In future dealings the businessman will be predisposed to act favorably upon this salesman's seemingly unselfish recommendations and the salesman will be first on the buyer's list for future selective exposure. This approach is based on the premise that it is better to gain a customer for a lifetime than it is to gain a single sale now. While one of the first three salesmen cited above may have gotten this initial order, the fourth salesman will ultimately succeed in building the trust and confidence for customer loyalty.

The fifth technique on the broad continuum of sales presentations really combines the best of all the others. This salesman will ask enough questions to understand the businessman's problem, his immediate objective, his long-range objectives, his overall business, and much of his personality. This salesman will sincerely analyze the various alternatives and concisely explain their merit and application. He will recommend a valid solution as an expert and he will have the greatest chance of persuading the businessman on the initial sale and, in addition, in future repeat buying situations.

Obviously when a buyer is aware of a problem and calls a salesman, he is predisposed to listen and has made selective exposure possible. It is not strange then than salesmen using any honest sales technique can persuade a businessman to buy under these conditions. Sales managers in almost

*Courtesy: International Business Machines Corp., Armonk, N.Y.*

FIG. 5. A sales representative talks to grain elevator operators about record-keeping problems.

every line of business continually try to develop more legitimate sales leads for their men.

## BUYER NOT AWARE OF HIS NEED

Unfortunately, leads are usually too infrequent to occupy a sales staff full time and most of a salesman's time is spent looking for businessmen who will give him exposure. How can one apply the principles of predisposition and selective exposure to developing new accounts?

An interesting side effect of persuasion is that when opinion conversion works at all, it is usually through a redefinition of the issues. It generally results from the reinforcement or building up of an associated but subordinate attitude, which causes this new attitude to dominate the many other existing attitudes and interests. In psychological terms, while a direct frontal attack is likely to hinder change, a side attack, which consists of creating a new opinion, is a procedure in which these selective processes are not likely to be operating.[8] In sales terminology, this is the problem-solving technique where the buyer is not aware that he has a problem.

The effective salesman analyzes his prospect's business in relation to the

[8] Douglas Waples, Bernard Berelson, and Franklyn R. Bradshaw, *What Reading Does to People* (Chicago: University of Chicago Press, 1940).

product to be sold. He attempts to find ways that can cut costs, improve service, increase profits, or the like for the buyer by saving time, money, space, or increasing turnover of merchandise for resale. Rather than jumping in with both feet and talking a mile a minute, he asks the businessman questions about his business and listens attentively. He compliments his competitor's brands and reassures the buyer by approving of the prospect's judgment in choosing such brands. He makes no claims about his product's superiority. However, he may capitalize on the feature that makes his line different from the competitors' if there really is a recognizable difference. The salesman attempts to get the buyer to talk about his business problems, a subject most often dear to the buyer's heart and likely to interest him. By offering to help him solve his problems, the salesman makes the buyer aware that he is making his own decisions and making them with expert advice. This is the soft-selling technique with no pressure evident as it is now taught in many graduate business schools throughout the country. It is based on the complete sincerity of the salesman.

Most businessmen are constantly looking for ways to improve their service, make better use of their personnel, make better use of their capital equipment, increase their own share of the market, reduce capital tied up in inventory, increase the rate of merchandise turnover, provide greater protection against possible losses, and so on. Any attempt to lay out a plan in one of these areas will be of some initial interest to the businessman. The sales audit is part of this technique. Here the salesman acknowledges the businessman is probably doing the right thing now but offers to study the situation and honestly compare current practices or costs with industry norms. It can be of interest to the businessman in the same way that an outside auditing firm will verify internal accounting practices. The report after investigation should be reassuring and can often be profitable as well by turning up minor problems that can easily be corrected.

Here is the effective salesman again, offering a sincere service to a businessman while his unlucky competitor is knocking on doors as fast and as long as he can, hoping to find someone who will listen to what he has memorized to say about a product. The effective salesman considers a service complaint as another opportunity to reinvestigate a problem while the unlucky salesman looks upon this type of call as a nonproductive nuisance that he would rather avoid. Whenever the effective salesman makes a detailed study of some phase of his prospect's business, he will know much about this unique firm that makes it different from its competitors and he will be able to talk the same language as the businessman and therefore be more acceptable in the future. He will have earned a place on that businessman's list for future selective exposure.

## EXPOSURE DUE TO COURTESY

Businessmen are generally nice guys, warm and friendly, and would really like to buy from most salesmen if it were humanly possible. Many of them hate to say no and certainly do not take any pleasure in telling a salesman he has lost an order. They will often see any salesman on his first visit simply to be courteous. This courtesy may be based on trust in the reputation of the selling company, its products, or even on a friend's referral. The buyer may also have a secondary motive such as to keep posted on new products and applications or to keep posted on what competitors are doing. He may simply wish to maintain good public relations for his own firm. Whatever his motive for seeing the salesman, the buyer is entitled to some return for his time invested and for his courtesy. This is an ideal time for the salesman to gain information in a friendly manner and to begin building the buyer's confidence in him by providing helpful information and offering services. If the prospect does not feel satisfied with the exchange for the time he granted, there may not be a second chance at exposure.

## LIMITS OF PERSUASION

Obviously there are definite limits of persuasion. Short of hypnosis and blackmail, a man simply will not do what he thinks is against his own best interests. One expert in the field of persuasion limits points out that in human relations, while appeals to noneconomic motives and appeals to unconscious motives seem to become more effective as knowledge of social science develops, on the other hand as the persuaders become more sophisticated so do the people to be persuaded. Since the knowledge of manipulation has become widespread among businessmen, there has been an increasingly effective use of the mechanisms of defense and escape or resistance to persuasion.[9]

Assuming techniques improve, one must remember that the audience will not remain the same. They gain in the strength of their resistance. After all, one begins learning to see through persuasion attempts as early as he begins eating baby food. When good old reliable father tastes baby's food and smacks his lips over it, baby may be led to taste. If the taste is pretty bad, an antipersuasion analyst is created. While parents are usually wise and unselfish concerning baby's welfare, children soon discover that

---

[9] Raymond A. Bauer, "Limits of Persuasion," *Harvard Business Review,* Vol. 36, No. 5, 1958, pp. 105–10.

parents are not invariably selfless or entirely accurate. An early bedtime for
the children may serve the parents' desire for social activity. Timid parents
overestimate the probability that a puppy will bite and that a kitten will
scratch and children find these things out. Most parents are then regarded
as often reliable dispensers of correct information but as occasional misleading manipulators of the truth. The trick is to discover when they are
manipulating. Long before the child starts formal schooling, he is aware of
the more obvious techniques of personal persuasion. Life continually
teaches him the more subtle appeals and how to resist them.

Attempting to determine which appeals to unconscious motives will be
most effective can be very frustrating because motivation research is not
the exact science the experts would like it to be. One story tells of a
consultant in consumer motivation who was studying packaging for a
maker of juvenile products. He stationed himself outside of a supermarket
and gave money to a number of boys with instructions for them to buy
anything they wanted. As the boys came out, the researcher eagerly
checked with each one to see what type of package had attracted him.
Every single boy came out of the store with a watermelon! Subliminal
appeals are subtle and complex and they are often missed by a large
number of the audience. They may also boomerang, as some individuals
respond negatively, or opposite to what is intended, to the unseen stimuli.
An amusing example of negative behavior in a marketing campaign occurred in November, 1963, in the area around Seattle, Washington, where
advertisements warned the public not to buy a certain kind of imported
nut which tasted bad and would be un-American to support. Within a few
weeks sales had more than doubled![10]

It is man's native intelligence, his indomitable spirit, and the learning
process that define the limits of persuasion. Because individuals vary in
proficiency and motivation, the limits of persuasion will also vary from the
highly gullible to the highly skeptical.[11]

## PROSPECTING FOR NEW ACCOUNTS

Persuading men in business depends upon more than knowing the
individual buyer and having the ability to communicate a message. Obviously the salesman must find someone to persuade. This is prospecting and
it is so apparent and so important that many salesmen fail to see it. A big
backlog of prospects is another key to successful persuasion. As soon as the

---

[10] *New York Times*, Advertising column, November 15, 1963.

[11] This conclusion is drawn directly from Bauer, *op. cit.*

salesman finishes working with one sales problem he can immediately begin another.

Effective salesmen do not think of prospecting as knocking on so many doors but as using creative imagination and thorough analysis. Some of the qualities needed to find prospects are a sense of the realities of a situation, an awareness of possibilities, and, finally, the ability to make a decision and take action. One popular story tells of the printing salesman who so highly developed his sense of the realities and his alertness that his customers and his competitors looked upon him as psychic. He was always on the right spot just before the order was to be placed. He was effective because he was alert and thought constantly about his prospecting.[12] Another famous story tells of a successful salesman having lunch in an exclusive club where he saw a father and son, both important industrialists in that city, and their lawyer lunching together. The salesman later telephoned the father for an appointment. Within three days he had written a sizable amount of business life insurance on father and son yet had never called on these people before and was the only life insurance salesman who did so at this time. How did he know they were ready to buy? Knowing who the people were was primary and being in a position to observe was also necessary. The point of this story, however, was the effective salesman's awareness of possibilities. He sensed the possibility that two industrialists together with their lawyer might indicate a business reorganization and he was right.[13]

Some sales managers recommend that their men spend at least 30 minutes each day thinking about where they can find more prospects and that they then compile a list which can be revised regularly. Other sales managers suggest a different list of prospects for each field of likely customers. Finding the influential buyer is clearly one of the keys to becoming an effective and creative salesman.

## PROSPECTING THE SAME INDUSTRIAL ACCOUNTS

Industrial salesmen generally call regularly on the same group of firms whether they buy or not and the question arises, Is their problem of prospecting so different? Not really. Industrial and commercial prospects fall into four major groups: (1) new concerns in the area or new in a particular line of business; (2) old customers who no longer buy for one

---

[12] Charles B. Roth, How to Make $25,000 a Year Selling (Englewood Cliffs, N.J.: Prentice-Hall, Inc., 1953).

[13] Frank Bettger, How I Raised Myself from Failure to Success in Selling (Englewood Cliffs, N.J.: Prentice-Hall, Inc., 1949).

reason or another; (3) firms who use the particular type of product but have never purchased from the one supplier before. (4) Finally, there are the present customers who can buy more of the products.

Getting new prospects is essentially the same in any line of selling but prospecting among the same group of concerns over and over requires creative, imaginative, development selling and an understanding of the processes of persuasion are important here. Getting old customers back into the fold is not as difficult as it might appear at first glance. They once had reason to place confidence in a particular company and the job of the salesman is to renew that confidence. In such a situation the salesman has something to start with and can plan an effective side attack—for example, to renew old acquaintances of his company—which is more effective in persuasion than a direct frontal assault.

The toughest prospects are those that have standardized on a competitor's product. However, when a salesman understands why persuasion works and how conversion works, he will be in a position realistically to add some of these names to his prospect list. Finally, the easiest to persuade are his existing customers. If the salesman has new products or new applications or new ideas for the use of old products, existing customers will buy more and more because they already have confidence in the salesman and are predisposed to accept his recommendations.

## NATURAL ATTRITION OF REPETITIVE BUYERS

Salesmen should remember there is a natural turnover of buyers within a company as well as a natural attrition of accounts away from existing suppliers. The law of attrition means simply that the same customers do not stay with one supplier indefinitely year after year.[14]

Businessmen often change their attitudes as they mature and experience satisfaction with some products and services while others fail to satisfy them. Things do not always look the same at age 45 as they did to the same man when he was 25. Customers grow old, get sick, and retire. Individuals that influence buying may change jobs, get promoted out of jobs, and for many other normal reasons are never a permanent obstacle to a salesman. Regular calls will make the salesman alert to such changes in personnel. Another factor which affects natural attrition is the many different people within a business concern who can influence buying policies. From the company president down to the receptionist in the outer

[14] George N. Kahn, "The 10 Biggest Mistakes Salesmen Make," *Sales Management* (booklet reprinted from a series of articles), 1962.

office, a few key people can exert the kind of influence the buyer may listen to and may make the difference between successful exposure and a cold turndown. These are the people the effective salesman learns to recognize and cultivate as his friends. For this technique to be successful, it must be done with tact so as not to offend the key or official decision maker for going over or around him. This is a variation of side attack using group norms which shall be discussed subsequently.

In many industries an 80 percent attrition of customers in five to ten years is common. Effective salesmen are insulated with patience, calmness, and knowledge. An account may buy from competitor old George Smith out of habit and loyalty but when old George Smith finally retires, the account may seek an entirely different supplier. The customer may change his own product line, creating entirely new requirements, or the firm may grow so large that old ways of buying are no longer applicable. Occasionally top management demands a shake-up and change for the sake of change. Existing suppliers are just as apt to fail on delivery or service as anyone else. The patient salesman who has been calling regularly will be most likely to be considered as an alternate supplier—particularly if he is sensitive to such internal problems.

While the law of attrition varies from industry to industry in the degree of turnover, it is applicable to almost every line of business. Prospecting among a limited number of accounts requires a greater understanding of the processes of persuasion than in an unlimited market. The salesman must keep in touch with old contacts and constantly strive to establish new contacts with buying influentials. With patience, the salesman calling on the same accounts over and over will ultimately achieve his goal of getting exposure to the right buyer in his field.

## SUMMARY

Selective exposure is the process of choosing messages that promise to agree with and therefore to protect the predisposed attitudes of an individual. Consumers will tend to expose themselves only to salesmen who can be expected to confirm their existing buying attitudes. Confidence in the source of a message seems to be a prerequisite to any persuasion attempt and is the initial goal of the effective salesman.

Businessmen will usually expose themselves to a salesman offering some new product or service in their field or when they are aware of an existing need. When the salesman offers a genuine service about which they may not have previously thought, the promise of satisfaction is often strong enough to cause them to listen. Most businessmen are reasonably polite and out of courtesy will see a new salesman on his first call.

Persuasion has limits defined by the buyer's intelligence, sophistication, and personal experience in resistance. An effective salesman must constantly search for new prospects and he applies the same basic principle of selective exposure to develop leads to noncustomers. Thanks to the natural law of attrition in sales, even seemingly impossible buying personalities and discouraging competitive actions are not permanent obstacles to getting a new account.

# 8

# The Prospect's Selective Perception and Retention of the Sales Message

Selective perception is the process of seeing or understanding certain selected information in a message that agrees with, or is compatible with, preconceived ideas, attitudes, and beliefs. An audience will hear and comprehend that with which it agrees and either not hear or not accept that with which it disagrees. The points of information one likes one can see at a glance but points of disagreement are often unintelligible or not recognizable. The unwanted opinion or information is obscure or dark and of doubtful meaning or may seem too ambiguous. Selective perception is a defense system of the mind which functions to filter out disagreeable information to protect one's self-image or one's preconceived beliefs and attitudes.

Retention is the secondary process of retaining, holding, or remembering the choice information contained in a message that is compatible with preconceived beliefs and attitudes. If an audience is compelled to memorize a message which is contrary to existing beliefs, it will quickly forget or confuse the message so as to make the meaning ineffective. When tested for recall of a simple message of this type, a person will not be sure of its content because the information didn't seem to make any sense to him or he felt the speaker could not be believed.

Actually it is impractical to attempt to separate the two processes because remembering or recalling depends entirely upon originally receiving and understanding the message and the only way one can test for original perception is to ask for a playback of what is retained. The two processes therefore are handled jointly although at any given time it may be one process or the other that is being illustrated rather than both.

113

## INITIAL INTERVIEW OBJECTIVES IN PERSUASION ATTEMPTS

Upon first meeting an audience, the persuader seeks favorable attention to his message and does not want distracted listening or hostile disregard. If an audience is unobservant, heedless, or inconsiderate, the message may never be heard, much less understood. Second, the persuader seeks favorable interest in whatever he is saying. He would like a degree of curiosity, an inquiring mind or an intellectual action. The third component in the persuader's objective in the initial meeting is some degree of personal involvement on the part of the audience. He would like his audience to be emotionally moved to include or permit his message in its personal thoughts. He would like the audience to actively take into consideration the various points of his message and not sit passively with the blank stare of a dead fish.

## TYPICAL SALES BEHAVIOR

Many sales manuals point out that if the prospect cuts the salesman off too soon, or if he fails to pay close attention to what the salesman says, it may be due to the salesman's getting off on the wrong foot. The effective approach in any given instance depends upon the interaction of the salesman, the product, the prospect, and the particular circumstances of the interview. The first 10 seconds of a sales interview are said to be vital to its success and they must win the prospect's undivided attention, awaken his self-interest, and make him want to hear what is to be said. Much has been written about proper clothes, a firm handshake, a friendly smile, and the like, all of which deal with making a good first impression. Many sales manuals point out the prospect must be directed to focus his thoughts on what the salesman is prepared to do for him.

Experiments have been conducted at Johns Hopkins University with a psychogalvanometer, or lie detector, to determine how long a prospect might listen to a sales talk and have the message register efficiently.[1] The findings indicated a three-minute fatigue point and the conclusion was drawn that after three minutes of listening to a sales presentation, the prospect wanted to talk and therefore would listen no longer. In addition it was also demonstrated that words affect people physically as well as mentally.

---

[1] Elmer Wheeler, *Tested Sentences that Sell* (Englewood Cliffs, N.J.: Prentice-Hall, Inc., 1937).

In attempting to excite the listener's imagination, salesmen often use key emotional words as the famous Wheelerism, "Sell the sizzle, not the steak."[2] Unfortunately every listener does not have the same understanding of a particular word as the speaker. When someone says cat, one may think of kitten; a hunter might think of a jungle animal; a construction engineer might think of an earthmoving tractor; a college man might think of a coed. To describe someone's behavior there are some 18,000 English words which refer to personal qualities or conduct—for instance, active, affectionate, aggressive, alert, alarmist, and so forth. Every word one hears is colored by his own life experiences. Words have different meanings and an individual's responses to them are conditioned by his own subjective experiences, memories, likes, and dislikes.

Some experts maintain that a salesman's vocabulary is the most potent tool in his kit. Words are the tools which can describe, define, explain, illustrate, and make visual the ideas of the product to the prospect. Words can open the interview, and words can close the sale. But in the face of all the difficulties of communicating, can salesmen really paint a word picture the buyer can visualize and understand? One interesting experiment in word pictures, the parallels between the use of stimulating words and the conditioned action or behavior that followed, was performed by a psychologist.[3] He attached electrodes to various muscles in the body of a subject and allowed the subject to lie on a couch in a darkened room, instructed to relax. The subject was then asked to imagine that he was swinging a golf club. On no account was he to move. With these directions, the experimenter obtained action currents from the muscles that would have been involved in full-scale overt performance of the commanded movement. No such action currents were obtained from other muscles in the body. An effective word picture, both literally and figuratively, really does move the listener.

Imagine a salesman leaving a businessman after having given a complete sales presentation which was well planned in advance but where no sale was achieved. Later, talking to his sales manager, he might say, "I don't understand what went wrong. He seemed interested and let me give the whole talk but when I finished he asked a stupid question which I covered very thoroughly in point four of our talk. I just couldn't get him excited enough to buy."

The sales manager would probably check over the things that make a

2 Elmer Wheeler, *Sizzlemanship* (Englewood Cliffs, N.J.: Prentice-Hall, Inc., 1937).

3 E. Jacobson, "Electrophysiology of Mental Activities," *American Journal of Psychology*, Vol. 44, 1932, pp. 677–94.

good first impression such as good clothes, good manners, a firm hand-shake, and a pleasant smile. He would ascertain whether or not the prospect was given an opportunity to talk frequently and that the salesman had confined his talk to three-minute sections. He would check for the adequate use of emotional words and he might ask, "Did you say this convincingly? Did you give your talk enthusiastically?" He might attempt to instill confidence and give encouragement by urging the salesman to go out and tell his story to more people because "nobody can sell them all." Notice the entire appraisal of the sales interview is from the point of view of the salesman's words and actions and not the prospect's point of view.

### Results of Typical Sales Behavior

Since conversation is obviously not necessarily communication, the salesman is often asked "stupid" questions because the prospect's attention has been blocked and too often the result is no sale. It would pay to probe a little deeper into this type of sales situation. Why would an intelligent businessman ask a "stupid" question which had been thoroughly covered in a sales presentation? Either he didn't hear what was said or he misunderstood what was said. How could this happen? Something said earlier may have captured his attention and blocked later points. The important question the salesman should have asked himself is, "What captured his attention?"

One can easily observe this phenomenon in his own reading. If one anticipates a point to be made, his attention wanders and he misses some clue in his search for confirmation of what he anticipates. Another variation one can observe occurs when an interesting point in his reading captures his imagination. If he reads on, his attention reverts to the earlier point and again he misses a clue for later conclusions. When he does get to the conclusions, they do not seem to ring true, for he has missed one of the vital steps in the author's logic. Is this a rare phenomenon or is it common? What light has the research of the social psychologist shed upon selective perception?

### METAMORPHOSES OF RUMORS

Psychologists have studied how oral messages change to fit the existing spheres of knowledge and attitudes of those who pass the messages along. In one phase of these studies, for example, a picture of a fight on a train, in which a white man is holding a razor and arguing with a Negro, was shown to subjects who were required to describe it to other subjects, who in turn were required to describe the action to others, and so on. In the course of these successive narrations, the razor typically shifted to the hand of the Negro. Material which does not fit the predispositions of a perceiver is likely to be recast to fit not only his span of comprehension and retention but also his own personal needs and interests.[4] A similar experiment was conducted showing pictures of typical attitudes with one fact completely out of place or wrong, such as an American Red Cross ambulance loaded with boxes clearly labeled "Ammunition." Subjects telling later of what they had seen most often described the boxes as medicines.[5]

A number of researchers have reported on studies which involve cartoons ridiculing racial and religious prejudice. Most often the messages were misperceived by prejudiced persons. The cartoons were described by the subjects as devices employed by the Jews to stir up religious strife or as devices which glorified the pure American lineage and the like. Misunderstanding was 250 percent more prevalent among the prejudiced than among the unprejudiced, and three times as common among those prejudiced who were least aware of the social implications of prejudice.[6]

## ECONOMIC AND SOCIAL OBSTACLES TO COMMUNICATIONS

There is also a relation between communication abilities and socioeconomic class which has significance for salesmen. The kind of supersophisticated advertising which appears in the *Wall Street Journal* and the *New Yorker* magazine is almost meaningless to lower status people. They cannot comprehend the subtle humor and are baffled by the strange art. They have a different symbol system and a very different approach to humor. This does not mean they lack intelligence or wit but that their communication skills have been shaped differently and they interpret what they see differently because of their experiences.

In a study of how people interpreted the expressions and motives of

[4] Gordon Allport and Leo J. Postman, "The Basic Psychology of Rumor," *Transactions of the New York Academy of Sciences*, Vol. VIII, Series II, 1945, pp. 61–81.

[5] Classical studies include: Muzafer Sherif, *The Psychology of Social Norms* (New York: Harper & Bros., 1936); Jerome S. Bruner and Cecile O. Goodman, "Value and Need as Organizing Factors in Perception," *Journal of Abnormal and Social Psychology*, Vol. XLII, 1947, pp. 33–44. The latter cites some 20 other earlier and pertinent investigations. Many of the earlier findings have been refined and extended by S. E. Asch, *Social Psychology* (New York: Prentice-Hall, Inc., 1952).

[6] E. Cooper and M. Jahoda, "The Evasion of Propaganda," *Journal of Psychology*, Vol. XXIII, 1947, pp. 15–25. Also see: P. L. Kendall and K. M. Wolf, *The Personification of Prejudice as a Device in Educational Propaganda* (New York: Bureau of Applied Social Research, Columbia University, 1946).

characters in a film extolling tolerance, *Home of the Brave,* similar findings are reported.[7] Responses were largely predictable on the basis of the subjects' individual scores on racial tolerance tests. This principle of selective perception was also brought out in a study mentioned earlier where adults were asked whether reports which they did read had convinced them that smoking was a cause of cancer.[8] The relationship was accepted or perceived by 54 percent of the nonsmokers but by only 28 percent of the smokers.

## FEAR-THREAT APPEAL

An example of arrested attention or blocked learning was clearly shown in a study of threat appeals.[9] The experimenters presented three groups of high-school students with three versions of an illustrated lecture on dental hygiene. All versions cited the dangers of dental neglect and recommended specific procedures of tooth care. The three versions differed only in the degree to which they emphasized the possible dire consequences of dental neglect. Tests before and after the lecture revealed that the recommended procedures were adopted most widely (36 percent) by the group exposed to the minimum threat version and least widely (8 percent) by the group which was most strongly threatened. Differences between the groups were still apparent a full year later. Thus a strong threat is in itself preoccupying and may hinder learning of the material in the communication.

Two other studies reported similar results and draw the conclusion that when fear is strongly aroused but not fully relieved by the reassurances contained in the persuasive communication, the audience will become restless, ill at ease, and will become motivated to ignore or minimize the importance of the threat.[10]

---

[7] D. M. Wilner, "Attitude as a Determinant of Perception in the Mass Media of Communications: Reactions to the Motion Picture, 'Home of the Brave' " (Ph.D. dissertation, University of California, Los Angeles Library, 1951).

[8] Charles I. Cannell and James C. MacDonald, "The Impact of Health News on Attitudes and Behavior," *Journalism Quarterly,* Vol. XXXIII (1956), pp. 315–23.

[9] I. L. Janis and S. Feshback, "Effects of Fear-Arousing Communications," *Journal of Abnormal and Social Psychology,* Vol. XLVIII, 1953, pp. 78–92.

[10] I. L. Janis and H. C. Milholland, "The Influence of Threat Appeals on Selective Learning of the Content of Persuasive Appeal," *Journal of Psychology,* Vol. XXXVII, 1954, pp. 75–80. B. Bettelheim and M. Janowitz, "Reactions to Fascist Propaganda: A Pilot Study," *Public Opinion Quarterly,* Vol. XIV, 1950, pp. 53–60. Particularly pertinent here is a study by Irving L. Janis and Robert F. Terwilliger, "An Experimental Study of Psychological Resistances to Fear Arousing Communications," *Journal of Abnormal and Social Psychology,* December, 1962, pp. 403–10. This study indicates a low threat version of an antismoking message produced less disturbance and more attitude change than the high threat version.

## SELECTIVE PERCEPTION AND RETENTION IN SALES

Assume a buyer listened to a brief memorized sales talk and could recite it back to the salesman as accurately as it was written. One must then conclude that he actually heard every word and apparently understood the meaning. If the salesman calls back several days later he may be amazed that the same buyer again asks a "stupid" question that was completely answered in the memorized talk. If an intelligent businessman could recite a sales talk one day, why would he completely forget a major part of that talk only a few days later? Obviously, having heard all of a message, he selectively remembers only certain parts of the message.

As an illustration, assume a salesman quotes a price that includes delivery charges in New York and New Jersey but the price is plus freight costs beyond that area. At this time the buyer says, "For example, our Chicago office would be that price plus freight from your Newark, N.J., plant. Is that right?" After full agreement on the quoted price, the salesman leaves. The next day when the buyer is ready to place an order not for Chicago but for Indianapolis and the salesman begins to add freight from Newark, N.J., the buyer reacts like a wounded bear, "But you told me this was a delivered price west to Chicago! Why are you changing now?"

Is this businessman a deliberate liar or a chiseler? Neither. He is simply exhibiting the all too common human trait of selective retention. In business parlance, this is referred to as a convenient memory. Another illustration occurs all too frequently in bulk pricing. The salesman tells the buyer that on orders over so many units or dollars, an extra discount applies. Subsequent orders for a single unit go back to the original price. The buyer will repeat and give examples clearly indicating his complete understanding of the bulk pricing arrangement. Later when he stops volume purchasing and is buying single replacement units, he may scream and holler about the higher unit price, "But we agreed if I bought so many units I would get the lower price on all subsequent purchases, regardless of the quantity."

## RETAINING SYMPATHETIC MATERIAL

This occurrence of selective retention was documented more than 20 years ago and it has since been redocumented a number of times. In one of the earlier studies, experimenters tested college students who were anti-communist and compared them to a group who were procommunist.[11] Both groups had to memorize two written passages. One passage was for and the other was against communism. The students were then asked to reproduce the passages and this process was repeated over a number of weeks. The results showed the material was more readily learned by the sympathetic group and more easily forgotten by the unsympathetic group.

A similar test of recall of certain documents published widely in the newspapers showed that persons who had recalled the documents were consistently found to be more likely to approve the position taken by the document while those who could not recall the documents, even when told the gist of them, were not sympathetic to the views in them.[12]

In other words, a salesman who seeks favorable attention, interest, and some degree of involvement on the buyer's part on his initial call too often goes all out to impress the buyer and stimulate him with emotional words and ideas and ends up losing his audience. Instead of getting orders he receives stupid questions or arouses no interest in his proposition. Selective perception and retention, the protective processes, are operating against this salesman.

## REALISTIC OBJECTIVES IN PERSUASION ATTEMPTS

An initial sales interview should be an attempt to gain effective communications between the salesman and the buyer. Effective communications include understanding, interest, attention, and a degree of personal involvement but it is a two-way street. A two-way conversation, in and of itself, is not necessarily synonymous with communication because when two people engage in a conversation, a good deal of what is said is never heard, and part of what is heard is misinterpreted. Often there is much less of a meeting of minds than is realized for the one who is talking has to compete with the inner voice of the listener. Each listener holds an idea in his mind and can hardly wait for his turn to speak. Some of what the speaker says gets through and the listener fills in the rest so that what is understood is different from what is said.[13]

All forms of selling, as well as modern viewpoints on communication,

---

[11] Jerome M. Levine and Gardner Murphy, "The Learning and Forgetting of Controversial Material," *Journal of Abnormal and Social Psychology*, Vol. XXXVIII, 1953, pp. 507–17.

[12] Herbert H. Hymann and Paul B. Sheatsley, "Some Reasons Why Information Campaigns Fail," *Public Opinion Quarterly*, Vol. XI, 1947, pp. 412–23.

[13] Jesse S. Nirenberg, "How to Reach Minds—and Hearts—When You Talk to People," *Sales Management*. December 19, 1958, p. 33.

point up the importance of getting and maintaining the listener's attention. Communication studies indicate the tremendous problems in attempting to maintain complete attention. Theoretical articles on education and selling both emphasize the importance of covering a single point
at a time, reviewing periodically, gaining understanding and acceptance
point by point throughout a presentation. This indicates why a memorized
talk often leaves a buyer unmoved. He may not have been allowed to
express an objection or raise a question and his attention to subsequent
sales points was lacking.

Education and sales techniques have long been compared. The sales
philosophy of the often-quoted John H. Patterson of National Cash Register fame is simply that selling is essentially teaching. If the prospect
understood the register, he would come in and buy it. Patterson stressed
that the major function of the salesman was to make the prospect understand the proposition. This was the big theme in the 1893–1900 N.C.R.
organization period under Patterson.[14] Modern articles also cite many
parallels between education, or the psychology of learning, and sales, or the
psychology of persuasion.

To be practical one must note the limit on such comparisons. Educators
are dealing primarily with a captive audience which is for the most part
well motivated to listen. Businessmen, especially professional buyers, are
for the most part pressed for time and will listen only as long as the sales
talk interests them. It is true that some teachers, including the writer, put
some students to sleep but the students are still captive for so many
minutes, interested or not. In addition, the student is committed to return
again and again for so many weeks. The businessman is not a captive
audience. He can terminate an interview any time he wants and most often
will not give a boring salesman a second chance at exposure. It behooves
the salesman, therefore, to perceive sharply the buyer's impressions and
reactions as he goes along and repeat or emphasize only when necessary to
reinforce—and then to do so in an interesting and entertaining way.

A good salesman is often compared to a good actor because he commands the complete attention of his audience and can get the listener to
feel he is part of the story. Here again is a one-way conversation to a
captive audience and this is almost impossible to achieve in a real business
situation. Telephones ring at the most inopportune times, business associates interrupt, and time is limited. The listener is rarely, if ever, com-

---

[14] "The Original Schoolmaster," Editorial about John H. Patterson in *Dun's Review
And Modern Industry*, December, 1963, p. 3.

**FIG. 6.** Auto manufacturer hears of advantages of using salesman's product in his cars.

pletely with the speaker in a business situation. A realistic objective for the salesman should be to gain effective communications with the buyer.

## EFFECTIVE SALES BEHAVIOR

Since a salesman or persuader initially seeks a degree of personal involvement on the part of the listener, instead of attempting to direct the buyer, the salesman might do better if he begins thinking in terms of what the buyer wants. The audience is predisposed to certain ideas, attitudes, and beliefs and the salesman must learn about these things before he can use language which the buyer will understand. It is the salesman's initial responsibility, therefore, to get the buyer to discuss himself in a permissive, uncritical atmosphere. The salesman must become a sympathetic listener and neutralize any feelings of hostility the buyer may have for yielding some of his precious time. The salesman should ask questions which encourage the buyer to discuss what he sees as his problems or goals in his role on the job or in his private life. By listening with interest and repeating back to the buyer to demonstrate uncritical understanding, supportive feedback in psychological terms, the salesman proves he is listening attentively to the buyer and is a nice guy who agrees with him. This helps to establish a close and sympathetic relationship, which is essential to any two-way communication. By producing examples that support the buyer's point of view, the salesman can create a feeling of togetherness and the buyer will realize the salesman is really paying attention and apparently does agree with him. The buyer will then be favorably disposed toward the salesman and be more apt to listen when the salesman talks because he will feel that the salesman must be a better, finer kind of person to appreciate the buyer's viewpoints. This is generally true, this willingness to listen because of the buyer's feelings of satisfaction from his conversation that create a sense of obligation on his part to return the salesman's compliment and at least listen to his story.

While the buyer is talking, the salesman tries to identify problems which his products or services will solve and thus provide the buyer with greater satisfaction than he is now achieving. He must search for the discrepancy between what is and what might be. Initially the salesman should search for areas in which the buyer wants to do better and become aware of problems for which the buyer's present behavior is not adequate or areas in which the salesman's product or service will produce greater contentment for the buyer. The most efficient way to learn of these problem areas is not to talk but to listen. The salesman must become aware of what is actually said, what is unspoken but intended, expressions, tone of voice, choice of words, and direction of the buyer's thoughts. He must stay with the buyer's interests.

When the salesman begins his presentation he must instantly realize when the prospect is blocked mentally and determine why he is blocked. If the prospect didn't hear a point and the salesman senses this, he can repeat. If the prospect misunderstood a point and the salesman realizes this, he can explain more fully in different terms. But more importantly, the effective salesman perceives that something said at one point may have captured the prospect's attention and blocked subsequent communication. The salesman must think as a computer and while continually feeding in new information instantly decide what captured the buyer's attention, whether the buyer reacted favorably, and if so, whether to take precious time to reinforce this point. If the buyer reacted unfavorably, the salesman must decide whether to draw out the fear or to ease the buyer's anxiety by modifying the information into a more acceptable form. The salesman must do this smoothly and naturally and quickly while he maintains an open communication channel with the buyer. This human computer or mental self-regulating process is also known as psychocybernetics.

## CONCLUSIONS

The predisposition of a businessman does not always have a bearing on the immediate sales situation. Selective exposure, selective perception, and selective retention do not, of course, occur among all businessmen in all communication situations. The studies and illustrations cited in this chapter typically indicate that one or more of these processes influenced part of the group but not 100 percent of any group studied. Often from 20 to as much as 70 percent seem to be immune from these selective processes. Furthermore, the selective processes appear to function imperfectly at times. Generally, they serve to reinforce existing opinions but on occasion they may actually encourage opinion change.

Granted the exceptions noted, the selective processes do occur extremely frequently and normally do serve as a protective umbrella over existing predispositions. These processes have been documented and they can be redocumented in scientifically controlled experiments. They illustrate why a businessman buys what he buys, but how can the salesman use this knowledge to switch the buyer to his products? The key to this problem lies in a study of the exceptions to the protective processes noted above and which will be considered subsequently.

## SUMMARY

Selective perception and selective retention are the processes of understanding and remembering only certain information in a message that agrees with or is compatible with an individual's predisposition. On their first call salesmen seek to gain favorable attention, interest, and personal involvement on the buyer's part. Typically, they go about it from their own self-centered point of view and ignore the prospect's inner feelings. They are overly concerned about first impressions and instantly capturing the buyer's mind. Words are the typical salesman's tools and he attempts to use them to paint a word picture for the prospect.

Unfortunately, the results of typical sales behavior is a complete lack of communication as the prospect asks "stupid" questions or misunderstands the message completely. A number of social psychological studies have shown that selective perception and retention are the protective mechanisms that cause such misunderstandings, whether they are based on personal characteristics and prejudices or based on economic and social beliefs and attitudes. A strong threat or fear can also block subsequent communications. People tend to learn easily what is compatible with their predisposition and to forget quickly what is not in agreement with it.

The purpose of the initial sales interview should be to create effective communications with a prospect and the salesman must learn to listen rather than talk if he wants to learn the language the buyer will understand. In a friendly manner he should try to get the buyer to discuss himself and dispel hostility. Through supportive feedback the salesman creates a kinship with the buyer and therefore is most apt to get a reciprocal hearing from the buyer when it is his turn to talk.

When the salesman gives his sales presentation, he uses principles of education and communication to gain acceptance of one point at a time. He is continually alert to recognize when the prospect is mentally blocked and decides instantly what to do about it while maintaining an open line to the buyer's mind. The selective processes generally serve to protect the buyer's predisposition; however, they do not do so in all cases and on occasion may actually serve to encourage changing attitudes. It is the study of the exceptions that will provide the clue to conversion.

# 9

## Selective Action: Conversion of Attitudes, Ideas, and Beliefs

People behave as they do to satisfy conscious and unconscious needs of their body and mind including contradictory desires and self-destructive drives. Inner goals may be rational or not but in whatever way these inner attitudes are combined people behave as they do because of these total attitudes. In turn, the beliefs of an individual, his ideas, opinions, and attitudes, are based upon the social and economic realities of his situation as he understands them and his total learning experiences throughout life. For a person to voluntarily change his behavior, he must first change his attitudes or beliefs. Holding an attitude serves the individual by enabling him to maintain his goal direction and not act at random contrary to his own inner drives. This goal direction acts to maintain homeostasis, inner balance, or peace of mind. Wildly vacillating moods and seemingly incongruous behavior serve the total inner needs of the individual and, viewed in this respect, all behavior is goal directed and constant.

What psychological action takes place in the individual in whom an attitude changes? Something must have disturbed his inner balance which cannot be rectified internally without changing one or more attitudes. The change in attitude then serves to restore the inner balance. The resulting change in behavior is still goal directed and the goal, homeostasis, is constant. Chapters 7 and 8 indicated what arouses defenses which seek to maintain an existing attitude and how these defenses operate on a selective basis. One is now faced with the question: What causes an individual to gain enough insight to change an attitude? In other words, what can cause the individual's inner balance to be disturbed so seriously that his existing ideas, opinions, attitudes, and beliefs will not compensate to restore the balance and he is compelled to adjust an attitude? The causes involve

126

additional knowledge, adjustment, value expression, and ego defense.[1] Each will be illustrated briefly below.

The four factors which will arouse an individual to change an attitude, and the resultant change, vary according to the motivational basis. For example, opinions and attitudes aroused by additional knowledge or clues associated with filling real physical and economic needs cause the individual to see new or modified beliefs as appropriate to satisfy his inner needs. If a machine breaks down, an optimistic production manager suddenly sees a new, faster-producing machine as being more appropriate to his personal success than a repair of the old machine. On the other hand, a pessimistic production manager with strong doubts as to his personal value will see a new, faster-producing machine as reducing the criticism and punishment he feels is inevitable. Each is apt to move toward the new attitude in this case.

Adjustment is a motivation activated by clues associated with new people or new situations which may cause stress or anxiety such as changing conditions in an industry or within one's own company. For example, a new vice-president in charge of production or a company decision to manufacture products in an entirely new industry would cause the optimistic individual to see the change as opening new opportunities; therefore, his sights had better be raised to meet the new situation. The pessimist would see the change as another chance to hide his ineptitude and postpone the fate which he feels is ultimately his just desert. By modifying or completely changing his attitudes or actions now he can put off the horrible results.

Opinions and attitudes which express value judgments are aroused by clues associated with personal values or self-image, such as in the case of the office manager who aspires to be appointed to vice-president. An optimist who thought well of his immediate superior might see a more critical attitude of this individual as ultimately cutting him down and favoring the office manager's promotion. He will be tempted to go out of his way to compile facts and figures which illustrate poor decisions made by his superior. A pessimist who also aspires to be appointed to the vice-presidency and thinks well of his superior may believe he will never achieve this goal because his immediate boss should have cut him back for poor performance. This pessimist may also be tempted to go out of his way to

---

[1] See Daniel Katz, "The Functional Approach to the Study of Attitudes," *Public Opinion Quarterly*, 1960, pp. 24 (2), 163–204. The reasons for holding or for changing attitudes are viewed in the framework of the functions they perform for the individual psychologically.

compile statistics to chop down his superior in order to reduce the criticism of himself which he feels is inevitable.

Ego defense is most easily illustrated to the reader by posing a question: Do you want to be exposed as an individual who is of weak character and stupid or as an individual who is of strong character and superior intelligence? In the selling situation the salesman indicates that if the prospect buys now it will be obvious to those people whose opinions the buyer values that he is strong and of superior intelligence and the opposite will be equally true if he fails to buy. The optimist will see the new behavior as appropriate to his promotional goals and the pessimist will see the new behavior as postponing the punishment which he fears. In each case these two men will see the relevant facts in a new light and be apt to change their attitudes to protect their inner balance.

In all fairness to the reader it should be pointed out that self-esteem can vary within one person on different topics such as family, job, intelligence, love, and so forth, and can vary on the same topic at different times. For example, on a given day when things go well the individual is apt to generalize and have high self-esteem in most categories; when things go badly the reverse is equally likely. It is also common to observe people who vacillate back and forth or tend to hold a middle attitude, pulled equally to each extreme.

The drives, motives, and needs of an individual affect his perception of the world. When one interprets the world he does so in the light of his own learning and current needs. The perception of an audience at an athletic contest is an illustration of this. People on different sides of the playing field very frequently perceive the same play or the same decision by a referee quite differently, one agreeing with it, the other strongly maintaining that the referee is blind. Similarly the prospect will perceive the salesman in terms of his own needs, expectations, and prejudices.[2]

The self-concept, or ego, suggests each person has a picture of what he is or who he is and includes his values, attitudes, and his perception of his skills and abilities. Adjustment mechanisms are more readily activated if an attack is directed toward a more central part of the individual's ego or self-concept. This would be more likely than if the attack were directed toward a more peripheral part of his self-picture, where there is less ego involvement. For example criticism of the athletic ability of a teen-ager might arouse stiff defenses if he viewed his ability on the playing field as an

---

[2] See Harold J. Leavitt, *Managerial Psychology* (Chicago: 1st Phoenix ed.; University of Chicago, 1962), particularly chap. iii, "Selective Perception."

essential part of his own character. On the other hand, criticism of the athletic ability of a 50-year-old businessman might not arouse defense mechanisms if he were not overly concerned about such an image. If one should hint at his questionable business ethics, strong defenses would be much more likely exhibited. In other words, an individual will defend himself if his own self-image is criticized.

One's ego, self-image, or self-esteem is not a fixed or constant picture but changes constantly as he gains knowledge, is forced to adjust to changing circumstances, revalues known facts, or is forced to defend himself against criticism. Current events will influence his view of subsequent ones. Thus an optimistic message which appeals to personal gain, spoken to an individual who at that moment on that topic has high self-esteem, will be more persuasive than a pessimistic message which appeals to preventing loss or postponing a punishment.[3] This conclusion reinforces the earlier principle of asking questions and drawing out the prospect to determine his self-esteem on the pertinent topic so that an intelligent decision can be made regarding the optimistic or pessimistic tone of the proposed sales message.

A simplified schematic illustration of this concept can be constructed showing the problem of the old behavior or the attraction to the changed behavior passing through one or more of the four factors which can influence change and the resulting behavior based upon seeing behavior in a new light or seeing changes in standards of judging behavior.[4]

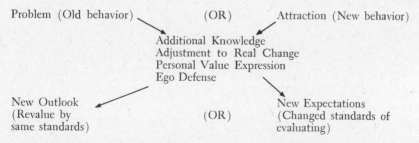

Problem (Old behavior)                (OR)              Attraction (New behavior)

Additional Knowledge
Adjustment to Real Change
Personal Value Expression
Ego Defense

New Outlook                                            New Expectations
(Revalue by                    (OR)                    (Changed standards of
same standards)                                        evaluating)

For example, if a two-gallon jug of oil were slippery causing frequent breakage (problem with old behavior), then the awareness of a two-gallon

---

[3] Howard Leventhal and Sidney I. Perloe, "A Relationship Between Self-Esteem and Persuasibility," *Journal of Abnormal and Social Psychology*, May, 1962, pp. 385–88. It was found that subjects high in self-esteem were influenced more by optimistic communications than by threatening communications while subjects low in self-esteem showed the opposite pattern.

[4] This schematic diagram was adapted from lectures by Professor Abraham Shuchman in market research, Spring, 1965, Columbia University Graduate School of Business.

jug with a top handle (added knowledge) would cause the buyer to revalue the source of supply of two-gallon jugs of oil. On the other hand, if a buyer were content with an insulator against heat and fire which caused loss of records and he then learned of an endorsement by the Underwriters Laboratory (additional), he would be apt to evaluate all such products on the basis of the presence or absence of the U.L. label, a new basis of evaluating the product.

## CONVERSION OF ATTITUDES DEFINED

Opinion conversion is the process which occurs when a subordinate or new attitude is elevated through reinforcement to dominate the matrix of attitudes, interests, and needs of an individual. When the prospect's sense of inner balance is disturbed sufficiently to cause discomfort or anxiety, he has three basic courses of action to relieve this tension: to move against people; to move away from people; to move with people, agree, and change his attitude.

When a buyer attempts to move against or become aggressive toward the salesman, the latter must divert the anger to an inanimate object and restore rapport with the buyer. The buyer must be led to see that arguing, fighting, and shouting at the salesman is fruitless because the problem will still remain. The inner conflict is strong enough in the buyer's mind but the choice of alternate courses of action are too balanced, or equally appealing, for him to choose. The tactful salesman must continue to reinforce the attitude which favors his recommended action and elevate it to a dominating position. This will make it easier for the buyer to decide in the salesman's favor.

If the buyer attempts to move away from or escape the salesman, he may tell his secretary that he does not want to see that salesman again. Repeat calls on the secretary and a little friendly charm will often persuade her to help the salesman gain another hearing. New sales information, such as a new account sold or new applications of the products, offer excellent reinforcing tools to convert this timid businessman who is, in reality, very close to buying.

Opinion conversion occurs when a buyer looks at the relevant parts of his problem in a different way and elevates a lesser attitude or belief to dominate the many and varied ideas, attitudes, and opinions he formerly held. The salesman has the responsibility to cause the prospect to take a fresh look at his problem and to see things in a different light.

## REINFORCING PROCESS

Out of all the competitive salesmen calling on him, the businessman finally moves and gives his order to one man. If the product, service, and salesman continue to perform as he understood they would, this account may become standardized on that product. The salesman must continue to visit and maintain warm, friendly relations which satisfy the buyer's personal needs just as the product must honestly serve the functional need. The new buying behavior is encouraged to become habitual and with the problem resolved the businessman can devote his time and attention to other problems. All the reinforcing processes and protective selective processes now work for the one successful salesman and the businessman will not readily reopen this particular issue.

These situations have been concerned with the buyer that had no existing favored supplier and was confronted by equally competitive products and salesmen. In commercial and industrial sales, it would be a rare situation when a buyer had no existing favored supplier. By the time a concern has grown large enough to warrant direct calls by a number of salesmen, it has established lines of suppliers that have served its purpose more or less adequately sometime in the past. The illustrations have shown the part the psychological forces play in the initial decision and how they reinforce existing suppliers to remain on a most favored basis. This is referred to as the buyer's loyalty to the supplier. In a sales situation, how can these same psychological forces work to persuade a businessman to buy a different product from the one he now buys and with which he is apparently satisfied?

## REACTION TO DIRECT FRONTAL ATTACK

The selective processes generally serve to reinforce whatever the businessman was predisposed to believe. If the group of men he is associated with conceive experimental change as a necessary and legitimate part of business progress, the businessman will most likely seek out new ideas and will be predisposed to remember those comments which bear upon this basic conception. Or if he thinks of himself as the watchdog of the company purse strings, he will want to be consulted before every expenditure of consequence and will listen and remember primarily the cost justifications; he will either not perceive secondary arguments for an expenditure or, if he does understand them, he will quickly forget them. Any direct frontal attack against such beliefs, such as, "Forget the initial cost for a moment and look at . . . ," are likely to backfire by stimulating the existing defenses into immediate and effective activity.

In other words, the basic forces of communication within the businessman all serve to reinforce his beliefs before the salesman arrives. Psychologically he is set to resist persuasion and will buy only what fits his preconceived notion of what he wants and why he wants it. This mental set of the buyer may include conscious and subconscious ideas and may include both rational thoughts and irrational desires or impulses. Overtly he will try to show only conscious and rational thoughts and behavior. If he has excellent insight into his own personality and maintains an open and fair mind, he will be better able to listen to a salesman and accurately judge the proposition offered. But one must constantly be aware the businessman will react in a predetermined manner according to his predisposition and the way in which his selective processes protect it.

In terms of his psychology, a direct frontal attack on an attitude or opinion of a buyer serves to awaken, organize, and stiffen his mechanisms of resistance and defense. He will become obstinate and angered at the direct or implied criticism of his judgment and professional buying behavior and he is apt to discredit the source of any such criticism. Once he mentally discredits the salesman, he will become committed to discrediting and doubting anything that particular salesman may say in the future.

## SIDE ATTACK

While there has been little current research of the effectiveness of side attack as contrasted to direct frontal attack, at about 1940 several reviews of this type of research were in substantial agreement.[5] Conversion could be far more easily accomplished by side attack, or creating a new opinion where none existed before, than by direct frontal assault on existing opinion. In other words, opinions are changed by making exceptions to general rules until the rule itself breaks down. Opinions can be turned gradually, point by point, but resist frontal or direct assault. If two opposing football players running at full speed meet head on, there is one loud collision. If they meet while running parallel, on an end run, for example, bit by bit they may turn the corner together. If the blocker has the edge, the ball carrier is sprung loose and if the tackler has the edge, the ball

---

[5] Douglas Waples, Bernard Berelson, and Franklyn R. Bradshaw, *What Reading Does to People* (Chicago: University of Chicago Press, 1940).

carrier must go inside of the end. Either way, the colliding of the blocker and the defender is less violent than meeting head on.

Recent studies of individual voters[6] and individual conversions to communism[7] indicate that an indirect approach does work. By attempting to convert opinion on a minor point which had little importance for the individual, the persuader was in reality attempting to create an opinion where none existed before. Since there is no obvious attempt to change opinion, the protective selective processes will remain inactive. When and if the new attitude develops sufficiently to challenge the old, conflict is likely to occur and may be resolved by conversion to the new opinion. In sales, the indirect approach is very common. A salesman gets approval on one point in his talk and attempts to build on it gradually to gain approval of other points. He gains limited acceptance of one product in his line and, after earning the buyer's confidence by performing satisfactorily, he attempts to gain approval on other products in his line.

The turning of an opinion, point by point, is a very subtle process. The process of increasing an individual's tolerance for a new type of message seems to increase his vague awareness and then his interest. He is then more apt to selectively expose himself to that type of communication and selectively perceive and retain more and more information which supports the new point of view. Sharp conflicts of attitudes may occur in the process; however, continued exposure to the persuader offers relief from the emotional disturbances caused by the conflict. Often an associated but subordinate attitude which offers greater satisfaction of the individual's personal interests by supporting one loyalty or one part of the conscience against another is elevated in this way.

## PERSUASIBILITY

Recent research strongly indicates some persons are, in general, more easily persuaded than others and that this seems to hold true regardless of the topic of persuasion.[8] The converse is also true, that some persons are, in general, less persuasible.

This ease of persuasion does not relate to the level of general intelligence but does seem to correlate to feelings of inadequacy or low self-

[6] Paul F. Lazarsfeld, Bernard Berelson, and Hazel Gaudet, *The People's Choice* (New York: Columbia University Press, 1948).

[7] Waples, Berelson, and Bradshaw, *op. cit.*

[8] Irving L. Janis, "Personality Correlates of Susceptibility to Persuasion," *Journal of Personality*, Vol. XXII, 1954. pp. 504–18.

esteem.[9] A number of studies—but certainly not all—have been able to redocument this probability. It does seem that a person in doubt of himself, insecure, and not willing to trust his own judgment would be more easily persuaded by a recognized authority in a given field. Once the authority had proved correct in any limited area, the insecure person would rely more and more on the authority for direction in the limited field and gradually in ever enlarging circles to many fields. A salesman who makes himself an expert in his own field can honestly speak with authority in this limited area. Once the businessman acknowledges the salesman as an expert, he will be more willing to follow other recommendations. If the businessman is highly insecure he will be more persuasible than other men for this one particular salesman. When a highly protected son suddenly is forced to take control of his father's business, this phenomenon may occur. If the salesman is wise, he will limit his influence to the area in which he is really an expert and advise the businessman honestly. Otherwise true friends of the businessman will intercede in his behalf and persuade him to "throw the bum out."

## EFFECTS OF CROSS-PRESSURES IN CONVERSION

Persons under cross-pressures have been observed to be particularly susceptible to conversion by personal influence but they are also likely to withdraw from the conflicting pressures and take no action at all. This may appear as a variation on the degree of persuasibility of an individual. However, it is normally of temporary duration, with doubts caused by external considerations rather than internal appraisal of self-esteem.[10]

In one of the voter studies mentioned earlier, special note was taken of voters who were subject to any one of a number of cross-pressures and its effect upon their voting behavior.[11] Two of these cross-pressures involved lack of political agreement among the voter's family and close associates and two involved his own basic attitudes on relevant political issues. Voters subject to any single cross-pressure tended to make their final decisions considerably later in the campaign than did those who were not so plagued. The longest delays occurred among those whose family and primary type groups lacked political agreement. In other words, the more personal the cross-pressure, the longer the conflict and indecision lasted. Those with

---

[9] Irving L. Janis, et al., *Personality and Persuasibility* (New Haven: Yale University Press, 1959), p. 237.

[10] Siegfried Kracauer and Paul L. Berkman, *Satellite Mentality* (New York: Frederick A. Praeger, Inc., 1956).

[11] Lazarsfeld, Berelson, and Gaudet, *op. cit.*

two or more cross-pressures were most likely to change their vote intentions and accounted for 64 percent of those who were actually converted from one party to another. Some recrossing of party lines can be assumed; however, the information available does not indicate how much. It can be expected that those who are firmly committed will be less susceptible than persons who are already in doubt. Those subjected to cross-pressures are likely to sway back and forth between two opposing authorities in a repeating process of conversion and reconversion. In sales, the persuasion attempt is called unfreezing the prospect; the conversion is called moving the prospect; and to prevent reconversion, the prospect is refrozen or encouraged to develop fixed buying habits and not reopen the issue.

This same voter study showed another interesting facet of human behavior. Tensions of multiple cross-pressures tend to render their victims less interested and even to cause them to belittle the whole affair. This indicates a basic pattern of human adjustment, or a typical defense mechanism. When a person is attracted toward and simultaneously desires to run away from a course of action, he often does neither but tries to change the subject or avoid the conflict altogether. For such conflicts of interest, the easy way out of the uncomfortable situation is simply to discount its importance and give up the conflict as not worth bothering about.

Such a person, divided by cross-pressures, seems to believe equally in two opposite attempts at persuasion. Conflicting groups pull both ways at once. The protective nets of reinforcement of predisposition and the umbrellas of resistance to persuasion are partially down, but sympathetic influences in both directions remain constant and approximately equal. Two good competing salesmen will often have this effect on a prospect. Unless this hapless victim of the tug-of-war loses all interest in the matter and remains aloof, he seems likely to vacillate to and fro between competing camps. To maintain his sense of inner balance or well-being, he must withdraw. Thus the conflict which caused all the bother is treated as really not being worth all the effort involved.

Giving up too quickly is one of the biggest mistakes business and industrial salesmen make. When a prospect is undecided, it is the persistent salesman that gets the order, and not the quitters, the almost half who give up after a single call on a business prospect. About 25 percent make two or three calls before quitting and another 5 percent make four calls and then give up. It is the lucky 20 percent remaining that make five calls or more and these men write 75 to 80 percent of the industrial orders.[12]

[12] George N. Kahn, "The 10 Biggest Mistakes Salesmen Make," *Sales Management* (booklet reprinted from a series of articles), 1962.

An effective salesman can't call back too often because on each call he has something new and interesting to impart to the prospect. Any willing salesman can learn more about how his product will help the prospect. He can study the prospect's firm and learn what its problems are and how he can help solve them. When a prospect is divided by cross-pressures, it is the quitter who concedes the order to the persistent salesman and the latter will write most of the orders.

## EFFECTS OF PRIMARY GROUPS IN CONVERSION

Primary groups to which the businessman belongs, or wishes to belong, serve as reinforcing influences which hinder change. The top management team, the clique within the company, the bright young vice-president's group are examples of such a primary group within a business. His family, neighbors, alumni groups, church, and political organizations or trade associations may also be primary groups which influence the businessman's behavior. Under certain conditions, influences from such quarters may be relatively inactive or may even serve, atypically, to aid and abet change.

Men who value their group membership are particularly resistant to any communications opposing the group norms and their resistance is intensified in regard to issues which are particularly important to the group. The reverse is also true. Conversion effects are greater among those who do not highly value their membership and in regard to issues which are not particularly important to the group. When a campaign aimed at conversion that has shown little success suddenly becomes effective for a particular individual, the bonds between that individual and some restraining group appear to break. This happens dramatically in espionage when agents suddenly go over to the other side. Analysis of such situations in the light of learning theory suggests that while adherence to the norms of the original primary group was rewarding, communications opposing those norms were resisted. When adherence to the group norm became unrewarding, or not in the true interest of the individual, the previously conditioned responses were apparently extinguished and the individual became newly susceptible to the communication stimulus and its promise of new reward. As one set of group norms ceases to play a restricting influence, a new set is developed which serves to impel change.[13]

When a businessman feels he is cut off from the group to which he belonged, not invited to some meetings, for example, he might accept and

[13] Elihu Katz and Paul Lazarsfeld, *Personal Influence: The Part Played by People in the Flow of Mass Communications* (Glencoe, Illinois: The Free Press, 1955).

act upon a proposition which some persistent persuader had worked on for a long while but which had no effect upon him while he felt he was a member of a cohesive group. Given a change in responsibility within his company, a businessman might decide the new, tougher job is not worth all the effort. Failure to achieve a production quota might cause a man to look desperately elsewhere for help. Whatever the cause, as a businessman's lot suddenly becomes unattractive in his own eyes, he will often look to new sources and listen to new sources of information with a new set of attitudes totally out of keeping with his previous orientation. Analogous to this might be the errant husband who seems to break all previous ties and suddenly go off with a young blonde.

Communications may stimulate group discussion which render norms more clear and which thus encourage conversions among loyal members who had perceived the norm incorrectly. A group of men within a company might work very well with some general principles to guide them, such as building a better mousetrap but at a high unit profit. Suppose the competitive situation forces a group discussion where the profit motive becomes primary and the group decides to cheapen the product in order to hold the profit high. One or more of the men who were previously loyal might now think less of the value of the group or might actually rebel. Group discussion may also encourage those privately inclined toward change by revealing the presence of an unsuspected minority in support of their position. Entire groups may occasionally be converted because the new point of view is in accord with a norm more basic than the one discarded. This same group of executives might decide a better product at a higher price would increase sales enough to maintain their high profit. If this mousetrap company had previously bought only the lowest priced raw materials to maintain a high profit, it might now suddenly switch suppliers and buy raw materials that would improve its mousetrap even though at a higher cost. Here the sales representative of the quality supplier who knew the situation in the mousetrap industry and was aware of internal strife at this particular mousetrap company might suddenly be rewarded for his persistence in being on the spot other salesmen had written off as useless because that company was loyal to its old-time suppliers.

## EFFECTS OF OPINION LEADERSHIP IN CONVERSION

Opinion leadership within the group can also influence change rather than reinforce old beliefs. The accountant, the lawyer, the sales manager, the engineer, the production manager individually are respected for their specialized knowledge. They can screen technical data in their fields and present a simplified view to the group. This view is sometimes biased intentionally and sometimes without the opinion leader himself being aware he is doing it. Since he is recognized as the specialist by the other members of the group, there is not apt to be any serious challenge to his recommendations. The key to selling a competitive product to the Better Mousetrap Corporation might be in persuading one opinion leader, not necessarily the entire staff or the purchasing department.

Opinion leadership can also influence change rather than reinforce beliefs in a group of competitive organizations such as insurance companies or banking institutions. Savings and loan institutions, for example, send their men to the same conventions and many of these men read the same newspapers, eat their business meals in the same restaurants, and buy the same trade magazines. A job well done for one opinion leader in the group is quickly and efficiently made known to others. This personal recommendation before the salesman makes his call causes other potential buyers to be receptive to a look into the proposition and to listen to the salesman. Selective exposure and selective perception now will tend to work for the salesman attempting to persuade a businessman rather than to work against him in resisting persuasion.

Studies have been conducted on this group effect and conversion in many diverse areas.[14] Consistent results were obtained in studies of opinion change in groups of Boy Scouts, religious groups, war prisoners, and Communist defectors; similar results were revealed in studies of voting changes, farm practices, and the purchasing habits of women. More pertinent here perhaps is a study among physicians who had adopted a new drug.[15] While the detail men or sales representatives were found to be the most common source of original information about a drug, medical colleagues were found to be the most common final source prior to the actual adoption of the new drug. In other words the flock waits for the leader's opinion before it will move.

---

[14] Harold H. Kelley and Edmund H. Volkart, "The Resistance to Change of Group Anchored Attitudes," *American Sociological Review*, Vol. XVII, 1952, pp. 453–65. Harold H. Kelley, "Salience of Membership and Resistance to Change of Group Anchored Attitudes," *Human Relations*, Vol. VIII, 1958, pp. 275–89. Edward A. Shils and Morris Janowitz, "Cohesion and Disintegration in the Wehrmacht in World War II," *Public Opinion Quarterly*, Vol. XII, 1948, pp. 280–315.

[15] James Coleman, Elihu Katz, and Herbert Menzel, *Doctors and New Drugs* (Glencoe, Illinois: The Free Press [forthcoming]).

## EFFECTS OF ROLE PLAYING ON CONVERSION

The conversion potential of a persuasive message appears to be intensified under conditions of audience participation and particularly among persons who are required, regardless of their actual feelings, to assume a role sympathetic to the point of view expressed. This successful technique to convert opinion has been shown repeatedly in the social psychologist's laboratory and is believed to have been employed by the Communists in brainwashing Korean War prisoners. Many salesmen confuse this technique with demonstration, which to them means showing the product and demonstrating how it works. To the psychologist, role playing means getting the prospect into the act. There is a major difference which shall be emphasized.

In a series of studies, male college students were required to present persuasive talks to fellow students without a script but after being permitted to read an affirmative argument first. Others were permitted to read aloud to their audience directly from the script. The results consistently indicate that the amount of opinion change in the speaker himself, produced through active participation, is dependent upon the amount he had to improvise and is not related to the amount of his own satisfaction in the job he had done.[16]

Role playing and improvising seem to be the techniques of brainwashing American prisoners of the Communists during the Korean War. A study suggests that overt agreement, conjured up for the specific occasion, may contribute to the ultimate actual conversion of the one urged to create talks contrary to his original views.[17] Similar findings are reported on studies of seventh-grade students who had to evaluate selected comic books;[18] on adults told to prepare talks favoring or opposing salary increases for teachers;[19] and internationally in Voice of America propaganda studies.[20] Subjects of these tests were found later to have selectively retained

---

[16] B. T. King and Irving L. Janis, "Comparison of the Effectiveness of Improvised Versus Non-improvised Role-Playing in Producing Opinion Changes" (paper presented before the Eastern Psychological Association, 1953), in Carl I. Hovland, Irving L. Janis, and Harold H. Kelley, *Communication and Persuasion* (New Haven: Yale University Press, 1953), p. 278.

[17] *Ibid.*

[18] Herbert C. Kelman, "Attitude Change as a Function of Response Restriction," *Human Relations*, Vol. VI, 1953, pp. 185–214.

[19] Claire Zimmerman and Raymond A. Bauer, "The Effect of an Audience Upon What Is Remembered," *Public Opinion Quarterly*, Vol. XX, 1956, pp. 238–48.

[20] Kracauer and Berkman, *op. cit.*

and improvised their arguments in accord with the audience they expected to address. Selective perception and retention are directed, in spite of the predisposition of the individual, toward the goal of the persuader.

In sales, this is the technique of getting the prospect into the act, using the demonstration as the pretext to get him to assume a favorable role. When a businessman listens to a sales talk, he employs clear, critical faculties to judge the merits of a talk and evaluate the proposal. When he participates, even partially, in a product demonstration, he becomes more of a biased witness for the salesman rather than an impartial judge of the facts. Seeing is more than believing in this case; it is selective learning. When a prospect is persuaded to participate there is a whole new attitude of mind. He and the salesman are working something out together and the prospect then becomes sympathetic rather than reluctant or uncomprehending. The prospect tends to put himself in the salesman's shoes and he sells himself.

In a number of studies, it was found that selective retention works in favor of the position the individual was required to assume, even if that position was contrary to his original views. Trying to gain status with the audience by excelling as a speaker seems to account for the internalizing of the overt behavior. In other words, while trying to convince others of a view contrary to his own, the speaker convinces himself.

## EFFECTS OF NEGATIVE SELLING IN CONVERSION

Negative selling is a special type of role playing in which the normal roles of buyer and seller are completely reversed and the prospect does the salesman's work. One technique for reversing roles works like this: "You probably can't afford this, Mr. Prospect, but I want to show you what our new product will do for you."

The reaction often is, "Who can't afford it? Let me tell you, young man. . . ."

Selling a marketing consulting service, for example, a college professor might employ this negative technique in the following manner: When a client suggests he might use their services, the salesman or professor in this case might ask, "Why?" This would put the client on the defensive and cause him to think of the many things he ought to know. The salesman could then suggest doubt and cause the client to be specific by asking, "What information do you need, for example?" After the client firmly establishes the need in his own mind, the professor could go on with this negative technique to explore ways to satisfy the need. He might ask, "But can't you get most of the information you need from existing sales reports?" The client would be apt to argue that existing records are not sufficient for his purpose. "Well then, can't your own salesmen in the field get this information for you?" Again the client would be expected to argue how impractical this would be. Reluctantly, the professor would finally agree to make the survey. The client would have sold himself and there wouldn't be any doubt in his mind why he needed the survey and why using an outside consultant would be the best way to get it. Not only is the customer forced to do the selling but he is put in a position of pleading with the expert to take the job, often even offering a bonus besides.

While many stories illustrate negative selling, they are hard to apply correctly as it is not likely that prospects will often act in the desired manner. Closer to a normal application of this sales technique is the one often described by many experienced salesmen. Early in his career, the young salesman called on a large buyer who had never given his company an order. The prospect bluntly told the young salesman he would be wasting his time trying to sell him. The salesman's reply was to the effect that he was not trying to sell the prospect but understood the prospect was an expert in that field and the young salesman simply wanted the expert to tell him how to sell other people. The stories all conclude the same. The tough old buyer, flattered by the young novice, completely sold himself and gave the salesman a large order.

In the field of political science, this technique is commonly used with the familiar phrase, "If you can't beat them, join them." When Franklin D. Roosevelt wanted Republican support for some of his congressional battles, he appointed Stimson, a prominent Republican, as Secretary of War. F.D.R. joined his political enemies by giving them star positions on his team. More recently, John F. Kennedy used the same technique when he appointed Republican Henry Cabot Lodge as ambassador to the hot spot of South Vietnam. One can assume that for similar reasons President Johnson continued the appointment when he assumed office. Professional politicians are well aware of this technique of persuasion; however, when handled with sincerity they willingly allow themselves to be persuaded.

Perhaps the concept of negative selling can be illustrated by the statement, "Things forbidden have a secret charm." A newspaper editorial cited this as an explanation of the huge numbers of tourists going abroad in view of an expected tax on tourism. "Even more charming than things already forbidden are those that tomorrow seem likely to be illicita."[21]

---

[21] Editorial, "Praevalent Illicita," Wall Street Journal, July, 1965.

When a salesman is not permitted to see the man who makes the final decision, he must persuade a subordinate to present his message fairly. Provided his job is *not* made too easy, even a hostile subordinate may become persuaded, against his original opinion. If the subordinate must improvise a fair presentation, he will gain status with both the boss and the salesman. What was formerly an obstacle to persuasion now becomes the effective salesman's asset. Competitive salesmen may submit letters or brochures which do not involve the subordinate and he will not become interested in their cause. The effective salesman will ask for a list of things the subordinate wants for his visual presentation. When handled with diplomacy and tact, the subordinate will then become involved and ultimately will be favorably inclined toward the position of the effective salesman.

The negative selling technique is a pure application of the psychological phenomena of reverse role playing. A businessman persuades himself by creating a talk or message that will persuade others. In the process, his predisposition, selective exposure to facts, and selective perception and retention of facts work to modify or change his opinion sufficiently to persuade himself.

## SUMMARY

Opinion conversion is the process in which a seemingly new attitude is built up to the point at which it looms over all other attitudes and causes an individual to take some mental steps to regain his sense of inner balance. Normally any direct suggestion that the individual has false or wrong beliefs will alert his defense mechanisms to the point that he will discredit the accuser and disbelieve anything he might say in the future.

A persuasion attempt that begins with a minor point about which the listener is not aware of any particular feelings and gains acceptance on this insignificant point has some chance of success. As minor points, seemingly of little or no consequence, are accepted the effective defenses of resistance lie dormant. Some people seem more easily persuaded on any topic than other people, due primarily to a lack of self-confidence. Whenever a person is torn between the advice of two friendly sources he tends to delay making a decision, if not to withdraw completely from the conflict.

The various groups to which an individual belongs tend to reinforce and protect his predisposition. However, when the group no longer serves his needs or seems to make sense, the same predisposition will encourage him to leave the group to find more satisfying norms elsewhere. Opinion leaders, those whom the individual respects and listens to in a given field, will tend to present material biased by their own predispositions and will thereby influence the individual to change to agree with the leaders' opinions.

Role playing is the technique used to encourage a buyer to create a persuasive sales talk, often against his previous opinions and beliefs, and thereby persuade himself. In negative selling, the buyer and seller reverse roles completely and the buyer acts the part of the salesman.

All successful conversion techniques depend primarily on lulling the defense mechanisms into inactivity and thereby gaining selective exposure, perception, and retention. Once having gained acceptance, new information is treated as if the subject were predisposed to receive and enjoy it. Conflicting but subordinate attitudes can be reinforced to grow in strength to dominate positions, and the subject effectively persuades himself.

# 10

# The Salesman and the Situational
# Aspects of Persuasion

Vanity or self-conceit plays fantastic tricks with one's memory; however, a quiet and private appraisal of self can be both awakening and educational. At any given moment a salesman holds a mental picture of what he is like as a person, with such traits as honesty, industry, intelligence, good humor, and so forth. At that same moment his customers also hold a mental picture of what he is really like as a person, including such human traits as greed, avarice, laziness, baseness, and so forth. In truth, the salesman is a small part of each of these extremes for that moment. As events occur to make the salesman and the observing customer more optimistic both mental pictures will become more realistic and the converse also applies while only a tiny fraction of either of these mental pictures holds true. This illusive truth is what one seeks in attempting to learn of his own strengths and weaknesses so he may improve and more nearly become the ideal person he desires. The building up of honest self-esteem is a difficult but necessary process if one is to become an effective salesman.

## SALESMAN'S PREDISPOSITION

The salesman's attitudes, ideas, opinions, and beliefs combine to predispose him to like certain personalities and certain phases of his job responsibilities and to dislike and possibly ignore other personalities and other job phases. From every exposure and experience in life he will have learned to expect certain things from people in various situations and he himself will behave in a predictable manner. To become more effective, he should study his own attitudes as they relate to people and to the various responsibilities of the sales job.

144

All of what has been said about the buyer applies to the salesman, no matter how careful he is to be open-minded and objective. The salesman is predisposed to like certain types of people and the selective processes will tend to operate in such a way as to protect the salesman's self-image. He will expose himself more often to his "kind of people" and he will more easily perceive what they are trying to do. He will remember from call to call what was really said and will act accordingly. Others who do not treat him according to his self-image will tend to confuse the salesman. He will not understand what they say and will not understand their motives. He will have difficulty remembering what was said or how the prospect reacted during the last interview.

The primary responsibility of a salesman is to help customers solve problems. The salesman's attitude must favor helping others above or at least before helping himself. There should be no conflict with such a noble attitude; however, many prospects and customers do not want the salesman's help in solving their problems. Helping people under these conditions can be difficult and may cause the salesman who has weak convictions to withdraw or leave the field. To be more effective the salesman must pursue his desire to help in ways which are acceptable to the customer.

Another duty of a salesman is to exercise financial responsibility. This includes discretion in handling his own expense account and negotiating adjustments in pricing or settling claims with customers. The effective salesman is willing to accept the results of his own decisions, operating on the principle of his long-term contribution to profit. Customers and prospects see an entirely different picture, sometimes feeling the salesman has unlimited money to burn and other times feeling he has no discretion whatsoever and is simply the tool of his manager.

Independence is another facet of the sales job which can be looked upon with differing attitudes. Most effective salesmen feel they are their own boss and enjoy the freedom of action this permits. Some salesmen and many observers would not want the responsibility of directing their own activities, as they are more comfortable following the orders of authorities. Still others believe the salesman is totally directed insofar as where and when he must visit and exactly what he is compelled to say.

Arguing and bargaining are often part of the selling job and both salesmen and buyers consider this phase as either an annoying problem or an enjoyable exercise in the ancient game of rhetoric. The salesman's negative attitude is quickly perceived by customers and they may react unfavorably. In this area of self-understanding, it is essential for the salesman to be enlightened if he is to be effective with those who enjoy bargaining as well as with those who prefer a single firm price without negotiating.

Travel, being constantly on the move, continually meeting new people, can be considered fun and a challenge or it can be thought of as a shallow and transient way of life with no family or community ties. Eating expensive meals in restaurants can be fun or boring depending on the quality of the food and the company. To the customer who rarely dines out, it may sound intriguing yet to the tired salesman it may seem painful. Clearly, the truth lies somewhere between the two. However, the attitude remains in the mind of the beholder. It is the attitude that colors the salesman's behavior.

To the customer, the salesman is the supplier. Any errors or problems, for example, in product quality, shipping, or invoicing, are his direct responsibility and he must take the blame. The salesman normally has little or no voice in such matters and is aware of problems only after they have led to errors which irritate his customers. Effective salesmen willingly assume full responsibility for every action of the company they represent and they make it their business to know its operation and policies to enlighten customers and reduce or eliminate errors.

Effective salesmen often listen sympathetically to customers' personal troubles and problems as a friend in need but they keep their own problems to themselves. This gives some buyers the impression that the salesman is a strong person to lean on emotionally and one who is discreet. Buyers will often try out their ideas on salesmen without fear of being ridiculed. These situations can be flattering to the salesman and harmless if he is aware of the nature of the relationship. It can also distort his self-esteem if he lets the flattery blind him to his own weaknesses.

Manipulating people is perhaps the most misunderstood and condemned practice of persuasion. Some salesmen enjoy manipulating people for the sense of personal power they feel or because it fills their need to prove themselves superior. Consumers are justified in fearing and condemning such behavior. Effective salesmen, however, look upon persuasion as being beneficial to their customers in the same way that parents persuade their baby to eat a proper diet. It is the fundamental attitude to which the salesman is predisposed that makes the difference between long-term effectiveness and shortsighted sales.

The pressure of sales quotas is another area of misunderstanding and the salesman's attitude can help to make his life more pleasant or more frustrating, which in turn will be reflected in his behavior with customers.

Assume a salesman goes over his quota for a given period, such as a year or a quarter. He then goes back to zero sales for the new period and must begin again. It may seem that no matter how well he does, he will still periodically zero out and begin again, never finishing the frustrating endless race. On the other hand, each period offers a new opportunity to excel, to gain personal recognition, and to be rewarded. Such opportunities rarely occur in other vocations.

Finally, there is the attitude toward the selling job itself. Many people consider a sales job something one does if he can't do anything else. Unfortunately, the extreme shortage of effective salesmen has opened the doors to many people who should not be tolerated in sales. Effective selling is something that perhaps one person in ten is capable of doing and considerably less than one in ten actually do perform effectively. A really effective salesman is quickly recognized and can advance rapidly in the marketing department to top management. The false popular image of selling need not mislead the confident and effective salesman.

The salesman's attitudes, ideas, opinions, and beliefs may be in conflict with each other and occasionally may be contradictory to his attempts at persuasion. If he acknowledges his faults he can attempt to correct them through self-development but if he cannot change, he is at least aware of these weaknesses and can avoid situations which will expose them. An effective salesman is on guard to control those human emotions which are self-defeating—such as greed, feelings of superiority, and boastfulness, for example.

## SALESMAN'S COMMUNICATIONS

When the salesman attempts to persuade others, he always expresses something about himself as well as refers to something external to himself. Inspection of these expressive meanings that accompany one's persuasion theme will help him further to understand why persuasive messages are effective in some cases and not in others. There are many sounds, words, and expressions that can be given different meanings simply by changing the inflection or tone of the message. The vocalizations of an individual function as expressive symptoms. For example, a particular cry of a baby may be interpreted as, "He is hungry," or, "He is sleepy." These noises operate as symptoms and cause adults to take appropriate action. Think how many ways a suspicious wife can say to her late arriving husband, "Working late again, dear?"

A shaky voice in an adult is an expressive symptom, more convincing to his listeners than the direct expression, "I am nervous or afraid." All his life a person learns to categorize certain expressive symptoms and, therefore, he can sometimes penetrate to a truth about a speaker which was not intended to be revealed. When a salesman is sefishly motivated the buyer is likely to identify the persuasive message as against his best wishes and so will not act as the salesman recommends. Thus the unwitting expressive symptoms often trip up the deliberately dishonest salesman.

Beyond expressive symptoms, the actual spoken word is subject to various interpretations. This refers to the hidden meaning of a word or phrase and not to the various dictionary meanings discussed earlier. Freudian interpretations are perhaps the most popularly known hidden meanings in American culture. Early in his career, Freud attributed hysterical neurosis in women to the early psychological damage caused by the incestuous seduction by their fathers. Further evidence convinced him that his patients had deceived him and he was too gullible. Then he developed another interpretation of their incest reports. They expressed that the speaker was not a liar but had unconsciously desired the reported seduction. It was a wish fulfilling fantasy, not an accomplished fact. Freud found slips of the tongue meant much more than simple fatigue and haste. They expressed suppressed desires. The *Reader's Digest* often prints "Freudian slips" and the layman listens with a sixth sense to a specialized language for such expressive symptoms. Such has been the popularity of Freud's views in America.

A salesman's attitudes and beliefs about buyers he contacts and about the obligations and responsibilities of his job, his predisposition, will materially affect his mode of operating by exposing him to his kind of people and by causing him to be confused when dealing with buyers who apparently look at things quite differently from the way he does. Whenever he talks to a buyer, even including the extreme case in which he is merely regurgitating a memorized talk, the salesman is bound to express something about himself. The change of emphasis on different words, the tone used, the degree of strength in his voice, the Freudian slips, all will tip off the buyer to most deliberately misleading salesmen.

## AUDIENCE IMAGE OF THE SOURCE

Earlier it was pointed out that children learn that parents are not always selfless and occasionally mislead. As the child moves out into the world he constantly tries to discover when others are operating in his best interest and when they are attempting persuasion against his interests. When a friendly uncle, for example, tries to influence the hesitant young nephew to join his firm, he attempts to convince the young man that he has mistaken his own interests. The uncle tries to introduce new information, without bias, for the sole benefit of the nephew. What is really the best interest of the boy is to learn a business thoroughly and become the boss instead of getting a job with higher starting pay which may lead to a dead-end future. Will the uncle be persuasive? He will only if the nephew previously has thought well of his uncle and can see his own interest agreeing with the picture his uncle paints.

Beyond the family and immediate friends, the problem of persuasion grows more complex. A message will be credible, a recommendation to action will be persuasive, to the degree that the source of the message, the salesman, is thought to be trustworthy. There are basically three components of credibility: intention, expertness, and trustworthiness. Intention, it has been shown, must be identified with the buyer's own best interest. Expertness is the professional selling technique of presentation and this will be covered in some detail in Part III of this book. Trustworthiness overlaps intention but goes beyond. First, the source of the sales message must be identified by the buyer as either neutral and disinterested or, more realistically, possessed of a self-enlightened attitude which shows he is devoted to the welfare of the buyer. Second, the salesman must be knowledgeable through training or experience. To the degree that the salesman is believed to have these qualities, the message will be effective.

Extensive investigations have shown that messages attributed to high credibility sources were more often considered fair and were believed than were the exact same messages attributed to low credibility sources.[1] For example, if the identical message was supposed to have been said by Lenin and by Thomas Jefferson, different degrees of acceptance appeared. Messages varied with bias and credibility were also tested and immediate differences of the same general order were observed, with the high credibility source persuasive in a ratio of better than three to one. Tests showed that after a month's passage of time, the number of those persuaded by the low credibility sources increased. Once the source was reinstated or renewed in the listeners' minds however, the differences between the two groups immediately reappeared.[2] In sales this indicates at least one reason why a neglected customer or prospect will drift to competitors. Regular

[1] S. E. Asch, *Social Psychology* (New York: Prentice-Hall, Inc., 1952).

Also see Helen B. Lewis, "Studies in the Principles of Judgments and Attitudes: IV. The Operation of Prestige Suggestion," *Journal of Abnormal and Social Psychology*, Vol. 14, 1941, pp. 229–56.

[2] Herbert C. Kelman and Carl I. Hovland, "Reinstatement of the Communicator in Delayed Measurement of Opinion Change," *Journal of Abnormal and Social Psychology*, Vol. XLVIII, 1953, pp. 327–35.

calls will renew the confidence a prospect places in the salesman. Once a salesman has earned the potential buyer's trust, he cannot sit back and wait for the buyer to call him in on a problem. With the passage of time the buyer will think less of his credibility unless it is renewed in his mind and this credibility is constantly reinforced by the salesman's friendly visits.

## SITUATIONAL ASPECTS OF PERSUASION

There are some contributory factors which affect conversion in many selling situations. Research points out there are some definite aids to persuasion, some definite distractions, and a number of qualified or conditional aspects which may apply. These include explicitness, two-sided presentation, stimulating fear to motivate, repetition, variation, cumulative effects, and canalization. Each of these situational aspects shall be discussed briefly.

### Explicitness vs. Implicitness

Research evidence strongly indicates that persuasive messages which clearly, emphatically, and explicitly state the conclusions desired are much more likely to be understood than those which allow the buyer to draw his own conclusions. Furthermore, action recommendations also seem much more likely to be followed when they are specific and explicit.[3]

One typical study, for example, gave identical messages to two groups except that conclusions were explicitly drawn in one but not the other. Persuasion in the direction intended was 48 percent for the explicit version with 3 percent boomerang effect, or a net conversion effect of 45 percent, as compared to only 19 percent persuaded in the control group and 11 percent boomerang effect, or a net effect of only 9 percent.[4] Such find-

---

[3] Dorwin Cartwright, "Some Principles of Mass Persuasion: Selected Findings of Research on the Sale of United States War Bonds," *Human Relations*, Vol. II, 1949, pp. 253–67. Cartwright concluded his study by stating the more specifically defined the path of action to a goal, the more likely it is that the path will be followed (p. 264).

Also Elihu Katz and Paul F. Lazarsfeld, *Personal Influence: The Part Played by People in the Flow of Mass Communications* (Glencoe, Illinois: The Free Press, 1955). It was found that the more specific the suggestion a personal contact makes, the more likely it is that his or her advice will be followed (p. 214).

[4] Wallace Mandell and Carl I. Hovland, "Is There a Law of Primacy in Persuasion?" *American Psychologist*, Vol. VII, 1952, p. 538. This study dealt with the advisability of devaluating currency which is not likely to be ego-involved, and on which the audience is unlikely to have strong preexisting opinions.

ings are quite consistent and in accord with a number of other studies.

In sales literature there is the oft repeated story told by many experienced salesmen that clearly illustrates the need for being explicit. The salesman had forced himself to the limits of his capacity by using everything he knew to persuade a stubborn prospect for several hours. He was about talked out and could think of nothing new to add. With nothing to lose but his frustration, the salesman blurted out, "Why the heck don't you buy my proposition?"

The businessman, equally frustrated by the ordeal, retorts, "Why the heck didn't you ask me? I was ready to buy an hour ago!"

This salesman obviously thought he had asked for the order many times and in many ways but to the prospect it was never clear, specific, and explicit. Hindsight indicates the buyer could have silenced the salesman earlier by ordering. To be effective, the salesman should give clear examples of the conclusions desired and avoid being vague or simply implying what action is desired. Inspirational sales literature translates and abbreviates this concept to state simply: Ask for the order.

## One Side vs. Two Sides of an Argument

Presenting only one side of an argument as compared with presenting both sides has been another subject of research on effective persuasion.[5] In general, investigators found that presentation of both sides of an argument was more effective in persuading the well informed but that one-sidedness was more effective with the poorly educated. Businessmen are generally well educated, and here one must include the self-made men who are often self-educated to a degree that is well beyond that of many college graduates. An illustration of this self-education is the vocabulary test of 150 words given in England where top executives averaged 143 correct words, one higher than college professors; 14 words higher than liberal arts graduates and 23 words higher than graduate engineers.[6] While this may be a small sample and the results disproportionate, even after one discounts a large percent, one must conclude that most successful businessmen do have the ability to put across their ideas to their associates with words. They are, as a group, well educated. One would assume therefore that a

[5] Carl I. Hovland, Arthur A. Lumsdaine, and Fred D. Sheffield, "Studies in Social Psychology in World War II," *Experiments on Mass Communication* (Princeton, N.J.: Princeton University Press, 1949), Vol. III.

[6] Earl Prevette, *The Power of Creative Selling* (Englewood Cliffs, N.J.: Prentice-Hall, Inc., 1954).

two-sided presentation to a businessman would normally be more effective in persuasion than a one-sided presentation.

Among men originally favoring the advocated view, a one-sided message proved a more effective reinforcement than a two-sided message.[7] In sales one often sees a man who is ready to buy but the unwise salesman seems to be a compulsive talker and proceeds to talk himself out of the order by confusing the prospect. If the buyer believes in the salesman and the product and he already favors a given purchase, then a one-sided presentation will be most appreciated for its brevity and it will be more effective. In the same vein, studies have also shown that a one-sided argument also serves as an efficient innoculator or insulator if the listener commits himself publicly after being exposed to the message.[8] If the businessman agrees with the salesman's proposal and goes out on a limb by recommending it to his associates, he will subsequently selectively hear and understand only arguments which support his declared position. He will be insulated or mentally protected against counterarguments.

Presenting both sides of an argument in an apparent but illusory impartial manner was also found to boomerang.[9] If the two-sided presentation is in any way suspect of bias, it becomes particularly ineffective. Omission of one relevant point against persuasive effort is more noticeable when presenting both sides. This is another concrete reason why complete honesty and sincerity are fundamental in selling. Another fault with presenting both sides is that if impartiality is too complete, the entire presentation may be without effect because the pro and con arguments may cancel each other out.

Studies have shown that when properly used, two-sided messages appear to be the most efficient innoculators against future argument. Normally, in commercial and industrial sales a buyer will call in a number of competing suppliers and try to withhold decision until he has heard them all. If the first salesman gives a two-sided presentation, he will steal the punch from subsequent sales stories as well as direct the buyer's mind to look at the others in a particular way. The salesman will anticipate competitors' counterattacks on his product and direct the buyer's attention to details favorable to the first presentation.[10] In other words researchers generally

[7] Hovland, Lumsdaine, and Sheffield, op. cit.

[8] Carl I. Hovland et al., The Order of Presentation in Persuasion (New Haven: Yale University Press, 1957).

[9] Hovland, Lumsdaine, and Sheffield, op. cit., p. 225.

[10] See Arthur A. Lumsdaine and Irving L. Janis, "Resistance to 'Counter Propaganda' Produced by One-Sided and Two-Sided 'Propaganda' Presentations," Public Opinion Quarterly, Vol. XVII, 1953, pp. 311–18.

agree a two-sided sales presentation is more effective when the buyer is to be exposed to subsequent competitive arguments or when the buyer initially disagrees with the salesman's position regardless of subsequent exposure. A one-sided presentation is more effective if the buyer initially agrees with the salesman's position or is not apt to be exposed to later counter- or competitive arguments.

In a realistic sales situation this is not as complicated as it may seem at first glance. Having given a one-sided or totally biased presentation to a businessman, the salesman can ask for the order. After answering simple objections without getting the order, the salesman might attempt to get the prospect to commit himself openly in favor of the proposition by recommending the purchase to his associates. If the buyer still indicates he wants to shop around, the salesman can go on to a two-sided presentation. If the sales interview is truly a two-way communication and the salesman is aware of the processes involved in persuasion, he need not talk himself out of the sure sale, nor will he quit too early on a tough sale when a little more effort in the right direction can be effective. Using this technique in closing a sale will be discussed more fully in Chapter 21.

## STIMULATING FEAR TO MOTIVATE AND ITS BOOMERANG EFFECT

A number of sales demonstrations are designed to arouse fear in the prospect's mind so he will buy the product to protect himself. But a series of recent studies consistently shows that the greater the fear stimulated in the listener's mind, the *less* effective the persuasion becomes.[11] One study previously cited showed the dangers of dental neglect and gave three identical persuasive messages for specific hygiene but in the three messages three different degrees of the fear stimulant were employed.[12] In the maximum threat version there was less than one-tenth change; in the moderate version there was about one-fifth change; and in the minimum threat version there was about one-third change. Upon retest, these differences persisted even one year later. The persuasion effect was shown to be in an inverse ratio to the degree of fear stimulated. Studies involving

[11] Carl I. Hovland, Irving L. Janis, and Harold H. Kelley, *Communications and Persuasion* (New Haven: Yale University Press, 1953). This study uses the term "Threat Appeals" (p. 56) which has become the standard terminology for content which attempts to persuade by frightening the listener.

[12] Irving L. Janis and S. Feshbach, "Effects of Fear-Arousing Communications," *Journal of Abnormal and Social Psychology*, Vol. XLVIII, 1953, pp. 78–92.

smoking and its relation to cancer have drawn similar conclusions.[13] A strong threat is in itself too preoccupying, which probably hinders learning other material in the message. With fear aroused but not fully relieved by later reassurances which were not perceived, the listener will tend to ignore or minimize the importance of the threat. The frightened listener employs the defense mechanism of withdrawal.

Market research shows that thousands of consumers who are in a position to fulfill long held dreams will simply continue to dream and not take any steps to buy what they want because they are afraid. For example, a young husband's first attempt to buy some fancy lingerie for his wife's birthday is a new situation for him. Young husbands are not sure how they should behave and they feel inferior, which distorts their perception of reality. They feel they will behave improperly or they may intrude and disrupt the store routine. They may also feel others will respond to their actions in such a way as to ridicule or hurt them. Any sales technique which increases this sense of fear, such as negative selling or snob effect, will boomerang. In the same way, the new bride prefers to shop in a self-service supermarket where she can look at the cuts of sirloin, round, or porterhouse without admitting she doesn't know what they are. She will not willingly expose herself to a smart butcher who might ridicule her ignorance. Buyers want reassurance, not fear stimulation or ridicule.

### Repetition, Variation, and Cumulative Effect

Research generally supports the view that sheer repetition of a message is effective in some forms of persuasion. One study of the effectiveness of repetition found that more television set owners than nonowners used each of the tested advertised brand.[14] Fewer owners used the brands not advertised on television. When a brand began to advertise on television its sales went up with the set owners while holding at a constant level for nonowners. Persons buying television sets increased their purchases of the advertised brands but not of brands unrepresented on television. Other studies have revealed that many people dislike television commercials and most people are well aware that the source of the message is biased and interested primarily in selling the product. Where all sources are equally untrustworthy but where some choice must be made, between razor blades,

---

[13] Charles F. Cannel and James C. MacDonald, "The Impact of Health News on Attitudes and Behavior," *Journalism Quarterly*, Vol. XXXIII, 1956, pp. 315–23.
[14] Thomas E. Coffin, "Television's Effects on Leisure Activities," *Journal of Applied Psychology*, Vol. XXXII, 1948, pp. 550–58.

for example, repetition is the first law of persuasion. It is reported that when a commercial is seen and disliked, the set owners still buy more of the advertised brand than when they do not see the commercial.[15] Since the buyer considers most competing brands about equal in value and since he must shave his face with one of them, he is most likely to say the name that comes most readily to mind. This is analogous to a free association test. Hot—cold. Knife—fork. Razor blades—Gillette. This does not mean that the buyer particularly likes the product or is truly persuaded to buy it for its merit but that his purchase of it is really an act of associative memory.

Studies of persuasion attempts directed toward changing attitudes and opinions of individuals generally agree that it is repetition with variation, not sheer repetition, that is effective. Several studies have found not only that varying appeals were particularly successful but also that a certain degree of ambiguity apparently increased the effectiveness of appeals by making them susceptible to various interpretations.[16] Persons given more than one type of reason to buy were found more likely actually to do so. This does not contradict the law of explicitness cited earlier. When asking for action, direct explicit instructions favor persuasion but when building desire a certain degree of ambiguity can be better. A buyer who is interested in a proposition can often see benefits that he may not disclose or he can feel advantages that he would be embarrassed to discuss openly. In this sense, discretion is the better part of salesmanship. If the subconscious motives are working for the salesman it is best not to tamper with them. If the salesman brings them to the surface, the buyer may be forced by his own sense of morality or logic to deny them and not to buy. In other words, probing these hidden desires may boomerang while some degree of ambiguity in this sense may aid persuasion.

Perhaps more easily recognized and understood concerning the ambiguity of an appeal is the campaign speech of a politician. It might run as follows: "Democracy is alive and must move ahead with vigor. We are free to live and love and laugh. We face the future with confidence and courage. We are American." These noble statements are almost meaningless but they can mean all things to all men; thus people with divergent views may be brought together in one political party. In a sales situation, the emotional appeal can be so general and ambiguous that the prospect

---

[15] Thomas E. Coffin, *The Hofstra Study: A Measure of the Sales Effectiveness of Television Advertising* (New York: NBC Research Division, 1950).

[16] Paul F. Lazarsfeld, Bernard Berelson, and Hazel Gaudet, *The People's Choice* (New York: Columbia University Press, 1948). Also Cartwright, *op. cit.*

can read into it added benefits without a specific analytical discussion. The final request for action, voting for the politician or buying the salesman's proposition, should be explicit, definite, and so strongly worded that there is no danger of its being misunderstood.

Listen to a favorite march or classical musical theme and notice how often it repeats and also how it repeats with minor variations. Once the listener begins to tap his foot or nod his head with the rhythm, he indicates his enjoyment. Upon repetition of the melody he is apt to smile. Repetition tends to reinforce his original preference.

Studies on cumulative exposure have generally been inconclusive. Repeating the same message 7 times may be as effective as repeating it 15 times.[17] Marketing specialists refer to this as the threshold of effectiveness or the minimum point at which a stimulus is just strong enough to be perceived or produce a response. One marketing survey of the Philadelphia beer market showed that an advertiser had to spend at least 10 percent of the total beer dollar sales in the area in order to gain some listener awareness. Anything less than this amount was not perceived by the audience and the advertising money was wasted. On the other hand, two exposures may often be no more effective than a single exposure. This may be due to two major factors. First, the listener may identify all messages beyond the first as identical and become bored with the subject. The second and more probable reason for the ineffectiveness of cumulative exposure is that the selective processes are operating differently in subsequent exposure. The first time through, a buyer may have listened and understood because he had a problem in this general area. Subsequent calls found him with new problems, perhaps more pressing and demanding of his attention, and he subconsciously stopped listening to the repetitive message. This again points up the importance of a salesman's understanding of selective exposure, perception, and retention. While social-psychological research has not demonstrated this point, it would appear likely that if a buyer repeatedly and willingly exposed himself to a varied sales message with selective perception and selective retention, he would be more easily persuaded than under conditions of simple repetition.

---

[17] A. D. Annis and N. C. Meier, "The Induction of Opinion through Suggestions by Means of Planted Content," *Journal of Social Psychology*, Vol. V, 1934, pp. 68–81. On the other hand, the effect of cumulative exposure to films on the same topic was found to be in all respects greater than the effect of a single exposure by Ruth C. Peterson and L. L. Thurstone, as reported in *Motion Pictures and the Social Attitudes of Children* (New York: Macmillan Co., 1933). Reshowing a film to clarify any questions raised by the audience was found most effective by the Commonwealth Office of Education, *The Effective Use of Films* (Sydney, Australia, 1950).

## Canalization

Studies have generally agreed that people are far more likely to be persuaded to fill existing needs than they are to develop entirely new needs.[18] Existing buyer attitudes can be directed toward new objects through familiar words and symbols. However, it is difficult, if not impossible, to direct attitudes to entirely new goals. If a woman wants more time in the afternoon to go shopping or to play bridge with her friends, she may be persuaded to buy a dishwashing machine for the free time it will provide but it may be very difficult to get her to accept the probability that a dishwashing machine can clean her pots better than she can do it herself.

The essential point of canalization is that a sales message which seems to promise the buyer relief from existing needs is more likely to be persuasive than a sales message which attempts to create new needs. A study of office managers, for example, showed that many bought new equipment primarily to get more work done by the same number of office people and not to make their employees' lives more comfortable or easier.[19] Convincing this type of buyer that ease and comfort would produce a greater volume of work would be difficult if not impossible. But persuading him that a piece of equipment will produce greater volume in spite of a lazy operator will be much more appealing to him.

## SUMMARY

The selective processes which operate on a buyer also serve to protect the salesman's predisposition and self-image. He will more readily expose himself to people he likes and avoid buyers who tend to confuse him. Whenever he talks to a prospect, he will unintentionally express something about his own attitudes. Since the buyer's confidence in the salesman is paramount in any attempt at persuasion, the salesman should be completely honest and sincere. The deliberately dishonest salesman will unwittingly give himself away because he is easily seen through and the false presentation is more apt to boomerang than to persuade.

[18] See Cartwright, op. cit. Also see Paul F. Lazarfeld and Robert K. Merton, "Mass Communication, Popular Taste and Organized Social Action," in Lyman Bryson (ed.), The Communication of Ideas (New York: Harper & Bros., 1948).

[19] Joseph W. Thompson, "A Strategy of Selling," in Steven J. Shaw and Joseph W. Thompson (eds.), Salesmanship: Modern Viewpoints on Personal Communication, (New York: Holt, Rinehart and Winston, 1960), pp. 21–2.

Specific and direct conclusions and requests for action are more effective than implicit or vague statements. Normally an open two-sided presentation is most effective in dealing with businessmen in a competitive situation. An extreme threat to stimulate a buyer's action should be avoided because the anxiety created during the presentation may block further perception or distort his perception so that he completely misunderstands and dismisses the importance of the entire proposition. Generally speaking, repetition with variation is effective as long as the buyer exposes himself and perceives the message. It is always easier to convert an attitude or opinion to satisfy existing needs and desires of an individual than it is to attempt to persuade him by creating new needs and desires.

The salesman's perceived intentions and trustworthiness are two of the components which determine whether a message will be persuasive. The third component is the expertness of the persuader, or the effective selling strategy and technique of presentation. These phases of persuading men in business are so important that Part III of this text is devoted entirely to strategy and Part IV is devoted entirely to techniques.

# PART III

## Sales Strategy: Planning a Sales Presentation

# 11

# The Stimulus-Response Theory of Selling

Most people are familiar with the prepackaged sales presentation of the door-to-door salesman. The customary spiel of the circus barker or the broadway sideshow crier are often simply amusing variations of the canned speech. They all have the same basis for their existence. Most industrial salesmen, selling to the same accounts over and over, look down with scorn on such a simple selling method. Oddly enough, however, experiments conducted in the field without the salesman's knowledge have consistently shown that many industrial salesmen give practically the same talk to almost every prospect. In one experiment, tape recordings were used to convince the most skeptical salesmen that their talks really were not as varied and individual as they had sworn them to be.[1]

## THE EXTENT TO WHICH PLANNED TALKS ARE USED

The canned sales presentation is widely used with forethought and knowledge—used intentionally—by marketing management in a number of industries. It is used in retailing, both in stores and in house-to-house outside selling. It is taught by most life insurance companies, mutual fund selling companies, stockbrokers, and real estate agencies. While these are generally consumer markets, this method of selling is also used extensively by wholesale salesmen calling on businessmen who are, for example, supermarket operators or appliance store owners; by medical detail men doing missionary sales work with doctors and dentists; by manufacturers' representatives doing long-term selling or missionary work for new building materials with architects; it is used widely in selling office machines such as

---

[1] Joseph W. Thompson, "A Strategy of Selling," in Steven J. Shaw and Joseph W. Thompson (eds.), *Salesmanship: Modern Viewpoints on Personal Communications* (New York: Holt, Rinehart and Winston, Inc., 1960).

161

electric typewriters, accounting systems, and furniture and filing equipment; it is used in selling textbooks to college professors; and it is used in selling industrial equipment directly for the manufacturer.

A salesman for a national drug company contacts doctors in his area to keep them abreast of the constant new developments in his field. These medical detail men are, in reality, missionary salesmen because the doctor is not expected to buy the product directly but hopefully will prescribe it for his patients, who in turn will actually make the purchase. To a number of doctors, office time is equated with money and they grant their time to the salesman only grudgingly. The salesman must be quick and to the point with his message. Not too long ago, one drug company departed from the industry-wide practice of sending out college graduates trained in pharmaceutical backgrounds and changed to less qualified men equipped with a six-minute memorized sales presentation. The presentation covered three new products and the salesman's choice of one of three additional products so that each product had only one and one-half minutes to be talked about. On the next visit, the salesman had memorized another six-minute talk on different products. The doctors reacted with both resentment and good humor. They attempted to break into the continuity of the memorized talks or to break up the presentation with jokes and comical facial expressions. The sales managers then instructed their men to go back to the first sentence and repeat the entire canned speech every time a doctor broke into the talk. The time-conscious doctors quickly learned to let the salesmen say their piece without interruption and get out. Although the doctors resented this sales approach, they did prescribe significantly larger amounts of the one company's drugs. Very rapidly almost every other drug company imitated the pioneer and today, for the time being at least, this is the typical sales method in that industry. Of course, detail men do have other types of accounts, such as hospitals and drugstores, and they have other duties and responsibilities. This is not an attempt to belittle the salesmen or the marketing policy—after all, they have both proven economical and effective.

Perhaps more typical of the planned talk is the one given by the man selling insulated safes to a businessman. The salesman is taught precisely what to say on the telephone to gain an appointment and he must memorize every word he will use in his sales presentation. The only variations permitted by sales management are in the numbers to be supplied by the prospect during the interview and the selection of memorized responses to objections at the close. A typical presentation, with the dramatic directions noted in the margin, would begin:

Good morning, Mr. _____, I am _____ of the ABC Company. I came in to talk to you about protecting your essential records from fire. Mr. _____, what would happen to your business if you lost your Accounts Receivable files and other customer records? In all probability you would be in serious danger of going out of business. Forty-three percent of businesses having fires *do* fail. Only 7 percent carry on without serious loss to the company. That is a startling revelation. I am sure you can appreciate the seriousness of it.

*Speak firmly and forcefully*

*(Pause after question)*

*(Pause to emphasize)*

Even though a building is constructed of fireproof materials, disastrous fires do occur; irreplaceable records are destroyed and business is seriously curtailed if not actually lost because people are guilty of overestimating their protection against fire. An insurance policy never replaces or pays for records that are burned up.

Let's look at these pictures. I'm sure you will recognize the names of some of these buildings. Even the Pentagon was vulnerable. Fourteen truckloads of valuable records were lost.

*Take out ABC News. Show prospect page one. Circle paragraph 4.*

Here are several different businesses which had fires in which records were destroyed. I'm sure you don't want to lose any of these records; accounts receivables, tax records, general ledgers, checks, and open orders.

*Point to pictures. Check each record as you mention it. Pause.*

You don't have to lose any of them, Mr. _____. ABC safes are proven protection against this loss. That is how these people protected themselves. Don't you think this is worthwhile considering?

*Point to undamaged records in ABC safe. Wait for answer.*

For 35 years ABC has recognized the need for this type of protection and has manufactured a complete line of safes. The first step to assure this protection is to determine which of your records are needed to maintain your business. After we know which records must be maintained we can select the equipment to house them.

Shall we look over your records together, or do you prefer to have your office manager do that with me?

*Trial Close*

The talk resumes again with a number of trial closes and more and more information, as much as one hour of one-way talking, and ends on this note:

Now Mr. _____, you can't always prevent a fire
but you can prevent losses due to a fire. You know
which of your records are essential. Why not decide        Look directly at
now how these records should be housed?                    prospect. Speak
                                                           firmly and force-
Note: If the prospect denies that his papers are worth     fully.
much, toss a couple of dollars on his desk and take a
handful of his mail and start to leave. He will admit
then how valuable these papers really are.

The objectives, in this illustration, are first to establish the value of
business papers; to establish the possibility of all prospects having a fire
regardless of the type of building they are occupying; to establish the need
for protecting valuable papers; to show the businessman how he can
conveniently protect himself against loss; to get immediate favorable action from the buyer. Notice a few of the emotional phrases—"what would
happen to *your* business if *you lost* . . . a *startling* revelation . . . *irreplaceable records* . . . *you* can appreciate the *seriousness* . . . *disastrous*
fires . . . *you* don't want to lose." These phrases emphasize the individual
and his personal loss. They are intended to convey the salesman's legitimate and sincere concern for the businessman. The poor man didn't know
he was leading such a precarious business life. Fortunately for him, the
hero happened along to save him from the brink of disaster.

As to the possible effects on the businessman, in practice a few will
actually be persuaded to study the matter seriously as the salesman suggests. The large majority of individual businessmen, however, will be
distracted by thoughts of fire prevention in the office and plant or possibly
what they might do in the event of a catastrophic fire. The few businessmen who permit the salesman to go through his entire presentation will
probably be surprised when he carries out the dramatic instructions at the
end. If their predispositions permit, and the salesman's manner is acceptable, they may laugh at his final gesture and think well of him. If so, the
salesman will probably gain future selective exposure from this prospect. If
the businessman's predisposition is such that he resents the manner of the
salesman of the intrusion into his time and privacy, he may very well resent
the salesman's final gesture and quietly or loudly resolve never to buy from
him under any conditions. The salesman may unwittingly have made a sale
for his competitor and the businessman is unlikely to expose himself to the
ABC Company's future representatives. One such salesman sold a safe
every working day for more than a month using a variation of this technique but more than half of the buyers subsequently would not accept
delivery and nonbuyers flooded the ABC Company with complaints.

*Courtesy: International Business Machines Corp., Armonk, N.Y.*

FIG 7. A dictating unit is demonstrated by a sales representative to a prospective customer.

## WHY IS THE STIMULUS-RESPONSE SALES METHOD USED?

Despite its obvious pitfalls, this sales technique is prevalent today in many industries, and generally with management's encouragement, because of the mass markets which have yet to be contacted. When selling a single product to a mass market one is working on the law of averages. The man who gets the greatest exposure to prospects and effectively presents his stimulus-response sales plan will get the most orders. Many life insurance companies teach this form of selling because practically everyone is a prospect. Large mutual fund sales organizations require their salesmen to learn a two-hour canned speech before they are permitted to make their first call. It includes every idea that sales management has found useful for selling mutual funds in a mass market. The result? New men can sell almost as effectively as old men. The salesman's problem is finding enough prospects who are willing to sit down and listen for two hours.

In today's competitive market, sales managers cannot hire good sales-men, as their cost is often prohibitive. To reduce selling costs and yet gain the market exposure it would like, sales management has resorted to hiring men who are not truly qualified and then giving these men the crutch of a memorized talk which was devised by successful salesmen.

## THE KEY CHARACTERISTICS OF CANNED TALKS

If a sales plan is written out for the salesman and he memorizes it word for word, it is called a canned talk. When the salesman uses only selective parts of such a presentation and then substitutes his own varied talks for other parts but still follows the preplanned outline, it is called a planned talk. If the prospect says one thing, the salesman plans to answer with a particular memorized paragraph. In either form, canned or planned, a fairly standardized type of presentation which they give to all prospects is developed by most salesmen. It becomes a matter of habit.

A canned or planned talk is a complete talk which is based upon management's idea of talks which have proven successful and in which the salesman controls most of what is said. Through a standard presentation, he seeks only positive reactions by covering all benefits and qualities of his product and by covering all possible objections before they can be voiced. Even the closing of the sale is precanned to outmaneuver and outthink the poor prospect. Whatever form it takes, the planned talk is designed to communicate as many buying benefits as possible to the prospect as soon as possible in an attempt to elicit a favorable buying response. All the possible facts are assembled and arranged in logical sequence to tell a complete story which is supposed to conclude with the prospect motivated to buy the package.

If the salesman is aware of the stimulus-response basis of a canned talk, there is nothing wrong with using such a presentation on the proper occasion. Unfortunately, too few salesmen understand the selling principle involved in a canned or planned talk, even when they acknowledge that is the technique they are using. These men are more concerned with giving the complete talk than they are with stimulating a favorable response. The salesman is trained to say many magic words and raise certain points which supposedly will appeal favorably to most buyers, who will respond with orders. "Open sesame."

The accepted psychological principle which makes this form of selling effective is explained by the stimulus-response theory. Pavlov's experiments in conditioning showed the effects of stimuli on a dog.[2] One can easily recall, he first used the sight of food to stimulate the dog's salivary glands. Then he associated sound, a buzzer, with the sight of food. Finally the buzzer alone would stimulate the salivary glands. In business, the salesman attempts to use words which will automatically trigger a desired response. Remember Elmer Wheeler's sage advice, "Don't sell the steak—sell the sizzle!" He writes of having tested 105,000 selling word combinations on 19 million people in a retail situation to make his planned sales talks "foolproof" through pretesting in the field. Wheeler's principle is not magic words but word magic which he explains and illustrates delightfully in his books.[3]

Earl Prevette tells how to go about building word magic to fit a salesman's individual product.[4] Boring and dull statistical data are described with warm feeling and emotional overtones so the prospect can actually sense the benefits of using the product. Bert Schlain writes, "Keep polishing your sales talk until every single word, phrase and idea is the very best for a particular job it has to do. You'll know you've reached that point when you are confident that, if a prospect lets you state your case, the order is practically 'in the bag!' "[5]

A good planned talk has an engaging beginning, a logical and effective presentation and demonstration, and, finally, as many as ten standard phrases to use in closing a sale. The sales philosophy is to use a standardized approach and presentation to all prospects but when it comes to asking for the order, a concession is made to the individuality of the buyer and alternate appeals can be used.

## THE ADVANTAGES TO THE SALESMAN AND TO THE COMPANY

The apparent advantages of a standardized presentation to the salesman are that it saves his and the prospect's time, which enables him to see more

---

[2] I. P. Pavlov, *Conditioned Reflexes*, trans. G. V. Anrep (London: Oxford University Press, 1927).

I. P. Pavlov, *Conditioned Reflexes and Psychiatry*, trans. W. H. Gantt (New York: International Publishers, 1941).

[3] Elmer Wheeler, *Tested Sentences that Sell*, 1937; *Sizzlemanship*, 1937; *The Wealth Within You*, 1955; *How to Sell Yourself to Others*, 1947 all: (Englewood Cliffs, N.J.: Prentice-Hall, Inc.)

[4] Earl Prevette, *The Power of Creative Selling* (Englewood Cliffs, N.J.: Prentice-Hall, Inc., 1954).

[5] Bert Schlain, *Big League Salesmanship* (copyright by National Sales Executives, Inc.) (Englewood Cliffs, N.J.: Prentice-Hall, Inc., 1955).

people on a given day; it provides logical order to his sales story, which makes it easier for the prospect to understand and follow; it enables new salesmen to speak confidently without fumbling for words, which earns the buyer's respect; it assure's a smooth and complete presentation, preventing the absentminded omission of any important points; and it leaves the salesman free to devote his attention to showmanship and to observe the prospect's reactions. If the presentation is well designed, a number of words or expressions will stimulate some prospects into a buying action automatically. It is a complete and automatic sales presentation which requires a minimum of thought on the part of the salesman and which, when told to enough people, will assure some degree of success.

The apparent advantages to the selling company include the easier recruiting of job applicants, selecting of the men for hire, and the training of new salesmen. These functions are all simplified due to the lower manpower qualifications which can be set. The men do not have to understand the intricacies of their product, the persuasion processes, the various selling techniques that could be available to them or anything of the psychology of personalities. Since standards are lower, hiring, training, and maintaining a sales force presumably would be less expensive. The company can also be more reasonably assured the desired message is being delivered to prospects and this in turn will eliminate or reduce salesmen's exaggerated claims for the product and much misinformation which causes poor public relations and subsequent service complaints.

## THE KIND OF PREPARATION REQUIRED

The burden of preparing an effective stimulus-response sales program is, of course, on the management of the selling company. It must analyze its expected market and its product benefits to the individual buyers. Through techniques similar to mass communications and advertising, management must build a sales presentation that is as interesting as possible to the widest possible market and yet be explicit enough to be understood by the prospect. The presentation must be built to encourage the buyer's confidence in the salesman as a knowledgeable source of information who is trustworthy, sincere, and likeable—the clean-cut, boy-next-door image. Since this type of selling is most often used on a single call, the presentation must pay particular attention to building action or motivation stimulus because once the salesman leaves the prospect the latter is not likely to get excited or interested in the proposition again. If the company has many diverse products, it must build presentations for each of them and if the salesman is expected to make repetitive calls on the same prospects, new presentations must be organized for each subsequent visit. This clearly is repetition with variation and, hopefully, with a cumulative effect.

The preparation of the stimulus-response talk by the salesman involves more than simple memorization of words and phrases from a written script or by listening to records and tapes or by watching sound movies and mimicking the actors. Earl Prevette compares the salesman to an actor rehearsing for perfection and he writes, "You must practice your Sales Plan until you know its every word by rote; until you learn to time it; until you sense the proper pitch and inflection to give each word . . . you will begin to feel your lines."[6]

The salesman must develop sustaining enthusiasm in his presentation and remember that even though he may have given his talk hundreds of times, it will still be new to each audience that has never heard it before. Finally, the salesman must be aware of the trial closes built into his talk and be aware of the buyer's reactions so that he doesn't talk himself out of the probable sale.

## DETERMINING THE EFFECTIVENESS OF STIMULUS-RESPONSE SELLING

A company entering a new market probably would be wise to imitate existing industrial practices, at least until its management develops sufficient evidence upon which to base a sound judgment. But new and old companies can use small and separate marketing areas to test the effectiveness of different sales methods or of different canned talks. Care must be taken to insure comparable market conditions, equal sales potential, identical timing and number of calls, identical supervision, and the like, so that as nearly as possible the only difference or variable is the sales method being tested. The sample markets must be large enough to be reliable and the time period must allow sufficient penetration. The acid test of effectiveness is, of course, the dollar sales volume divided into the total selling costs, which should include recruiting, selecting, and training salesmen as well as the obvious costs of supervision and ongoing sales compensation of the men. This was the method used by the various drug companies cited earlier in this chapter to evaluate the effectiveness of stimulus-response methods. Another determining factor regarding effectiveness might be the time required to cross the threshold and to saturate an area. The highly competitive gift stamp companies generally work an area to get as many

---
[6] Prevette, *op. cit.*

merchants to participate as quickly as possible and once the point of diminishing returns is reached, the stamp company moves its creative sales force out and attacks a new area. Different canned presentations prove more or less effective depending upon the speed with which the area can be covered. Finally, but of high importance and validity, would be marketing surveys, sampling techniques of prospects' reactions to the stimulus-response talks. For example, if sales were up 10 percent in an area but hostility jumped up sharply to, say, 50 percent of those who heard the talk, this would make the next canvassing that much harder to gain exposure. Here the cumulative effect would definitely boomerang.

## THE DISADVANTAGES TO THE SALESMAN AND TO THE COMPANY

For the stimulus-response system to be successful, most prospects must react in the same way; they must respond to cues or stimuli in a certain way. The salesman dominates the sales interview and gives his complete talk with little regard for the prospect's viewpoint. The salesman who employs the pure stimulus-response method of selling ignores the independent working of the prospect's mind. As illustrated earlier, individuals really are very different in their predispositions and this materially effects what they perceive. Obviously then, the stimuli the salesman plans to use must vary not only with the individual prospect but with the present state of the prospect's mind.

Another disadvantage of the canned or planned talk is its lack of two-way communication. The prospect is forced to be passive and he learns little or nothing about the individual salesman. Each representative from a given company sounds pretty much like every other representative. There is little to build confidence in the individual salesman even if the presentation is nearly perfect and its appeals generally close to the mark. A prospect without confidence in the source of a message will be difficult to persuade. Because of this factor, stimulus-response salesmen prefer to work on a referral basis, from friend to friend or from accepted authority, such as a certified public accountant, to the businessman.

Due to the limits of the attention span, a prospect who is not given a chance to speak may soon lose interest in the sales presentation. Even the best of listeners want to participate in conversation and resent salesmen who monopolize a conversation. As if this were not bad enough, to compound the error, salesmen often override the prospect's attempts to object and put off all questions until they are covered in the sequence of the planned talk. This causes the prospect to listen selectively for the answer to his objection or question and he will miss almost everything else that is said. When the salesman's conclusion is reached, it does not seem logical at all to this prospect who selectively heard only part of the talk.

Probably the most important disadvantage of the stimulus-response talk is that it is product oriented or based upon the product and the product benefits, which more often than not are of little or no concern to the businessman. He is interested in his real or imagined problems and does not want to listen closely to a salesman who will bring up additional problems. While the product, its benefits to the user, even the general ideas, may truly help the businessman, unfortunately the salesman is not permitted to change the language of the prepackaged talk to suit the mental set of the particular buyer.

From sales management's point of view there are disadvantages in teaching the stimulus-response method of sales. Since the job qualifications are lower, problems are inherent in the inferior men hired. Turnover is usually higher, as misfits and malcontents are not properly screened out in the recruiting and selection of salesmen. Sales effectiveness is not nearly as high as it might be under another method and the total sales costs for twelve inferior men, for example, might easily be higher than the total costs for six superior salesmen. When the inferior men master this selling technique, their employer normally does not teach more advanced selling techniques and the men feel trapped at this level. They may either slip ever so gradually into boredom and ineffectiveness or quit suddenly for a more challenging job elsewhere. It is difficult to inspire salesmen, to get them to be enthusiastic, after they have been trained to sell mechanically.

## SUMMARY

While most people are familiar with the canned talk of door-to-door salesmen, few people realize the extent to which this same method is used to persuade men in business and professions. Doctors, lawyers, college professors, and businessmen in general are constantly exposed to prepackaged talks, and some of these are quite subtle while others are blunt and obvious. These planned talks may be designed to be simply informative— to pack the salient points into a concise period. More normally they are designed to stimulate a buying response through the use of emotional overtones and logic that is channeled to lead in only one direction. Businessmen react very much the way homeowners do to door-to-door salesmen.

A few who are in the market do buy but most businessmen give a quick brush-off to the salesman using a canned talk.

This technique of sales presentation is used in business primarily because it is the quickest way to get a product exposed to the large markets as yet untapped. Less qualified men are hired and with minimum training they can often go out and sell almost as effectively as the old men. These memorized talks are based upon the product or service and not on any one prospect's individual need. The logic is preplanned and positive reactions are sought along the way to the precanned close which is designed to outmaneuver the prospect. The effectiveness of this method of presentation is based upon the accepted psychological principle of stimulus-response. Certain words, phrases, and ideas stir the prospect's imagination and he responds in a favorable manner.

The advantages are more apparent than real. They include: saving time, building confidence, and providing a smooth and complete presentation. A sales company can broaden its job qualifications and more easily recruit applicants, select men, and speed up the training process. It can get the desired message delivered to the market quicker and presumably at a lower unit cost. Preparing an effective S-R talk includes market research, product and benefit analysis, and techniques of mass communication, or one message of interest to the widest possible audience. Unlike advertising, a canned talk must motivate buying action immediately. The salesman must learn the talks as an actor learns to live his part and sustain enthusiasm no matter how many performances are given or how restless the audience appears.

The effectiveness of this type of presentation can be determined by test marketing and cost analysis, time analysis of market penetration, and by market surveys. Unfortunately, the disadvantages often outweigh the benefits. People normally do not respond like sheep and all go in the same direction when stimulated. Since it is impossible to plan what all prospects will think, say, or do, the presentation is designed to force a chain of thought and make the listener passive. Due to the brief attention span of enforced listening, most prospects tune out and fail to follow the logic or hear the stimulus which is supposed to motivate buying action. By their very nature, these S-R talks must be based upon the product and not what any individual prospect may want to hear at any given moment. There is little or no provision for tailoring the preplanned package to the mental set of the listener. A company actually creates problems when it intentionally hires inferior men. Turnover is higher and sales effectiveness is lower, which causes sales costs to rise alarmingly in the long run.

The following is reprinted with the kind permission of Dow Jones & Company, Inc., Community Sales Program, Circulation Field & Phone Sales Division, Princeton, N.J.:

## SELLING BARRON'S NATIONAL BUSINESS & FINANCIAL WEEKLY

OPENING: "Good morning, Mr. Wilson, this is Mr. Smith calling for Dow Jones, publishers of The Wall Street Journal, The National Observer, and Barron's National Business and Financial Weekly. I wanted to check with you to see if you're reading a copy of Barron's each week." (Pause for response).

THE BASIC SALES APPEAL: "Barron's finds that (businessmen) (executives) (professional men) are as much concerned with the meaning of economic and political developments and how they *affect* the course of business and the value of investments as they are with knowing about these events in the first place."

"Barron's analyzes effects domestic and world-wide happenings may have in business and finance. Consequently, it is widely used by (businessmen) (executives) (professional men) for charting the future course of their business and personal financial affairs. Dow Jones is the world's largest business-news organization and Barron's Editors have access to more basic information than any other writers of business and financial trends."

"Each week in Barron's you receive popular features like THE TRADER written by Harry Nelson, who is known as the Dean of Financial Writers, The BUSINESS FRONT, THE WORLD AT WORK, NEWS AND VIEWS OF INVESTMENTS, and the STATISTICAL SECTION . . . the finest compilation of market information to be found anywhere including the major exchanges, and complete over-the-counter markets."

"There's more to Barron's, of course, but this gives you an idea of how Barron's provides investors and readers with the necessary tools to help them understand the meaning of the economic and political developments of today."

CLOSE: "Mr. Wilson, the kind of information Barron's supplies each week, if purchased in report form, would cost hundreds of dollars a year. Yet you can put this reliable investment-news service to work for you for just 30 cents a week. I'd like to have you test Barron's either at your office or at your home. Which would you prefer?"

## THE LEAVITT EXPERIMENT*

### One-Way versus Two-Way Communication

In its simplest essentials our problem is to clarify the differences between these two situations: (1) One person, A, talking to another, B, *without* return talk

* (Reprinted from *Managerial Psychology* by Harold J. Leavitt by permission of the University of Chicago Press. Copyright 1958 by The University of Chicago.)

from B to A; versus (2) conversation from A to B *with* return conversation
from B to A. The differences can be clarified best by testing one method against
the other. Here is such a test situation:

The pattern of rectangles shown here is an idea you would like to tell some
B's about. Suppose you try to communicate it *in words* to a half-dozen of your
friends who are sitting around your living room:

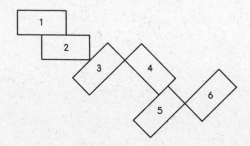

Assume that the rectangles touch each other at "sensible" places—at corners or
at midpoints along the line. There are *no* touch points at any unusual places.
All the angles are either 90° or 45° angles; there are no odd ones. This pattern
of rectangles is an idea comparable perhaps to a complicated set of instructions
you may have to give to a subordinate or to the definition of a policy that you
would like to pass along or to the task of explaining statistical quality control to
a sales manager. This idea can be communicated to others under (1) one-way
or (2) two-way conditions.

If you are the communicator, these are your one-way instructions:

1. Turn your back on your audience so that you cannot get visual communication back.

2. Give the audience blank sheets of paper, so that they can listen and draw
exactly what you are communicating. Ask them to try to draw as accurate a
picture of the pattern of rectangles as possible.

3. Describe the pattern of rectangles to them *in words* as fast as you can.
The audience is not permitted to ask questions, or laugh, or sigh, or in any
other way to communicate back to you any information about what it is
receiving.

This game is a good parlor game, if you can find some people to try it on.
Try it, time it, and then check the accuracy of your communication by
determining whether or not your audience has drawn what you have described.
If they received what you tried to send, so their pictures match the test picture,
then you have communicated. To the extent that their pictures do not match
the one in the drawing, you have not communicated.

Two-way communication can be tested for contrast in the same way. The
same rules apply, and here is a similar test pattern:

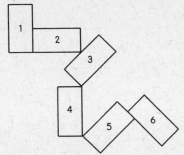

This time the basic job is the same, to describe the pattern verbally so that the people who are listening can draw it. But here are the differences:

1. This time you may face your audience.

2. They are allowed to interrupt and ask you any questions they want to at any time they want to.

Try it this way and time it. The differences between what happened the first time and what happened the second time are the differences between one- and two-way communication. (The order in which the two methods are used does not matter.)

Under experimental conditions these findings have emerged from this game: (1) One-way communication is considerably *faster* than two-way communication. (2) Two-way communication is more accurate than one-way, i.e., more people in the audience correctly reproduce the drawing under two-way conditions. (3) The receivers are more sure of themselves and make more correct judgments of how right or wrong they are in the two-way system. (4) The sender finds himself feeling psychologically under attack in the two-way system, because his receivers pick up his mistakes and oversights and *let him know about them*. The receivers may make snide remarks about the sender's intelligence and skill, and, if the receivers are trying very hard and taking the task seriously, they may actually get angry at the sender, and he at them. (5) The two-way method is relatively noisy and disorderly—with people interrupting the sender and one another, with the slowest man holding up the rest, and so on. The one-way method, on the other hand, appears neat and efficient to an outside observer, but the communication is less accurate.

To put it another way, one-way communication is not likely to be communication at all. It is more likely to be talk. One can talk by passing words out into the air. Those words don't become communication until they enter meaningfully into somebody else's head.

# 12

# Formula of Mental Steps Used in Selling

Formula selling is selling in a preplanned design with the persuasive sales points timed or geared to formal mental steps of the buyer. There is popular agreement among sales executives and national sales schools that these steps encompass such things as attention, interest, desire, conviction, and action, although there is no general agreement among psychologists on the actual existence of a series of mental steps. The formula selling theory at least admits there is a series of aspects in the persuasion process, however, and this is an improvement over the assumption of the stimulus-response selling method that the right word will automatically produce a sale. In operation, the formula method requires the salesman to dominate and control the interview, maintain attention on a desired phase of the product or application, and guide his pace of presentation by the buyer's response. The prospect's participation is limited primarily to his reaction to what the salesman presents.

## EXTENT FORMULA SELLING IS USED

Formula selling is predominant in industrial sales and is more applicable to business sales than to retail or consumer markets. Where the product or service being offered is complicated and difficult to understand, the formula method of selling predominates. Whenever a salesman calls repeatedly on the same accounts throughout the years, this method is most common. Whenever the salesman has a number of products in the line of goods he is offering, this method enables him to vary his talk on each visit while still maintaining a set selling pattern as a guide. Industrial supplies and equipment, office supplies and equipment, manufacturer to wholesaler, wholesaler to retailer, petroleum and chemical products, and many related services are typically sold through a formula method presentation.

176

The junior salesman who has memorized his stimulus-response planned talk can use this more advanced theory of selling by applying selective portions of his talk at the opportune moment, tailored to a specific individual prospect. He can use some degree of creativeness and imagination.

A salesman for an oil company, for example, selling to service station owners normally offers tires, batteries, and accessories in addition to gasoline and oil. While the service station is often married to the oil company —that is, under contractual agreement to purchase the company's products exclusively—unless the operator can be persuaded to promote sales actively, the products will simply sit on the shelves and gather dust. It is the salesman's job to get this customer to move more of his merchandise. On a particular call the salesman may plan to increase the sale of snow tires. Assume that from previous calls and notations on his account card, the salesman knows the station owner likes hunting and caters to a number of sportsmen. The planned sales interview might go something like this:

| | |
|---|---|
| TBA SALESMAN: | Good morning, George! This cool September air feels good for a change, doesn't it? Won't be long before you can go out hunting again! Are you going to get out much this year? |
| PROSPECT: | Hello, Pete. No, I doubt if I'll be able to spare much time and I can't afford an extra relief man but I sure would like to. I hear the pheasant are thick up at Connie's Farm. You know, he leaves the oats in the fields a couple of months longer than he should just to attract pheasant? |
| TBA SALESMAN: | Boy, that's planning! He must love hunting, too. But those farm roads are rough on a car. You know, a hunter around here could really use snow tires to get through the mud once he gets off the main roads. |
| PROSPECT: | He sure could! I had them on my old car last hunting season and I got in and out of some mighty rough places. |
| TBA SALESMAN: | You know, George, with all the customers you have that are interested in hunting—I was just thinking you might work up a really effective snow tire promotion. Look, suppose I get you some poster size pictures, hunting scenes, and car towing pictures, and we put them at the pumps and here in the station. Wouldn't a lot of your customers get curious and begin talking hunting—just as we did? |
| PROSPECT: | You know, that's not a bad idea. Maybe we could work up something at that. What kind of a deal have you got? |
| TBA SALESMAN: | I'll get you the pictures all right—no problem there—and I really do have an attractive offer for you on our snow tire line. [The salesman then quotes sizes and prices and |

recommends the size of the order.] "These quantity prices are good only until the first of next month, George. You see, we want to distribute as many snow tires as possible before the season starts. After that, every dealer screams for same-day delivery on a single set of tires and our costs shoot up. You can understand that. Does this order look OK to you, George? If so I'll get busy and round up some good posters for you.

The dialogue might go on much longer, with objections and negotiations; however, this brief sketch illustrates the formula method. To get favorable attention, the salesman planned his initial conversation around the approaching hunting season. To maintain interest, the salesman planned to swing naturally into a discussion of the muddy roads and the practical value of snow tires. To build interest into desire, the salesman planned to show the dealer how to interest his customers to buy tires and, finally, to get action, the salesman worked up a firm order with a pricing deal limited to a specific date. Clearly, the discussion could have veered off at many points but the salesman had his formula and would have tactfully attempted to stick to his planned presentation of snow tires. Another situational problem in this particular line of business is the constant interruption of the sales talk due to cars pulling into the station. Timing the sales points and getting the buyer's desired response can be difficult but notice how casual and offhand the presentation sounds. On follow-up calls, the same salesman can bring up other features and benefits of snow tires without fear of contradicting himself or of boring the prospect with exactly the same canned talk.

In another field, office machines, the formula selling method works in much the same manner although the prospect normally has no fixed source of supply. On the first call, the formula salesman must make use of market research and motivational research for clues to his preapproach and approach. A sales interview on the first call might proceed as follows:

SALESMAN:              Mr. Campbell, I've asked to see you because I happened to come across a letter typed in your office the other day that gave me an idea. The letter was neatly typed and its message was perfectly clear but it just didn't seem to carry the degree of importance we all want. Here is your letter and here is the exact letter typed on our new electric with executive type! Notice how this version clearly stands out —it seems to command respect and attention! I'm sure you agree, don't you?

OFFICE MANAGER:        Well, perhaps one copy does look better but most of our work requires a lot of carbons and we are more interested in them—but I do like the looks of your letter.

| | |
|---|---|
| SALESMAN: | I'm glad you mentioned carbons. That's one of the tremendous advantages of our new electric—the fact that it can make more and better carbons than any manual machine. Here are four copies of your same letter—notice how clear they all are. |
| OFFICE MANAGER: | But how do I know you didn't make three more originals to get these extra copies? I've been burnt before on this sample type of thing. I don't know. |
| SALESMAN: | I certainly wouldn't want to mislead you. What I suggest is for you to test this new machine for yourself. I'll have a machine sent over and show your secretary how to adapt to it quickly. Then you be the judge of the results—fair enough? |

Before the interview, the salesman knew little about the buyer personally but he had obtained a simple letter written by him. Motivational research had turned up the five most common reasons why a businessman switches to electric typewriters and the salesman planned his presentation accordingly. The plan was flexible enough to cover all five common motivations—better looking letters; more and better carbons; increased typing speed; better accuracy; and various convenience factors—although only the first two were directly called into play when the salesman wisely stopped. This clearly illustrates the flexibility of the formula presentation. The attention device was to arouse curiosity about a specific letter the office manager dictated. Talking about the buyer is an excellent way to gain his favorable attention. In this oversimplified illustration, it leads directly into interest. An objection, "But our work requires a lot of carbons," is easily turned to an advantage to build desire and, finally, the buyer's very doubt is turned into a test of honesty, which is the action desired. Action in this case is limited to approval of a trial use or demonstration of the machine in the prospect's office. The next call will also be preplanned by formula to reassure the office manager and build his confidence in the salesman and the product. After one machine has been purchased and found to be satisfactory, this salesman will be trusted by the buyer and be in a position to urge standardization of this account on the one brand of electric typewriters. The salesman converts the prospect's attitude of suspicion and distrust, gradually, point by point, to an attitude of open-minded fair trial, to limited acceptance of one machine, and, finally, to complete standardization because the prospect believes from his new experience that this one salesman is honest and trustworthy and the product really does serve his need.

The formula method of sales presentation assumes the mental steps a buyer goes through are attention, interest, desire, and action. The salesman will not ask for an order until the prospect has gone through the previous steps and not until he senses strong desire on the buyer's part. If the buyer's reactions are quick, the presentation may be quick but the normal course of the interview is quite lengthy and allows the buyer to participate in a limited way in a two-way conversation. The salesman attempts to direct and control the conversation and confine it, as much as possible, to the product he is selling. On later visits, he will bring up many different points, build his knowledge of the buyer's predisposition and reinforce whatever favorable attitudes and sales points he had achieved earlier. Each visit is preplanned to cover certain points, different reasons to buy, but the formula remains constant. With imagination, a good salesman using the formula method is thus able to make a fresh and new sales presentation of his product each time he visits the same prospect.

## JUSTIFICATION OF THE USE OF FORMULA PRESENTATIONS

Formula selling grew out of the difficulties of the stimulus-response method of presentation. Early in the twentieth century, new inventions and products were sold on an educational basis through memorized talks. About 1900, a number of successful salesmen analyzed their own experiences and decided most of their orders fell into the AIDA pattern. The need was obvious for greater flexibility than a memorized talk permitted, yet they felt guidelines for the salesman were essential. Their then-new formula still required the salesman to control the interview and the presentation is, therefore, basically salesman oriented rather than customer oriented. The customer's reaction determines the timing of the presentation and each sales presentation can vary considerably from all previous ones. Most books written through the first half of the twentieth century on salesmanship, speech, and public interviewing techniques use a formulized theory.[1]

A National Sales Executives, Inc., handbook, *Your Career in Selling*, gives five mental steps that must be taken in the prospect's mind before the sale is made. They are: curiosity, interest, conviction, desire, decision or

---

[1] The slogan, "Attract attention, maintain interest, create desire," is credited to E. St. Elmo Lewis in 1898 and at a later date he added the fourth term, "get action." The fifth term, "satisfaction," was added to the slogan by A. F. Sheldon in 1911. See Edward K. Strong, Jr., *Psychological Aspects of Business* (New York: McGraw-Hill Book Co., Inc., 1938). The word "confidence" was inserted between "desire" and "action" by W. D. Kitson, *The Mind of the Buyer* (New York: Macmillan Co., 1940). Kitson holds that there are six distinctive stages in the sales process: attention, interest, desire, confidence, action, and satisfaction.

action.[2] Bert Schlain, in his book *Big League Salesmanship*, illustrates formula selling by the following six basic points: theme, promise, problem, solution, proof, and finally, action.[3]

However classified, categorized, or subdivided, the essential elements in formulized selling remain the same. The Sales Analysis Institute has been teaching this method to several generations of successful industrial salesmen throughout the world. They begin with the premise that most businessmen are logical in decision making and that all men are motivated by self-interest. Each sales school has its own specific and detailed method of moving through its formula and the prospect signals the salesman is taught to observe. The formula is tailored not only to a given industry but also to a specific sales company.

## PSYCHOLOGICAL FOUNDATION—REFRACTORY PHASE

This formula strategy is based upon the psychological concept of refractory phase which helps the salesman with the problem of timing selling points within the interview. In communication, refractory phase means an impulse or message traveling along a nerve fiber, like an electrical current in a telephone wire, which in effect ties up that line in such a manner that it cannot carry another message until it recovers from the previous one. After each impulse the nerve must rest for a very brief period, which is called the absolute refractory phase, and no message can pass over the nerve fiber. If another stimulus or message is applied during this rest or recovery period, it will simply delay recovery and make the nerve rest longer. As the nerve recovers, it will first respond only to a stimulus which is stronger than normal, only gradually going back to normal.

This psychological concept of refractory phase, as applied to selling, is actually an old friend, selective perception. A salesman may speak to a person and not be heard or understood because the prospect has his mind on another topic or is still considering a previous statement. As in teaching, the salesman must get acceptance on one point at a time and focus the prospect's attention on one idea at a time. For this reason, effective salesmen advise showing pictures without printed copy so they can continue talking and directing the prospect's attention. If printed copy is shown to a prospect, the salesman should remain quiet or both his picture

[2] National Sales Executives, Inc., *Your Career in Selling* (no date). This organization is now the Sales and Marketing Executives International with headquarters in New York City.

[3] Bert Schlain, *Big League Salesmanship* (Englewood Cliffs, N.J.: Prentice-Hall, Inc., 1955).

message and his verbal message will be lost. To pace his presentation, the salesman should pause after each point and often ask a question which will reveal the prospect's understanding and willingness to go on to another point. As Frank Bettger cautions, a sales talk may take seconds or it may take several hours.[4] Another necessary method of gauging the pace is careful observation of the prospect's actions, and what he doesn't say is often more important than what he does say. The prospect is encouraged to talk but the salesman attempts to confine the conversation to the specific point he wants the prospect to consider at a given time.

## ADVANTAGES

Clearly, formula selling utilizes the advantages of the canned or planned talk in that the salesman uses preplanned expressions and speeches so he can speak with confidence and conciseness as well as use tried and proven key emotional words to motivate the prospect to action. In addition he can be more creative and imaginative in the employment of these words. The prospect's response, or lack of response, guides the pace and steps of the formula salesman but it is the latter who controls the progress and direction of the conversation. This method of selling takes considerably longer than the simple stimulus-response method, which automatically rules it out for many types of retail and consumer applications, but it does have advantages in persuading men in business. The salesman now is tuned to one individual prospect at a time and is permitted to vary his sales presentation accordingly. He can keep to one topic and does not have to fumble for the right words. He still has a definite sales plan.

This sales technique is an improvement in training the junior salesmen who have learned their basic product knowledge and product applications and have memorized their planned talks. They are ready to participate in more creative sales; they are ready to use their imaginations and their understanding of human nature as it applies to any one particular prospect. This understanding is the foundation for developing an organized sales talk which will be flexible or adaptable to each of the many different prospects the salesman will meet under varied situations. The basic advantages of formula selling over stimulus-response methods are: it is tuned and tailored to the individual prospect and permits some, although limited, prospect participation. It provides a more natural, logical, and complete

---

[4] Frank Bettger, *How I Raised Myself from Failure to Success in Selling* (Englewood Cliffs, N.J.: Prentice-Hall, Inc., 1949).

sales presentation. It confines the sales interview to a single topic at any one time and thereby saves time.

## CHARACTERISTICS OF FORMULA SELLING

In formula selling the salesman first gains favorable attention and converts the prospect's attention to positive interest. The interest is built into intense desire for the product, which is turned into conviction about the entire proposition. Finally, the prospect is encouraged to act upon his conviction. Attention is generally achieved through the buyer's self-interest and in building desire future benefits to the prospect are stressed. Hand in hand with desire for the benefits is conviction and, therefore, quality aspects are stressed such as how and why the product will deliver what the salesman promises. "The office girls will be happy and do a good day's work with this machine *because* it has done away with the exhausting manual. . . ."

There are a number of variations of what constitutes the mental steps in a prospect's mind. Psychologists, successful salesmen, and sales trainers often disagree with each other and among themselves regarding mental steps, the use of logic, the use of suggestion, and interpreting intuitive behavior or impulse buying. Edward Hagarty, author and sales trainer, states the AIDA sales formula is one of the most effective in preparing visual presentations but he also recommends the following formula: "Make the prospect dissatisfied; suggest your remedy; answer his questions and ask for action."[5] Sales magazines abound with case history types of illustrations and examples of formula selling and they often compare the steps to a good game of golf or drawing a series of cards as in poker.

Formula selling often includes a list of the various general types of prospects, such as the silent type; the procrastinator type; the opinionated type; and so forth. Then for handling each of the types there are specific general strategy rules such as: ask questions, summarize benefits, flatter, and so forth. In reality, any such consolidated list as the "ten types of buyers" is highly impractical as are the specific strategies of "handling" them. This classifying of buyers blinds the salesman to the individual subtleties so necessary for professional selling which are covered thoroughly in Chapter 6 regarding the buyer's predisposition.

Demonstration is used in almost every type of selling. However, it is particularly important in formula selling for two major reasons. First, a

---

[5] Edward J. Hagarty, "How You Can Make Your Own Visual Presentation," *American Salesman*, August, 1958, p. 38.

demonstration normally involves the prospect's sense of sight, sound, and touch. These additional senses employed properly will direct his attention and reduce distractions which block his perception. Much of the literature on how to sell includes and often emphasizes demonstration. Second, if one can get the prospect to play the part of a happy owner of the product, he will literally persuade himself. Many sales manuals begin with the advice, "You have got to tell 'em." Later, they advise, "You have got to show 'em to sell 'em." The effective salesman goes one step further. He gets the prospect to use his product or feel he is the happy owner and this salesman uses the powerful, tested, persuasive technique of role playing discussed in Chapter 9. Even if the prospect is against the sales message, if he can be induced to tell why he should buy it, he will often persuade himself. "Tell 'em?" Yes. "Show 'em?" Yes. But add one more line, "Get 'em to tell you!"

## PREPARATION REQUIRED

When using the formula method of presentation the salesman has greater choice of sales material as well as choice of sequence and stress, or emphasis, to be employed in a given situation. Because of this large degree of personal choice or discretion, he must be more intelligent, more imaginative, and certainly better trained. His training must include product knowledge, product applications, the formula his company uses and how they want it employed, some aspects of persuasion, and a degree of depth in analyzing a buyer's responses. He must be adept at thinking on his feet, fielding questions from any quarter, and in the use of his imagination.

Preparation for formula selling includes a detailed analysis of each product handled and each technical detail, such as the gauge of steel used or its particular form and shape, must be directly related to a user benefit. Why is the product made this way instead of another way? What resulting benefits are exclusive with this product as compared to the competitive products on the market? In this way, the salesman can confidently answer any question on product technicalities and can also develop a philosophy of company purposes and goals which is so basic to imaginative, creative selling. Training of industrial salesmen often takes from six months to several years before the men are permitted to make their first call. Putting a man out too early, before he is adequately prepared, can be very expensive even if he is on a commission basis. This is because any sales lost are not only lost for that time but generally for many, many years in the future. Once an account decides to standardize on one product, it is very difficult to reopen the issue and persuade the account to change again.

A sales organization cannot easily change from stimulus-response to formula selling. Preparation on the company's part involves a new and detailed analysis of the new sales job and a written job description to provide specifications for hiring. Recruiting must be done on a higher level, generally among college graduates, and selection must be extremely discriminating. Because of the high quality man desired, starting salaries must be firm and competitive with other vocations. Training is lengthy and must be complete to be economical in the long run. Those who do the training should be education-minded as well as sales oriented so that what is taught is of long-range value to the salesman and his company. Finally, a great deal of patience is required to supervise and motivate the trainee over an extended period of nonproductive activity in the company classes and the early months out in the field trying to sell.

## EFFECTIVENESS OF FORMULA SELLING

While formula selling is in general an obvious improvement over stimulus-response selling, it too has many drawbacks. The disadvantages, unfortunately, outweigh the advantages. People in general, and businessmen in particular, do not regularly think in a formal set manner. Formulas assume all prospects think alike, while in reality this is not the case. They may work in four out of ten situations, for example, but this is falling back to the law of averages used in stimulus-response selling. Industrial selling, persuading men in business, generally does not have an unlimited number of prospects, hence has no such averages to fall back on. The limited potential market requires that every account be seen repeatedly in an attempt to sell more goods and services to old accounts and to develop new accounts.

More importantly, in its pure form the formula method of presentation is a salesman-controlled situation and certainly most businessmen sense this. They often resent being directed and resist anything they suspect of being pressure. The entire presentation, from approach to final close, is product oriented rather than customer oriented. The prospect may easily become aware of the salesman's interest and consider him a biased source not to be trusted. As has been proven again and again in experiments, the source of a persuasive message must be perceived as a completely unbiased authority, or else acting unselfishly in behalf of the prospect, before the prospect will be persuaded.

A final word of caution in using formulized selling: The salesman must know people. He must know how to interpret the individual prospect during a given interview. He must literally think on his feet and employ the proper part of his planned talk for each and every variation in the prospect's response. By knowing the prospect, the salesman can antiicpate which benefits will be most apt to appeal and which phases of his sales talk to play down or omit entirely. Unless the salesman is sensitive to the buyer's unspoken feelings he too often misses what is really on the prospect's mind and therefore cannot possibly penetrate the prospect's protective umbrella of selective perception.

## SUMMARY

Formula selling is the method of presentation which assumes there are definite mental steps a prospect takes before buying and keys the sales arguments to the prospect's continuing responses. It is used extensively in nonconsumer fields, particularly in business and industrial selling. It was created to overcome the objections of the canned speech and is based upon the psychological concept of refractory phase. A single sales point or idea must be accepted before the next point is introduced or everything that follows will be mentally blocked. Formula selling uses the advantages of stimulus-response selling, such as confidence and conciseness and key emotional words to motivate, but combines these with creativity and imagination to permit the salesman to adapt to each individual prospect. This improvement is necessary when attempting to persuade men in business as they are generally more objective and sophisticated in their buying behavior.

Formula presentation generally includes such concepts as gaining favorable attention by focusing on the prospect; building interest and desire by stressing the benefits of the product; encouraging conviction by logically explaining how the product will produce the benefits; and, finally, motivating the desired action through key emotional words and objective and compelling logic. Grouping of buyers into types and evolving specific strategies for handling each type are often characteristic of formula selling. However, the validity of this practice is questionable. Demonstration is also characteristic of formula selling to maintain focus or attention on a point to be considered, to clarify difficult concepts, and to motivate the prospect to play the role of a happy owner.

The salesman must be recruited, screened, and selected with greater care than in stimulus-response methods of selling as he will have to rely more on his own judgment when alone in the sales situations. He must be more intelligent and imaginative as well as sensitive to the buyer's responses. Training in product knowledge and formula application clearly takes much longer than simply memorizing a talk. The sales company must analyze its job specifications as well as its hiring and training procedures and then adjust them to fit in with the higher quality salesman desired.

Formula selling, while clearly an improvement over the stimulus-response method of presentation, still has limited effectiveness. Businessmen, indeed people in general, do not think alike or in a set pattern. One man may in one situation accept logic while in another situation he may be more responsive to suggestion. He may act intuitively with varying degrees of insight or he may act on impulse with little or no insight. All of these reactions can be used interchangeably by the same man under various conditions. Since the presentation is basically product oriented or salesman oriented and dominated by the salesman, there is inbuilt resistance caused by the prospect's feeling of being pressured and directed which automatically arouses his suspicions and distrust. Obviously, the formula salesman, to be effective, must be sensitive to people and know how to interpret their reactions and adjust to their moods and needs as he goes along in his presentation.

# 13

# Want-Satisfaction Sales Strategy

One of the so called "secrets" of salesmanship is to find out what the other fellow wants and then to help him find the best way to get it. The want-satisfaction theory of selling holds that a want or need must be discovered from within the buyer's mind and then brought to his awareness. The salesman simply acts as the buyer's agent to show him how to satisfy this need through the purchase of the salesman's goods or services. This is popular in life insurance sales literature and is often referred to as "hitting the hot button" which motivates the prospect to buy. In its pure form, product considerations are secondary and once the salesman "hits the hot button," the buyer persuades himself to move heaven and earth to satisfy his need.

In the second half of the twentieth century, the want-satisfaction theory of selling has taken the lead in popularity over the formula theory of selling. The sales presentation is based on the prospect's self-interest, his "hot button," the emotional motive that carries the strongest appeal for him at that instant. This motive may relate to his personal role in life or to his organizational role in business and the sales presentation must be balanced with a composite of facts, figures, and proofs. However, the emphasis is on satisfying his emotional wants. The presentation has a dual purpose: the salesman must first create in the prospect's mind a definite need and then he must show how his product fills that need. John M. Wilson of National Cash Register puts it similarly, "The selling process must encompass the art of finding needers, dissatisfying them into wanters, and satisfying them as buyers."[1]

There is little agreement as to the number of wants or the relative importance of each want within an individual. Wants which impel people

[1] John M. Wilson, *Open the Mind and Close the Sale* (New York: McGraw-Hill Book Co., Inc., 1953).

to buy will vary in intensity from person to person and at different times within the same person. The various wants of an individual compete for satisfaction. The strongest want is that which creates the greatest tension for a particular individual at a particular time and, therefore, the most intense demand for satisfaction. The salesman's job is to determine which emotional wants are likely to exist and which are the dominant ones. According to this theory of selling, a constant appeal to the prospect's dominant wants for satisfaction are most likely to bring orders.

## THE EXTENT TO WHICH WANT-SATISFACTION IS USED

This technique is used most effectively by experienced salesmen who have enough self-confidence to permit the sales interview to go in many directions as a true two-way conversation. In fact, the buyer is encouraged to do most of the talking and the salesman becomes a good listener, "looking" for the keys to unlock the hidden want from the buyer's mind. While it is used particularly in selling insurance and autos and similar consumer merchandise, it is growing in popularity in most industrial selling to businessmen. Recently a national magazine reported industrial firms starting two training programs: one for engieeers to learn selling and the other for salesmen to learn engineering.[2] As part of the training programs, to anticipate what the customer really wants in an emotional sense, a number of these companies send their salesmen to state universities to study the need-satisfaction theory. The technique based on this theory can apply to all types of selling but it is used primarily on large prospects because of the length of time it takes to develop any one sale and to develop a substantial total sales volume.

Frank Bettger tells this anecdote about his early selling days.[3] A successful businessman in his sixties, with more than adequate life insurance for his family needs, brushed Bettger off when he approached the man. Impulsively Bettger asked,

. . . surely you must have some interests outside of your family and your business. Perhaps a hospital, religious work, missionary or charitable work of some worthy purpose. Did you ever consider that when you die your support will be withdrawn? Wouldn't this loss seriously handicap or even mean the discontinuance of some splendid work? (He didn't answer my question, but I could tell by the expression on his face that I'd struck oil.)

---

[2] "Business" section, *Time*, September 13, 1963.

[3] Frank Bettger, *How I Raised Myself from Failure to Success in Selling* (Englewood Cliffs, N.J.: Prentice-Hall, Inc., 1949).

According to Bettger, the prospect actually supported three foreign missionaries including one in Nicaragua administered by one of his sons and his daughter-in-law. Bettger took a blind stab and accidentally hit the "hot button" and found out what the man wanted. Later he went through his sales presentation and whenever the prospect objected to the cost Bettger steered the conversation to the wonderful work the foreign missionaries were doing. Finally the prospect bought, "as he knew he must." Thereafter, Bettger tells, he thought of selling as helping people get what they want. It inspired him, gave him courage and enthusiasm. He developed a sales plan which would discover a man's wants and he began to sell not life insurance but "satisfaction." His personal selling success story is perhaps one of the most widely read and known in sales today.

## ORGANIZATIONAL ROLE

A national financial company that specialized in making small family loans to individuals hired a young executive to be director of personnel. One of his duties included obtaining the proper office equipment to enable the employees to do their jobs effectively. A salesman of high quality dictating machines, who had been calling on this account for years without getting an order, visited the new executive and was told they had just standardized on a competitor's product. The executive stated the decision had been made by his superiors, corporate officers, before he was hired and readily admitted he had not compared machines himself. Faced with this problem, the discouraged salesman left to ponder his future course of action. Within a few days an article appeared in the *Wall Street Journal* announcing the consideration of a merger between this financial company and a larger one. The machine salesman sensed a second chance in the offing and approached the new executive on a want-satisfaction basis.

SALESMAN:     Mr. Strong, I read of your possible merger and I wondered, since you are a new executive here, what it might mean to you personally?

PROSPECT:     Well, John, I wonder myself. We don't know any more than what you yourself read in the newspaper.

SALESMAN:     It must be quite a kick in the stomach—leaving one job for another only to find the new one might be dissolved soon.

PROSPECT:     Well, you can't figure everything in life. I was hoping—the president hinted pretty broadly when he offered me the job—to become a vice-president here within two years but now it looks as if I'll be out of a job.

SALESMAN:     Do you know the executives of the other company at all?

PROSPECT:      Well, I met a few the other day. They came to look us over.

SALESMAN:      As I recall from my sales calls there, most of their executives are quite old. You know, they just might need young executives like yourself.

PROSPECT:      Really? Do you happen to know who is in charge of personnel over there? Is he old?

SALESMAN:      I have met him but I don't really know him. He looks to be in his late sixties at the very least.

PROSPECT:      Say, there may be something in this merger for me after all. No, I guess not. I'm not here long enough to have gained any recognition and they probably wouldn't recommend me.

SALESMAN:      I don't know about that. Obviously if the merger goes through they will need someone here that knows the personnel and equipment and is energetic enough to work out all the details of integrating the two work forces. I doubt if their old fuddy-dud wants all that work.

PROSPECT:      You have a point there. If only I could have gained some recognition before they started this merger talk. I've barely got the personnel records and functions straightened out. This has taken all my time. I haven't been able to make much of a name for myself yet.

SALESMAN:      Mr. Strong, suppose you were taking them over instead of them taking you over. For your area, what information would you want from their personnel man?

PROSPECT:      Well, I'd want a list of job specifications and locations so that I could eliminate as much duplication as possible. Then I'd want a list of their equipment for the same reason and I'd also want to know what prices or contracts they buy under in order to standardize the two companies on single suppliers most economically.

SALESMAN:      Well, I can tell you from my own experience with them, they may be larger but they have grown by buying small concerns, not by developing business or talent on their own. They have darn few records of equipment and a very hit-or-miss buying philosophy. Since most of their purchases are decentralized, they have every business machine made and they are of all ages.

PROSPECT:      If that is the case, they certainly can use my experience and energy! Boy, would I like a crack at that job! I could save the company ten times my salary every year. Do you realize the efficiencies that could be worked out? Man that would be a challenging job I'd love!

SALESMAN:      Suppose we work out an inventory and replacement schedule here for your machines and equipment and set up a few national contracts to replace on a volume basis. Wouldn't that be of interest to these other executives when they come to look you over next time?

PROSPECT:      It sure would show up that other personnel director that they

have! You know, it might work at that. Let's go to lunch and
see what strategy we can work out to speed this thing up.

In this oversimplified illustration, the prospect had a problem with his
organization role in the new merger. The salesman, through directive
counseling, tactfully turned the businessman's thinking from a pessimistic
attitude to one of optimism and suggested where the prospect might still
satisfy his craving to become a vice-president. The "hot button" was
pushed and the man was ready to take on a mountain of work to achieve
satisfaction. Clearly the two men will become honest friends and sometime
later, perhaps days or even weeks, the subject of dictating machines will
come up. The businessman is well aware of the salesman's ultimate
motives; however, he is grateful for the encouragement and help received
and he will be appreciative of the salesman's friendship. The odds are very
favorable that the two companies will standardize on this salesman's
machines.

## PERSONAL ROLE

Many years ago, when frozen foods were being introduced in volume in
supermarkets, the owner of a chain in the Austin, Texas, area was considering installing complete frozen food departments in his ten stores. This
sizable prospect attracted salesmen from most of the large suppliers and
the quotations submitted were highly competitive. The businessman was
satisfied they were all about equal and there would be no particular
advantage in leaving his existing suppliers. One salesman, working south
from Chicago, arrived on the scene late but before the order had been
given out. It was his habit to read the local newspapers whenever he stayed
overnight in a hotel, looking for business leads of course, but in the lonely
hours he read the sports, political news, and even scanned employment
articles. Upon arrival in Austin, the salesman went immediately to see the
businessman and was told the buying decision had been made but the
order had not been placed. The prospect did not wish to discuss it further
or waste the salesman's time and energy simply making out a quotation
comparable to the many already received. The salesman, perhaps intuitively, asked, "Mr. Webster, you aren't by any chance related to the boy
who played halfback at Oklahoma a few years ago?"

PROSPECT:     That's my boy! Do you know him?
SALESMAN:     No, but I saw him play and I followed his career in the news-
              papers for years. He was the most natural running back I have
              ever seen! My territory goes from here to Chicago and believe

me, thanks to your son, they know the Webster name along the whole belt.

PROSPECT:    What games did you see? Do you remember that 93-yard run he made in the big game?

SALESMAN:    I sure do remember—everybody does. You know, I think the best play he made in his career was not in running but the key block he threw to spring the fullback loose against State.

PROSPECT:    You'll have to excuse me now. I have to go to the bank to arrange financing this expansion but I would like to talk to you some more. Could you meet me for lunch?

Oversimplified, this story illustrates a want, the personal need of the father, being satisfied by talking with a knowledgeable salesman. The businessman wanted the reflected glory of his son's illustrious sports career. The father lived through the achievements of his pride and joy and the salesman, after discovering this, stayed on that topic exclusively. He increased the businessman's desire to talk about it and, indirectly, emphasized the personal importance of reflected glory this role played in the father's motivations. Since all the salesmen were submitting substantially equal proposals, the businessman achieved no particular satisfaction from dealing with any particular one but here was a man that knew and was interested in the sports career of his own son. The salesman must be a superior person to recognize what the prospect recognizes as being important, someone it would be pleasant to know better. As the story is reported, after a pleasant lunch talking football the salesman got the order and the buyer only then asked, "By the way, what company did you say you represented?"

## PERSONAL ROLE OF OLDER MEN

Influential businessmen are apt to be older than the average sales prospect and as such it might be wise to illustrate want-satisfaction selling to this group. The influential businessman described here can be as young as 50 but he is an exceptional man and has earned his independence through personal success and prestige. A study of the influential senior citizen shows he is apt to have more surplus dollars in his pocket and greater freedom of choice, not being limited by the social patterns of his equals. He is often a member of a board of directors, owner of a successful business, or, in other words, in a position to influence other orders. In addition he is nearly always a figure of authority to some members of the middle-aged and younger groups.[4]

4 Ernest Dichter, "What the Older Man Wants When He Buys," American Salesman, August, 1958, p. 82.

What does the study show of the wants of older people? They want to feel included in society and not set apart. They want to be needed—for opinions on the salesman's product, for a testimonial of his product, for their influence with others. They want to make up their own minds and they glory in their independence. They want to do things their own way, not being satisfied with older existing ways of doing things. They want something new—not to keep up with others but to get ahead of others by being first with something others haven't heard about yet. They want to be young again and they are not content with their memories, particularly errors of omission or regret for things that weren't done at all in their youth.

In the competitive foreign sports car market in the United States in 1963, the Standard-Triumph Co. of Britain's Leyland Motor Corp. surveyed U.S. buyers and found the average age of its TR-3 buyer was 47 years. To satisfy the wants of this older purchaser, the company decided to put roll-up windows and more comfortable seats in its new TR-4. The appeal was to senior citizens who wanted to be young again but with the comforts due their age. The Triumph's TR-4 and Spitfire in the U.S. have overtaken the second best-selling auto import and moved from the red into profitable black on the profit and loss statements for 1963.[5]

If by getting the senior citizen to talk about himself the salesman develops the feeling that as a younger man the prospect should have done something but didn't, the salesman can help him to substitute a pleasant experience now for an unsatisfactory memory. While motivation researchers can highlight specific markets and general needs and wants, it remains for the salesman to draw out and develop the individual's wants. Each prospect can be very different in some major aspect and he is always different in many subtle ways.

## PSYCHOLOGICAL FOUNDATION FOR WANT-SATISFACTION SELLING

This technique was developed because the stimulus-response and the formula methods of presentation were too product oriented and no matter how good the sales talks may have sounded, many prospects simply didn't care to listen to, or act upon, the persuasive messages. Salesmen experimented with talking to the buyer about his interests, experiences, and desires until they could find a clue which would indicate a personal need or want that their product could fulfill. This evolved into a strategy of sales

---

[5] "Business" section, *Time*, September 13, 1963.

presentation in which the product is either ignored completely or is a low secondary factor while the buyer is encouraged to talk out his interests and needs in life and the salesman basically listens. It is based on the psychological premise that self-interest is the primary motive in any man's behavior and if the salesman can determine the prospect's primary motive and show how he can satisfy this need, the buyer will not be able to resist persuasion.

Personal wants may vary from self-punishment caused by guilt feelings to a desire for universal recognition caused by unfounded feelings of self-importance. Organizational wants may vary from a desire for high profits to pay dividends to a desire for low profits to frustrate union negotiators. Clearly, individuals in the same market research group can have varied and often opposite motives for their behavior but they will generally act in their own interest as they see it. Each prospect will normally have a number of desires which are often contradictory in nature. A man may want to be the objective, cold, unemotional, and logical boss and at the same time he may want to be the friendly, gregarious buddy to all employees.

In its pure form, the want-satisfaction theory of selling can be psychological manipulation of a prospect. One motivating factor, one basic personal want or need, is reinforced by the salesman to the point that it dominates all others in the prospect's mind for that moment. Since the salesman offers immediate relief or satisfaction to reduce the unbearable tension, the prospect is practically self-compelled to act as the salesman desires. In practice, it should be noted, this pure form of want satisfaction rarely if ever occurs.

## CHARACTERISTICS OF WANT-SATISFACTION SELLING

The primary difference between this method of persuasion and the others covered previously is that it is fundamentally customer oriented and the product is secondary or is completely ignored until late in the conversation. Unlike the salesman giving canned talks or following a formula presentation of product sales points, the want-satisfaction salesman basically listens and the customer is encouraged to do most of the talking. The question and answer technique of drawing a prospect out of his protective shell is also characteristic of want-satisfaction selling. The salesman is primarily concerned with getting the prospect to talk so he can discover the prospect's wants and he does not use a lawyer's technique of asking leading questions to guide the prospect into a trap by his own conclusions.

A salesman uses questions to direct the prospect's attention to broad areas of information in which the salesman is interested. He uses questions to get information about specific facts or to see how the prospect habitually solves various problems. His primary purpose in asking questions is to communicate interest and stimulate a free flow of talk. When a businessman begins talking he may be general and hesitating, deciding whether or not to say what he really has on his mind. He may make some light remark or be thinking out loud in an attempt to clarify his own ideas. He may even say the opposite of what he means in an attempt to conceal his true feelings. Some people, negative in nature, do this habitually even when there is nothing to be gained. The salesman, therefore, must draw the prospect out without jumping to conclusions.

Drawing out techniques taught by psychologists such as Dr. Jesse S. Nirenberg include asking questions that require an explanation for an answer; asking the prospect to explain more fully; repeating his last few words and remaining silent which is an unspoken request for him to continue.[6] By interpreting back, saying back in different words what he thinks the prospect meant, the salesman can strip away ambiguities, too-broad generalizations, and other camouflages and uncover what is really on the mind of the prospect. A salesman with a limited amount of time will generally try to cover a few areas of information. When more time is available or on subsequent visits, he will want to inquire into a number of topics. Usually he should have planned the general areas in which he is interested and the sequence in which he will introduce them.

The asking of specific detailed questions may cause the prospect to feel that if the salesman wants to know something he will ask for it. Thus, he tends not to give additional information which would be useful. Since the salesman cannot think of everything that there is to ask, and since one of his jobs is to get the prospect to talk rather freely, he must use broad rather than specific questions. One kind of broad question is called open-ended. An example would be, "Tell me how you got into this industry, Mr. Jones." Although such a question directs the prospect's attention to the area of the beginning of his career, it gives him complete freedom to pick out whatever he wishes to discuss. One man may begin with his college preparation and the reasons for his choice. Another man may begin by talking of the "fickle finger of fate." And still another may choose to

⁶ Jesse S. Nirenberg, "How to Reach Minds—and Hearts—When You Talk to People," *Sales Management*. December 19, 1958, p. 33.

emphasize the social contacts which influenced his career. The advantage of such a procedure is that it lets the salesman see the kinds of things that the prospect considers it important to bring to the salesman's attention. This permits the latter to make some judgment about the prospect's values and about things he thinks will impress the salesman.

The salesman does not always have to ask a question formulated in a complete sentence. Sometimes the simple phrase, "Then what?" is enough to encourage the prospect to continue talking. Another useful device is to repeat a key word or phrase used by the prospect. For example, "I just didn't seem to be making the progress that I should so we decided it would be best if I tried another industry." The salesman replies, "We decided?" "Well, I mean my wife and I talked it over and she thought. . . ."

To help the prospect elaborate his remarks, another kind of open-ended question is, "Could you tell me more about that?" Another useful question is formed around some unclear word or phrase used by the prospect. For example, "What do you mean, 'pretty good progress?'" Such questions often turn up unexpected bits of information. Salesmen must learn that the specific meanings they attach to words are not necessarily the same as those understood by the prospect.

Questions that begin with "Why" and refer to feelings and desires of the prospect are usually not very satisfactory. A question such as "Why did you choose this particular company for your career?" often brings superficial answers. Such questions may often be rephrased into ones that begin with "What?" For example, "What led you to join this company rather than some other?" This puts the emphasis on what the prospect sees as advantages rather than upon his hidden feelings or desires. As a general guideline, questions should not lend themselves to a "yes" or "no" or a very short answer because they produce little useful information. Leading questions should also be avoided because they may influence a prospect to answer with information that will please the salesman rather than reveal something about the prospect.

Dr. Nirenberg also cautions the salesman not to interrupt the other person as it frustrates his effort to communicate and he may stop trying.[7] Interruption implies that the salesman is more interested in his own thoughts than in the prospect's and can't wait for his turn to speak. The prospect may not feel like competing for the salesman's attention. This blocking of the prospect's expression of emotion will frustrate and irritate him. The best way to drive a prospect's wants into hiding is to resort to a

---

[7] Nirenberg, op. cit.

cross-examining approach. To draw the prospect out, the sales interview must be an easy give-and-take discussion. It is a two-way street and the salesman's willingness to reveal his own attitudes often encourages the prospect to reveal his.

Once the prospect's problems are revealed, the salesman must make the buyer aware that he understands and sympathizes with the prospect's side of the picture. To do this, the salesman must have so much confidence that he doesn't talk about the product or service that he is selling. Once the prospect is aware of his need, the salesman presents a solution to satisfy the wants. At this point, the selective processes of perception and retention will aid persuasion. The salesman will be considered a friendly source of authority, if not unbiased, at least primarily concerned with the benefit of the buyer's interest. The businessman can now be more easily persuaded to do what he wants to do. Frequently the businessman will also require a logical presentation to justify his action and a well-prepared sales plan will quickly and efficiently justify his acting now.

The projective technique is also characteristic of the want-satisfaction method and is borrowed from the Rorschach Inkblot Test but modified as a market research tool.[8] The salesman shows the prospect a series of pictures without any writing, using the pretext that they may be used in future advertisements, and asks for the buyer's reactions and recommendations. The pictures might show people with the new equipment but obviously not using it. When prompted, the prospect most often will project his own thoughts into the innocent and noncommital situations pictured. "These people look as if they are talking baseball or sex and delaying getting to work in the morning." Or he might say, "Obviously the boss stepped out and the mice will play while the cat is away." He might reverse this idea and say, "It looks like the damn machine broke down and stopped these people from producing." Such projective techniques can be extremely effective in eliciting the businessman's inner thoughts and attitudes, such as hostility toward fellow workers. However, it takes considerable understanding and training to handle this technique tactfully and intelligently as well as to interpret the comments made. It does provide a convenient transition to the personal opinions of the prospect and, properly handled, will encourage him to speak out along such lines.

In the W-S method, the final presentation is oriented on the spot to reinforce one motivating force within the prospect to dominate all other

---

[8] H. Rorschach, *Psychodiagnostics* (2d ed.; Berne, Switzerland: Verlag Hans Huber, 1942). For material on the use of projective devices in marketing, see G. H. Smith, *Motivation Research in Advertising and Marketing* (New York: McGraw-Hill Book Co., Inc., 1954).

Courtesy: E. I. du Pont de Nemours Co., Wilmington, Del.

FIG. 8. Salesman and manufacturer talk over results of material being used in manufacturing process.

considerations at that moment. Reinforcement normally consists of building happy images, "selling the sizzle and not the steak." The W-S salesman doesn't sell foreign sports cars; he sells an image of youth. He doesn't sell transportation tickets; he sells romantic intrigue. He doesn't sell dietetic foods; he sells an image of a handsome or youthful waistline. He doesn't sell insurance; he sells happiness and peace of mind. He doesn't sell common stock; he sells the power of wealth. He doesn't sell clothes; he sells the admiration of others. He doesn't sell products; he sells the images, the intangible emotional pleasures the buyer receives when making his purchase. He makes his strongest appeal to the emotions and generally leaves the logic of the mind to the formula salesmen. It is a subtle method of persuasion and often the buyer is not aware of why he was persuaded. The salesman builds friendship to the point of camaraderie and the prospect rewards him for his personal interest with an order.

## ADVANTAGES OF WANT-SATISFACTION SELLING

This is clearly an improvement for the prospect over the product-oriented sales presentations because the discussion centers on the prospect's immediate interests, needs, and wants. It is an advantage to both the salesman and the prospect because it is a natural, friendly, easygoing two-way conversation without the frequently expected argumentation, aggression, and often obnoxious behavior of a forceful and dominant salesman. The W-S salesman becomes a friend to the buyer. It is an advantage to the salesman in that the final presentation is adapted to the individual prospect at the time the prospect is definitely interested and motivated in his area. Since the buyer has revealed some of his predisposition, his selective processes of exposure, perception, and retention can now favor persuasion. When the "hot button" is discovered and pushed, the salesman and the prospect are going the same way and both want to achieve the same purpose, to satisfy the buyer's wants. For having evidenced sincere interest in the prospect's wants and welfare, the salesman becomes a trusted source who is more readily believed and whose persuasive message is, therefore, more easily accepted. It is an advantage to both the salesman and the prospect in repeat buying situations because the entire buying-selling relationship is natural and friendly for both participants and the buyer has no feeling of being taken or persuaded to do something against his own best interests. Finally, it is an advantage to the selling company which gains access to and orders from top business executives who would not otherwise have taken the time and listened to a product-oriented sales presentation because they were not previously aware of an interest or need in this area.

## PREPARATION OF THE WANT-SATISFACTION SALESMAN

Clearly, a customer-oriented sales presentation demands considerable knowledge of, or intuitive insight into, the psychological motivations which influence an individual's behavior. In order to discover what will motivate an individual at a given time, to find his "hot button," the salesman must be a master in the technique of getting a prospect to talk, drawing him out of his protective shell, and learning of his predisposed attitudes, ideas, and beliefs. This is a form or application of the psychiatric technique of directive counseling. The "patient" is encouraged to volunteer information about himself and the "psychiatrist" interprets the information and helps the patient to see it in a new light, to understand what it is that is bothering him; what he needs to feel better; what will satisfy or make his life more pleasant and fulfilling again. Obviously most salesmen must be trained in the psychological processes of motivations and the techniques of discovering them as well as interpreting them in a form and manner that is acceptable to the prospect. Clearly, this is a job for an educated and trained listener, not for a compulsive talker.

Next, the salesman must be trained in the psychology of persuasion so that once he discovers what will motivate a particular prospect, he will know how to communicate his ideas in terms meaningful to the prospect in attempting to convert his attitudes to ones more favorable to the salesman. This refers to getting the prospect to see his needs or wants in a new light and reinforcing that idea which places one want in urgent need of satisfaction. Normally, the salesman must be extremely self-confident because in using this technique he must befriend the prospect and gain his trust and confidence in order to be "helpful" and "advise" the buyer to make him aware of a problem and its "urgent" need of satisfaction. Only after these attitudes have been established in the prospect's mind does the salesman begin talking of his product as the correct solution.

Finally, the salesman must know his product and its applications primarily in terms of satisfying the prospect's inner or personal needs. He must be as well versed as either the stimulus-response or the formula salesmen although he may use this detailed knowledge only on rare occasions. Sales made by the want-satisfaction presentation often leave the buyer unaware of what product or service he is actually getting but with a strong feeling of confidence in the man to whom he gave the order. The details of the product are secondary to the satisfaction the buyer feels. Whatever questions about the product do arise, however, must be answered clearly and correctly to maintain the atmosphere of sincerity and confidence.

Obviously, the sales trainer must be more of a psychologist than a product-oriented salesman. The trainees normally are college graduates at least in their late twenties or early thirties with a substantial background of business experience and an interest in psychology. Some salesmen with little formal education use this method intuitively; however, it would be difficult, if not impossible, to screen reliably a group of applicants for such intuitive behavior. The time, effort, and cost of hiring and training such men would be difficult to evaluate. The time it takes to prepare a college graduate with business experience to sell in this manner is considerably longer than the methods previously considered. Companies generally plan an expensive two-year training program which frequently includes a sequence of college courses in psychology. They feel they cannot afford the luxury of sending younger, less trained men into the field only to lose orders from repeat buyers of expensive goods and services.

## EFFECTIVENESS

To predict the effectiveness or value of this method of sales presentation, one must consider its advantages and disadvantages in relation to the cost of the product being marketed. Clearly it takes an entirely different recruiting, screening, and hiring practice from the product-oriented methods and difficulties arise immediately in the determination of what constitutes a "good" listener. An effective training process is very long and expensive. The salesman must know his product and the psychology of selling, and he must be well practiced in the techniques of projective psychoanalysis and directive counseling. He must be able to make the hidden needs and wants clear and acceptable to the prospect. Without proper technique, the entire effort may easily boomerang.

It normally takes considerable selling time to develop the needs and wants of an individual prospect, to say nothing of an entire group of prospects. Businessmen often will not grant this much of their time when pressed with other problems which demand more immediate attention. This increases the selling costs both in the cost of a single call and in the time it takes to develop a sale. This method demands complete sincerity but due to the time element, salesmen become impatient and too often are tempted to jumpt to quick conclusions. This lack of sincerity and patience normally shows up just as clearly as do dollar signs in the salesman's eyes and immediately arouses the buyer's suspicion and undermines his confidence in the source of the message. The want-satisfaction method of selling requires a delicate touch, without any pressure the prospect is aware of. Any word or action which hints that the salesman is manipulating the prospect will boomerang and all will be lost. Prospects that sense they are being used, manipulated, or toyed with will rebel against the salesman.

## SUMMARY

The want-satisfaction theory of selling is common in consumer goods and services such as insurance and mutual funds and is often used intuitively by senior salesmen in business. It is growing in popularity in the field of industrial selling, particularly where the goods and services represent a substantial investment. In a market where product and service differentiation is difficult or impossible to obtain, competitive salesmen are most often judged on a personal basis. The buyer looks for the man he can most easily get along with. The appeals may be based upon the personal wants of the buyer or upon his organizational role, that is, what he wants for himself within his company. The psychological principle of the primacy of self-interest is the foundation for this selling theory.

Fundamental to this theory is a customer-oriented presentation rather than a product- or salesman-oriented prepared talk. The prospect is encouraged to do most of the talking while the salesman listens. To encourage the prospect to divulge his inner wants, the salesman uses the projective technique and the question and answer method. Once the needs are discovered, the salesman attempts to elevate one motivating force into a dominant position in urgent need of satisfaction. He generally does this by building images of the emotional satisfaction to be achieved by taking action immediately.

The advantages of this method of persuasion include the following: The discussion centers on the prospect's interests as he sees them and this encourages selective exposure. It is a friendly easygoing two-way conversation which encourages selective perception and retention. The final product presentation occurs when the prospect is already interested and motivated toward the suggested solution and both salesman and prospect are going the same way to satisfy the prospect's needs. The salesman is trusted and more readily believed and the prospect feels his buying action is definitely in his own best interests. Busy executives will often take time to talk about themselves when they might not take time to listen to a product talk about something in which they had no interest.

To prepare salesmen to use this method of persuasion, many companies hire college graduates with considerable business experience and put them through an intensive but lengthy training course which is more psychologically oriented than product oriented. The salesman must have a deep understanding of directive counseling, motivations, and the psychology of communication and persuasion. His technical product knowledge should be oriented to fitting emotional wants of the prospect.

Without proper technique, the salesman may not understand, interpret, or have the prospect understand his own motives and the effort may easily boomerang. It often takes a lengthy interview to develop the strong wants of an individual prospect, despite what the oversimplified examples might lead one to believe, and many businessmen simply will not give up this much time from their busy schedules. Selling costs are extremely high, which limits the want-satisfaction attempt basically to goods and services which represent a substantial investment. The salesman cannot be impatient and jump to conclusions for he will show his lack of sincere interest and arouse suspicion which is self-defeating. This fault also applies if the salesman is not subtle and shows any sign of manipulating the businessman against his own best interests.

◆    ◆    ◆

## SELLING THE NATIONAL OBSERVER*

*OPENING:* Hello, Mr. Wilson, this is Mr. Smith calling for Dow Jones, publishers of the Wall Street Journal, Barron's and The National Observer. I wanted to check with you to see if you're reading a copy of The National Observer each week. (Pause for response.)

*THE BASIC SALES APPEAL:*   I'm glad to hear that, Mr. Wilson, because
(If prospect has read)            you already know what a great variety of
(the paper.          )            news The National Observer covers each
                                  week . . . and how *understandable* the editors make that news. In fact, many people are saying that by reading The National Observer regularly they are beginning to understand what's going on in the world and national affairs for the very first time.

*CLOSE:* I'd like to invite you to start reading this important new publication on a regular basis, Mr. Wilson. May I have delivery started for you?

*THE BASIC SALES APPEAL:*   Oh, you haven't heard about The National
(If prospect has not)            Observer, Mr. Wilson? Well, it's a brand
(read the paper.      )            new *family* newspaper published every week
                                  by the publishers of The Wall Street Journal.
It's new in concept too . . . designed to give you *more* information in less reading time and to help you understand the news. The National Observer covers all kinds of news . . . national and world affairs, sports, fashions, medicine, science, TV and movies . . . just about everything of interest to the alert intelligent reader.

*CLOSE:* I'd like to invite you to try The National Observer, Mr. Wilson, to see if you don't agree that it's the most informative and interesting newspaper you've ever read." May I have delivery started for you?

---

* The above is reprinted with the kind permission of Dow Jones & Company, Inc., Community Sales Program, Circulation Field & Phone Sales Division, Princeton, N.J.

## FOREIGN FLAG AIRLINES

Foreign flag airlines solicit freight business in New York City primarily from freight agents. Mr. H. Lerner, a new salesman for one such airline, was asked to prepare a memorized presentation and a want-satisfaction presentation for their sales force. In addition, the sales manager asked how the airlines might dramatize their service and for a list of typical objections and answers. Mr. Lerner submitted the following report: (Company identification has been eliminated.)

## MEMORIZED PRESENTATION

Actually these few minutes could prove to be very profitable to you. I realize that you must see about 30 of us fellows from the various airlines every week. And each one of us gives you the same line about direct and frequent service to the flag country. But do you know, Mr. Rightman, that I'm not even going to discuss shipments to my country because I know that we are going to get that traffic anyhow. After all, nobody can equal the frequency of direct service that my company offers between New York and our capital. What I'm after, quite frankly, is some of your freight moving from New York to Western Europe.

Now, serving our clients is as important to us as I'm sure it is to you. So let me show you how we can help you in this regard. You know, we are the small airline with big airline services and facilities. We fly Boeing 707s and 720s exclusively on our transatlantic routes. However, the really big advantage of shipping with us is that should anything go wrong, as can and does happen with any shipment sent via any carrier throughout the world, our system is still of a size where tracers are immediately answered and the cargo is immediately located.

Also, notice our late departures. (Show schedule.) Here, for example, we depart at 2200 (10:00 p.m.) which means that any problem arising in your office during the late afternoon—as they so often do—could still be taken care of in sufficient time to be delivered to JFK Airport to make this particular flight.

Therefore, you can see that by using my airline you are not merely fulfilling your basic obligations to your client but you're actually going one step beyond. In view of this, I'm sure you'll want to try us at your earliest opportunity.

Now tonight we fly the route to London, Rome, and our capital. If you'll pick up your phone and dial OL 1–2345 and book whatever cargo you have to these destinations, you'll see what we can do!

## WANT-SATISFACTION
## PROGRAMMED PRESENTATION

In order to determine the specific requirements of the individual prospect in question, the salesman asks some very pointed questions. Based on the answers to these questions, the salesman is in a position to offer a tailored service to the client.

    1.Q. What is the nature of the cargo that you handle for most of your clients?

    A. Anything from steel bars and tractor parts to delicate electronic equipment.

    2.Q. What destinations do they (your clients) generally ship to?

    A. Mostly to London, Paris, Zurich, Teheran, and Johannesburg.

    3.Q. By and large, what the the weights of the individual shipments you handle?

    A. They generally run from 900 lbs. to a ton.

Well then, Mr. X., I see that we are in an excellent position to do business together. We not only have the necessary equipment to handle your specific type of cargo, we also have regular flights to the specific destinations that you mentioned. Furthermore, the capacities of our cargo holds on our passenger aircraft are sufficient to hold the quantities you ship. In addition, our jet-smooth passenger planes are perfect for that electronic equipment you mentioned.

Why not book today's shipment with us? See how easy it is. Just pick up the phone and dial OL 1–2345. You'll find us to be the airline that is made to order for you!

## DRAMATIZATION

Unlike some other products and services, it is very difficult to dramatize the advantages of using a particular airline. Of course, one can cite the shortcomings of the competition, but this is not only considered unethical, it is actually dangerous. In reality, those same problems of lost cargo, overflown destinations because of weather, and so forth can plague any airline. And if these problems are used to illustrate shortcomings of the competition, they can easily boomerang.

However, there are some rather unique ways of illustrating an airline's capabilities. Every once in a while the airline takes the opportunity of inviting various guests on a free flight to a new destination. It is at such times that clients are "wined and dined" and the airline's potentialities are clearly dramatized.

## OBJECTIONS

Wherever possible, it is always desirable to anticipate the prospect's objections so that they can be answered intelligently.

The following are some typical objections in this business and some of the ready answers provided:

    Q. We use only the flag carriers of the country of destination.

    A. It is sometimes detrimental to follow any particular policy to the exclusion of all other possibilities. It is always better to make use of two airlines to a particular destination rather than the other way around. In short, it is unwise to put all your eggs in one basket.

Q. The customer pays the freight charges and therefore routes all the cargo.

A. In that case, I'm sure you won't mind my soliciting your customer. May I have his name and address?

Q. We are quite happy with our present service, why should we change?

A. It is always wise to have something or someone to fall back on. Won't you let us serve you in that way?

◆  ◆  ◆

## MORSE FIELD REPORT: PHILCO CORPORATION,*
### (Philadelphia, Pa.)

The use of "electrolized" drills—drills "armored" by an exclusive process of the Morse Twist Drill & Machine Co. for cutting tools—is resulting in great savings of time and money by the Philco Corporation, Philadelphia, in the construction of the Philco-2000 electronic data computer.

Hundreds of small holes must be drilled in each of more than 18,000 printed circuit cards which make up the "brain" of the computer. The drilled holes permit placement of wires and transistors which power this data processing system.

Many of these cards are made of a highly abrasive epoxy resin glass fiber. When first developed, it became apparent to Philco engineers that this material was far too abrasive for ordinary drills. Various types of conventional high-speed and carbide drills were tested and found inadequate—some even snapping in two when brought into contact with the work.

The cost of drilling increased at the Philco plant. Not only were replacement drills becoming expensive, but work had to be stopped while changes were made, and the actual drilling slowed down in hope of protecting drills from breakage.

After exhaustive testing, Philco learned the drill which provided the durability and long life it needed was an "electrolized" drill supplied by the Morse Twist Drill & Machine Co. of New Bedford, Massachusetts. This Morse drill is a conventional tool which has become subjected to a confidential process which "armors" the tool with an alloy allowing it to drill through highly abrasive materials without deteriorating its cutting ability.

The basic structure of the drill is not affected by electrolizing, and only a few

---

* The above is reprinted with the kind permission of Morse Twist Drill & Machine Co., a Division of Universal American Corporation, New Bedford, Massachusetts.

cents is added to the cost of each high-speed drill. It is estimated that the process increases a tool's life up to ten times.

The supervisor of Philco's circuit card drill section, Edward Rosowski, said of Morse drills: "We find that the electrolized drills rarely break, even if they are lowered onto the work incorrectly. The abrasive wear seems not to affect them, and they certainly hold their cutting edge for a long period of work.

All in all, the use of the Morse tool has meant a great savings to us in both production time and money saved."

# 14

# Problem Solving and the Service Concept Used in Selling

## DESCRIPTION

Problem solving, or mood selling as it is occasionally termed, has evolved from the customer-oriented method of want-satisfaction selling but has gone beyond it in true sincerity. It is based upon building the prospect's confidence in the honest service that the sincere salesman can provide. It is dedicated to the primary benefit of the prospect by developing the true business needs and then thoroughly investigating all feasible solutions, projecting their applications, and selecting the most likely solution. The salesman lets the chips fall where they may and recommends the most likely solution even if this does not include purchase of his own product.

## THE EXTENT USED

While this method of persuasion is used by some experienced salesmen in almost every sales field, it is relatively rare in general sales. On the other hand, it is quite common in technical fields where production or engineering services are important. When a product has an easily demonstrated superiority over all competitors, it would be an effective technique to use with a completely honest two-sided presentation. However, obvious product superiority is usually short lived and the basic approach would soon have to be changed radically.

The foundation of problem solving as a technique of persuasion is true sincerity without equivocation or mental reservation. While the salesman is with his prospect, nothing else in the world can be on his mind besides the immediate problem of the prospect. Every phase of the problem and

209

every factor which may be associated with or affected by the problem is openly discussed and evaluated. The salesman helps the prospect to define his own wants and needs but he does not stop here or jump to hit the magic "hot button" to get his order. He goes beyond simple want-satisfaction to aid the prospect to consider several possible solutions and to project their possible applications into the future. The salesman honestly encourages the prospect to decide on which solution is most feasible and to act or delay accordingly.

## Jenns Packaging Machine Corporation

Years ago a senior salesman representing a packaging machine company called on the plant engineer of a chewing gum company in Long Island City with the idea of automating the manufacturing process. The plant engineer, always on the lookout for ways to increase efficiency, took time out to see the salesman in the reception room. The two men discussed the raw materials used, the existing type of equipment, and the necessary steps involved from unloading raw materials to shipping finished goods. The plant engineer felt there was too much handling of materials between processes but knew of no machines on the market to relieve the situation. The salesman asked if he could tour the plant and ask questions in order to work up some suggestions. Since the salesman talked the same language as the plant engineer and seemed to be something of an expert in the materials handling field, the plant engineer readily agreed.

On his first tour, the salesman mentioned several ideas but could not discuss them fully with the prospect until he talked with his own machine engineers. On subsequent visits, he obtained additional technical data such as the handling speed of various components, their size and floor space, and ceiling height required. He inquired why certain machines were used instead of different ones and about the company's experience with the different machines. He explained his ideas to the plant manager and together they explored the number of variations possible at each step. The salesman worked up a materials flow chart showing how and where raw materials progressed to final packaging and how most of the existing equipment could be tied in directly to a continuous belt system. One bottleneck neither the plant engineer nor the salesman could solve immediately and it seemed this would frustrate their efforts. The salesman investigated all the equipment manufactured and with his own machine engineer worked out ways his company could adapt several machines on the market to serve its purpose.

Finally he submitted detailed floor plans, specifications, and quotations showing several ways to accomplish complete automation of the manufacturing and packaging operation. Raw materials would be put in at one end and, without being separately handled again, would move continuously until they came out of the packaging machine in cartons ready for shipment. The two men discussed the advantages and disadvantages of each solution and finally agreed upon one which would pay for itself and was the most practical. The salesman got his order for nearly one-half a million dollars for the packaging machine plus the continuous belt equipment, and some unknowing manufacturer of the problem machine also received an order for almost one-quarter of a million dollars.

Clearly no canned speech or formula presentation could have sold this expensive packaging machine, nor could psychological pampering of the plant engineer cause a company to change its entire manufacturing procedure. It took a salesman who was sincere and willing to investigate a vague problem, narrow it down to specific objectives, and work hard and long to find a solution. It took honesty in analyzing the various machines and methods. Recommending the purchase of another manufacturer's machine for the bottleneck took courage because this increased the final expenditure by 50 percent and might have jeopardized the entire effort.

## Chemical Sales Company

Very recently, a chemical salesman called on a large aircraft manufacturer attempting to introduce new plastic materials to the machine engineering group. Neither the chemical company nor the tool engineers had ever used plastic materials in tooling before although the chemical company had gotten promising but limited test results which showed the plastic had some of the major properties desired by tool engineering. Any desired shape could be inexpensively molded from a plaster cast and the material was dense enough to withstand considerable stamping pressure and hold its own shape within fine tolerance limits. The plastic could then be tooled, that is drilled, tapped, and so forth, as easily as metal. One big unknown was how long the material would hold up in a stamping production run as even steel dies must be refaced after a number of parts have been stamped out under tremendous pressure.

A small group of tool engineers agreed to do research with the plastic material and the salesman asked for security clearance to work with the men. Their initial problem was to cast a large shape, such as a tail section of an airplane, and maintain constant density and strength. The salesman phoned his own plant daily and had them experiment and vary the formula according to the needs of the tool engineers. New materials were shipped regularly, together with engineering data regarding room temperature and cooling times required. Finally a large casting of the desired strength was achieved and the experimenters ran a simple stamping test of a few parts successfully. The tool engineers were elated and ready to order the plastic in bulk but the salesman would not take the order! He requested a plastic die facing be used on the next production run of less than 50 pieces to determine its longevity. The tool engineers agreed and when a production order for 25 pieces came through they cast the required die facing and ran the test. The 25 pieces came out exactly as specified and the machine was allowed to run longer. The 35th piece showed signs of variation and the 40th was definitely rejected. The experimenters had established fixed limits under certain pressures and were now on safe grounds to recommend the plastic. The original plastic casting could be duplicated at a unit cost considerably below older methods and for short-run production; substantial money and time could be saved. The salesman got his order, the gratitude of the tool engineers, and the customer's recommendation of his services to the entire industry.

Obviously, the sincerity of the salesman and his willingness to work with the prospect to solve the problem was essential in this sale. Notice, however, when he had a chance to grab an order and run the salesman did not. This man insisted on a test to determine the practical limits of his product and in so doing he ran the risk of losing the sale. Only when production tests proved the materials really were applicable was this salesman content. In the future these tool engineers will believe what this salesman says about his other products. He is one of them, accepted as their friend. Confidence based upon proven service to the customer is the foundation of this type of selling.

### Office Furniture Company

Product application need not always be technical to use the problem-solving techniques with sincerity. A common advertisement in the office furniture industry has the heading, "Make us prove we can save office space for you!" Office planning and layout work has evolved into a specialty as much as factory layout. A good office equipment salesman often knows more about job functions and the space and equipment requirements of office workers than the architect who designs a company's entire building.

Recently a desk salesman approached the office administrator of a large insurance company who was looking for additional floor space. The salesman suggested a study of existing space and equipment as well as the possibility of new equipment in the existing space. The administrator readily agreed and worked with the salesman surveying each job and each department for expected expansion requirements in the next five years. All information was then transcribed onto new floor plans showing existing equipment rearranged with room for expansion as well as new plans with new equipment. The costs of moving, painting, and electrical and telephone work was included for each of the alternatives and a projection into the future was made to determine the probable time limits of expansion. After honestly appraising the alternatives, the salesman recommended the continued use of existing equipment under the new floor plans.

Top management saw the proposals and realized that another group of people in a second office building they rented could be immediately brought into the one office at a considerable savings in rent. The salesman got his order after replanning the combined office staff for consolidation in the one building.

Since most salesmen are specialists in their narrow field, they are very often experts in related problems and can suggest alternative courses of action with honest appraisals that the prospect is not normally aware of. Sincerely solving problems can be an effective sales presentation in many nontechnical fields simply because the salesman is more knowledgeable in his field than is the buyer. Many accounting machines, office copy machines, and printing machines are sold because of a problem-solving technique, honestly applied. When a salesman is selling simple products, often nothing astonishes prospects more than his common sense and plain honest dealings.


## WHY PROBLEM-SOLVING TECHNIQUES ARE USED

While the customer-oriented want-satisfaction theory, covered in the previous chapter, seems to be a definite improvement over the salesman or product-oriented presentation, in practice it is too often attempted by men not proficient in the fundamental psychological techniques so necessary, and therefore the crude persuasion attempt is easily seen through and resented by prospects. In addition to the problems of adequately training salesmen, the market is gradually shifting its emphasis to younger minds willing to accept buying responsibility and this creates additional prob-

FIG. 9. The salesman is backed up by a team of 39 specialists that can meet
any selling problem that arises.

lems. Most college graduates of business administration today are schooled
in the scientific method of making business decisions which is quite
comparable to the problem-solving technique. These are the young men
who will be among the future business leaders. One day they will make the
buying decisions. They welcome this sincere approach from a salesman,
particularly when he is an expert in some detailed or technical phase of a
problem. Their attitudes toward salesmen in general indicate a predisposition the salesman should be aware of in order to encourage persuasion and
not mobilize defenses.

In one study of college seniors,[1] almost half of those questioned thought that large scale production causes aggressive selling and results in the high standard of living in this country. Less than one-quarter believed that aggressive selling causes the high production. Only one-fifth believed that sales makes consumers happy and about one-quarter judged that people would be better off if there were fewer salesmen and another quarter qualified their answers to fewer of some kinds of salesmen. In other words, they do not credit selling in general with much social and economic contribution to the American way of life. In probing attitudes regarding salesmen's ethics, it was found that over one-quarter felt sales jobs require more compromise with the truth than some other jobs and an additional 60 percent felt that some kinds of sales jobs require compromise with the truth. In other words, some 85 percent felt that salesmen exaggerate, tell part-truths or are insincere. The third area studied was the attitude toward sales as an occupational status. Less than half the college seniors felt a college education was needed for sales jobs and of seniors with marketing majors, slightly over half would even consider a selling job. This study concludes that college seniors think of most salesmen as contributing little of social and economic value to our way of living; as being insincere and self-interested; as being educationally inferior because sales jobs do not need a college education sufficiently to justify them.

The results of another study indicated several similar prevalent misconceptions about the salesman's job.[2] General college students tend to think of the salesman as a drummer, slippery, here-today-gone-tomorrow, living by his wits, and ready to make a buck by any means. In general they showed a lack of knowledge of salesmen and, consequently, a lack of confidence in them. Those students planning a sales career were only slightly more accurate in their conception of a salesman. These students viewed the salesman as holding a self-centered point of view instead of the professional salesman's customer-centered point of view. The traditional portrait of a salesman as an irresponsible pitchman seems to be slow in dying, even among college students preparing for a sales career.

---

[1] William M. Borton, "What's Wrong With the Way We're Selling Sales Careers to Collegians," *Sales Management*, March 15, 1957 (an interdepartmental doctoral study using psychology, sociology, economics, and marketing—conducted on two California campuses).

[2] J. Donald Staunton and the Editors, *American Salesman*, "I Didn't Raise My Boy to Be a Salesman!" This report is based upon a nationwide survey of campus opinion as printed in *Management Review*, March, 1958, p. 9. By permission of The American Management Association, Inc.

These attitudes, indicative of the predisposition of college seniors, illustrate why a professional salesman must build confidence through sincere problem solving and why canned talks and formula presentations often fail. The basic methods of selling are correctly recognized as salesman oriented and incorrectly this confirms the buyer's predisposed poor attitude toward salesmen in general. This also points out the danger of the want-satisfaction method of selling. The prospect is often predisposed to distrust the salesman and he is listening and looking for any sign that will confirm his original although false belief. If he senses he is being manipulated, he will shake off the persuasive arguments and retreat under his protective umbrella and selectively perceive the salesman's interest as being very different from his own.

Going beyond the young buyer, the hard realities of costs and competition have produced a demanding boss. Often a higher executive than a purchasing agent makes the ultimate buying decision and dealing with a corporate vice-president calls for a sophisticated salesman. In terms of persuasion, the man using a mood of complete sincerity in problem solving is building confidence in the source of authority. After repeated exposure, the businessman will know with the certainty of personal experience that this salesman operates entirely in the best interests of the prospect. He will learn to trust the salesman completely and sooner or later will give him whatever orders he asks for, knowing that the salesman will protect the businessman's best interests.

## CHARACTERISTICS OF PROBLEM SOLVING AND MOOD SELLING

All phases of this technique of presentation are directed toward building confidence. Before the initial approach, the salesman studies his individual prospect, the current economic situation, the particular business and the industry. When he makes his first contact he is prepared to offer a genuine and specific service to the prospect. He is open and direct and makes his first impression one of complete sympathy and agreement with the prospect, not attempting to sell anything or even talk product.[3] Later in the interview, or on subsequent calls, he draws the prospect out of his protective shell enough to discuss his problems in business. As in want-satisfaction selling, he uses questions to probe areas of business wants, needs, and desires but makes no attempt to lead or direct the prospect's thinking. He

[3] Edward C. Bursk, "Low-Pressure Selling," *Harvard Business Review*, Vol. 25, No. 2 (1947), pp. 227–42.

then analyzes the need and gently makes the prospect aware of a specific problem. The prospect at this point actually spells out the problem in detail and what he wants to change from. From here on, the technique is very different from the others covered earlier.

Once the prospect understands his own problem, the salesman encourages him to examine as many possible solutions as are feasible, not just the salesman's personal decision or just the products he represents. Each plausible solution is thoroughly investigated, with the salesman participating in the legwork and honest appraisal. Then each solution is projected into the future to determine as accurately as possible the net short-term and long-range effects. On this basis, the choice of likely alternatives is narrowed down and a selection can be made more intelligently. In the persuasive situation, this is a two-sided presentation by the same source of authority and the arguments must be strictly unbiased to be effective. It is the salesman's responsibility to honestly protect the prospect and recommend that course of action which is in the prospect's best interest. The entire sales presentation is clearly customer oriented.

Another characteristic of this type of selling is empathy or identifying of oneself with another in order to understand him better. Women sales personnel, apparently with intuition, honestly place themselves in the prospect's shoes and feel what they would really do if faced with the same problem and alternatives.[4] This feeling or attitude is transmitted to the prospect and a single identity is established between buyer and seller, both going the same way for the same purpose. This similarity to the perceiver is more easily recognized, for example, when a New York GI overseas meets another New Yorker and feels he has met a long-lost friend. Once established, this empathetic feeling generates a degree of confidence in the buyer that would not be possible otherwise. The salesman must forget his primary job of selling for a living and the danger is that he is often apt to agree with the prospect about not buying when he really should buy.

Also characteristic of the problem-solving technique of persuasion is the emphasis on business decision making as it is taught in business schools in many leading colleges. This encompasses the diagnosis of the problem, or narrowing down generalities to specific objectives; the evolution of alternative solutions, or investigating as many feasible alternatives as possible; the projection of results, or forecasting both immediate probable results and long-term likelihoods; and finally the choice, or desirable alternatives as they relate to objectives. This entire process, ideally, includes the effect of

---

[4] Richard A. Yahraes, "Can Saleswomen Teach Men about Selling?" *American Salesman*, May, 1959, p. 50.

personal and corporate objectives on the interpretation of problems, creative thinking, and "idea-producing" techniques; the place of statistics,
probability, and logic in decision making; and the nature of value judgments in many business decisions. In other words, if the salesman can fit in
with the type of thinking the businessman is taught to respect and admire,
he is more apt to be accepted and have a persuasive effect on the businessman.

## VALUE ANALYSIS[5]

Modern engineering and purchasing techniques have evolved a system
known as value analysis which is quite similar and compatible with the
problem-solving sales method. Value analysis is concerned with identifying
unnecessary costs that do not affect customer features or use: those properties, features, or attractive qualities that cause prospects to want to own the
product.

Due to the rush of an original marketing effort, many costly methods
and materials get incorporated into a final design. In the competitive
marketplace, the sales force demands products or product improvements
quickly. There is little time or patience for adequate market research,
design engineering, production engineering, and packaging. There is, therefore, much opportunity for later savings through value analysis.

In modern industry this function is usually a full-time job and should be
independent of the purchasing department, which is concerned with the
cost of acquisition and has suppliers to which it is loyal. The value analyst
should also be independent of the engineering and manufacturing personnel, who have certain tolerance demands which may not be related to the
marketability of the product. If these people aren't smart enough to help
the value analyst through participation, the salesman should be big enough
and sophisticated enough to educate them to the fact that the value
analyst is helping others and explain why he is doing so. This will help to
gain their confidence and friendship for subsequent exposure to his sales
presentation.

A formal value analysis plan includes seven steps and various sales
representatives are expected to aid at several points. The first step for the
analyst is orientation or locating possible areas to search for cost savings.

---

[5] From the viewpoint of modern engineers and purchasing agents, value analysis is
the philosophy applied to cost reduction techniques which use the problem-solving
sales strategy. See L. D. Miles, *Techniques of Value Analysis and Engineering* (New
York: McGraw-Hill Book Co., Inc., 1961).

He is concerned with how much is spent for a given item and how often the purchase occurs. The second step is a search of existing information and covers supplier costs, methods and costs of processing in the plant, specifications and tolerances, how the product is used, and what customer features the part or process generates. Salesmen often have customer services or technical handbooks and they can develop useful information from their own research and development people. Salesmen can also help the value analyst in the third step, which is speculation or a brainstorming session designed to blast useful ideas from the subconscious mind. It often involves ignoring what has been done in the past in favor of a new material or process for the future. The fourth step is analysis of each of the speculative ideas, and here again sales aid is expected to get facts, figures, and alternatives. At the fifth stage, a program is planned to allow proper time to design, engineer, test, "de-bug," procure materials, and schedule the manufacturing process. The sixth state is the activation of the formal plan and the value analyst actually bird-dogs internally to keep materials, new tolerances, and all other phases of the plan coordinated. Finally, a formal summary is made which shows what was done and what was achieved.

In a large industrial concern, this value analysis program can easily save upwards of $1 million annually. *Purchasing* magazine devotes one annual issue to value analysis and has literally hundreds of value analysis cost reduction case histories, including articles on the vendor's role in V.A.[6] The General Electric Company originally pioneered this engineering and purchasing system and its use is currently being encouraged by Secretary McNamara in the U.S. Department of Defense. Currently RCA uses this system to hold costs down and to improve its many products.[7] Value analysis is being encouraged in the late 1960s to play a major role in company profit improvement and few purchasing departments, however small, have any excuse to ignore it.

While value analysis is growing in popularity, it is estimated that fewer than 10 percent of businesses currently use this philosophy and of those that report using it, few have a full-time program. A salesman who cooperates fully with a value analyst over a period of months or years must still submit a competitive bid to purchasing when the prospect is ready to order. Customer loyalty at this point often breaks down in favor of the lowest bidder. Still, it would seem foolish for a salesman not to cooperate

---

[6] *Purchasing*, May 5, 1966. Entire issue entitled, "1966 Value Analysis."

[7] John Vande Water, "RCA's New Concepts In Value Buying," *Purchasing*, May 18, 1964, p. 34.

with a value analyst because in the process he will gain much knowledge of his prospect and have opportunity to befriend many important people who may influence the final buying decision.

## PREPARATION

The emphasis in training for problem-solving techniques obviously is on technical knowledge of the product and how it relates to user benefits, with thorough schooling on the technical qualities which substantiate any claims made. The product may be manufactured in a certain size or from a certain gauge of steel for reasons of economy and the salesman not only knows why it is produced in this way, he also knows where he can request minor changes to suit the customer's needs and where the basic costs will change radically. In other words, the salesman knows his production limitations, both physical and financial, and how they will apply to likely customer requests. Knowing why the plant operates as it does, the salesman understands the philosophy of the company and can anticipate the fields or areas in which he can modify or change his standard product and the areas clearly beyond the product's limitations.

The salesman's training includes the psychological processes of persuasion covered earlier but the emphasis is on building confidence in the source of the message, the authority in the field. Knowing why, in this technique, is much more important than knowing how. This relates directly to the scientific decision making noted above. Each step of the persuasion process, including the suggestion of alternatives which are feasible from the customer's point of view, must be related to objective facts and justified accordingly. In this process, the salesman who is gruff but technically correct is more persuasive than the smooth or nice guy type of salesman who is too general or loose with the facts.

Second only to technical knowledge in this technique of presentation is the ability to communicate in an educational sense. The salesman is supposed to be more of an expert in his limited field than the prospect but he must make his ideas simple and understandable to the business executive who may not be familiar with the technical terms involved. Making technical data clear and understandable to the novice is a skill which can be taught in a training class and its importance cannot be treated lightly in preparing salesmen for their field experience. The salesman must state his idea, illustrate his idea, and then restate his idea in different terms if necessary for unless the prospect understands what his suggestion is and appreciates the minute technical point on which the idea swings, all the

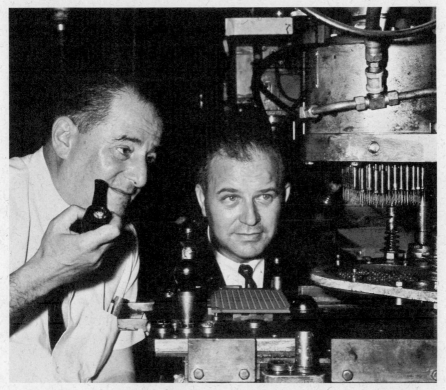

*Courtesy: Morse Twist Drill & Machine Co. New Bedford, Mass.*

**FIG. 10. An installation that he sold is inspected by a salesman.**

clear, scientific thinking involved may be lost to an audience that understands a different language.

## EFFECTIVENESS

The advantages of problem solving in a mood of sincerity include those of want-satisfaction and go beyond. Both are customer oriented and directed toward the mutual goal of solving the customer's problem. In the problem-solving case the attention is directed primarily to business problems in the technical sense. The final sales presentation in both cases is created to serve the individual prospect and in the problem-solving technique the use of a two-sided argument completely without bias is essential and is generally more acceptable. The problem-solving technique builds long-range confidence in the source of authority which is primary to any repetitive attempt at persuading men in business. Selective exposure, selective perception, and selective retention should operate to favor persuasion whenever the salesman operates in a truly sincere manner, holding his prospect's goal higher than his own compensation.

In problem solving, it takes considerable time to develop the various solutions feasible for an individual prospect and businessmen may not extend the necessary time to permit an objective appraisal. Often, other problems, more pressing, prohibit them from giving adequate time or thought to solutions suggested. On occasion businessmen may use the salesman's effort and intelligence without any promise of the reward of an order in the immediate future. Due to this time element, a salesman's own impatience will often cause him to bypass a thorough probing of alternative solutions to a problem and defeat his own image of sincerity. Without complete confidence, suspicion will be aroused and the buyer may pick out the good points of the salesman's suggestions with no sense of obligation to reward him. In addition, any pressure from the sales manager to get orders this month instead of some future date must be hidden from the prospect. Economic pressure on the salesman from his boss as well as from his personal family needs must remain secondary in the prospect's mind regardless of the salesman's need. Perhaps the greatest reason this method of selling is not as effective as it might be is that too often the salesman is sold. He becomes so involved in being completely fair and unbiased in his two-sided presentation that he is ineffective as a persuader. There is always the danger of an empathetic salesman honestly advising a competitor's product or, for the wrong reasons, advising that no purchase be made. Experienced sales managers have seen many good salesmen develop to this mature level of presentation only to lose heart in their own product or company because they feel their customer's needs are even greater for another product than their own. But by definition, salesmanship includes getting favorable action and financial priority as part of the persuasion process. No one has time or funds to purchase everything he could possibly use and it is the salesman's job to get priority for his product as long as the prospect can honestly benefit by its use. It takes common sense and a level head to draw the line between practical use of a product and either overselling or underselling.

## SUMMARY

Problem solving is the technique of persuasion based upon complete honesty, giving consulting service in a technical sense, primarily for the benefit of the buyer. While it is used occasionally in nontechnical fields, this method of persuasion is common in engineering or technical fields. It is an appealing sales method primarily because businessmen in general and future buyers, the young college graduates in business administration in particular, are predisposed to suspect salesmen of selfish motives. Using this method, the salesman offsets his suspicion and builds confidence by producing an honest service which is clearly understood by the prospect. The buyer must learn from personal experience that a particular salesman operates entirely in the prospect's best interests.

The primary characteristic of this method is a mood of sincerity or complete honesty. The salesman offers a legitimate service of problem analysis, investigation, and recommendation of one solution regardless of who may get the order. He puts himself in the prospect's position and exercises his judgment based upon his technical knowledge which normally is superior in his field to that of the prospect.

Obviously this method requires the salesman be thoroughly prepared in a technical sense as well as in the broad applications of his product so that he can offer a legitimate service to the customer as an expert in his field. Since he is dealing in technicalities, the salesman must be particularly adept at communicating his technical ideas to prospects who often have only broad general knowledge. Every suggestion must be understood and accepted from the customer's point of view regardless of possible over-whelming technical logic which he may not perceive.

When the sale is of a technical nature, this method of presentation is fundamentally applicable, particularly when the size of the investment justifies the amount of time and effort involved. As competitive products become more nearly equal, with less demonstrable advantages, this method is less effective. The urgency for quick decisions often causes salesmen to become impatient and recommend only one solution or causes businessmen to demand and get an answer before adequate investigation and honest appraisal can be made. In either case, the salesman undermines the confidence which is fundamental to this method of presentation. Unfortunately, a completely sincere effort with a two-sided presentation is truly so fair and unbiased that it is often completely ineffective in persuasion—not only is the prospect left on the fence but often the salesman himself is left with doubts concerning his own product or company.

◆　　◆　　◆

## SAFETY SELLS A PRODUCT*

The technical and competitive aspects of industry today are such that special customer service sometimes is a product's chief selling point. A case in point is tetraethyl lead, the anti-knock compound refiners add to gasoline to improve octane count and performance. Du Pont's TEL and its competitor's are chemically identical. The price is as low as either is able to get it. Du Pont's principal opportunity for an advantage lies, then, in offering special services. To provide them, Du Pont backs its TEL salesmen with a group of 39 specialists.

TEL, even in minute quantities, is hazardous to refinery employees. With that in mind, Du Pont goes far beyond the customary technical and marketing aids. To safeguard refinery and transit workers, Du Pont offers as well the wide range of special safety services. Over many years these Du Pont services, supplementing the refiners' own safety program, have built an enviable record: In the entire U.S., there has never been one case of lead poisoning recorded among refinery personnel blending concentrated TEL with gasoline.

## MORSE FIELD REPORT: ULTRA-SONIC PRECISION CO., INC.†
### (Mt. Vernon, N.Y.)

Mr. Lawrence Hofmann, president of the Ultra-Sonic Precision Co., Inc., manufactures carbon moulds up to ½ inch thick used in the manufacture of transistors and other fine electronic components by RCA, Texas Instrument, Motorola, Sylvania and other similar firms. He is one of the many hundreds of manufacturers throughout the country who have learned to turn to Morse for the solution of cutting tool problems. Morse was recommended to Ultra-Sonic by a friend of Mr. Hofmann who operated a manufacturing plant in New Jersey. The friend said that he had had a cutting tool problem and the Morse organization solved it for him.

Tom Spindler therefore called at the Ultra-Sonic plant and was presented the problem of extending drill life. He obtained details of the equipment used, rate of production and other operating factors, and samples of the materials to be drilled.

After weighing all factors, it was apparent that the problem was one which could be solved best by electrolized drills, and this type of tool was suggested.

There then followed a series of in-plant tests under ordinary working conditions. Results were tabulated by Ultra-Sonic management, and checked by the Morse representative.

These test results equalled or surpassed the benefits estimated by Morse, and the production drilling line was equipped entirely with Morse electrolized drills.

This is but one instance of the service and assistance which is available from the Morse organization. Morse maintains engineering salesmen in every state who are capable and willing to make any cutting tool problem their own. If the problem is particularly complex, a Morse salesman or distributor can

---

* The above is reprinted with the kind permission of E. I. du Pont de Nemours Company, Inc., Wilmington, Delaware.

† The above is reprinted with the kind permission of Morse Twist Drill & Machine Co., a Division of Universal American Corporation, New Bedford, Massachusetts.

call on the Morse plant for technical, engineering and designing help. Morse sales service engineers spend much of their time in the field on such calls.

The moral of the story is easy to see: don't keep your cutting tool problems —give them to a Morse Man!

## GREAT COMPANY FILTERS

Industrial water engineers are concerned with filtering equipment for water which enters their industrial process as well as waste treatment equipment for after plant use disposal. With government interest in restoring the purity of our rivers, industrial filtration systems have become big business. For the most part, buyers are engineers, technically trained and relatively sophisticated. Mr. Kenneth Mason, an experienced salesman for a water conditioning company, prepared the following sales talks to help train new salesmen:

### PLANNED SALES PRESENTATION

Sir, I would like to thank you for this opportunity to talk to you about the Great Company Filter.

This filter is the only one of its kind. It is by far the best on the market. It can do the job of filtration faster, more effectively, and cheaper than any other filter on the market at the present time.

It is fully automatic; it offers automatic backwashing which occurs at a loss of five feet of head result across the filtering media. There is only one valve per unit and no backwashing pump is needed. The filter also has many benefits not available in competing filters. They are as follows:

It is capable of standard filtration:
    Heavy duty and high rate filtration
    Coagulation filtration
    Cotalyzed oxidation filtration

We are the only company which produces one filter capable of these varied types of filtration. All competitors offer different filters for different filtration.

As for our competition, they claim that their filters have no valves. They try to show this as a good point; but it is actually one of the weakest points of their filters. Having no valves their filters cannot be interlocked to permit simultaneous backwashing of multiple-unit plants. Their filters also need extensive piping because the initiative of backwash is due to natural siphon.

On our filter we use a one-piece bolt which makes replacement quite simple. Our competition uses about twenty-five (25) pieces of wafers and spacers that are bolted together. This makes replacement very difficult.

Many of the companies in your field have already installed the Great Company Filter in their plants. All of them have been satisfied with the results of the filter. I am sure you see the many ways in which this filter could benefit your plants and cut down on operating cost.

Sir, our filters are available in many different sizes and we have one just suited for your needs.

Shall I send one of our engineers over to help you decide on just what filter you need to solve your filtering problems?

## THE PROBLEM-SOLVING PRESENTATION

Mr. Gibbs, I want to thank you for the opportunity to discuss my product and to help you find ways in which your company may benefit by using it.

I can show you how our engineers have helped some of the other companies in your field. Filtering can be a major problem in the chemical business as you well know. My company is putting out a new series of filters. These filters are capable of handling many types of filtration.

We have done surveys for some of the other large chemical companies and they have found the results very satisfactory. In one company we found them using a vertical pressure filter with a 12″ diameter. The filter cost them $250,000 installed. It was functioning well but was too slow. The company was going to buy an additional filter. After our survey we advised them to buy an 18″ diameter filter. Our price was $60,000 installed. When put into use they quickly learned our filter had a flow rate in G.P.M./sq.ft. of 2.1. The filter they had been using had a flow rate in G.P.M./sq. ft. of 1.8. This has made them one of our very satisfied customers.

Sir, we would like to make a survey for your company. We are sure it would be worthwhile to you.

Okay? Thank you. Our engineers will be here Monday morning.

(Two weeks later in Mr. Gibbs' office. The survey has been completed).

SALESMAN:    Mr. Gibbs, here is a copy of the survey. In this report our engineers have pointed out what they considered a problem area in your filtration system.

PROSPECT:    Well, Mr. Mason, after reading this report I find it to be very complete and I must agree with your engineers on one point. We have been having a hard time with the filtration of the cooling water used in connection with our acid purifiers. My company engineers agree with yours and feel that the filter you suggested may be the one we need. When could your company have it installed and ready to operate?

SALESMAN:    Mr. Gibbs, we can have the filter ready to operate in six weeks. All we need is your say-so.

PROSPECT:    All right, Mr. Mason—have your men start work as soon as possible.

## DRAMATIZATION OF SALES

Because of the size of the product we are selling, the only way in which a sales presentation could be dramatized would be through the use of charts and diagrams.

In order to show the prospective customer how Great Filters would benefit his company, we have many diagrams showing cutaways of our filters. The diagrams point out the major parts of our systems. They show the simplicity of construction and explain how this helps customers save. The diagrams show why our equipment is easier to service. This is one of the reasons why, when using our equipment, customers save money. We also point out the adaptability of our filters to many different types of filtering.

These diagrams are a great help when telling a customer of the saving he will effect through the purchase of our product. We are able to show him why and how the filters operate.

## ANTICIPATED OBJECTIONS AND LIKELY ANSWERS

1. Q. Would it not be very costly for me to install the Great Company filtering system in my plant?
   A. The Great Company Filters are less costly to install than most other filters now on the market. This can be backed up by comparing our price list against those of other companies.
2. Q. Won't it require a higher trained person to operate the filters?
   A. The Great Company Filters are fully automatic. Back washing starts automatically depending on the condition of the filtration bed. This eliminates the possibility of a mistake being made by an operator.
3. Q. But if your valve is fully automatic, does this mean it can't be operated manually for special jobs?
   A. Sir, the filter is automatic—true: But when needed it can be operated manually. In fact, sir, the manual controls on this filter are more responsive than those on most manual filtering systems.
4. Q. Wouldn't this filter require more space than the other filters on the market? Wouldn't I need a larger area than I am now using?
   A. This is one feature of our filter that is completely exclusive. Our filter is a multicompartment filter. It is made of a number of small compartments. This makes it more compact than any other filter now being made. It requires less headroom and can therefore be used in places where it has not been possible to use filters before. This as you can see would enable you to utilize space which you could not before utilize.
5. Q. The cost of this filter must be great compared with that of the filters I am now using?
   A. On the contrary, sir, the installation cost and the unit cost of our filters is less than that of the filters you are now using. In fact, the cost is much less. In one instance our system saved the city of ABC, Illinois almost 50 percent of the total cost of buying and installing a filtration system. This is, of course, a great saving; but many other towns and companies have saved quite a bit by using the Great Company system.

# 15

# Depth Method Sales Strategy

## DESCRIPTION

In the third part of this text one can see the continuum of sales methods, ranging from the extreme of the completely salesman-oriented canned talk to the opposite extreme of the completely customer-oriented, problem-solving or mood selling approach. All of these presentations were illustrated primarily in their pure form. In practice they do overlap, blend, and intermingle but generally at random and without premeditated design or purpose.

Depth selling, as it is taught in a few leading graduate business schools, combines the best features of all the other selling methods but does so with forethought and intention. The salesman analyzes his individual sales prospect and problem, creatively thinks of as many of the various combinations possible in his selling methods, and mentally projects their applications into the future. He decides from the few likely probabilities which method to apply at each stage of his sales plan. This effective salesman always has his personal goal firmly in his mind—to sell more of his goods and services to more people who can truly benefit by their purchase. He is a positive "take-charge" person who can diplomatically get others to work with him to get things done. He is responsible to his customer, to his boss, and equally to the factory and service people who depend on his sales at a fair profit for their livelihood. He is the sales professional who runs the team of experts from his own company and he calls for individuals to support him when and where he feels it is necessary. He is the expert who not only knows how to sell but also knows why his persuasive efforts will succeed in a particular application.

## EXTENT USED

The successful salesmen in almost every field—consumer, retail, whole-sale, manufacturer, door-to-door, inside or outside selling—are usually the experienced professionals who are strongly motivated to succeed and to keep on succeeding. Every prospect is a personal challenge to their individual talent and ability to make a new friend, build confidence, and get the order. These men most often will use a combination method of presenting their persuasive message and they will vary it according to the individual prospect at any particular time. They know from personal experience that some things will have a better chance for success with one prospect than the usual or standard company method. Looking back at some of the selling fields already illustrated, one will readily see that different methods of presenting the persuasive message were not only possible in each case but often were desirable. Depth selling can be utilized in practically every field of persuasion as the successful professionals have proven.

## Selling to the Consumer

A successful insurance salesman who normally uses a memorized talk might study a prospect and feel that this businessman will listen and act only on the advice of an old friend. The salesman will search out a mutual friend and study the businessman's likes, dislikes, and ambitions and later arrange an informal meeting such as a lunch. His words and actions will emphasize everything the two men have in common, particularly as it relates to their life experiences, to establish a similarity to the perceiver and illustrate how they think alike and have comparable ambitions and goals. He will arrange a number of such meetings and actually woo the prospect with praise and attention. At each meeting he will endeavor to learn more about his prospect's predispositions and personal ambitions as well as to increase friendship and build confidence. When he feels he has a legitimate appeal for life insurance, he will build a custom sales presentation for this particular businessman and he will establish a setting or situation where the subject will come up naturally and smoothly, if possible will be brought up by the prospect himself. As one friend to another, the salesman will present his message in a manner of giving honest advice. Assuming the proposal has merit for this businessman at this time, the prospect will selectively perceive and retain the salient points that have the greatest appeal for him. Since he is so predisposed, he will probably check with the mutual friend for confirmation of his opinion of the salesman's character and honesty although he will in fact be tending to do what he wants to do —buy from his new friend.

Notice, while the actual sales message may be memorized or may follow a predetermined formula, the entire sales presentation includes learning what the prospect wants and how the product or service can better satisfy it, building up a trust and friendship for the persuader, and involving the prospect in a role-playing conversational situation. The ultimate objective is to sell insurance, to be sure, but the professional salesman here uses the processes of persuasion to aid in making a friend and then helping the friend achieve something he wants in life. If a salesman uses this depth approach, or combined sales method, in consumer products or services, it has an effect very much like the repeat sales in industrial selling in that the buyer gains confidence in the salesman and gives him introductions to other friends, referrals and leads to additional prospects. Once the prospect is persuaded to do what he knows is best in his own interests, persuaded in an acceptable manner by his own standards, he then gains confidence in the salesman and will try to help his new friend get additional legitimate sales.

## Selling to the Retailer

The salesman employed by one tire manufacturer has the duties and responsibilities of helping the local franchised tire dealer manage his business profitably. This includes modern approaches to merchandising, buying and pricing, personnel management, advertising, promotion and display, customer relations and services, and often training the dealer's salesmen, providing materials for sales meetings, and technical aid in advertising layout and copywriting. It may on occasion include advice on funding his accounts receivable and equipment and many other basic independent retailer functions. This salesman must be more expert in the management of a retail operation than his dealers. His investigation and analysis of the various problems of one retailer must be thorough and his recommendations must be sound and practical, and yet he must aid the retailer without seeming to tell him how to run his own business. This is selling tires in depth! If the dealer is successful, the manufacturer's representative will move more of his tires. Whatever the salesman can do to make the dealer more successful, he should do. His effort, his goal, is identical with that of the dealer. He becomes the technical authority, working for the dealer, to increase volume, efficiency, and dealer profits.

Very often the franchised dealer is a former manufacturer's representative himself and he will be expert in this field although, as times goes on, more and more out of date. It takes a tactful and intelligent young representative to tell the old timer what and how to change in order to keep up with a changing market in highly competitive times. The individual dealer may be more interested in maintaining a good name in his community than he is in earning a higher profit. The pride of ownership may indeed be a stronger motive in this individual than making money. If the manufacturer's representative recognizes this motive, he may stimulate the dealer's interest in sponsoring local events which will enhance the prestige of the dealer. Extra profits will enable this dealer to do more sponsoring; hence the attempt to increase sales volume is well justified on altruistic grounds.

Each dealer normally will have slightly different background, personal experience, business problems, local market conditions, and personal ambitions for himself and his family. Each dealer is predisposed to behave in a predictable manner when exposed to stress caused by conflict. By knowing each account, the salesman can avoid initiating upsetting ideas and conversation and he can truly help the dealers by suggesting improvements they are likely to listen to, understand, and accept. Knowing what the dealer wants, the salesman can offer legitimate services which will help him satisfy his wants to a greater extent and he can plan his sales presentation in a manner that is likely to have the greatest appeal to the particular dealer. The manufacturer's representative can move more of his merchandise, help the dealer to become a greater success, and, over the years, develop many true friendships.

## Selling to the Manufacturer

The man representing an international oil company might attempt to sell machinery lubrication products to an industrial concern. After investigating and analyzing the general market, the salesman studies the larger prospects and narrows his attention to one prospect at a time. For a particular concern he tries to learn such technical things as what their machines are, what their breakdown experience has been, what competitive products are being used, and how his product or knowledge or service can be better. Finally he attempts to find out, not who issues the order, but who makes the buying decision for lubrication products in this particular plant. Some of this information can be learned before the first call but more often it will be gained as the result of a series of calls.

Once he learns the identity of the man who makes the buying decision, the salesman attempts to find out as much as possible about that individual's predisposition and what it is he expects or would like the lubrication products and service to accomplish. Knowing what criteria will be used to judge the product and service, the salesman can then build his presentation. If a problem exists, clearly he can offer his technical services to help solve it, but if none are apparent then he must find out where and how he can improve service or better satisfy the prospect's needs. Incidentally, most buyers will not switch to a new supplier simply to get a lower price although they may use such a quotation to force their existing supplier to lower his price. The new salesman may find one single lubrication product of his which serves a particular need better than the existing supplier's product. If he bases his appeal on the motivating factor within the prospect—such as time between changes or less downtime—he may easily gain a small order.

Once his product and service in this limited application have proven valid and reliable, the salesman is more readily accepted and believed on future occasions. On each subsequent call he may bring the buyer useful technical information such as the type of equipment and machinery used in similar plants or new production methods being tried by others. In any event, he attempts to build friendship and legitimate confidence in his technical knowledge and interest in the prospect's welfare as well as to get to know the buyer on a personal basis. Should the existing supplier fail to perform on product or service such as delivery, the newer salesman will be in an excellent position to get an order. More likely, however, the existing supplier will gradually neglect the customer, making less and less personal calls for what the old salesman considers automatic business. Gradually the new salesman will supply more and more of the repeat orders.

The depth salesman investigates the situation and the buyer, searching for any area in which he can offer a legitimate service. Once he gains some acceptance, he increases his knowledge of what the prospect is attempting to do and continually searches for alternate ways to do it better. In the process, he builds the buyer's confidence in him and increases his own image as an authority in his field. He builds friendship and mutual trust upon which later persuasion attempts will be based.

## CHARACTERISTICS OF DEPTH SELLING

Depth selling, as a method of presenting a persuasive message, is characterized by four basic points. It is customer oriented in its overall plan of persuasion but it is flexible enough to include stimulus-response, formula method, and want-satisfaction whenever and wherever applicable. It is based upon building long-range confidence in the salesman's motives and trust in his technical knowledge. It is a service-oriented approach aimed at satisfying the business needs of the customer, solving business problems, and building a satisfying personal relationship ranging far afield of the salesman's products. Finally, characteristic of the depth selling method is the emphasis on discretion rather than on sincerity. While a buyer may honestly need professional advice in some phase of running his business, pure sincerity may very well anger him and cause him to disregard everything the salesman may say both in the field of his technical advice and in the product he is attempting to sell. The professional salesman using this method of persuasion is well aware of the limits the prospect sets regarding the areas he will either seek or listen to advice. The limits may change as the two men get to know each other better but the professional salesman makes no attempt to change the buyer's behavior other than getting an order and helping the buyer when he asks for help.

The professional salesman knows his own product as well as his own plant engineers and he can readily state why its technical features are as they are. He knows the product applications and limitations. He knows his competitor's products, their advantages and disadvantages. He knows his market and keeps abreast of developments in which his customers are likely to be interested.

The professional salesman knows why the predisposition of the businessman may influence his acceptance of what is done or said. Before he plans his approach to a particular businessman, he learns as much as he can about the man, his company, and his industry. He learns as much, that is, as is consistent with what he is attempting to do and gauges his time and efforts accordingly. He will then know if the businessman is relatively old or young and possibly how he feels about his age, his role in the business, and his family image. He now knows why certain appeals are likely to be effective and can project the probability of subsequent events in the sales plan based upon which initial appeal he selects. With this forethought he can intelligently decide what his approach will be based on and why it should work.

The professional salesman's knowledge of the process of selective exposure in persuasion leads him to think through the various ways he might get an audience with this particular prospect and how each way will affect subsequent events in the overall sales plan. From his investigation of the businessman he knows why some approaches will be better than others to gain an audience and he can narrow down the alternatives and select the one that will be most likely to succeed both initially and in its subsequent effect.

The depth salesman understands the process of selective perception and therefore he knows why this particular businessman is more apt to see and understand one type of presentation than others. He is aware of the very short time span of attention and the effects of the refractory phase in selling. He is adept at drawing a businessman out and getting him to talk about himself and his business problems. He can see beyond the immediate prospective sale to the ultimate goals and purposes of his prospect.

All of the above processes are thought through before attempting to approach a particular businessman at a particular time. A tentative sales plan is constructed based upon the available known facts. When he makes his first move, this salesman does so with deliberation and confidence. As he makes his initial contact and moves into his opening questions and statements he adds facts to his earlier investigation. He keeps an open mind and regularly weighs additional known facts against various alternative plans of action. He encourages the prospect to talk of his needs, wants, and desires and the salesman tries to figure out how to best satisfy them. Gently and with discretion he makes the prospect aware of his needs and how this salesman's product will help to satisfy these needs at this time. The salesman is in a position to judge whether a one-sided argument or a two-sided argument will be more persuasive at this time and he can act with confidence accordingly. He balances his emotional appeals through suggestion with clear, concise logic. He proves himself a qualified expert in his field by both his questions and his presentation. He makes the prospect aware of his genuine concern for the prospect's best interests and benefits as well as the proper application of his product. Everything he does builds the image of a likable expert who is primarily interested in the buyer's benefit. He builds confidence every step of the way.

Knowing the processes of selective hearing and retention, this salesman checks as he goes along and can determine why some points seem blocked and what to do about getting them accepted. The entire sales interview is a two-way friendly business conversation with attention directed primarily to the businessman's needs and how best to satisfy them. If there is any legitimate fact that the buyer needs to make an intelligent decision and the salesman cannot supply it at that time, there is no pressure or attempt to ride roughshod over the objection. If the prospect has a legitimate reason for not buying that the salesman cannot answer, he openly admits it. He keeps the door open for exposure on subsequent visits and allows himself time for more investigation and study.

The professional salesman looks at pressure as a continuous line from high positive pressure, such as the salesman-oriented, fast-talking presentation, through zero pressure in the center to low or negative pressure such as the lengthy, customer-oriented, "cabbage-to-kings" conversation. Each customer and each sales interview with the same customer may require more

Courtesy: International Business Machines Corp., Armonk, N.Y.

**FIG. 11. A sales representative discusses possible application of his office machines with a customer.**

or less of either positive or negative pressure. For example, some people on occasion love to argue and bargain. They will not respect the salesman if he does not accommodate them and play their little game, if he gives in too quickly or is too firm and too rigid. The professional salesman knows his prospect and why he should vary the sales pressure on a given occasion. The key to the type and degree of pressure is that the prospect should never feel he is being forced, manipulated, or used in any way against his own best interests.

The sales interview, or series of interviews, serves to build the buyer's confidence up to the point that he likes and respects the professional salesman and acknowledges that he is an expert in his field. The prospect becomes convinced that it is his own best interest that is paramount with the salesman and they are both trying to achieve the same result. With the proper mixture of emotional appeal and logic for this particular business-man at this time, there will be no feeling of undue pressure being used. He will reach the desired conclusion and act to satisfy his need. He will be persuaded to help the professional sell more of his goods and services to more people who can truly benefit by their purchase. The businessman will get into the act, play the role of the salesman, and mentally sell himself.

## ADVANTAGES OF DEPTH SELLING

Since depth selling is a combination of the various methods, it can have the sum of the advantages of each method without their disadvantages, as well as the additional benefits of many sales techniques that do not logically fit into any one of the other methods. This selling method is based upon an understanding of the psychology of persuasion and each aspect of persuading one man is given adequate thought before the pros-pect is approached. This increases the amount of exposure and perception the salesman will achieve, no matter which general selling method he later employs. Since one of its characteristics is a customer-oriented attitude, then problem solving and want-satisfaction are automatically interwoven in the sales presentation whenever applicable. The presentation is directed toward the buyer's self-interest; hence selective perception and retention are more likely to operate in favor of persuasion than against.

The depth salesman is highly sensitive to the changing moods of the prospect and can employ whatever technique best serves his purpose at a given moment. For example, he may use a stimulus-response talk to provide clear and concise logic to reinforce a prospect's emotional decision. He may use pure suggestion without logical facts to activate a prospect who indicates impulsiveness. He may quote a single but firm price and never vary from it or, on the other hand, he may quote a price intention-ally high knowing the buyer wants to bargain. Being flexible, the depth salesman's presentation can vary continuously to suit the changing ele-ments in a persuasive situation. He is not bound by a memorized talk or the arbitrary rules of a formula and can, therefore, custom-tailor his presentation to the individual prospect at the given time, place, condition, and mood.

Since building confidence is also characteristic of this type of presenta-tion, the prospect learns to recognize the salesman as an authority in his field who is trustworthy and believable. This is essential to persuasion.

Building friendship is also characteristic of depth selling and this, too, aids persuasion, primarily because the salesman becomes similar to the prospect in some fundamental way. In any professional selling, this similarity to the perceiver is established in order to gain additional leads and recommendations or repetitive orders as the case may be. The salesman is honest; however, he exercises discretion in what he says or omits so as not to lose an order—by being too critical or telling the prospect how to run his own business, for example. The depth salesman is fully aware of his own goal— to sell more goods to more people who can truly benefit—and will maintain faith in his product and company. He will be loyal to his customer but equally loyal to his own company and aware of his responsibilities to the many people who back up his efforts.

## PREPARATION OF THE SALESMAN

To be properly trained in the depth selling method and to cultivate an attitude of fair-mindedness and the wisdom of discretion, a man must be educated, responsible, and mature. His formal training should include knowledge of products, particularly as they relate to customer benefits and the technical qualities which substantiate the claimed benefits; knowledge of the policies and procedures of the selling company so that he understands why things are done as they are and can cooperate to achieve the stated purposes; knowledge of the selling company's history, reputation, and objectives so that he can relate his own job to his responsibility to others in the company; and finally, knowledge of the market, which includes both customers and competitors, so that he can recognize potential prospects, locate and contact the influential buyer, and handle objections smoothly.

Beyond knowledge, but equally as important, the training should include the development of skills such as the psychology of persuasion applied to the various methods of selling; the skill of servicing an account, representing the customer, and making legitimate adjustments when needed; the skill of operating equipment, giving demonstrations, and teaching personnel of new customers how to use the equipment properly so they can obtain the maximum benefit from their purchase.

Work habits should also be included in the formal training program because depth selling is perhaps the most varied, flexible, and time-consuming method used. The salesman should become an adept analyst of each individual prospect, his potential, and the related time and effort to devote to each one. He should become a self-starter, an independent and industrious worker, a problem solver with imagination, and a continuous student of people and persuasion. Such things as routing and frequency of visiting customers and prospects should be taught so that the salesman understands why he is told to do such things and can cooperate because he sees it is in his own best interest to do so and not because some person in the home office arbitrarily said so.

This leads to the final element in preparing a man to use depth selling: creating proper attitudes. This should be woven through the entire training program and serve as the salesman's motivation to become outstanding. Knowing what purposes he serves, why such purposes, goals, policies, and procedures are of value to him and to society and knowing how to do the job correctly can often motivate a salesman more than money. Personal recognition, friendships with fellow workers and with customers, and the personal pride in a job well done are equally important in establishing proper sales attitudes and motivations.

The preparation of salesmen to use the depth selling method should include knowledge, skills, work habits, and attitudes and the training should be a continuing program. It is a large job both in time and management effort. Successful salesmen in many fields have been self-educated in this method through their own experience of trial and error. However, as company knowledge and attention are directed to these training problems, much improvement and time savings can be realized.

## EFFECTIVENESS OF DEPTH SELLING

Evaluating the depth selling method is difficult because, in relation to the total number of salesmen, very few men use this method. However, analysis of observed sales behavior, speeches, and written articles by successful men indicates the depth selling method is particularly effective. Observing individual salesmen on a number of calls for several days indicates the highly successful men more often than not use the depth selling method. With premeditation they analyze the individual prospect and with designed purpose they select a selling method for each different case. By analyzing the top 20 percent of a sales force, the men who write 75 percent of the orders, and observing many of these highly individualistic and successful salesmen with their prospects, one is struck by the salesman's sensitivity to his customer and his flexibility in the attempt at persuasion. Listening to sales managers boast of their own sales success, one is quickly aware of the imaginative versatility of these men and how they personally employ the depth selling method. Analysis of sales literature also leads one to believe there is no single way to sell successfully but a blending of methods, usually with forethought and design, to go beyond the simple application of product and into a problem-solving area.

Occasional success stories of a salesman using a shortcut to easy sales generally represent a misleading appraisal of the actual facts. Honeyed words and false promises sooner or later are seen through and while the salesman may have gained an order he has also lost a customer. If a sales message is irritating and the prospect resents it, he may still buy the product due to an immediate need but he will have no product loyalty whatsoever and will be highly susceptible to counterpersuasion. For example, in the sale of highly competitive drugs and medications, studies have shown that the final buying influence is not the detail man giving his six-minute memorized talk but other doctors. These influential doctors probably have known the local detail man for years and have established friendship with and confidence in him. These doctors read more of the literature on experimental drugs and keep their knowledge current. They will give the respected detail man time and ask pertinent questions and will understand his message. These doctors are the final persuaders of their fellow doctors and the detail man simply operates on a memory association basis. Does your patient need cortisone? Remember the XYZ Drug Company!

Most highly effective salesmen appear to use a premeditated analysis of their prospect and the business, an imaginative choice of alternative courses of action and appeals, their projected probabilities, and, finally, the decision to act based upon knowledge and experience. Once begun on a given course for a particular businessman, these effective salesmen can and do change as additional knowledge is gained or the situational conditions change. This is effective depth selling.

As Harold J. Leavitt wrote.*

In a long-term relationship, when A knows he must go on living or working with B *after* he has tried to change B's behavior, he may proceed with caution no matter what his personal ethics. His own dependency on the others in the relationship serves as a built-in governor on his influence techniques, even if his conscience doesn't.

## HOLLY MERRITT AND COMPANY, CPA SERVICES

While there is an obvious need for accounting services in business and industry there is also tremendous competition between consulting companies.

---

* Reprinted from *Managerial Psychology* by Harold J. Leavitt by permission of The University of Chicago Press. Copyright 1958 by the University of Chicago.

The ideal client is one who has outgrown his old accounting system but, due to the pressing problems of growth, has not studied the accounting problem. Substantial savings can be achieved for a client which easily justify the consultant's fee. Partners in the accounting firm often sell this service, beginning with only an introduction from a mutual business friend. In this case, Mr. Richard Bayer, partner in the Holly Merritt Company, has made a telephone appointment with Mr. John Martin, principal in a manufacturing business. The initial interview proceeds as follows:

Good afternoon Mr. Martin! My name is Richard Bayer of the Holly Merritt Company, certified public accountants. I'm very pleased to meet you. I appreciate your allotting this time for us to get together and I assure you that our discussion will prove to be a profitable one for you.

As you undoubtedly know, no matter what kind of business we're in, we all have two major problems with which to deal. First, we must run our business as profitably as possible; and second, we wish to plan our tax status so as to pay as little of our profits as possible to the tax authorities.

In your particular case, your everyday concern will be to see that your production meets your orders on time; that shipments are made on time; that every sale is invoiced; that your receivables are collectible and collected; that you have enough money at the proper time to pay your suppliers, to purchase new equipment and materials propitiously; and last but not least —that you come out of all this with a worthwhile profit.

Our services are designed to assist you in accomplishing all of the foregoing so that the fees which we receive are more than made up for by the money which we will save you.

How do we accomplish this?

First, we will set up your books and operations so that they complement each other and serve to protect all your assets such as cash, receivables, and inventory.

Second, we will help you plan a budget so that you have money when you need it in order to take advantage of discounts, material and equipment purchases, and plant expansion.

Third, we will continuously review your factory, office, and bookkeeping operations for revision as your needs change.

Fourth, we will help you set up your corporate structure and operations in a manner which will afford you the lowest amount of taxes to be paid.

And now, Mr. Martin, we've done enough talking. It's time we got down to work. If you will be so kind as to direct me to the record-keeping department, you can resume your duties and I'll get the profit ball rolling. By the end of the week I can have some preliminary suggestions for improvement for you.

The next week, Mr. Bayer returned by appointment to present his findings to the prospect. Here is his presentation:

Good morning Mr. Martin. Our report has been completed and I would like to preface it by expressing my gratitude for the invaluable cooperation extended to me by you and your staff.

Because the main objectives in instituting our investigation were to help you increase your profit and decrease your taxes, we have concentrated our efforts on reviewing your record-keeping system and your corporate structure.

After reviewing your record-keeping system, we concluded that you have outgrown it to some extent and it is not doing the kind of job you want it to do. It is also too costly.

All your records are being kept manually; the volume of work involved requires excessive labor hours and increases the possibilities of errors. For example, at present your bookkeepers prepare the invoices, record them in the sales journal, post to the accounts receivable ledger, and prepare the monthly statements—all in separate, time-consuming operations.

Secondly, we have concluded that your corporate structure, though expedient to you in the early years of the business, has become impractical from two standpoints. First, your increased income and expanding facilities have forced you as a Subchapter S or small business corporation to be taxed quite unfavorably. Also, as a Subchapter S corporation you are quite limited in seeking new investors to provide you with additional capital for operations and further expansion. To help alleviate the record-keeping problem, we can have several types of systems installed for you—either manual or machine aids. These aids will undoubtedly reduce your clerical costs and increase the protection of your records. We know this to be a fact as we have performed the same services for other manufacturers in your line, such as companies Crown, Zenith, and American, with whom I'm sure you are quite familiar.

As to your corporate structure, we are convinced that you should repeal your election to be taxed as a partnership and actively seek the new investment you require by increasing your capitalization through the issuance of a preferred class of stock. This step will accomplish three definitely advantageous objectives: First, it will enable you to accumulate, without tax penalties or specific reserves, $100,000 for expansion or working capital; second, it will permit you to acquire the additional investment that is necessary for your desired expansion; and third, it will require you to relinquish neither your rights in nor control of the corporation.

We know that these are giant steps we are asking you to take. But judging from the tremendous success you've accomplished in building this business to its present status, we also realize quite well that you are foresighted enough to appreciate the need for and significance of constructive change, investment, and expert advice. We would consider it a privilege to help you grow to your expectations.

# 16

# Selling to Groups and
# Team Selling Methods

Due to automation industrial selling today is more technical and complicated than ever before. This has its obvious economic effects; it also has psychological and social ramifications within a company and a community. The unit size of some orders runs well into the millions of dollars. Just to provide the physical housing and accessories for such machines can easily exceed $500,000. New technically trained personnel have to be brought in and old ones retrained. The working hours must often be changed to keep the new "monster" on a steady diet. New accounting and statistical reports are now possible and new forms often require legal approval. New production, packaging, and distribution controls are now possible. The new machines affect practically every department and every person in a business. Very few men are qualified to make intelligent buying decisions in all of these areas.

## TEAM BUYING

Team buying has evolved to fill the need for so much knowledge in so many diverse areas. The team can be a permanent organizational setup with a staff of qualified experts or it can be a temporary group composed simply of the various department heads involved in a single problem. Many large corporations have one group that tests and appraises products for their achievement of standardization. A second group decides on time priority and where replacement equipment shall be used. A third group decides when the budget will permit the expenditure. A fourth group does the actual buying after it gets requisitions properly endorsed. Each group functions in its own area of responsibility. However, the leaders often will meet regularly to maintain similar objectives and efficiency. In the normal course of events, a professional salesman follows his proposal from one group to another and he is qualified to speak as an expert in each of the fields of primary interest. His selling job—the why and how of persuasion —remains fundamentally the same.

The RCA value analysis team, mentioned in Chapter 14, is usually made up of a buyer, a mechanical engineer, an electrical engineer, a cost estimator, a production man, and a value analyst. In a group like this, no matter what the discussion, there will always be several emotionally detached people. When the engineers feel strongly about a technical point, purchasing and cost people will not be emotionally involved and will be able to consider the problem objectively. Each member begins to realize that others don't consider his hotly defended views as important as he does and he begins to take a more considered view himself.[1]

Tomorrow's more sophisticated customer and the combination of talented individuals on such buying committees demand the salesman have a deeper product knowledge, more knowledge of the customer's business, and a more sophisticated sales approach to meet the higher level of audience education. Such developments indicate tomorrow's salesman will have to be more inquisitive and more imaginative. He will work more and more with groups of specialists and he has to be prepared to address this more sophisticated audience. In order to make a clear and convincing presentation, the salesman will have to make a keener and deeper analysis of his prospective customer's needs. Since there is apt to be a larger dollar volume involved, the effort in investigation and homework is fully justified. The salesman of tomorrow will have to learn as much as he can from the engineers, scientists, comptrollers, legal, and other specialists on his own company's staff.

People who are in contact with one another in large organizations tend to form small informal groups offering members the satisfaction of sociability, spontaneity, and a sense of belonging.[2] These people must learn to get along together to be effective and they soon realize that the scientific approach is to get information from all sorts of sources. One major source of information is the vendor. For the supplier, the increasing cost of the sales call will force executives to focus their talents on larger or key accounts.

---

[1] John VandeWater, "RCA's New Concepts in Value Buying," *Purchasing*, May 18, 1964, p. 45.

[2] See George C. Homans, *The Human Group* (New York: Harcourt Brace & Co., 1950); also A. Zaleznik, *Worker Satisfaction and Development: A Case Study of Work and Social Behavior in a Factory Group* (Boston: Harvard Business School, Division of Research, 1956).

## SELLING TO A GROUP OF BUSINESSMEN

By investigating the prospective company—doing the brainwork before the legwork—the salesman knows what the proper sequence of contact and approval must be. He learns as much as possible about each of the individuals he expects to contact and he relates their predisposition to the area for which they are responsible. He plans his approach and initial appeals on the basis of his understanding of selective exposure. Each group wants a different type of information and the emphasis must change as the proposal moves along. From each contact, however, the salesman draws out additional information about this company and each of the groups and individual contacts. The salesman may use many combinations of sales techniques as his proposal moves along, depending upon whom he is dealing with at a given moment. Still his story must be consistent and check out 100 percent true and sincere whenever these various contacts get together without the salesman. Since the effective salesman is basically honest and completely sincere, he need have no fear in this respect. For example, the production and distribution people will be interested in how the product works, how it will fit in with their existing systems and services, and how they can benefit by using the product. The accounting people will be more interested in how the product will pay for itself, how long it will take to write it off their books, and how payment can be made to their best advantage. The purchasing people will be most interested in learning why this product is superior to any less expensive but similar product and whether it will reduce complaints back to them about machine downtime and service calls. The professional salesman knows more about each of these areas than his individual contacts in the prospect's company. He can speak with confidence and direct their attention to the area in which they are basically interested. He has no need to contradict himself or to be insincere.[3]

Every step of the way the professional builds the prospect's confidence in him as an authority in this field. He preplans his approach and every step of the sale to use the processes of selective exposure, selective perception, and selective retention to his advantage. Normally he must use a two-sided argument because of the extended time involved and the size of the order, which will encourage competitive bids and arguments. He attempts to get each contact into his selling act at the contact's own level and at the

---

[3] For the sociological point of view on group and other relationship problems in industry see Burleigh B. Gardner and David G. Moore, *Human Relations in Industry* (Homewood, Illinois: Richard D. Irwin, Inc., 1955).

next level. For example, he might say, "Thanks for your approval, Mr. Production Manager. I wonder if you could suggest how I might handle this proposal when I talk to your people in accounting next week?" Whenever he gets approval, the professional finds some way to reinforce the favorable opinion through role playing and how to enlist that contact in his cause and wishing for his success.[4]

Once he has successfully run the buying maze of such a large company, the professional can return with confidence to meet many old friends within the corporation. He can present additional products and gain acceptance more easily. He has switched from being an outsider viewed with suspicion to a favored source. He has earned the prospect's respect for his honesty and sincerity and he jealously protects the confidence that the buyers place in him. He is the expert to whom they look for any information in his field and he serves them in any way he can.

## PSYCHOLOGY OF PERSUADING A GROUP

Persuading a group of people is much more difficult than persuading an individual. However, the theorems of persuasion discussed earlier were tested on groups in laboratory conditions and the same principles do apply. Each individual in a group has certain predisposing ideas and knowledge which will influence how he individually reacts to any attempt at persuasion. The selective processes of exposure, perception, and retention will all normally operate to protect the individual from change. It is the salesman's duty to reach the individuals in the group and encourage each man to speak out so that the salesman knows what each one wants. The salesman can then use the selective processes to aid and abet persuasion. Even if the group is sitting together in one room, the salesman should get each one to voice his opinion or objection sufficiently for the salesman to understand the individual.[5] He should then make separate appeals to the unique needs of each person and present a two-sided argument which is discreetly fair and honest. He should make the benefits of his product alive and real to each man and make the need seem so great that delay in buying will be more expensive than ordering today.

In other words, when selling to a group, the professional salesman sights in with a rifle and persuades each individual separately. He does not blast

---

[4] The research on communications nets can be found in: Alex Bavelas, "Communication Patterns in Task Oriented Groups," in H. Lasswell and D. Lerner, *The Policy Sciences* (Stanford, Calif.: Stanford University Press, 1951).

[5] For technical summary of research on communications net see M. Glanzer and R. Glaser, *Techniques for the Study of Team Structure and Behavior* (Pittsburgh: American Institute for Research, 1957), Part II.

with a shotgun of mass communication and rely on the law of averages. The professional salesman uses his knowledge of the predisposition of each person he contacts to have the selective processes of persuasion work in his favor.

## TEAM SELLING[6]

A product or market may be so technical and complex that one man cannot possibly be an expert in all areas. A number of large corporations have evolved team selling to serve the many facets of buying problems. Ideally, it works like this: The professional salesman in the field learns of a problem in an area in which his company should be interested. He feeds back this information to his research and development people and maintains contact between them and his prospects. Once a product is developed, the salesman is a key man in determining the marketing policy. When the product has been field tested and is finally ready to be sold, the professional salesman heads up the selling team of experts. He has first-hand knowledge of his prospect; therefore, it is he that designs the overall selling strategy for this particular account. He knows which experts he will probably need and decides which personalities will best serve a particular part of his sales plan. From here on to getting the order, the professional salesman operates exactly as he would on a team of buyers except that he normally has one or more assistants at his elbow to fill in the gaps in his own technical knowledge.

The professional salesman might call on his engineer to go along on one call and his accounting expert to go along on another call on the same prospect. Since these experts are not trained as salesmen, the group leader explains the purpose of the specific call and how it fits into his overall sales plan. His expert must understand the persuasion processes at least well enough to know when to be silent and when to let the professional salesman field the questions and direct the prospect's attention. The professional salesman is in charge of team selling because he knows the "why" of persuading a particular prospect. Those that know the "how to" will be called into the sales plan as the professional team captain sees fit.

## TEAM SELLING IN THE CONSTRUCTION INDUSTRY

Several men working together for a single large order is common in highly technical fields or where the product is custom designed and built to

---

[6] Leon Morse, "The Sound of A Different Drummer," *Dun's Review and Modern Industry*, August, 1963, p. 26. Morse points out that team selling is a movement that is snowballing and he cites a number of specific companies using this sales strategy.

the customer's specifications. An item such as the common brick used in the construction industry can often be sold successfully by team effort. Normally the future owner hires an architect to design a building and the architect specifies the exact materials he desires. He then solicits bids from general contractors to do the entire job. These contractors, in turn, solicit bids from subcontractors to do the plumbing work, the electrical work, the masonry work, and so on for the various trades. The mason contractor or the general contractor may purchase the brick but it must meet the architect's specifications. The architect may be strong and insist on exactly what he had originally specified or he may be weak and accept a number of substitutes as equal in quality, color, and finish. Occasionally the building owner will insist on a certain material and the architect and various contractors may go along with the decision. In most cases the architect will insist on the specified brick; hence he is the one to be persuaded for future jobs. When the architect is not insistent, the influential buying decision may be made by any one of a number of men in any one of several firms.

In team selling, one man may spend most of his time contacting several hundred architects and doing missionary work to get his brick specified on future jobs. He will have the technical knowledge necessary to discuss various contruction materials, methods, and costs and he can advise the architect on such technical phases as the economical use of reinforced brick masonry or using clay masonry insulated cavity walls, for example. While his goal is to have the architect specify his brick, his discussion might easily include such things as interest rates, price trends, depreciation and maintenance costs, income taxes, initial construction costs, framing and foundation problems, building space occupancy, speed of erection, air-conditioning costs, heating costs, insurance rates, and real estate taxes. The ultimate cost of building walls can vary from about $5.00 per square foot of wall area for masonry cavity wall to $9.00 for metal panel wall to $30 for double plate glass. Clearly the esthetic value of whatever type of construction is chosen will vary with the amount of money available. All of these factors must be appraised before the architect makes his decision to specify a particular material. As the salesman gives such aid and service to the architect, he builds confidence and friendship so that when the actual choice of brick is to be made his suggestions are more readily accepted. The architect may then specify his color and finish for face brick, for example.

Once the general contract is awarded, a second salesman in the team may already be on friendly terms with the successful bidder, as most of this man's time is spent getting to know contractors and serving their interests and needs. The emphasis here is on construction scheduling and initial costs, and discussions might center on such things as the latest construction methods and material handling equipment. The contractor is interested in spending the work and in anything that will reduce his building costs. If he has learned from experience that this salesman gives accurate delivery information, that he is reliable and trustworthy, he will be more apt to order from him than from another less familiar salesman. If the masonry subcontractor is directed to buy his own materials, the same salesman in the team would normally contact him in the same manner.

Occasionally the ultimate owner of the building may intercede in behalf of a friend to request a certain manufacturer's brick. This contact is normally maintained by a third man in the selling team who has many influential friends in high company positions. He is the man that keeps in touch with old college and fraternity friends, joins the right athletic and country clubs, and is constantly in the proper social activity making friends wherever he goes. This executive salesman may spellbind a social audience with a discussion about the historical background of the brick industry, going back to the time of Sargon of Akkad, founder of the Chaldean Empire 4,000 years before Christ. However innocuously he does it, this salesman gently makes all of his friends and contacts aware of his business without seeming to talk business. When he hears about any construction activity, he attempts to influence the owner, on a friendship basis, to request or recommend his product.

In this simple example, the three basic areas of contact are quite different and yet complementary. The team focus is on people, not on product. They attempt to persuade men in business on each job as it moves along from one buying influential to another. While any one member of the team may get the order, usually it is a result of their combined efforts. Ultimately price, quality, and delivery are the deciding factors. However, in this highly competitive field it is common for five or six suppliers to submit nearly equal bids, and the salesmen themselves make the difference. In practice, of course, each man in the selling team over the years will develop many friends among both architects and contractors. The nice guys get the order—those salesmen the owner, the architect, and the contractors like to work with.

Team selling was used initially in the competitive building material field of metal facade panels. Manufacturers of stainless steel, porcelain enamel steel, and aluminum and gold anodized aluminum panels had to get city building codes changed before architects could specify their materials. This pure missionary type of selling went on simultaneously with team selling as illustrated here.

Courtesy: National Cash Register Co., Dayton, Ohio.

FIG. 12. A salesman demonstrates the applications of his machine to a group of department heads.

## TEAM SELLING AUTOMATED EQUIPMENT[7]

In the field of material handling, automation has complicated the sales effort to the extent that several selling teams must often work together to integrate their various systems. For example, in one large bakery recently constructed a computer system makes a continuous check of the production process every 15 seconds. The complete system took two years to develop and meshes automatic baking and other plant operations with those of the business office. The data-control center also masterminds a

---

[7] This is adapted, with the kind permission of the editors, from Thomas J. Murray, "Systems Selling: Industrial Marketing's New Tool," *Dun's Review and Modern Industry*, October, 1964 p. 51. Describing the Honeywell 610 digital computer control system at the kitchens of Sara Lee in Deerfield, Illinois.

warehouse as large as a football field. Snapping out 80,000 instructions every three seconds, the computer directs the flow of these materials into the plant, memorizes these movements so that inventory can be updated, stacks as many as 7 million cakes, picks six orders concurrently, and prints a record of each shipment for the business office.

Designing and building the complicated system taxes the ingenuity and patience of architects, engineers, consultants, and designers. The sales team of the automated warehousing equipment company, for example, had to work with the sales team of the solid state computer which controls the entire operation. Each equipment supplier had to use a battery of experts and often to conduct experiments in untried areas because this was to be the most advanced plant in the food-processing industry. The cost of the complex, some $22 million, justified the team selling efforts.

A team effort is often required to install automated equipment properly because so many people must be trained to feed the "monster" data in the form it can understand. The sales engineer directs the training purposes and objectives; however, he generally has a staff of teachers who may spend from several months to a year or more doing the actual instructing of the buyer's personnel. Often, at the discretion of the sales engineer, a technical expert is loaned to the buyer for a year or two after the initial training period to insure proper utilization of the expensive equipment.

## TEAM SELLING OF SPECIALTIES

Large prospects in many fields often demand more service than any one salesman can perform. For example, in specialty selling such as office furniture and filing equipment large buyers often demand a unique design exclusively for themselves. Design and production engineers must be brought into the selling situation. Experts must lay out the floor plans to obtain the optimum use of available space, heating, ventilation, and lighting. Interior decorators are generally used to determine wall colors, floor colors, and furniture colors as well as to select draperies, carpets, and upholstery materials. Specialists in record management are occasionally used to create a retention and destruction schedule in conjunction with working out the filing problems and flow of work in an office. If the account is buying for a number of locations on a national basis, the shipping and delivery personnel, decentralized warehouse, and installation personnel must all be coordinated. Normal it is the sales executive who selects which expert will be used on a particular job and at what time. He coordinates their activities both before and after the sale. While he captains his selling team, he also represents the customer to his own office and protects the customer's best interests in areas such as quality, price, delivery, installation, service, and necessary training of personnel.

## REASONS FOR TEAM SELLING

Due to the tremendous growth and accumulation of knowledge, there has been a natural trend toward specialization. It is often quicker and more effective to select men who are good salesmen and teach them the technicalities their business requires than it is to attempt to teach technicians to become good salesmen. Because of this, good salesmen become the team captains who are supported when and where necessary by a staff of technical experts.

Often the problems inherent in large scale production, national distribution, installation, and service are such that one man cannot be expert in all phases. The very size of the order may be enough to tie up a company's facilities over an extended period. Delivery may have to be negotiated in a series of units to enable the plant to schedule its production time and maintain service for its other customers. Clearly, the salesman would not normally be expert in these areas and he would need help.

In some industries, a sale may require a multitude of details which must be analyzed and then synthesized. The sheer bulk of work involved may be too great for any one man; hence he is assigned a staff to work under his direction. In fire and casualty insurance, for example, the underwriter may direct his field engineers to study factories in several states in an attempt to reduce poor risks and improve safety for one customer.

Finally, team selling has evolved as a premeditated method of persuasion because of the large geographic areas where a single customer may do business. If purchasing is decentralized or if orders can be placed locally at each of several plants and offices, clearly the selling company should coordinate its efforts and records in order to keep track of friends within the customer's office as they are transferred and promoted. A testimonial from one division manager is often very influential with another division manager. If, on the other hand, purchasing is centralized, that is, all orders are issued only from the home office, then the more requisitions from the field that specify a particular brand, the more apt the home office will be to look favorably on that product. Once the product is purchased, proper installation, training, and service at the various field locations will aid future attempts at persuasion.

## CHARACTERISTICS OF TEAM SELLING

Team selling, as the name implies, is a group effort usually coordinated by an experienced and very capable sales executive. It may involve several salesmen attempting to persuade different men of the same company or of different companies working on a common job. It usually involves a staff of technical specialists who may provide advice, appraise a problem, or handle the tremendous amount of details involved in some selling situations.

The executive salesman who directs the team effort generally uses the depth selling technique and varies the approach depending upon the situation and people involved. For example, he might direct a group of salesmen in field offices to call on all branches of a particular company and give identical sales presentations to plant managers. He might arrange a business luncheon between himself and several key executives in the home office of the prospect. He might direct one of his own plant engineers to contact one of the prospect's engineers to study a given problem. Every step is premeditated and selected with knowledge and purpose so that little or nothing is left to hit-and-miss chance or to the law of averages. Selling equipment that costs millions of dollars is most often depth selling on a team basis.

## ADVANTAGES OF TEAM SELLING

Clearly the primary advantage of team selling is that the proper knowledge and effort can be brought to bear to aid in persuading men in business. Since the knowledge and effort required is often beyond the limits of any one human being, a staff of experts can be utilized to create the feeling of authority and trustworthiness so essential to persuasion. The executive salesman attempts to establish friendly relations with each of the buying influentials and this also aids in persuasion.

The company using team selling has better control and direction of its salesmen and the type of business it wants solicited. The executive salesman who captains the team also serves as a trainer for the men under him and he gets to know personally many of the important people of his own company. He learns the practical limitations and facilities of his company and this experience makes the team captain an excellent prospect for top executive jobs. Fortunately, there is a growing trend toward such placement, so that there is room at the top for effective men.

The customer gains by receiving the proper analysis of his problems by experts in each technical field involved. He gains nationwide service as required and very often has the product tailored to suit his individual needs. He gains the advice of recognized authorities and very often saves considerable money by instituting recommended systems, procedures, and equipment which may be incidental to the main product under consideration.

When properly directed, team selling can be effective and economical for both the customer and the selling company. Strict cost accounting should be utilized to keep track of the amount of time spent by the many individuals involved. With the cost facts known, intelligent decisions can be made regarding allowable time for study of problems or training customer personnel, for example. Since the buyer ultimately pays for all the services rendered, he too should be interested in keeping track of and controlling all selling costs.

## PREPARATION FOR TEAM SELLING[8]

The individual salesman who directs the team selling effort must be trained for depth selling and must, in addition, develop some broader character traits. Depth selling, as previously noted, requires a mature, responsible, well-educated man who is trained in knowledge of the product, knowledge of the company policy and procedure, knowledge of the company history, reputation, and objectives, and knowledge of the market. In addition to knowledge, this man needs to develop the fundamental skills of persuasion, servicing accounts, operating the equipment, and teaching others. Being responsible and mature, he will have acquired the proper work habits and attitudes and will be strongly motivated to succeed.

The team captain must be prepared to handle a number of influential decision makers from one large prospective company at the same time—similar to playing five games of chess simultaneously. He must be prepared to lead his own staff of experts and assistants firmly but diplomatically and he must be prepared to coordinate many details, ideas, and problems all at the same time. Socializing with prospects and customers is used in most forms of selling. However, it is particularly important in team selling because of the high level executive contact. Taking an office manager to lunch is quite different from taking a group of vice-presidents out for a

---

[8] For an overview, see Leon Morse, "How to Create a Salesman," *Dun's Review and Modern Industry*, December, 1963, p. 46.

night on the town. This is amusingly illustrated in the following anonymous joke about the government's 1963 tax and expense account regulations:

The trouble with those boys in Washington is they've got no idea of all the
work some businessmen have to go through to get business. You can tell that
from the example they give of how a businessman ought to report his entertainment. The example they sent out reads this way: 'Lunch with Jones, Green,
Brown, and Smith, Trustees of P.Q. Real Estate Investment Board. Discussed
architectural plans submitted for proposed Claremont Apartment Building. No
other persons entertained.'

Now, that's fine and dandy, if you're entertaining trustees, but if you're
entertaining the clowns I have to do business with you've got to go into all the
sordid details or you don't get your deduction. To demonstrate that point, I am
going to read from a carbon copy of an expense account I have just turned in,
following the new Washington rules. It says:

'Dinner with Buckman, Dietzel, and O'Brien of Ajax Machinery. Discussed
retooling. Buckman says, 'Why don't we have another round, a double this
time.' More discussing and drinking. Dietzel says, 'Why don't we go to some
place where it's a little livelier.' We go to the Orangutang Club. More
discussion and drinks. Buckman says Ajax needs heavier casings. O'Brien says,
'Speaking of casing, he's been casing two girls at the corner table, and why
don't I ask them over?'

I get the girls over . . . Lucille and Roxy. More drinks, more discussion.
Dietzel starts figuring retooling costs on tablecloth. Waiter objects. Dietzel tells
off the waiter. Manager, eight diners object. O'Brien says he and Dietzel will
clean out the joint if manager and diners are not careful. Tip waiter ten bucks
not to call police and leave for Lucille's apartment.

Reach Lucille's apartment, discuss contract date with Dietzel. Lucille tells
Buckman to come in off fire escape. Buckman says him Tarzan, her Jane. Big
guy upstairs says, 'Jane better get Tarzan off fire escape or he will call police.
O'Brien sick in kitchen sink, tie caught in garbage grinder. Jerk O'Brien loose,
get Buckman off fire escape. Give Lucille $15 for miscellaneous damage, leave
for hotel.

Stop at Club Hotsy for six nightcaps and listen to Buckman's plans to get rid of
his partners while O'Brien and Dietzel are having a foot race in parking lot.
O'Brien falls asleep in shrubbery and Buckman gets into fight with the bartender.

Arrive at hotel 4:00 A.M. O'Brien, refreshed by sleep, crawls through lobby,
baying like a dog. Buckman knocks over potted plant, bust of Conrad Hilton.
Dietzel takes over elevator. 4:30: catch Dietzel and get all of them to room.
Buckman starts calling old Army buddy in San Francisco. Leave. Cost for
evening—$247.58. Return to hotel 11:00 A.M., wake Buckman and others.

Buckman asks what happened. Tell him. Get rush order to retool Ajax Machinery.'

Now that's exactly what happened and I've got the bills, three waiters, a manager, eight diners, two girls, a bartender, an elevator operator, a house detective, and a check from Dietzel to prove it. If Washington thinks I didn't have to entertain them that way to get the order, they don't know Buckman, Dietzel, and O'Brien.

## EFFECTIVENESS

If the product, system, or service to be sold is so technical or so complicated because of the size of the order, then team selling is very effective. When the prospect demands more than any one man can possibly know or physically handle, then team selling is particularly effective. Whenever a large prospect has decentralized purchasing spread over large geographic areas, team selling serves the purpose. The only true alternative to team selling in such cases is an inside service department to back up the outside salesman. The salesman then becomes the middleman and attempts to communicate his own service department's knowledge and limitations to the prospect and the prospect's needs and problems to his service department. As noted earlier, direct face-to-face communications are difficult enough but any element of indirect communications, of a third party interpreting each message back and forth, is bound to be less effective and much more time-consuming.

Team selling—bringing the staff of experts into direct contact with the prospect and his problems—is effective whenever the size of the order justifies the high selling cost. It need not be a blind gamble and the risk should be calculated precisely before such a decision is made. The selling company should set up cost accounting for its entire sales and service departments and compute exactly how much time and money can be invested to seek a large order. Once proper budgeting is established, controls should be introduced to check periodically the progress of a selling team and to aid the team captain by giving him cost facts upon which he can intelligently revise his sales strategy as the situation changes.

## SUMMARY

Team selling is most often used to get the largest orders, it is often used in technical fields, and it is occasionally used when introducing new products where missionary work with one group must go hand in hand with the direct sales effort with a second group. Technological progress, the tremendous growth of knowledge and resulting specialization, enables industry to turn out new products and materials in a seemingly endless parade. This specialization often demands a team of knowledgeable men to present a complete sales story. Automation of plant and office creates problems that appear to be quite different from any past experience; hence both the buyer and the seller have evolved teams to analyze, interpret, and synthesize the many details involved. Some buyers today are capable of placing orders large enough to tie up the entire production and distribution facilities of a supplier and this involves the seller's top management in all divisions if he is to maintain the company identity.

Team selling is characterized as bringing a staff of experts and sales assistants into direct contact with the prospect and his needs and problems. The team captain is the executive salesman who coordinates the team effort and directs its activities. Most often depth selling is the method of presentation or sales strategy used to guide the proposal through a buying maze.

The customer benefits by having the proper knowledge and resources of the supplier applied to his needs and this creates respect and builds confidence. He gains nationwide service and, due to expert advice, often realizes substantial improvements in fields not directly related to the main problem. The selling company also benefits by having its executive salesmen in direct control of the entire sales effort, which should minimize costly trial-and-error procedures by the younger salesmen as well as aid in their training. The broad experience of the team captains makes them excellent prospects for future broad management jobs.

The team captain should be a mature leader who is trained in depth selling and has the knowledge of his own company, his product, and the market. He should be skilled in persuasion, servicing accounts, operating the equipment, and in teaching others. In addition he should be adept at handling many details and people simultaneously and be able to entertain high executives socially.

Properly applied, team selling is very effective and its cost is justified by the size of resultant orders. A well-directed staff of experts and assistants who are brought into direct contact with the prospect can more quickly and effectively achieve the desired results than can a similar staff in the seller's home office.

# PART IV

# Techniques of Practical Selling

# 17

# Qualifying Prospects and the Use of Telephone and Direct Mail as Aids to Personal Selling

A problem common to many salesmen is deciding where to go on a particular day to get an order. Knowing where to find prospects, how to judge them, and how to get in touch with the right person often seems to be more than half of the sales effort. Another problem is the time wasted through trial-and-error testing of a sales message and of the salesman's ability to persuade prospects. There are telephone and direct mail techniques which can be used to pretest the effectiveness of a message and to determine the prospect's degree of awareness and conviction in advance of the personal call by a salesman.

Another reason for the increasing use of direct mail and telephone as aids to personal selling is the continuing shift of the population to the suburbs and the ever expanding metropolitan areas. New branch stores open and additional local plants and distribution facilities are constructed in an endeavor to keep up with population moves. Poor downtown parking facilities and the difficulties in mass transportation have caused many people to rely on mail and telephone service. Due to the increase in the number of working wives and the increasing number of husbands with more than one job, many companies have developed selling plans to make customer contact easier by mail and telephone.

The increased use of the telephone in business and industrial selling has been caused by increased selling costs required to maintain a company's share of the market in an expanding population. If 200 industrial accounts represented 5 percent of the market in 1966, then 400 such accounts might be required in 1969 to hold the same 5 percent share of the market. If a company's goal is to increase its share of the market 9 percent, for example, then 750 accounts might be required in 1968. As the market grows in population, more and more new accounts are required for a company simply to hold steady its share of the market.

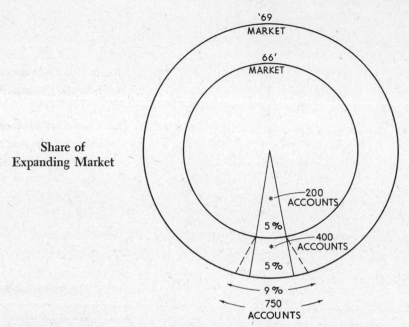

Share of
Expanding Market

In this illustration each salesman will have to double his effectiveness to enable the company to hold its share of the expanding market and more than triple his effectiveness to gain 9 percent of the new market. Clearly this demands more efficient use of selling hours.

Suppose a salesman with excellent knowledge of his customer and his business needs drives 75 miles to an isolated location to present a new product. He may find his buyer is attending a convention in Chicago or the plant is closed due to a strike. Rather than waste half a day or more, might it not be more expedient to telephone first? Such obvious waste of time is not limited to the new salesman or to small suppliers. Continuing surveys by consultants of the telephone companies regularly find experienced men representing large, well-directed sales organizations in both city and country territories wasting an alarming portion of their selling time.

Average Industrial
Salesman's Day

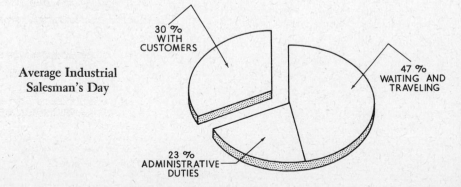

This simple diagram shows that the average salesman spends less than one-third of his time with customers, and this includes time spent making service calls as well as time spent with people in the customer's concern who are not decision makers. Since the future will demand more effective use of time, salesmen should combine written communications and telephone communications with face-to-face communications. There are advantages other than time savings which can accure to the intelligent use of these additional customer contacts.

## DEVELOPING CUSTOMER ORIENTATION THROUGH INSIDE SALES ON THE TELEPHONE ORDER DESK

Through tradition, many companies are organized by product line and they have sales specialists for each group of products. Customers with requirements in several product areas are forced to deal with several salesmen from the same vendor to fill their needs. This product-oriented approach is rapidly being replaced in many industries by the concept of customer orientation which means each salesman is now expected to handle the total needs of his group of customers.[1] He becomes a specialist for a particular customer trade or customer industry. This salesman is expected to have sufficient specialized and technical information to render informed service to his particular trade on multiple product lines. The home office specialists provide technical advice and counsel to selling personnel.

This kind of service is better than having various product-oriented salesmen calling on a customer because the customer can look to one salesman to serve his total needs instead of having several different representatives calling on him to discuss different products from the same supplier. It is less confusing to the customer and the one salesman has the opportunity to become more thoroughly acquainted with the customer's people and operations. The salesman can do a more complete job for the supplier and, due to the increased knowledge and understanding of the customer, he can render more valuable service to his customers.

One problem that sometimes arises with this type of selling occurs due to the absence of the salesman when the customer needs him. "Sorry, the man who handles your account isn't in. May I take a message?" While it may be logical for the salesman to be out in his territory, it is of no help to a frustrated customer. To overcome this difficulty, many companies have created a telephone order desk and utilize this as a training device for new salesmen. Each outside customer-oriented salesman has a twin salesman on

---

[1] A complete description of such a transition and the use of the telephone as a training device is described by R. W. Seeley, "Why Every Salesman for Columbia-Geneva Has an 'Inside Double,'" *Sales Management*, June 15, 1956, pp. 62–64.

the inside to handle his customers when they call. He is always there and he is familiar with each account. This team arrangement frees the outside salesman to devote a major portion of his time to field contact work and the inside salesman has the responsibility of securing all information required for orders and inquiries. The two men keep in daily contact and share their information.

Customer service provided by the inside man usually takes the form of writing up routine orders, expediting shipment of old orders, developing price and delivery information, and answering billing questions. The gathering of information by the inside salesman may involve contact with product specialists in other departments. Through these contacts the inside salesman learns the many technical details of his products directly from experts while customer inquiries teach him their needs and typical demands. Inside men are responsible principally for service and they learn to talk the customer's language. Long before they become outside salesmen, these inside men are able to understand and communicate with customers. Through customer contact, the outside man obtains the information or questions and passes it on to his inside counterpart. The inside man is in a position to discuss the customer's interests on an equal footing with the outside representative. Since the contacts between the two men are frequent, they become interdependent and work out the solutions to their problems together. The new man has the guidance of the senior man while the customer benefits by the direct attention of both men. This personalized service to each customer draws the customer closer to the selling company because the team effort results in good service on all orders. For the selling company this team technique builds a pool of well-trained candidates for outside sales. To the customer, continuity of contact with one or two individuals who are thoroughly familiar with his account, his problems, and his needs and interests is very important. It saves him time and unnecessary explanations and does away with delays, frustrations, and irritations. This technique recognizes the importance of the individual customer by serving him as he wants and needs to be served.

Personal salesmen, properly trained in telephone techniques, can devote more working hours to actual sales talk and less to waiting room delays and traffic snarls. Although there are more than 50 million telephones in the U.S., the instrument itself is merely a tool for bringing good salesmanship to bear on prospects. Even good outside or personal salesmen must be taught good telephone usage and the telephone companies in most areas offer expert advice and training programs without cost.[2] Simple rules for the inside salesman include:

---

[2] The author is indebted to Mr. Brendon Stave, communications consultant, N.Y.

1. Answer the telephone promptly.
2. Identify yourself by department and name.
3. Speak pleasantly with warm friendship in your voice.
4. Offer assistance and secure the information wanted.
5. Get accurate data on customer name, billing address, and specific merchandise desired.
6. Encourage the customer to call again and thank him.
7. Keep your promises to find answers to his questions and be sure to call back.

## BUILDING SALES MESSAGES THROUGH DIRECT MAIL
## MEASUREMENTS OF EFFECTIVENESS

Commonly used forms of direct mail are letters, announcements, catalogs, folders, envelope and package enclosures, house organs, postcards, and circulars. Normally, direct mail copy should have only one idea to a mail piece, with short sentences, small words, and pictures. Often five or six pieces mailed a week apart are necessary to make an impression and to sell an idea. Special campaigns should be used for each product line and for each objective.[3]

While direct mail is often used to make direct sales, it is generally more effective when used to obtain inquiries and leads for salesmen. Direct mail is often an inexpensive way to reach distant buyers and to build up weak territories. When it is desirable to reach all buyers at the same time direct mail can be most effective, such as in announcing price changes, new products, and new product uses and in preselling prospects in a limited geographic area. Mailings are too often a hit-and-miss attempt to locate people who are actively in the market for a particular product. Results should not be measured by the number of inquiries one gets but by the number of qualified leads that can be turned into sales.

Before developing the mailing package, one must decide what his objective is. If one knows what he is trying to accomplish, he can custom-tailor his message to fit his needs. If one is attempting to activate wholesalers and retailers, the message must be compatible with their motives which could include: making money, taking advantage of special opportunities, increasing their sales, having pride in distinctive merchandise, and desiring to be

---

Telephone Company, for much of the material on proper application & techniques of the telephone in business.

[3] For an excellent application of this technique selling trucks to businessmen see Bill Doyle, "$30,000 a Year—and More—As a Ford Salesman!" *Ford Crest News*, January, 1965, pp. 11–13.

the leaders in their field. The promotion pieces probably should contain information on how the products benefit the buyers, what makes the products a better buy, how they can contribute to the profit picture, how much the products cost, and where they can be bought. Assuming the object is to solicit inquiries, the promotion piece should make it easy for the prospect to respond. People who inquire usually are ready and able to buy. They are interested in the product or service or they wouldn't respond. A little initiative on the part of the salesman can turn many inquiries into sales. The salesman can build the initial inquiry into a strong desire to buy by supplying information pleasantly and enthusiastically and making it easy for the prospect to buy.

Once the benefits and customer motives are known and it is decided what appeals are to be used, it is necessary to draw up a list of basic facts about the company that support the planned appeal and will make people want to do business with the company. The foundation of direct mail copy can be based upon the reasons why the products are better than or different from competitors' products. The appeal can be based upon customer services such as credit policies, speed of service, technical know-how, special packaging, or other unique features offered. The appeal can also be based upon company image which would include the individual executives, the long company history of giving satisfactory service to customers, the brand name products handled, indicating reliability as well as the size of customer order which can be handled and financed easily. In developing the mailing campaign, a series of ideas in logical sequence must be evolved, with each individual mailing designed to communicate only one idea.

After each message is carefully planned, its effectiveness can be measured only if certain formal testing procedures are followed. Evaluation is essential if sales messages are to increase in effectiveness. A selected sample of subjects must be chosen which is truly representative of the entire customer target group. By picking a random sample, each prospect has an equal chance of receiving the mailing and pure chance determines the specific name. This technique minimizes the possibility of the mail going to an unrepresentative sample which might easily yield misleading results. An alternate technique would be to intentionally pick a group in which high interest would be expected and test the message appeal on this highly biased group. If this high interest group did not respond to the message, it might obviate the need for a large mailing with that message.[4]

As the mail campaign develops, it is often possible to check the effec-

---

[4] For greater depth and understanding see E. Jerome McCarthy, *Basic Marketing* (Homewood, Illinois: Richard D. Irwin, Inc., 1964), particularly Chap. 4.

tiveness of different messages through the use of split sampling techniques. By dividing the sample into four equal groups, several different messages can be prepared and the results evaluated. The chances of outside influences and competitive actions should be the same for all four groups; hence any difference in results should be indicative of the degree of conviction which the message carried. In this way one can learn whether a particular message was convincing and to what degree. Statistics can be compiled regarding the degree of conviction to be expected in advance, with nonprospects as well as prospects for each series of messages.

## DEVELOPING SALES TECHNIQUES AND LEARNING TO TALK THE CUSTOMER'S LANGUAGE

A number of companies have developed specific mailing programs for each of many different lines of business in which their prospects engage. If

*Courtesy: Sperry & Hutchinson Company, N.Y.*

**FIG. 13. A shop owner discusses business with a salesman**

the salesman wants to interest a food store owner in changing from a clerk-service operation to self-service, there is a campaign designed to convince him he should consider the change. Individual campaigns are designed for doctors, dentists, druggists, gas station owners, department stores, and insurance companies. Such preplanned mail campaigns reduce guesswork and save time for the salesman. These mailing pieces are very successful in selling ideas because the ideas, the copy, and the dramatic effects are all slanted and custom-tailored to the prospect.[5] They talk his language and discuss his business interests.

Most industrial direct mail programs are coordinated with a personal selling plan. These mail campaigns are among the first steps used to arouse interest and prove a need exists. This procedure is effective because the prospect has been presold on the company and the idea before the salesman makes his direct call. The salesman follows up mailings with personal calls and makes calls between mailings whenever possible. Becoming familiar with such customer-oriented ideas and language is excellent training for the inside salesman.

Besides learning to talk in terms which have specific meaning for a particular group of prospects, the sales trainee working on a telephone order desk, or as the inside twin to an outside salesman, soon learns to handle common customer objections and problems which are typical of each trade that he serves. He should learn to handle complaints cheerfully and effectively befriend the customer to convert complaints into additional orders. Through direct mail campaigns and actual work experience on the telephone desk, the sales trainee builds his own knowledge and increases his self-confidence. Before his training is complete, he literally knows more about his customers' problems in his specialty field and how to solve them than they do themselves. He can become the expert in his field and provide legitimate service to all his accounts.

In learning to talk the customer's language, the salesman should not forget that conversation should be a two-way communication. The customer should be encouraged to talk freely of his business problems and particularly of the areas in which the salesman may be of some help. If the salesman knows and understands the customer's terminology, and point of reference, he can more easily put himself in the prospect's shoes and appreciate the problem as the prospect sees it. The effective salesman can then suggest a solution by using words and phrases which the prospect himself used, and understanding will be more complete. Selling with such training becomes easier and more effective.

---

[5] See Lawrence G. Chait, "Power of Direct Mail," *Sales Management*, October 5, 1956, concerning a consumer survey by R. L. Polk & Co., New York.

## LOCATING PROSPECTS

The importance of knowing where the market is located for a particular product or service cannot be overstressed. If the sales manager does not identify groups of customer targets, then the salesman must. He should also identify specific individuals within companies to minimize wasted time and increase his selling effectiveness.

Most selling companies have lists of customers that buy over and over again as well as those that once purchased some merchandise or service but did not stay active. They usually have lists of noncustomers whom they would like to serve. These lists are very often incomplete and out of date because of the constant movement of companies and of personnel within each company. The local post office can provide a list checking service that will help keep a mailing list accurate and up to date.

Outside of the company records there are numerous possible sources of prospect names. Mailing lists are prepared by name brokers and can be as broad or fine as desired. Such lists include auto registrations, college graduates, doctors, nurses, dentists, voter registrations by precinct, as well as many other specific groups. Names can be obtained from published business directories such as Moody's, Standard & Poor's, and Dun & Bradstreet. Often trade publications will sell their list of mailing names, titles, and addresses. Since there are literally thousands of such publications, each designed to appeal to a specific group, a list probably exists for most products imaginable. With a minimum of cost, a list of names can be compiled from telephone books and the yellow pages. If names are grouped geographically, salesmen can increase their daily calls by as much as two or three times the average because little travel time is wasted between calls.

If the prospects are in a merchantile endeavor, Dun & Bradstreet will probably have a complete listing by city, county, or township showing the company size, line of business, sales volume, principles and their titles, and other useful information. Prospecting by the Standard Industrial Classification (S.I.C.) code number can be very useful in many selling situations. Each line of business has a separate number and related businesses have similar numbers so that a clerk can leaf through such a directory and pick out only those names which apply. This service is also provided by Dun & Bradstreet through the use of punch cards and business machines which will print selected data.

## QUALIFYING PROSPECTS

The initial question to be asked about each name on any list is, how good a prospect is this name? Qualifying prospects is time consuming and risky at best but it is necessary to save selling time. There are three basic questions which must be asked about each name. First, does the person or company have a need for the product or service? Second, does the person have the ability to finance such a purchase? Finally, is he willing to purchase assuming the benefits can be demonstrated?

A need for a product does not mean the person cannot survive without it but, more realistically, can the purchaser benefit by acquiring the product? Clearly, one does not need a large, expensive new car to obtain transportation; however, he might very well desire such an automobile. Can the suspect afford to acquire the product? Many people desire expensive things but cannot realistically finance such purchases. Since most lists of possible prospects are practically endless, the salesman would be wise to spend his time in the presence of those people who not only desire his type of product but can afford it. Finally comes the problem of the spend-save aspirations of the individual. Normally, if a person can afford a needed product he can be persuaded to spend his money to obtain it. However, very often people will deny themselves because they lack confidence in the future and feel more secure with saving their money or line of credit and doing without needed products. Occasionally, social norms cause people to buy quite differently from what one might expect. For example, in some well-to-do communities an expensive new automobile is looked upon as being ostentatious and a symbol to hide a basic inferiority complex. In these communities, the old rich families prefer two used autos which symbolize to their peers that they have so much wealth and feel so secure that they do not have to show off. The newer rich in the same communities often imitate the older families to gain social acceptance.

Through the judicious use of direct mail campaigns and good telephone procedures an effective salesman can save his time and that of the person being called. He can eliminate suspects and identify prospects. This reduces effort spent in making personal calls on people with no need or want from the product or service and insures more time to be spent with potential buyers. It can be an inexpensive way to qualify prospects.

## PROSPECTING OBJECTIVES

Besides qualifying prospects, the effective salesman utilizes direct mail and telephone for other purposes in developing sales prospects. His immediate goal, for example, may be to create an endless chain of prospects by having each customer supply him with the names of five additional prospects. These in turn will each be asked to supply five new names and the geometric progression quickly builds an infinite list. When he contacts the individuals on his list, the effective salesman attempts to develop extra appointments on a legitimate basis. Another objective might be to develop inquiries and leads or to invite prospects into a showroom. In any event, prospecting is a good way to maintain contacts and to develop goodwill for future business.

In almost any line, the salesman who uses direct mail and the telephone wisely and effectively an hour or more a day will spend more time in the physical presence of his prospects rather than less. In that hour he will set up appointments, avoid wasting time in travel, visiting when the prospect is absent or too busy with other problems, and long waits in reception rooms. The effective salesman will also make follow-up calls and letters to provide that extra nudge to indecisive prospects. He will utilize these tools to create goodwill and increase the number of people he contacts to many more than he could possibly see in person. If he does this regularly over an extended period of time, the effective salesman will far outsell the salesman who does not use the telephone and direct mail services.

## DISCOVERING THE BUYING INFLUENTIALS

When direct mail includes a return postcard with personalized fill-ins required indicating the individual's name and company title, it can be most effective in revealing who the buying influence really is. The telephone has a greater effect because of the psychological "nature of the beast." For example, when someone knocks at the door, most family members continue with their activities hoping someone else will answer the door but when the telephone rings most family members rush to answer it. This seems to be applicable to office routines as well and busy executives will usually take a moment to answer their telephones. If they do not have the power of decision in the area in which the salesman is interested they will often refer him to another executive who might be interested. Most people are genuinely helpful in this respect as long as the request is cordial and brief and they will direct the salesman to the proper parties. Top executives can be reached directly by telephone where they might not be accessible otherwise. It is very difficult to ignore a ringing telephone. Another variation of the telephone technique is the telegram message which requests an interview and states a telephone call will follow. A telegram denotes the importance the salesman places on the expected interview and predisposes the busy executive to take time to listen to the sales message. In each of these approaches there must be an element of news and the presentation should be brief and businesslike, getting directly to the point without preliminaries before and prospect feels a need for defenses. In the absence of a news angle, there is no reason why he should give the caller any further attention.

Such techniques can be used to discover and communicate with the buying influentials but they can sell only the idea of a personal interview. Normally they cannot be used to close a sale but only to open a sales interview—and nothing more. The manner of speech, the tones and the enunciation, are planned to arrest the prospect's attention, build his interest, inspire his confidence, and motivate him to give the salesman an appointment.

## REDUCE SELLING EXPENSE AND INCREASE SALES

An effective salesman shows each customer personal attention and he personally thanks each customer for placing an order. A follow-up after a particular purchase has been made is pleasing to most people because it indicates the salesman really cares about their use of the product and is not concerned only with getting them to order. Such follow-up calls often generate additional business immediately and can often provide additional prospect names. A satisfied customer is frequently the best source of qualified prospects and his enthusiasm for the product is genuine and easily believable to his friends.

Telephone and direct mail are used effectively to cover outlying accounts in a large territory where customers and prospects would otherwise be neglected. An offer to be of service to such accounts is greatly appreciated and suggestions or reminders of special events that are coming up may promote interest where none existed before. These distant accounts are often invited to attend a special demonstration to be given in central locations which the prospect has occasion to visit. This personal attention given to each account can be obtained without frequent personal visits, thereby reducing selling expenses. When inquiries develop in an outlying district, extra telephone calls may easily pave the way for additional appointments in that area with a minimum of time wasted. The effective salesman does not state that he plans to be in the area anyway but rather he tells his prospect that he wants to make a special trip out his way to see the prospective customer specifically for a given reason. If the prospect agrees, he will be predisposed to listen carefully to the salesman because it appears important enough to justify the long trip. A number of prospects can be contacted in this way and appointments made according to the route planned. This will increase sales and divide the traveling costs among several customers rather than be a burden on the single inquiry. Often delivery expenses can be divided in the same manner and this provides another good reason for contacting old distant customers who may be inactive at present.

In some lines of business special seasonal or pricing deals are offered periodically and old customers may be given an opportunity to shop the sale merchandise before it is offered to the general public. Even stable items are occasionally turned over on a special deal simply to bring new models into the showroom or store and these specials provide excellent material to solicit business from inactive accounts or hesitant prospects. Since the price is usually lower than normal, selling expenses become extremely critical, making telephone and direct mail solicitations more attractive.

It has been pointed out that telephone and direct mail techniques can effectively reduce the amount of time spent waiting in reception areas, and time wasted traveling and in traffic snarls and delays. However, of even greater importance to the salesman is that these techniques can also be used to increase the speed of the first timely contacts. When events change which may affect the prospect's business, a timely contact can be most rewarding to the salesman, and customers appreciate the special attention they receive. If the salesman hears of a customer who is experiencing some trouble, he can phone him and offer help in a number of ways beyond his own product or company services. Such behavior is often rewarded at a later date by a loyal customer who is grateful to the salesman who thought of him as an individual and not as another account number on a card in the office. An effective salesman considers each prospect as a friend, a neighbor, and a confidant and he attempts to maintain warm, friendly contact on a regularly scheduled basis. Often limited time prohibits making regular personal visits to every account and the telephone and mail provide the necessary personal touch between direct calls.

## LIMITS OF TELEPHONE AND MAIL USAGE IN PERSONAL SELLING

In telephone solicitations, the salesman is judged by voice alone and poor tones and lazy enunciation can ruin the best of messages. The buyer cannot see the salesman so his appearance, the product he sells, and the various visual aids used in personal selling are of no value. Everything hinges on the voice of the salesman over the telephone so it is necessary to choose words more carefully and to paint better mental pictures of the benefits which the buyer will be offered when he sees the salesman in person.

There is no way for the salesman on the telephone to know what is going on in the presence of his prospect, nor is there any visual hint of his reaction to the message. If the customer does not hear clearly or understand correctly he may not bother to ask the salesman to repeat but may simply refuse to see him or talk further about his proposition. Most people in business are very conscious of time passing while talking on the telephone and they want to determine the facts quickly and free the telephone lines. This often causes quick impulsive decisions which may be unfavorable to the salesman.

Most telephone solicitations are designed to be dominated by the salesman and the prospect is given only a minimumal opportunity to reply in an unexpected manner. The conversation is planned to follow a definite channel and it is assumed that as long as the message is clear, concise, well illustrated and dramatically presented, its reception will be satisfactory. Unfortunately, this is not always true. This theory fails to take into account that for communication to be effective it must be two way. There has to be feedback for the salesman to ascertain the extent to which the message has actually been understood, believed, assimilated, and accepted. The listener must regard the message as having a positive value for him or it will fail in its purpose. Studies of communication and persuasion stress the importance of feedback and indicate its presence is essential for the message to be effective.

Another problem in telephone solicitations is the question of unethical practices and the invasion of privacy. A few companies use high pressure tactics and fraudulent gimmicks which arouse the public to demand laws be passed which make telephone soliciting illegal. Portland, Oregon, and Phoenix, Arizona, are examples of cities that have tried to pass such laws but dropped the idea. Occasionally one reads of a citizen filing suit against a sales company for invasion of privacy and it becomes newsworthy because of the public is in sympathy with the individual and against the company.

It is certainly desirable to prohibit unethical practices in telephone selling. However, the answer is not outlaw telephone selling because a few concerns abuse the practice. Perhaps control and regulation making the selling company legally liable for specific unethical and fradulent practices would be a sounder approach. The proper use of the telephone by legitimate companies for legitimate purposes should not be interfered with in order to punish the few that abuse the practice.

A third area which limits the use of the telephone in personal selling is the buyer's reaction. One well-published authority in this field flatly states, "Makes appointments *only* when the interview is necessary . . . when it requires more than a few minutes, when you hope for the buyer's undivided attention—or want to give him time to prepare data to help him discuss his needs with you."[6]

This buyer is firmly against making unnecessary appointments because the buyer is likely to think the salesman places too high a value on his selling time. He is against the use of the telephone when the salesman does not know the buyer and he indicates that some buyers may be inclined to assume that the salesman is just plain lazy or merely trying to keep out of the rain. Such suspicions are often justified and the effective salesman would be wise to use the telephone with discretion.

Direct mail has two basic limitations when applied to personal selling. First is the degree of attention which the prospect pays to such literature and second is the impersonal nature of the message. Do people receive too much mail? Just how much mail does the average family receive daily—including all the bulk rate product and service solicitations sent out by American business? A study made in 1957 revealed that the average U.S. family gets less than one piece of mail per day! Even the upper income family received only three pieces per day.[7] While this may still hold true, the important point is not the actual amount of mail received but how the family feels about the amount of mail it does receive. If a family in the upper income group received 900 pieces of mail solicitation in a year they might well ignore most of them even though this averages out to less than three pieces of mail per day. Regardless of the physical count of mail pieces, it is common for people to refer to such solicitations as "junk mail" which is often thrown away without being opened. To compete for the prospect's attention under such conditions requires a specialist and considerable money. The cost of direct mail in the United States runs close to $2 billion annually according to the Direct Mail Advertising Association.[8]

The second limitation on the effectiveness of direct mail is the impersonal nature of the message even when it is tailored to a specific target group such as doctors. To compete for their attention many companies use both handwritten and typed fill-in notes to personalize their mail. How-

---

[6] Joseph Gentile, *Some Do's And Don'ts of Selling As One Buyer Sees Them* (New York: Dun & Bradstreet, Inc., 1955), p. 29.

[7] See Lawrence G. Chait, "Too Much Mail?" *Sales Management*, July 5, 1957, p. 16.

[8] See, "Candy and Gum Makers Will Spend about $60 Million," *Sales Management*, March 4, 1960, reporting figures by the Direct Mail Advertising Association.

ever, the basic message is the same for everyone on that mailing. Many busy people recognize this and resent it.

The standard form letter is comparable to the standard memorized sales talk. It attempts to solicit a response due to a preconceived stimulus which is designed to appeal to a certain number of those people who are exposed to it. This is attempting to sell by the law of averages and is directly contradictory to personal selling which has as its major advantage the ability to adjust the sales message to fit each individual as feedback indicates.

A standard form letter can be useful in personal selling when it is used as a basis for writing a personal letter to an individual regarding a problem that the selling company has handled before. The salesman can save time and put his ideas over more succinctly if he has a battery of form letters from which to draw selected passages that seem to apply to the specific situation he is facing. His letter then becomes personal and is adjusted to fit the individual prospect and answer his specific questions or doubts.

The use of the telephone and the mails have serious limitations as aids to personal selling and must be undertaken with a great deal of discretion. However, when used properly they can develop customer orientation, build effective sales messages, and develop good sales techniques. In some fields they are good tools to use in locating and qualifying prospects and in practically every field they can save time and reduce selling expenses while increasing sales. Good manners, intelligent sales messages, avoidance of high pressure, elimination of fraudulent gimmicks, and the proper timing of calls may well help to secure better public acceptance of such practices.

◆   ◆   ◆

## JAY BROWN: PROSPECTOR IN A BUSINESS SUIT*

Justin Brown, a field representative working out of Reno, Nevada, likes to talk about S & H Green Stamps. During these conversations, he uses two words with amazing frequency—*enthusiasm* and *prospecting*.

He's very enthusiastic about S & H Green Stamps; he has been highly successful in creating and maintaining this same degree of enthusiasm among his accounts. And he's a prospector, in many respects, like those Nevada silver miners who invaded Virginia City in the 1860's.

In Jay Brown talk (everyone calls him Jay), prospecting means looking for

* The above is reprinted with the kind permission of the *Sperry and Hutchinson Company Magazine*, New York, N.Y., March/April, 1965.

new S & H accounts. He diligently pursues this, always maintaining an active list of 100 good prospects. "When I sign an account," he explained, "it is replaced on my top 100 list by another good prospect. When it's apparent that I'm not going to sell a prospect, that one is replaced."

Jay Brown signs a lot of accounts. During 1964 he increased his field representative managed sales by more than $143,000 over 1963. (Field managed sales are accounts managed exclusively by an individual field representative). This was tops among all S & H field representatives.

The big year pushed Mr. Brown's field managed sales to more than $600,000 —twice the amount the territory had when he took it over three years ago.

How did he do it? "By setting definite goals for myself for the year, then breaking that down into goals for each month." For 1964, Mr. Brown had lofty goals: Sign 100 accounts and increase field managed sales by $110,000. He did that and then some, signing 109 accounts and increasing field managed sales by more than $143,000. Mr. Brown is soft-spoken, conservative in dress, and really looks more like a college professor than a phenomenal salesman.

"I make a list of calls—both service and prospecting—that I must make each week. Then I call on all of them," he said. To do this, Mr. Brown starts his day at 8:00 A.M. and works until at least 6:00 P.M., often later. Paperwork is handled at nights and on weekends.

## SERVICE, SERVICE, SERVICE

Mr. Brown places great emphasis on serving accounts. "In my opinion," says the transplanted Easterner (he grew up in Rochester, New York), "providing service is just as important, if not more important, than prospecting. If you keep present accounts enthusiastic this helps sign new accounts."

His existing accounts are among the best contributors to his top 100 prospect list. "If you keep them enthusiastic about S & H's service, they like to see neighboring noncompetitive businesses give the stamps." (Mr. Brown tells the story about a downtown Reno shoe store operator who took stamps after several calls. That man provided Mr. Brown with several prospects, and consequently, three new S & H accounts in the same area.)

"I feel," claims Mr. Brown, "that effective selling of S & H's service is basically a one-two situation. First, keep existing accounts enthusiastic and happy. Second, knock on plenty of doors. They work hand-in-hand."

Mr. Brown enthusiastically works to keep accounts enthusiastic. "I learn all I can about my various types of accounts. I read trade publications of all sorts, keep abreast of all the business developments in my area, and take a personal interest in their business," he explains. "I try to provide any hints I can that might help an account. After all, my job is the same as his—to increase his business. And S & H Green Stamps do that!

"Effective use of signs, posters, advertising, and other promotional materials helps increase the account's business and advertises S & H at the same time," points out Mr. Brown. "This is all part of S & H's service." Mr. Brown has built a friendly relationship with his accounts. "This leads to prospective clients," he emphasizes. "My accounts are always giving me good leads!"

Mr. Brown signs 50 percent of his prospects on the initial call. "The main reason for this," he pointed out, "is that when I go prospecting, the business has a real good potential of becoming an account.

Mr. Fred Acord, District Manager (South San Francisco), is enthusiastic about Jay Brown. "You can't have a success story without a good man," he says. "And Jay, among other qualifications, has dedication, ambition, and drive."

Mr. Acord explained that Mr. Brown always sets goals for himself that are just a little higher than the goals the company sets for him. "And he always reaches them," Mr. Acord explained. "Any salesman must make a lot of calls to be successful. Jay makes more calls than just about any salesman I have ever known. That's the heart of his success story."

Helping accounts has helped Mr. Brown, according to Mr. Acord. "He does a great service job," stressed Mr. Acord, "I've never heard of an account of his running out of stamps or promotional materials—and he covers a lot of territory." He covers 45,000 square miles to be exact. Mr. Brown has to keep on the go to cover his territory of Northern Nevada and the Lake Tahoe region of California, much of it sparsely populated.

## HE TALKS TO EVERYONE

"I'm a little short on people," says Mr. Brown, "so I talk to all of 'em." This approach led to signing such varied types of accounts as a bowling alley, beauty salons, motels, a Chrysler-Plymouth dealer, flower shops, an upholstery business, a television repair service, and a glass and window business, just to name a few.

"One of my most extraordinary accounts," Mr. Brown proclaims, "Is a general store in Gabbs, Nevada. That's a mining area and as you'd expect the store caters to miners. It sells almost everything and its nearest competitor is 58 miles away."

After several calls Mr. Brown sold the owners. The store's sales increased 18 percent during the first six months with S & H's service.

Another unusual account is a tiny grocery store in Genoa, Nevada, known simply as The Store. It's the oldest store in Nevada, in the oldest settlement in Nevada. Both were founded in the early 1850's and Genoa, which was at one time the capital of Nevada, is now a quiet mountain hamlet of 75 residents.

He has accounts at the other end of the scale. The Eagle Thrifty Drug and Grocery Markets, for example. The five stores do a lion's share of the business in the Reno-Sparks area (Sparks is Reno's sister city) and all of them give S & H Green Stamps. "They opened their first store in Sparks, in early 1964," Mr. Brown explained. "And it's going great guns, too!"

Mr. Brown is especially proud of an account in Gardnerville, Nevada. "I worked on Miller's Food Market for a full year," points out Mr. Brown. "I finally signed the account in late 1963. The market had a 30 percent increase in volume during 1964. Needless to say, the owner is enthusiastic about S & H and doesn't mind telling his business acquaintances about it. It's really helped me in Gardnerville!"

# 18

# Getting the Interview and
# Opening the Sale

A final buying action is caused by the interaction of the motives which a prospect is predisposed to possess and the mechanisms which will permit action, such as his motor and muscular capacities, his sensory capacities, and his intellectual powers of recognizing and understanding his needs. The actual buying process is also determined by the product or service itself, the various selling influences which may be personal and nonpersonal, and other influences such as relevant external events. In other words, practically every experience in a person's life helps influence a final buying action.

A businessman with certain ideas, attitudes, and beliefs may, as he commutes to work, read an advertisement in his morning paper. If he is favorably impressed by this message he becomes slightly different from what he was before he read the message. Later in the week he may have lunch with a friend who says nice things about the brand of product advertised in the paper. This experience will change the businessman slightly again and he may now believe that if he ever buys such a product, he probably should buy this particular brand. He now has a degree of conviction about the brand. Finally, the businessman visits a store for the purpose of buying entirely different items and, coincidentally, he sees a large product display in the store featuring the very brand he has read about and his friend has said nice things about. This may be sufficient to precipitate immediate buying action. Now the question arises: what caused the buying action? Clearly, many interrelated events each acted to influence the buying behavior.

Before a salesman can get an interview and attempt to open a sale, he must analyze the purpose of his initial interview with each individual prospect. What degree of conviction does the salesman hope to achieve on

277

this particular call? In some lines of business, the salesman desires to cause immediate buying action on the first call. He wants to know only what will precipitate those people who are already predisposed toward his product to take action and buy. However, many sales interviews cannot realistically be expected to result in an order on the salesman's first visit. What other purposes or objectives might a salesman have for requesting an interview with a prospect? There are at least nine general areas which effective salesmen consider before attempting to get an interview.

## PURPOSES OF A SPECIFIC INTERVIEW

*To Obtain Information.*  Research on an individual prospect, or possibly a group of customer targets, can provide fruitful information to build a sales presentation or to adapt a general sales story to a specific prospect. Specific areas of interest might include how they use that type of product or its alternative and substitute products; how they feel about quality and price generally and if possible about this particular line of merchandise; what the backgrounds of the particular company and of the particular buying influentials are; what competitors are actively promoting this concern and what degree of acceptance do they seem to have; how this company or prospect is different from others. When an effective salesman plans his interview to obtain information, he is basically searching for areas of similarity between himself and the prospect which he can later develop to get to know and understand the prospect personally. He introduces himself and attempts to build friendly mutual respect between himself and the prospect.

*To Discover Problems or Needs.*  Effective salesmen perfect their skills of observation and techniques of questioning to aid prospects to discuss willingly their needs and desires. These salesmen are attentive to everything to be seen and heard in the presence of the buyer which includes not only what the prospect says but also the manner in which he states his feelings. Effective salesmen exhibit a sincere interest in the prospect in a natural, warm, friendly way and they avoid any attempt to sell their product on such a call. The purpose of their visit is to scout the area and create a feeling of trust and confidence which can be mutually felt by both the prospect and the salesman. Together they search for areas of problems or needs of the prospect and at some later date solutions may be suggested. The salesman is an uncritical listener and encourages the prospect to do most of the talking. Prospects are often flattered by such an unexpected contact with a salesman and willingly escort him through the office and plant in a personal guided tour. Thoughtful silence on the part of the salesman indicates he is honestly studying the prospect's operations. Should he observe an apparent waste or wrong method of operation he might ask why the prospect does it this way instead of some other way. Whatever answer the prospect provides, the salesman remains uncritical— for example, by saying, "Yes, now I understand. That's interesting." This professional attitude will make it possible at a later date to bring up the same point with specific facts, figures, and interesting illustrations which clearly tell the prospect that the salesman has given personal attention to the prospect's problem and considerable thought to finding a better solution.

*To Develop Awareness.* Often customer needs or problems are obvious to the expert salesman in the field but they have not been noticed by the individual with the need. Small companies grow and their needs change as their size changes. However, pressing operating problems prevent management from stepping back and reevaluating their systems and methods of operating. Due to population shifts, markets can change so gradually that businesses catering to the public often do not appreciate the difference in demand for their products and services. An alert salesman who specializes in one line of business can quickly recognize trends and patterns which the local concern may overlook. New equipment and techniques are constantly being introduced which can materially affect the profit or provide other benefits to a prospect. The salesman is the authority in his field who can advise the prospect on the latest developments in his specialty.

If the purpose of the visit is to develop awareness in the prospect's mind, the planned discussion should center around the prospect's opinion of events and how they relate to current reality. It is presumed in this type of interview the prospect is perfectly capable of reasoning through his problem once it is brought to his attention. The discussion is intended to bring out all the salient points regarding the changed circumstances with some indication of the losses or other disadvantages of continuing in the old manner. This type of sales interview is often referred to as "seed planting" or putting the germ of an idea in the prospect's mind which will later grow to fruition and ultimately to a sale.

*To Offer a Legitimate Service.* Many sales strategies are based upon the honest concept of providing a true service to prospects and the purpose of the interview is simply to get permission to make a survey or to study an area which may or may not turn out to be a problem. Insurance salesmen have used this strategy with notable success for many years by developing a program for each individual prospect which indicates the minimum coverage the prospect himself wants at different points in his life, such as protection for his young children when his earnings are low, extra funds later for their college education, retirement funds for himself, and possibly a guaranteed income for life for his widow. This personalized comprehensive life insurance program is planned for the individual as a legitimate service to help him get what he wants at the time he needs it. The initial interview is to obtain all the necessary personal information about the prospect and his personal requirements and no attempt is made to sell at this time.

Highly complex computer systems are often sold by using the same sales strategy. The first interview is intended to get permission to explore the possible application of new techniques to achieve certain benefits which the prospect desires. The salesman often requires the assistance of a staff of legal, accounting, and production personnel to analyze the situation and evaluate costs and benefits to be expected. Clearly, no attempt to sell can be made during an early interview because there is not sufficient data upon which an intelligent decision can be made.

In selling to a retailer, an offer to study his inventory problems of size, styles, and variety may be the purpose of an initial interview. Limited storage and display space with unlimited product offerings from wholesalers and manufacturers represents a common problem to retailers. As noted earlier, sincere offers to help construct effective advertising; to promote additional store traffic; to lay out traffic flow within departments; to control inventory, expenses, and the like are all common and effective customer services which may be the purpose of the sales interview.

Accounting services are often introduced on the basis of a free survey of procedures which become the basis for a later sales presentation. The financing of accounts receivable also involves the free survey or study. Office systems and management consulting services are normally based upon a preliminary survey or audit of existing operations. Many consumer products lend themselves to this type of sales strategy and the large department stores have successfully used such services and surveys to promote air-conditioning units, furniture reupholstering, carpeting, and many other household items.

*To Submit Recommendations.* Many products are not technically involved or complicated to the point of requiring a preliminary survey but can be legitimately offered on a regular and routine basis. The salesman for such products will often learn of new methods and procedures from one customer and want to pass this information on to his other customers and

*Courtesy: E. I. du Pont de Nemours Co., Wilmington, Del.*

**FIG. 14. Client is shown use of protective coatings by industrial salesman.**

prospects. Such recommendations and suggestions normally relate to his product and its use which increase the benefits to the owner. Groups of customers, all in the same line of business, for example, often have common problems and seek solutions to fit their particular needs. Whenever the salesman can suggest improvement, he serves a legitimate function for the buyer and is a welcome visitor.

*To Provide Nonsales Information.* An effective salesman builds his image of being a friendly authority whenever he can with his prospects and customers and this often involves taking an interest in their problems in areas outside of his immediate product offerings. Customers have occasional requirements which are not easily answered and the service-oriented salesman is quick to find facts and do preliminary research work which will benefit his customers. This may involve products of a personal nature for various executives in the customer's company or it may be directly related to the operation of the business. However, the salesman becomes an assistant buyer and gathers information and facts which will aid his customer in making a wise decision. Articles in trade journals, newspapers, and magazines may be of interest to certain individuals and if they have not seen the articles, they will definitely appreciate the salesman's interest and personal attention to their needs.

*To Offer Trial Use of a Product.* Some products and services are difficult to evaluate prior to being used in a real situation and salesmen find it difficult to develop the degree of conviction necessary to cause a buying action. The purpose of their interview then is focused upon a fair trial use of the product or service. Such offers normally include a money-back guarantee with complete cancellation privileges if the buyer is not fully satisfied with the benefits derived at the end of the trial period. While this is very similar to direct selling, notice the emphasis in the purpose of the visit is not to convince a prospect to buy but merely to try. The salesman need not be as talkative or dominant when he is honestly willing to let the product speak for itself in actual use.

*To Handle a Complaint.* While the majority of salesmen attempt to be fair and complete in their claims about their products, some misunderstandings do occur and customers do complain. If the purpose of an interview is to handle a complaint, the effective salesman will utilize this opportunity to clear up the misunderstanding and to resell the product. Once the buyer states his problems they are already lightened. When the salesman shows sincere interest in correcting whatever seems wrong, the buyer is inclined to like the salesman. He will be more apt to listen to a correct presentation about the product which permits clearing up misunderstandings. Effectively handled, this often provides the opportunity to sell additional products, either then or at some future date.

## IDENTIFYING THE BUYING INFLUENTIALS

Just as it is difficult to isolate the cause for an immediate buying action with an individual, it is often equally difficult to determine who actually makes the buying decision, who else may influence the buying decision, and to what degree the various influences affect the ultimate action. In a simple consumer purchase of a television set, for example, father may set a dollar limit and mother may fix furniture and styling limits. The children may indicate a strong preference for a brand which their friends have. Neighbors may relate their good and bad experiences with previous brands. The television repairman, who advised buying a new set instead of having costly repairs done on the old set, may strongly indicate a brand preference from the standpoint of his future business. The salesman in the store may talk glowingly about a particular brand for which he receives an extra bonus for selling that week. Each of these influences are superimposed upon the predispositions of the individual members of the family. Their past experiences will color what they see and understand from each of the influences to which they are exposed. In addition to all of these personal influences are such nonpersonal influences as advertising, store promotions, convenience of the store or other outlet, and economic reality.

In a business situation the personal buying influentials become even more confusing. A receptionist may be influential relative to which salesman gets in to see the buyer. A department head may have a need but not the authority to place an order so he is limited to placing a requisition with someone else. A buyer may gather information and competitive pricing data. A comptroller or treasurer may determine the priority of expenditures. Another department head may argue for or against a given proposition even though he has no personal or business interest in the purchase. Staff specialists such as systems men, methods experts, and standardization committees may exert some influence. Outside experts, such as a certified public accountant or an interior decorator, may voice an opinion of the product offered. Top executives who do not normally concern themselves with such purchases may intervene due to personal friendship with a vendor or due to simple whim.

Dr. A. R. Oxenfeldt of Columbia University Graduate School of Business has analyzed the various buying influentials and offered an enlightening matrix which helps to clarify this problem.[1] He distinguishes the influences over the actual purchase as follows:

The Specifier—one who states the required product or service.
The Constrainer—one who limits how much can be spent.
The Voter—member of a group who is permitted to participate in the decision.
The Information Supplier—one who gathers factual data for others.
The User—the person for whom the product is actually procured.

---

[1] Alfred R. Oxenfeldt, *Executive Action in Marketing* (San Francisco: Wadsworth Publishing Co., Inc., 1966).

The Buyer—the person who places the order.
The Vetoer—one who may refuse to accept the conclusions of others.
The Kibitzer—one who volunteers unsolicited opinions.

Perhaps one should add a grouping called "The Screener," or the one who influences what information or what informant shall get through to any of the other buying influences. This would add people such as receptionists, secretaries, and various assistants to the original list.

An effective salesman learns to recognize the various buying influentials and to cultivate their friendship as early as possible. Besides the static relationship of the buying influences at any given instant in time, there is also the interaction of these people at different periods in time, with considerable changes in which person wields the power. Even the office boy of today may become Mr. Important someday in the future and he will remember how he was treated by various people within his company as well as by visiting salesmen. While it may seem obvious that the effective salesman will attempt to see the most powerful buying influence, many experienced salesmen overlook the obvious. Mr. Frederic C. Decker, publisher of *Printers' Ink*, recently reported the following experience:

The other day I called on the operating head of a rather large publishing company. He's an advertiser of ours and a man with whom I am well acquainted but I had never before made a formal business visit to his office. The purpose of my call was very commercial. I was interested in selling more space and both he and I knew it. But after we had talked for a half hour or so he leaned back in his chair and said, "Would you believe it, Fred, that you are the first representative of an advertising magazine, except for one space salesman, who has ever been in my office?"

Shame on ad press editors, publishers, and ad managers who haven't been doing their job. And hooray for that one space salesman, God bless him, who had made a call on the man who calls the shots in his company.

How rare he is, the space rep who has the confidence, the gumption, the ambition—or whatever it might be—to knock on the executive office door. Too often he stays in the more comfortable and less rarefied atmosphere of the lower levels at the agency or the advertising department. And as long as he dares not, or elects not, to venture up into the offices where final decisions are made he is missing so much in a business which holds its rewards for the man who is astute and venturesome enough to seek them.

He fails to realize two simple things. The first is that he'll just naturally be more successful when he makes his calls on the people who have the power to say yes and make it stick. Secondly, these are usually the easiest people to sell. They aren't lint-flickers and decimal-point hounds. Their viewpoints are broad and they are interested in conceptual approaches and creative appeals. They welcome ideas and people who have them. They respond to constructive analysis of their own problems, and solutions offered by good media.

The legendary figures of media selling, the Barron Colliers and the Mortimer Berkowitzes—these men learned their lessons early and capitalized on it quickly. They made sure their job was done at the lower levels, and then did it at the upper levels, too. And when they got upstairs they found they had little competition. Few of their space-selling confreres trod the carpeted halls and knocked on the paneled doors.

And the salesman today will find that the same rule holds true. That's why it is easy for the good man to be successful. So many of his competitors let the business go by default.[2]

## HANDLING BUYING INFLUENTIALS

Every identifiable buying influence has an opinion of the importance of his own job and a self-image which he would like to have recognized by others. The effective salesman treats every individual in his customer's organization as he would like to be treated himself. He attempts to befriend each buying influential and to demonstrate recognition of their individual importance by listening attentively to whatever they might say and to encourage their development of sound opinions favorable to his cause. Each of these individuals has a predisposition which influences his opinion of others and each has an organizational role which he attempts to play. By being an uncritical listener, the salesman can often learn of their ideas, attitudes, and beliefs which are relevant to his proposition. With such understanding he can then befriend each buying influence so that all of them will recognize the salesman as a friendly authority who is there to help them and their company succeed.

Every job from office boy to the president of a company is important and interrelated with all the other jobs. Production, engineering, sales, service, accounting, administration, and line or staff functions are vital to the smooth operation of any business. As noted earlier, the salesman's message to each buying influential must be compatible with each individual's predisposition, yet the various messages must be compatible with each other in the very likely event the various buying influentials get together and compare notes.

## LEARNING OF A PROSPECT'S NEEDS

Depending upon the purpose of the sales interview and the nature of the buying influential, the key to gaining selective exposure is to offer a

---

[2] Reprinted with permission, from Frederick C. Decker, "Publisher's View," *Printers' Ink*, September 10, 1965.

message which promises to agree with or to be compatible with the predisposed nature of the prospect. In order to understand the individual, the salesman must learn of his needs, wants, and desires which his product or proposition can help to satisfy or which the salesman as a problem solver can help to answer. It should be clear from the analysis of sales strategies that a prospect's needs are most often developed from a two-way conversation which enables the prospect to discuss his interests and problems as he sees them.

By paying careful attention to everything that is said and the manner in which the prospect emphasizes his points, the effective salesman can learn much about the prospect's current needs or desires. A trained observer can often pick up cues from the physical surroundings of the prospect which include the furniture and equipment, the use of space, lighting, decor, colors, fabrics, style, work flow, temporary storage, the amount and condition of inventory, the upkeep of buildings, machinery, and equipment. Such things communicate an image which many companies are vitally interested in. They often communicate much about the buying influentials who acquired such possessions. The type of people employed by a company, their age, dress, and industry often provide clues to the alert salesman regarding the wants and needs of his prospect.

## SOURCES OF INFORMATION

Before the salesman attempts to obtain an interview there is considerable homework which can be done to learn of the prospect's needs. Dun & Bradstreet, Standard & Poor's, Moody's, and similar reporting firms often publish an astounding amount of information about the principals of a business as well as the operation and financing of the business. Articles on both companies and individuals appear regularly in the *Wall Street Journal* and the *The New York Times* as well as in many other daily newspapers and weekly news magazines. Trade journals frequently report new developments and personal histories which provide tremendous insight into the behavior of certain prospects. Often a prospect's company publishes a house organ which notes not only personnel activities in the business but outside social events in which the important executives engage. The prospect is generally well known in his own marketing field and other customers can often provide biographical background information which will help the salesman to understand him. Employees of the prospect are occasionally willing to discuss their executives with insight which would not be available elsewhere. Other salesmen in noncompetitive lines who now sell to the prospect and have successfully run the buying maze are often willing to trade their knowledge for that relating to a different concern. Finally, there are usually historical records kept by the selling company which may give clues about the past behavior of prospects and which may be indicative of future behavior. Much of this fact-finding or initial research or homework can be done before it is necessary to contract an individual for an interview. After the facts have been obtained, the salesman, or in some cases the sales manager, then diagnoses these facts to determine how the company's products or services can help solve the prospect's problems. This analysis serves as the foundation for the preparation of a request for an interview which is apt to be compatible with the predisposition of the prospect.

## OPENING THE SALE

Having done his homework, the effective salesman is now in a position to become an expert, or authority, in his field. He knows the right person to contact for a given purpose and he at least knows enough about that individual to have some idea of what is apt to appeal to that person. He can begin by being a friendly authority with a specific individual in a particular company.

The salesman will mentally put himself in the prospect's position and attempt to see his problems and goals as the prospect himself views them. How can the product or service offered help the prospect to achieve his goals as he understands them? After several likely ideas are formulated, the salesman should then try to appreciate the extent to which the prospect is already aware of the problem and its solution. This may be tentative at this point of planning; however, it is a necessary step to enable the salesman to request an interview on an appealing basis. Being empathetic will enable the effective salesman to appreciate more fully the prospect's position as the prospect himself views it.

Whatever plan is evolved from the myriad of known detail, it must be sincere as the request for an interview must ring true if it is to be successful. If savings in time seems to be the most appealing of motivations, then the reasons for achieving time savings must be real and not simply apparent. The long-term contribution to profit must guide the salesman in his selection of appeals. Once deceived, a person will not willingly be duped a second time. This is equally important to one-call closers because in due time their reputation precedes them and they must be sincere if their sales company is to be effective over a long period.

When the initial contact is made, the salesman should be prepared to encounter some initial resistance and be prepared to meet it. The prospect will have been thinking about other business problems or occurrences and it may take a little time to put him into a receptive frame of mind. It is wise to let the prospect get something off his chest and be done with it rather than to have it bottled up inside of him blocking any additional ideas. Often things are not nearly so bad once the person has spoken out —in fact they may seem trivial and of no consequence and so disappear. An effective salesman is prepared to be an uncritical listener to his prospect and to let the effects of catharsis, or talking out, clear the prospect's mind.

Perhaps the most important key to opening the sale is an excellent verbal ability. Good communications in selling means using the kind of words, both in level of difficulty and in manner, which the prospect himself uses so that the salesman will be understood. Whatever appeal is to be used to gain an audience with the prospect, it should be communicated to him in terms which he understands and it should sound agreeable to him. The words figuratively paint a picture which he can see, understand, and like.

## CONTACTING THE PROSPECT

As noted in Chapter 17, the telephone is most often used correctly to set up appointments with prospects for high priced or complicated propositions which will require considerable time or which will require some preparation by the prospect beforehand. It is used incorrectly to set up appointments for routine visits where the sales message is stale or stereotyped.

More commonly, the salesman makes a direct personal call, gives his message to the receptionist, and waits his turn with other salesmen. It is this message that is all-important in determining the salesman's order of entry and the frame of mind in which the prospect is apt to receive him. A variation of the direct call without an appointment is a follow-up call after mailing promotional literature. This promotional literature may or may not have resulted in a response from the prospect. However, in either case it is presumed the prospect has been exposed to the sales proposition and has some awareness of the purpose of the salesman's visit.

Prospects who are difficult to meet in their businesses are often amenable to social contact, particularly if this is arranged through a mutual friend. Meeting by chance, but not really by chance, is more often suspected and resented than it is acceptable. Direct referrals with a note of introduction from the third party are often the best way to gain an audience with the prospect. The use of the third party's name without his permission can easily backfire of course. However, a simple statement about the third party being a satisfied customer should not offend either party and may be of genuine interest to the prospect.

## CHARACTERISTICS OF A GOOD SALES OPENING

An effective salesman will have studied his prospect before contacting him and will have tentatively identified the idea for motivating this individual. He will have selected his appeal for this prospect to activate his acceptance of exposure. This often takes the form of a teaser or promise of reward or satisfaction for the prospect in exchange for his valuable time.

Generally it is to the salesman's advantage to state the shortest period of time it will take him to convey his intended message. "Mr. Rightman, it will take only five minutes of your valuable time for me to show you how you can. . . ." This implies that if the prospect is quiet, the entire interview or visit will be finished in five minutes. If the prospect does become interested he can extend the length of the interview or, alternately, it is at his option and he need not be prepared to argue with the salesman to get rid of the nuisance, if that is what he thinks of the salesman.

Another characteristic of a good sales opening is an instantaneous establishment of rapport or an agreeable respect and understanding between the salesman and the prospect. While the ability to achieve this may be in part due to intuition, it is most often due to the homework done by the effective salesman, plus his keen attention and observation of details and the surroundings of his prospect. Experience in meeting new people under many differing circumstances will enable any attentive person to develop this trait.

Normally a good sales opening goes directly to some reference to the benefits that will accrue to the buyer or to a reference to an area which has been a problem for him. This shows the prospect right at the beginning of the interview that the salesman is thinking primarily of the buyer's interest and is not forcing the salesman's product or service without regard to need. Closely allied to the salesman's exhibiting some knowledge of the prospect's interests should be an indication that the salesman has studied the prospect's needs or problems and is qualified to discuss them from an authoritative or expert point of view. The prospect is much more apt to put confidence in and listen to the salesman who has studied his individual needs than he is to believe something so general that he suspects it to be canned or stereotyped.

If the salesman exhibits friendly self-confidence through his manner and words, he will be more believable and can honestly show his personal pride in himself and in his selling proposition. This feeling or attitude should be communicated quickly to the prospect. The purpose of the salesman's interview is to offer something which will realistically benefit this particular prospect. Mutual respect and admiration between the buyer and the seller are highly desirable to increase the creditability of the message.

## TECHNIQUES FOR OPENING A SALES INTERVIEW

In many lines of business, a direct statement about the product is normal and expected to begin a sales interview. The manufacturer's representative calling on the retail store owner, for example, is expected to show the new styles and to offer various price lines. There is no reason to be devious or cute in such a situation. A salesman covering a large geographic sales territory may want to phone ahead to conserve time in the next town he plans to visit. "Mr. Rightman, I am George Friendly of Partytime Dresses and I will be in your city tomorrow to show you our spring line. Could you arrange to be free around ten o'clock?"

A direct product approach is normal and effective in many lines of selling and is usually appreciated by professional buyers in practically every business. They appreciate direct statements and concise sales presentations as their time is most valuable and they are keenly aware of it. Their job is to see many salesmen and to compare the value of various competitive offerings. They are apt to resent a discussion which strays too far from the direct product offering.

Unfortunately for many lines of business, prospects do not welcome salesmen but consider them a necessary evil or an intrusion on their busy schedules. A busy architect, for example, must specify many products for various jobs and most often maintains up-to-date files on the various materials available to him. He avoids direct contact with salesmen as much as possible in order to devote his time to the business of planning. It takes an approach which is different to interest such a prospect. Arousing curiosity is one such approach if it is well planned and executed. "Mr. A.I.A. Experience, can you tell your clients what the newest floor covering material being used in government buildings is? Do you know what manufacturer's service will cut your planning costs in this area in half?"

A more common approach today is the premium method which offers the prospect a token gift to gain his initial interest. The Fuller Brush Company has popularized this approach around the world and it is used with slight variation by the many concerns which offer products at house parties. The hostess is given some premium, the guests are treated to a free dinner or fashion display, and all participate in a friendly social occasion.

In business, the premiums vary from personalized pens and brass name-plates for the desk to extensive visits to distant factories or important installations. These all-expense-paid tours are basically a premium or gift offered to the prospect simply to get him to listen to the sales message. More often this approach takes the form of an offer of a legitimate customer service such as the sales audit or free survey noted earlier. Many companies have found this approach very effective.

The referral approach is perhaps the most effective because the prospect's mental defenses are not apt to be aroused if a respected third party has suggested the salesman call on him. The salesman then becomes a source of information much more apt to be heard, trusted, and believed. "Your friend, Mr. Important, suggested you might be interested in this because. . . ." Such referrals must be legitimate to prevent a boomerang effect and, unfortunately, they do not occur often enough to keep most salesmen busy full time.

Woven through most of these approach techniques is an implied promise of reward to the prospect. This promise of satisfaction for time spent can be used directly as an approach. "Mr. Rightman, if you will listen to my suggestions and proposition for just five minutes, I can assure you that regardless of whether you buy anything or not you will gain several moneymaking ideas which you can use in your business." The promise of satisfaction can be much more specific and relate directly to facts and figures about a problem known to exist with an offer of possible new alternate solutions.

The various approaches conceivably could each be used by one salesman attempting to sell one company under different circumstances developed from outside investigation. For purposes of illustration, assume a salesman for an aircraft distributor noticed a newspaper article about a new sales record set by a company that might be a prospect for a business plane costing over $60,000. The salesman might use trade journals or professional reporting services to find out about the company and its executives. Assume the homework indicated this prospect sold to distributors in small cities up to 1,000 miles from the home office and the vice-president in charge of sales traveled this route more than half of his time. Additional study might disclose he traveled by regular scheduled airlines and normally rented an auto when he reached his destination. Perhaps through other salesmen, further investigation disclosed that while this vice-president was highly respected for his marketing ability, his own company would not authorize any purchases he might attempt to make on his own. The treasurer might be the source of financial power in this company.

Armed with this knowledge, the aircraft salesman decides the vice-president in charge of sales would be able to exercise the buying influence of a specifier and the purpose of the initial call would be simply to produce awareness. He might also decide, of the many possible appeals, the basic appeal should be to a combination of increasing sales and saving considerable travel time. The salesman must now face the choice of approaches.

He might offer a premium or a detailed analysis of the travel time spent visiting each distributor with comparable data using a company-owned aircraft. Such an approach would be based upon an offer to show this vice-president how to gain one extra week of time each month.

He might offer simply to suggest ways to increase sales or save time generally if the vice-president would take ten minutes to investigate a new concept in business travel. Such general promises to justify the time requested should indicate to the prospect satisfaction for his time spent.

Selling an expensive aircraft might easily justify the time and effort it might take to develop a source of authority which could be used as a referral from either old satisfied customers or other interested third parties. This might take a much longer period of time. However, if the prospect was on the road as much as indicated, perhaps he could not be contacted for several weeks or months and the salesman could use this time delay most effectively in contacting possible referral sources.

Using the curiosity approach, the salesman might develop a teaser campaign designed to make the prospect remember a certain date and keep it open. This might take the form of weekly token gifts and messages hinting alternately, first at increasing sales, then saving time, reducing selling costs, and building company prestige but without identifying any product or selling company. The only connecting thread between messages would be that each would conclude, "Remember March 9th and keep it open." The final message would invite the prospect to a private showing on March 9th at the ABC Aircraft Company. Properly planned, teaser campaigns have had highly successful results.

Finally, the direct product approach might be the most effective. By mailing colorful promotional literature to the prospect, a degree of awareness might be stimulated to a point sufficient to warrant a direct request to see this vice-president about the time savings to be realized by the company purchase of a twin-engine aircraft.

Assuming the interview with the sales vice-president was successful, the salesman might then face the problem of selling the corporate treasurer. An entirely different emphasis of appeals would probably be required and the initial approach to the new buying influential might also vary. The salesman would now have much greater and more accurate information in addition to having a friend, the sales vice-president, on the inside. If he continues his homework and pays attention to details, each step should become progressively easier.

## SUMMARY

The creative salesman realizes there are varying degrees of awareness and conviction which precede a buying action and often a sales interview does not attempt to close a sale. There are many legitimate purposes of a specific interview and they should be handled differently.

Buying influentials have different viewpoints and should often be handled entirely differently. In repeat buying situations, the roles of the various people may change as time passes and the effective salesman is attentive to such changes and is prepared to adjust to meet new situations. Developing information about prospects and their needs is essential in high capital investment purchases and is effective in most smaller purchases. There are many sources of information about prospects which can be developed with brainwork long before the legwork begins.

An effective creative salesman is armed with the knowledge of the purpose of an individual appointment, the buying influence of the person to be contacted, the effectiveness of the alternate choices of contact, the initial objectives to be obtained, and the various basic approaches which he may use. Clearly, the possible combinations of these various areas is a geometric progression and the likelihood of success of a particular set of decisions depends ultimately to a large extent on the amount of energy and thought the salesman is willing to devote to earning his sale.

# 19

# Impressing Sales Appeals on a Prospect

## THE NEED FOR DRAMATIZING SALES POINTS

A few people are truly eloquent and can spellbind their audience with words and gestures. These people can succeed in many fields but are rarely found, except briefly in passing, in sales careers. On the other hand, professional buyers often find after listening to five or six competitive sales presentations that a bad salesman sounds about as effective as a good salesman. The messages are practically the same, the claims are almost identical, and the subtle digs at each other are all too common. The prospect is often more confused after listening to the salesmen than he was before seeing any of them. Something dramatic is lacking when all sales presentations sound alike.

*Breathe Life and Vigor into the Message.* Great speakers, national leaders, famous stage and screen personalities distinguish themselves from their lesser known competitors by projecting, or emotionally reaching out to the audience. Will Roger delivered his philosophy with quiet humor while playing idly with a cowboy's rope. The audience was an equal part of his great act and quickly appreciated his sincere manner. Presidents Roosevelt and Kennedy had this ability to project themselves emotionally into the hearts of their audiences while talking to their minds. One of the greatest speakers in modern history, Sir Winston Churchill, could speak to an emotionally cold and detached House of Commons and arouse their emotions to a fighting pitch. Outstanding personalities are rarely born with this talent to project to an audience; they must learn it. Early in his childhood, Churchill was labeled a failure by his teachers. He had to work most of his lifetime at being the great speaker and writer which he succeeded in becoming. With all the professional writing assistants on his staff, President Roosevelt is reported to have revised his final drafts of political talks as many as seven times, searching for precisely the right phrase and word. It is not easy to breathe life and vigor into a message but when it is done with dedication and an understanding of the audience, it becomes so outstanding that even those who might disagree with the point of view expressed are sincerely compelled to respect the speaker's view.

*To Inject Speaker's Personality.* As noted in Chapter 7, a message is often judged by the assumed creditability of the source of the message. If a sales message contains no hint of the personality of the salesman, it may not be taken seriously by the prospect. The message would be as effective on a tape recording or radio commercial which can be mentally turned off, and very little of what is said is ever heard. The source of the message should become part of the total communication so the prospect can judge the salesman's expertness, his authority to talk on this subject, his friendliness, his interest in the buyer's welfare, his understanding of the buyer's needs and problems, and his sincerity. When sales messages are equal in all other respects, the prospect must decide on the basis of the individual salesmen. Which man would he like doing business with and being exposed to again in the future? Clearly, the man who can inject the personal touch which appeals to the prospect will be more successful than the others who appear stereotyped.

*Focus Attention.* By dramatizing a sales message, the salesman directs the prospect's attention to a specific point and the prospect's critical attitude is focused upon the phase of the sales presentation which the salesman is attempting to make. Due to the short attention span of most individuals, unless some dramatic action is taken to hold the mind which tends to wander, the sales message will be lost. An effective salesman is prepared with several dramatic actions which he can employ to regain attention when he senses he is losing the buyer's interest.

*Gain Selective Perception, Retention, and Recall.* Occasionally, a simple, logical sales presentation is understood and remembered. However, it is rare when any person can concentrate so thoroughly as to exclude all interfering internal thoughts of all other problems and external diversions —such as a pretty secretary walking by. More often the prospect is not attempting to listen that carefully and he will miss a number of basic steps in the simple, logical sales presentation. When the conclusion is reached, it does not make sense to him. The effective salesman is prepared to emphasize certain points in his presentation with dramatic action which really focuses the prospect's attention for that moment. Later recall by the prospect will invariably be aided equally by the action he saw and the words he heard spoken.

*Change of Pace.* Any lengthy sales presentation can become boring if one person tends to dominate the conversation. If a number of competitive sales presentations emphasize the same basic points and make the same claims, the prospect is bound to be bored. While repetition is normally effective in persuasion attempts, in this situation it could prove fatal for the repeating salesman. Repetition with variation will be effective but the variation in this case should include an element of surprise, a real change of pace and something dramatic. It will serve as a welcome change and break the monotonous regularity to which the prospect has been subjected.

## TYPES OF VISUAL MATERIAL USED BY SALESMEN

The tools of the salesman's trade consist primarily of visual aids which are used to supplement his personal efforts in adapting to each prospect's individual requirements. Just as he may know literally thousands of facts about his product and company but use only a selected few in a given situation, so he may carry literally thousands of pictures, charts, graphs, and other visual materials but use only a selected few for a specific purpose.

Visual aids with the sales presentation generally are more effective than the spoken word alone. This is analogous to the appeal of television which practically commands the viewer's attention compared to the radio which may be playing but can be virtually ignored. One often turns on the radio in the morning to hear the weather forecast so that he may dress appropriately for the day. In the preoccupation of preparing for the day, he often misses the weather report when it is finally broadcast. In the same manner, a prospect may think he is tuned in or listening for a particular point in a sales presentation and still miss it completely when it is finally stated.

Drawings and pictures are common visual aids and they are often the best way to communicate important details of a product. Photographs are used the same way but can be used more effectively when illustrating the product in use by other satisfied owners. Photographic enlargements can illustrate most clearly how a detailed product might fit into a larger scheme of things, such as how a small electric motor might be used in conjunction with a large, mass-production assembly line.

Films and slides are often used to increase the three-dimensional effect or to illustrate a time sequence of actions which makes it easier to understand the product or to appreciate its uses. For group presentations the overhead projector and the opaque projector are effective in pointing out interesting details which would otherwise be lost without the necessary magnification. Film can be stopped and a pointer used to focus attention on one detail at a time. If motion is important, the film speed can be varied to accentuate the critical movements.

Charts and graphs are best used to picture statistics where dry facts and figures might be boring or difficult for the prospect to visualize and understand. If an automobile traveling at a series of predetermined speeds requires progressively increasing distances to come to a full stop, how much more easily it can be appreciated if one sees a green bar two inches long representing stopping distance at a safe slow speed, a yellow bar four inches long for a higher speed, and a red bar eight inches long for the highest speed. Similarly, if increased profits are to be stated in relation to the number of feet of shelf space, a graph with an incline is quickly understood at a glance. Many functions of business management require graphs and charts to illustrate complicated statistics to top management which might not otherwise take the time to puzzle through them for understanding. Busy executives appreciate such timesaving presentations as long as the statistical data is readily available to verify the graphic claims. Work flow charts and organizational chain of command charts can quickly portray line and staff functions and responsibilities which words alone can rarely make clear. If the sales proposition involves difficult concepts, as in management consulting services, such visual aids are a tremendous benefit to communications.

Technical manuals can be useful to the salesman to insure all information is available to answer any questions which the prospect may raise during a presentation. These manuals are generally in loose-leaf form which permits the addition of the latest and most complete information. This can be impressive to a skeptical buyer of technical products. Such loose-leaf manuals also permit leaving the selected specifications with an interested prospect so he may study them after the salesman leaves. A danger in using such manuals is that the salesman may focus the prospect's attention on boring product details rather than on interesting user benefits. A weak salesman is tempted simply to read the details to the prospect rather than boldly interpret the technical data into meaningful generalizations which will apply to this particular prospect.

Models and miniatures are often fascinating to many people who find the printed and spoken word difficult to understand. This is particularly true if English is a foreign or second language to the prospect. He may be too embarrassed to ask the salesman to say everything again more slowly or he may not be interested enough to work at understanding the salesman. Most people enjoy handling and inspecting a miniature and if it has moving parts, they will generally activate the mechanism and become curious about it and interested in the point it is designed to illustrate. Of course, if the product itself is tiny, as many new electronic components are, an enlarged model might serve the same purpose of focusing attention and increasing understanding.

The product itself or an important component of the product can be used to demonstrate physically its superiority, uniqueness, or applications easier than words or pictures might. Many products are too large or heavy to be carried by the salesman but by prior arrangement with the prospect they can be delivered to his business and later demonstrated as they would look or be used in his own shop or office. A variation occasionally used by creative salesmen is to demonstrate by choosing an old piece of equipment the prospect is now using and showing him how a new unit would have additional features or automatic features which would reduce costly labor, wasted energy or materials, errors, or whatever the new model really would accomplish. The salesman must be both knowledgeable and eloquent to carry out such a dramatization. However, it is most effective because every time the prospect uses the old equipment thereafter, he is apt to be favorably reminded of the salesman and his dramatization.

Sales portfolios or a series of pictures which help the salesman tell his story are common tools of the mutual fund sales companies. They help direct the prospect's attention, aid the salesman to tell his story in logical sequence, and generally insure the honest presentation of facts without exaggeration or misleading statements. Each picture or drawing is accompanied by a brief headline of the customer benefit and some smaller print explaining or qualifying the claims. Since such literature must be filed with the Securities Exchange Commission, the printed words take on added creditability and they are often much easier to understand than the formal prospectus which actually offers stock for sale.

A manual of standardization can also be used to dramatize a particular sales presentation in special cases. A problem common to many salesmen is how to get a customer to standardize on his product exclusively throughout the country instead of using several competing brands at different locations. Standardization in the plant or factory has been firmly established in the United States for many years and it is gaining in acceptance in the office, warehouse, and branch store. The home office must establish the standard for various levels and then communicate this information to all related points in the organization. This problem of setting standards and then reproducing the information so that it is understood by all is often so complicated that many prospects hesitate to establish such a program. If the selling company has successfully standardized other accounts in the past, a customer's manual of standardization which shows the exact items

*Courtesy: International Business Machines Corp., Armonk, N.Y.*

**FIG. 15. An executive learns of storage capacity of computer from salesman.**

permitted to be requisitioned might help the new prospect visualize how easily he could accomplish the same thing.

## ADVERTISING AND MERCHANDISING AIDS
## AT POINT OF PURCHASE

Many sales campaigns are attempts to tie in national advertising expenditures with point-of-purchase display expenditures at the retail level. For example, an advertisement featuring a picture of the product with colorful balloons floating above might be copied for a store display featuring an oversized facsimile of the product and real balloons. A store window might be decorated to reproduce physically the picture in the national advertisement. Before the store owner will permit such displays and win-

300 TECHNIQUES OF PRACTICAL SELLING

dow decoration, he must be convinced the space requested will yield the greatest benefits to his store regardless of the benefit to the national supplier. Under these conditions, the supplier's salesmen normally would have advance copies of the advertising and store displays proposed, together with the facts and figures indicating the type and size of the audience expected and probable floor traffic to be generated by such a campaign. Local advertising campaigns might be tied into the national promotional plan with the manufacturer possibly sharing the cost of the local advertising. Here again the salesman would probably have visual aids already prepared showing how the store name would tie in to the national copy.

A variation often seen in advertising is the national advertisement by the manufacturer with a list of store names under the caption, "Where to Buy It." Assuming the offer is made equally to all outlets, this practice is a fair one and often permits the territory salesman to gain window or floor display space he might not otherwise expect. A blank advance copy of the national advertisement becomes his visual aid and if he is successful the store will often receive an enlarged copy of the finished advertisement with an arrow pointing out its name. This enlarged copy is then proudly displayed at the point of purchase.

Copies of advertisements are used in a special way in personal selling. To a number of people, a national advertisement is somehow proof of claims made because the ensuing liability prohibits false claims, or so the false reasoning seems to go. The very fact that the advertisement is published seems to lend authority to what the salesman says. While this reasoning may be unsound, a national brand name does carry considerable investment and the manufacturer is not apt to risk such an expenditure with false or misleading statements.

An advertisement in a quality magazine psychologically lends prestige to the product offered in the same way that placement in an exclusive department store is interpreted as a type of endorsement for the product. Many consumer products are sold to the retailer on the basis of national advertisements in quality magazines with an enlarged point-of-purchase copy of the advertisement emblazoned with the trademark of the magazine, "As advertised in . . . ."

The same psychological factors apparently are at work in advertisements that appear in technical or trade journals of the type the prospect is apt to be familiar with or read regularly. Such readership is apt to be self-selected —for example, all chemical engineers—and the advertisement is slanted or biased to appeal to that particular audience. Later when the salesman uses a copy of the complete magazine as a visual aid, it is not only a form of dramatizing his presentation, it also lends prestige to his products in the minds of some prospects. For many prospects, seeing the ad in the trade magazine reminds them of having seen it before and often this is a pleasant association.

## IMPRESSING APPEALS TO PROSPECT'S VARIED SENSES

Audiovisual presentations are used by almost every sales organization to involve the prospect's sense of sight as well as his sense of sound. If appealing to two of the prospect's physical senses is more effective than appealing to only one, doesn't it make good sense to employ other appeals when they are appropriate? The five physical senses are sight, hearing, touch, smell, and taste. The more senses a prospect uses to identify a proposition, the more effective the sales message will be.

Touch is the easiest of the senses to employ after using the audiovisual aids because the product itself or small samples can be carried and handed to the prospect. At times, creative imagination is necessary to demonstrate effectively through a sense of touch. For example, if a safe salesman carried a sample of the insulation material, a prospect could physically touch it but since it looks and feels like wall plaster it would communicate little meaningful information. Suppose this salesman handed the same prospect a partially burned ledger card with crisp black ashes about to crumble off the edge. He might also place a burning match under a small piece of steel plate which would quickly transmit heat to the prospect's finger. Whenever the prospect sees or handles burnt paper or a hot pot or roasting pan in the future, he may remember this sales demonstration.

Many products have a distinct odor which is unique to them alone, such as the nice clean smell of a new automobile or the smell of top grain leather in furniture and luggage. Other products have no direct odor but are associated with other events or activities which people can easily identify by the associated odor. Ladies' wear is pleasantly associated with perfume and a number of department stores subtly use this association to attract attention to various departments within the store. Hospitals have a distinct odor which can be associated with some products for cleanliness and personal hygiene. Chemists have recently accomplished wonders in this field and they can scent product samples or paper stationery to communicate a message which is pleasant to the prospect. Used with polite discretion, such an appeal can be both enjoyable and effective in building a lasting impression of the sales proposition.

Appeals to the sense of taste are generally confined to the selling of spices and related food products and little has been done to date to capitalize on the psychological phenomenon of association in the same way that it applies to odors. Taste and odor are very closely related as we all quickly appreciate when passing a bakery or when a holiday roast comes out of the oven. The familiar phrase is, "It smells so delicious it is mouth-watering!" The airlines are now using this idea of associating taste with their product—transportation—by appealing to the gourmet to have his favorite exotic food on board the plane. In personal selling, some men entertain their clients at exclusive clubs or restaurants both to impress the client and to cause him to compare every other nice restaurant with the one he visited with the salesman. Using the sense of taste to associate pleasant attitudes with a product may be difficult to apply but it would seem foolish not to use it when it is available and appropriate to the individual selling situation.

## WHEN TO DEMONSTRATE A PRODUCT

The timing of a product demonstration depends primarily upon the purpose to be accomplished and, secondly, upon the situational aspects at the moment of the sales contact. Dramatization and demonstration can be used to attract initial attention, to regain lost attention, as well as to narrow or focus attention on a particular phase or feature of the selling presentation. Demonstration can be used to increase the clarity and under-standing of a complex product or service. This can be illustrated by the analogy of giving a friend directions to a restaurant in the country. A simple map drawn on plain paper will be more effective than a page full of written directions. A demonstration can be used to obtain greater concen-tration on the salient points of a presentation. A file cabinet, for example, has only one basic moving part, which is called the slide. By demonstrating the construction and operation of the various bearing surfaces, the sales-man directs the prospect's attention to the major or outstanding difference in competitive products.

Some demonstrations are designed to change the prospect's awareness to conviction because, while he may doubt the spoken word, seeing the prod-uct perform under realistic conditions is tantamount to believing. This type of demonstration is much more vivid than words by a possibly biased salesman and the prospect is not apt to forget what his own senses told him. A demonstration can also be used to illustrate a point much more quickly than in the time it would take to tell the same point. For example, a quick and simple sketch of furniture in a room is much easier for a prospect to understand than a lengthy word description of the various furniture pieces in relation to each other and in relation to the different walls, windows, and doors.

A prospect will often attempt to carry on other activities while listening to a salesman talk in the honest belief that he can do both things well at the same time. Rather than argue the point, the effective salesman is prepared to demonstrate his product or service in such a way that it will cause the prospect to devote full attention to the sales presentation. A variation of this divided attention problem arises when a prospect is honestly interested in the sales proposition but the telephone and business associates continually interrupt the chain of thought. If the demonstration is vivid enough, business associates are more apt to postpone their interruptions and the prospect himself may ask the switchboard to hold his calls for the next few minutes. As an alternate course of action, the salesman can attempt to get the prospect away from his normal work station by showing him how the product really works in the shop, the plant, the warehouse, the selling department, or wherever it is normally used. Another condition under which it might be more favorable to demonstrate a product would involve taking the prospect to visit another customer's business to show him the product in use as well as the benefits to the user. Finally, the salesman can invite a busy prospect to his showroom for a demonstration either as an adjunct to the lunch period or outside of the customer's normal working hours. Busy people often are the best prospects because once they see the product demonstrated, they quickly appreciate any timesaving factors and they are personally motivated to obtain such benefits for themselves.

The purpose of all demonstrations should be to relate and adapt to the individual prospect's needs or problems and to show how the product or service can best satisfy them. Any planned demonstration causes a salesman to deliver an orderly talk and even a mediocre salesman will often find his efforts producing rewarding results when a planned demonstration replaces his plain sales talk. On the other hand, an effective salesman who can adapt to each prospect's individual needs will find the added dramatization produces excellent results.

An audiovisual presentation or product demonstration is also indicated when the sales proposition must be given to a group of buyers simultaneously. Such a demonstration should be planned so it will be understandable and interesting to the audience. The salesman should learn as much as possible about the general aims, interests, abilities, and capacities of the various members of the audience. This will make it easier to eliminate technical terms that are not familiar to the audience and to omit details which are of no interest to them. The purpose of a group demonstration is to convert raw data of facts, figures, and concepts into a form that an audience composed of people with different interests can grasp quickly and favorably. A planned question and answer period, both before the demonstration covering what the audience will see, and after the demonstration to summarize, is often essential and is generally most effective.[1]

## HOW TO PREPARE FOR A DEMONSTRATION

The foundation of any demonstration is an analysis of the objective to be accomplished for each individual prospect. Just as the method of getting an interview can vary with the purpose of each interview, so can a demonstration vary with the objective to be accomplished with each prospect. An airplane salesman, for example, demonstrating the short field takeoff and landing capabilities of his plane to a sale's vice-president who might specify what make he wanted, would be quite different in his sales presentation from the same salesman demonstrating the cost-cutting benefits of a company-owned airplane versus using regular scheduled airlines and auto rentals to a corporate treasurer who could veto the entire proposal. Too often a demonstration is thought of as simply showing the product to a buyer. Clearly, different buying influentials are interested in different aspects of the entire selling proposal. A demonstration of statistical facts and figures about a product should be quite different from a demonstration of the operation of a product designed to appeal to the operator or user of the product.

The demonstration should be planned together with the accompanying verbal message. The salesman should ask himself several questions. What motivations can be stimulated by demonstrating the product? What can be done to involve the five senses of the prospect so that he can be more quickly and favorably impressed with what he sees? If he is already motivated to purchase this type of product, what are the outstanding features of a particular brand which, when demonstrated, will cause the prospect to select or choose that specific brand of product or that particular supplier?

---

[1] A. A. Lumsdaine found that the amount learned from certain parts of a film could be increased substantially by directing the viewers' attention to those parts before the film was shown. A. A. Lumsdaine, "Attention Directed to Parts of a Film," in Mark A. May and A. A. Lumsdaine, Learning from Films (New Haven: Yale University Press, 1958).

Once the message has been outlined in a sequence which will complement the demonstration, effective language must be employed to put some meat on the skeleton. Certain points will probably be made intentionally before, during, and after the demonstration to provide the salesman an opportunity to employ repetition with variation. Assuming the prospect is reasonably well educated, it is likely the salesman will want to employ a two-sided argument in his demonstration and let the prospect be the judge of the soundness of his recommendations. This point was explained in Chapter 10.

The salesman should then practice the talk with the demonstration and smooth out any obvious difficulties in coordinating the two so the end presentation becomes a true audiovisual presentation. He should practice the presentation until it feels natural and logical but he should also remember that, as no two prospects are exactly alike, no two demonstrations should be exactly alike. The effective salesman is prepared to adapt his demonstration to the prospect's needs and supply whatever dramatization is necessary spontaneously as the situation dictates.

Finally, an equipment check is essential to avoid later embarrassment. If film is required, the salesman should be sure it is the right film; it is in good condition and wound properly; the projector and sound equipment work properly; and extra accessories are packed including an extra lamp, adapter plugs, extension cord, clean lenses, and the proper screen for the type of room, lighting, and number of viewers. If an overhead projector is to be used, transparent slides should be in the proper order and clearly marked for quick identification. Tape recordings should be wound properly, with each tape clearly marked and ready for immediate playback. While these things may seem obvious, many a salesman or public speaker has been embarrassed and near panic when his mechanical equipment failed to work due to the omission of such simple precautions.

## GETTING THE PROSPECT TO PARTICIPATE

If the salesman can get the prospect into the demonstration, the prospect will no longer be able to sit in cold detached judgment as he will automatically become part of the selling team. The prospect's cooperation in making the demonstration work will encourage him to desire its success because a convincing demonstration will in part reflect on his ability as a performer. He is no longer a part of the audience viewing the demonstration but has been transformed into a participating actor.

This role-playing effect, well documented by the psychologist Dr. Jacob L. Mareno, was covered earlier in Chapter 9. Even hostile audiences, such as prisoners of war, have been induced to change their attitudes against their own will when playing the role of the persuader of their associates. A prospect with much less ego involvement than the prisoners of war is more readily persuaded when he acts out the part of a satisfied user of the new product. He will tend to internalize the reasons which will make his acting more realistic and believable. Once the prospect shows or acts out the benefits of acquiring the new product, he is well on his way to being convinced that actually acquiring it is the best action he can possibly take. Clarity and understanding change awareness into belief and this in turn increases his desire to act.

Prospects often hesitate to participate in a demonstration. However, if the planning includes a role for him to play, it will seem more natural and not an imposition. For example, if a fire extinguisher is to be demonstrated in a large G.I. can, the salesman might start the fire and ask the prospect to stand by with the extinguisher for safety. Once the fire is blazing the salesman can ask the prospect to prove to himself how easily the extinguisher works. Having once used the extinguisher, the prospect will know with the certainty of direct personal experience how quickly and efficiently it works. No amount of words will ever be as convincing or as impressive to this buyer. Appeals to save time will often encourage a hesitant prospect to help the salesman demonstrate his product as will any operation which requires more than two hands at the same moment. On occasion a skeptical attitude can be used to ask the prospect to check something for himself so that there is neither distortion of facts nor room for any error.

## TECHNIQUES FOR CONDUCTING A SALES DEMONSTRATION

When a customer has agreed to a demonstration, it is essential for the salesman to check the physical facilities for such necessary things as the location and type of electric power outlets, controlling switches, seating arrangements, acoustical effects of the area, adequate space, ventilation, and similar items. If the demonstration is complicated, the prospect should be cautioned to plan sufficient time for a proper appraisal and possibly to arrange to have as many of the interested parties present as possible. If special machine operators are to be used, the demonstration will be more convincing if the prospect's own people are used whenever this is possible. If his shop foreman tries the product and likes it, the prospect is more apt to look favorably on the proposition than if an expert from the sales company does exactly the same things.

Finally, no matter how obvious things seem to the salesman who is an expert in his demonstration, the prospect should be prepared for what he will see. When people watch an industrial movie, for example, they will often concentrate on the people involved when really it is the manufacturing process which was intended to be illustrated. No sales aid is so obvious that some members of an audience will not look for the wrong things and completely miss the desired message. The prospect should be told of what the demonstration will consist and what points are critical or especially important to look for or to be studied carefully.[2] During the demonstration these points should be noted by the salesman verbally so the prospect really sees with his own eyes—and therefore believes—exactly what is considered to be the most important things instead of trivial or incidental details. When the demonstration is complete, the salient points should be reviewed again in summary form and the discussion opened to gain the prospect's voiced approval.[3] Once on record, as noted in Chapter 10, the prospect is not apt to waver due to later influences.

A variation of the demonstration technique is the trial offer which involves using the product under typical or normal conditions in the buyer's office, plant, or store. The salesman should prepare the user as well as the person making the buying decision. He should instruct the user or operator in ways to reduce effort and optimize the operations and should actually guide him through the initial attempt. After the operator has successfully accomplished the proper use, he should be permitted time to perfect his movements. Later, when the salesman returns at the conclusion of the trial period, he should again review the outstanding points and attempt to gain the prospect's open statement of approval.

## CREATING A FORMAL SUBMISSION OR PROPOSAL

In some lines of business it is common for prospects to ask for a written proposal before they will place an order. Even after a particularly effective sales presentation and demonstration, the prospect will often react very favorably and agree to purchase the product but qualify his approval with a casual request for a formal proposal. Typically, he may say, "That was a

---

[2] Military trainees made a learning gain of 10 percent when the instructor called their attention to important points to be learned and to the importance of learning these points. Carl I. Hovland, A. A. Lumsdaine, and Fred D. Sheffield, *Experiments on Mass Communication* (Princeton, N.J.: Princeton University Press, 1949), pp. 141–46.

[3] Wittich and Fowlkes found that 78 percent more material was learned by the discussion techniques over showing of a film alone. Also 28 percent more was learned over the method that only introduced and prepared the class for the film. However, these techniques required considerably more time. (Walter A. Wittich and John Guy Fowlkes, *Audio-Visual Paths to Learning* [New York: Harper & Bros., 1946].)

good demonstration. I like it and I'll buy it. Send me the prices for the exact items and quantities we discussed and I'll send you the order by return mail."

The temptation is to simplify the work and send the prospect only the information he specifically requested without any additional selling effort. Orders have been received by doing this but even more orders have been lost by doing so. The experienced salesman, having done this much work for an order, will not want to leave the last opportunity to chance. He will prepare a formal submission or proposal which continues to sell and reassures the prospect that he is making a wise decision.

The formal proposal is normally written to an individual in a warm and friendly manner. It can safely be assumed that other buying influentials will read the proposal before the order is actually placed. These other influentials may not be familiar with the product, the demonstration, or the rationale behind buying the product now, in this particular brand, or from this particular source. All major selling points are reviewed in the formal proposal and necessary pictures and charts are included to justify any claims or to clarify the specific choice of models or optional features which the prospect has selected.

The tone of the proposal is positive. For example, "When you receive your new ABC machine, you will quickly realize the benefits which we discussed yesterday, namely . . . ." For the benefit of other buying influentials who were not present earlier, the proposal should answer their probable questions which might include financial arrangements, instruction of the ultimate user, and other related information.

The actual quotation typically includes a referent to the catalog page number where the item is described, the stock number, the quantity desired, a brief word description in terms which will be meaningful to the prospect, the unit price, and the extended price. After the itemized list, a total should appear indicating earned discount, if any, delivery and installation agreements, and other details unique to each line of business.

The conclusion of the formal proposal should reassure the prospect of his correct decision to obtain the best product to fill his needs. If applicable, the proposal might include mention of the continued efforts of the salesman to help the buyer achieve optimum benefits after delivery. The proposal normally ends on a note of thanks which makes it easy for the prospect to initial his approval on a copy and return it or simply to telephone the purchase order number to expedite his order.

The length and form of the formal proposal would depend upon the type of proposition offered and the relative buying influence of the individual prospect. The salient point here is not to lose a sale by default after coming so close to a verbal order. A little more selling effort used in creating an effective formal submission can reduce the last-minute slips and increase the number of sold orders.

The formal submission or proposal must act as the complete selling presentation with the necessary dramatization and formal detailed quotation for an unseen audience that may never actually see or hear the salesman. It should be tailored specifically to the one prospect and be as personal as business cordiality will permit. If the friendly contact is the only one ever to see it, he can hardly be offended if the salesman shows he really wants the order and is still willing to work hard to earn it. When competitive proposals are received, the salesman who covers all points is more apt to receive favorable action than the low bidder who submits a short quotation which could be interpreted as a lazy or lackadaisical attitude which leaves much open to doubt in the buyer's mind.

◆　◆　◆

## VISUAL AIDS*

*The Master Copy*
In the field it's a good idea to carry the past five front pages of *The Wall Street Journal* with you on a call and use it in your presentation. The master copy is best injected into your talk when you describe the *Special Reports* as you can turn to each of these front pages and show the prospect each report— and at the same time he will see the great variety of stories The Journal covers in one week.

*Special Reports*
You will be sent from time to time samples of the five Special Reports appearing in *The Wall Street Journal* each week, printed on 8½ x 11 forms which demonstrate how these reports could look were they printed and sold separately. This Visual Aid effectively demonstrates in your presentation the value of having these reports on the front page for easy checking each day, rather than as just another magazine letter to pile up on a man's desk.

*Headline Sheet*
Each month you will be supplied with an 8½ x 11 sheet showing sample headlines from the previous month's *Wall Street Journals*. This aid allows you to demonstrate quickly the wide range of topics found in *The Journal* in a month's time (effectively shows *The Journal* is not a financial but a business paper for all business men).

---

* The above is reprinted with the kind permission of Dow Jones & Company, Inc., Community Sales Program, Circulation Field & Phone Sales Division, Princeton, N.J.

# 20

# Understanding and Dealing with Objections

A very popular belief is that the real selling begins after the demonstration and presentation ends and the prospect offers his objections. While this point of view is often correct, it is only part of the total selling picture and can be very misleading. Prospects often object early and throughout a sales presentation, not just at the end, and they do so for a variety of reasons. Some objections are real while others are merely excuses. Many objections are common to various products and services; others are unique to one particular brand of product. An effective salesman understands the reasons behind objections, is prepared to deal with them, and recognizes which strategy and which technique to employ in a given situation.

## WHY PROSPECTS OBJECT

Objections begin the moment a salesman requests an interview and often continue early in his presentation. The listener feels he is not a prospect because he is not aware of any need or problem in the salesman's area of specialization. As the presentation develops and the listener begins to appreciate the value and probable cost of the offering, he may feel he cannot afford the product regardless of how attractive it may be. The listener may be of such a nature that he would deny himself the pleasure or benefits of acquiring a product to maintain a feeling of security by keeping his cash in the bank. A listener may not have the authority to make a decision but may feel very reluctant to admit he is not as important as the salesman seems to believe he is.

Assuming the listener honestly believes he is not a prospect, a salesman selling to mass markets might be well advised to save his time and move quickly to the next prospect rather than waste a disproportionate amount of time attempting to gain a small sale. On the other hand, selling to a limited number of prospects often involves repeat calls and such objections must be overcome before the salesman will be effective. If the salesman is guided by the principle of his long-term contribution to profit, he will realize it is to his advantage to capitalize on his selling efforts already expended in developing friendly relations with the nonprospect. The effective salesman offers friendly advice and suggestions to the buyer and in return is rewarded with suggestions for legitimate leads either in the same company or in other companies. This policy also enables the salesman to return in the future when conditions change and the company becomes a true prospect.

*FEAR*. It is a common phenomenon for people to be suspicious and to resist any suggestions made by strangers, as noted in Chapter 3. Many people want to feel they know the salesman and understand his motivations before they will warm up enough to trust what he says or place any confidence in his claims. They want to feel the salesman is honestly looking out for their welfare before they are willing to conduct any business with him.

A closely related fear is the danger of the unknown in anything new. The prospect knows from experience the advantages and disadvantages of behaving as he now does but he does not know with comparable certainty what may happen if he changes his behavior to buy something new. Some people are continually perplexed by this fear of making any decision because it may be wrong. Rather than choose between alternate courses of action, they tend to do nothing. This effect of cross-pressures was covered in Chapter 9. The prospect will make light of the sales proposition and dismiss it as trivial or without any meaningful consequences for him.

Another fear is that of hurting existing friendly suppliers. Many sales stories indicate a fight or mental contest between adversaries but, in truth, much industrial buying and selling is done on a friendly and loyal basis. A recent editorial in a magazine for professional buyers pointed to this feeling and gave as its defense, "We can't crack the whip on people we've had pleasant long-term relationships with . . . . It's not right. It's not ethical."[1]

It is a fact that some buyers fall into comfortable relationships with salesmen and often identify their best interests with the suppliers' interests. When conditions change and competitive pressures increase, these buyers find it difficult to do a tough, professional job of purchasing. In simple

---

[1] Editorial, *Purchasing*, April, 1963.

terms of human relations, they do not want to hurt their friends. This is an admirable quality of character and is exactly what the successful supplier wants since he has spent years in cementing the good relationships between companies by supplying many extra services. Such loyalty, however, can be severely criticized from a professional buying point of view, both internally by other buying influentials and by competing salesmen.

*Rebellion Against the Salesman.* More popular in literature is the buyer's repulsion of the individual salesman. While this may be a carryover from the early life experiences of the buyer because of the high-pressure, fast-talking, here today—gone tomorrow type of salesmen, it is more apt to be due to some current sales behavior. As buyers become more sophisticated, they rebel against rudeness and overaggressiveness by salesmen. Since there are usually more possible suppliers than the buyer can possibly use, the buyer quickly rebuffs those salesmen whom he finds it unpleasant to be with. Such personality clashes normally have a more substantial basis than the mere whim of the prospect.

A salesman that begins an industrial contact with a pleasant welcome but after a number of calls has offered little or no help to the prospect can quickly become a pest to the buyer for calling too often without relating to the needs of the buyer. A variation of this rebellion against the salesman involves the overeager salesman who insists on telling his story when the prospect does not have time to listen. It is difficult for some salesmen to realize their customers have duties other than buying and are too busy to devote time immediately to any salesman. The customer must operate his business, handle his personnel and financial problems, keep materials and paper work flowing, and perform numerous other business activities. Many of these problems demand his attention and action immediately while the salesman's proposition can be investigated some time in the future. The same rebellion shows up when the prospect does have time but not the interest in a given proposition when the salesman calls. If the buyer is preoccupied with another business or personal problem he may not want to confuse the issue in his mind by introducing a second problem which some salesman wishes to raise. He is against interference in his thinking process but not necessarily against the salesman's proposition. If he is pushed or cajoled at that moment, he might very well rebel against the salesman personally while at another time when he has resolved the first problem he might welcome the same sales proposition.

Generally prospects rebel against a salesman because the salesman has neglected to encourage the development of the prospect's inner feelings or personality. The prospect may know the supplier very well and may even know the salesman but he feels slighted because his feelings have not been given an opportunity to be expressed. His sense of self-importance has not been catered to sufficiently to justify being friendly toward the salesman. He feels the salesman does not know him, understand him, and respect him enough and he will hold off conducting any business until the salesman proves he honestly respects the prospect. These feelings may or may not be conscious in the buyer's mind but they are very real and represent a considerable obstacle to any sale.

*Want More Information.*   As a sales presentation unfolds or is completed, many prospects object to buying simply because they do not understand the presentation or the actual offer being made. When a prospect says "No" at this point, he may mean that he will not buy because he doesn't understand or that the presentation does not seem complete. This type of objection is, in reality, a request for more information in order to make an intelligent decision. The prospect may be leaning toward a purchase but he wants to be reassured on some doubtful points. He may be seeking additional reasons which will logically justify his impulsive inclination to place an order. Occasionally a prospect will want a product or service for reasons which he feels do not constitute a socially acceptable rationale. For example, a man might want a product which would increase his sexual attractiveness but he might not be willing to acknowledge such a supposedly base motive. Thus he might object to placing an order until he could honestly tell himself that the product's primary purpose was to improve his health or peace of mind.

Other objections which are indicative of the lack of information are those which say the value offered is not equal to the sacrifice required. The benefits of acquiring the product from this supplier must outweigh the loss of cash in buying or the discomfort of doing without, or the unpleasantness of switching suppliers. Very similar objections arise when a buyer is considering several purchases but does not have enough financial ability to buy all the products at the same time. His problem then is to establish a priority of needs and his objections to the sales presentation may seem like comparing apples and oranges. Actually the buyer is weighing the benefits of acquiring product A first against the benefits of acquiring product B first.

*Desire to Bargain.*   Some buyers want to be quoted one firm price and be reassured that everyone else must pay the same price. They may attempt to bargain but only to test the firmness of the price offering. Other buyers want to be assured first that the product is right for them and then they take great delight in negotiating the price arrangement. Such prospects judge their own ability or prowess in buying by the amount of discount they can obtain. If the salesman is too firm and refuses to discuss price negotiating, these prospects feel the best part of buying is being denied to them. The actual price agreed upon is really less important than the enjoyment of bargaining. A variation of the desire to bargain is the prospect's desire to be wooed. A businessman about to place a large order is often wined and dined by competing salesmen and he naturally enjoys the chase for his business. He is courted for his attention and favor much the same as the belle of the campus. If he cannot bargain on the price arrangement, at least he can enjoy the treats that go along with being wooed. By raising objections, he can put off a decision, prolong his pleasure, and sometimes cause the salesmen to make their offerings more attractive than originally quoted.

## HIDDEN MEANINGS IN OBJECTIONS

From the above description of some of the reasons prospects object, it should be clear that any simple reply by a buyer can be interpreted in a number of ways. Earlier it was noted the phrase, "Working late again, dear?" could be intended to exhibit many different feelings in the speaker. Said sympathetically, it might mean concern for the unfortunate man who worked extra hard to support his family. Said in a friendly tone and manner, it might mean encouragement for the young man working hard to get ahead in business. Said quizzically, it might mean curiosity or simple interest in the activities of the man. Said with a knifelike edge, it might mean suspicions were aroused and a justification or explanation demanded. The same phrase could be said with sarcasm, meant as a positive statement for which no response was desired or expected.

This problem of communications must be solved if the salesman is to handle objections from a prospect effectively. In a self-confident and friendly manner, the salesman should draw the prospect out of his shell enough to understand what it is that he objects to and why. Simple objections may cover hidden meanings such as the prospect's bias against the salesman as an individual, against the company he represents, or against the entire industry—such as banking, for example, which the prospect may feel is a parasitic institution. The simple objections may hide socially unacceptable motives or they may hide the individual's personal need to feel important and to be respected. While many things can be taken at face value, a prospect's objections should be carefully probed and analyzed before any quick standard or memorized answer is given.

## EXCUSES VS. REAL OBJECTIONS

Some prospects are reluctant to hurt other people's feelings and rather than say no directly, they offer a number of face-saving excuses to get out of the situation politely. As soon as one such excuse is offset, another one equally false is put forward. Excuses which jump about indicate only a cover for a more basic underlying real objection which prevents the prospect from acting as the salesman suggests.

If a legitimately qualified prospect listens to a well-planned sales talk but then offers lame excuses, the effective salesman should attempt to clear away the smoke screen or camouflage and bring the real objection out into the open. A popular sales technique recommended to accomplish this is to ask the prospect, "If we solve that problem, Mr. Rightman, will you order? If not, then tell me, what else is really bothering you?"

Another problem the salesman must face is the determination of whether the objection is based upon reason or emotion because the strategy in dealing with these two groups of objections would probably be vastly different. Real emotional objections must be handled tactfully and often indirectly but if the objection is real and rational, the salesman can analyze the buyer's statement directly for logic, for projection into the future and likely consequences, as well as for alternate methods to achieve greater satisfaction. These methods can be used openly with the prospect's full knowledge and participation.

## COMMON OBJECTIONS

*Price.* On lost order reports that salesmen file with their managers, the one objection that outnumbers all others put together is price. This is true of competing companies often selling at virtually the same price. The customer states the price is too high; the price is out of line; he can't afford to spend that much money; he wants an optional feature at the standard price; he is looking for a cheaper model; the margin of profit for resale is too small; he would rather wait for prices to come down; he would rather wait for a special sale or discount. When the order is finally placed with a competitor, the unsuccessful salesman feels he lost the deal on price.

*Product.* Some prospects are honest enough to state openly frank and and critical objections about the product itself. They think the' quality is poor or inferior to competing products being offered; the design is not attractive or nearly as appealing as other products; the construction or assembly appears sloppy or faulty; the size seems wrong for the purpose they had in mind; the color tone or shade is not as attractive as that of another brand; the materials are not what they wanted. It is a rare occasion when a salesman will report an order lost due to an inferior product but the objection is voiced by prospects very often. Training in product knowledge generally prepares the salesman to offset this type of objection.

*Service.*   Slow delivery or broken delivery promises are perhaps the most common complaints or objections about service, particularly when sales are good. Other meaningful objections which are raised by prospects regarding customer services include credit terms; management services of training dealer salesmen, aid in preparing local advertising, aid in creating inventory and financial controls, aid in planning floor layout and paper work flow or customer traffic flow; facilities to make it easy for customers to shop and purchase; delivery, operation, and maintenance instructions; factory trained mechanics, service personnel and equipment facilities; and many more. These things were noted in Chapter 4. To one prospect, any one or combination of these services may make the difference between a typical sales presentation and an especially appealing offering. Such objections are very real and practical but the effective salesman is prepared to meet and overcome a buyer's hesitation with alternative services which for a particular prospect outweigh the apparent shortage or disadvantage.

*Company.*   Occasionally, through either direct or vicarious experience, a prospect will be predisposed or prejudiced against a brand name or the supplier's name. "Once I advertised and it failed; therefore I know with the certainty of personal experience that advertising is a waste of money." This analogy illustrates the fallacy of the company objection which begins, "The last time we ordered from your company, we received . . . . In either case, the prospect once had a degree of confidence in a sales offer and the results failed to meet his expectations. From this unique or at least very limited experience, the prospect generalizes that in all future cases the same disappointment is likely to occur. Alternately, a prospect with no direct experience may have heard of a similar experience by a respected associate in business. This vicarious experience becomes internalized to the point where the prospect honestly believes he knows the danger of dealing with a particular supplier. The effective salesman can draw the prospect out and have him state the cause of his belief or objection. When stated in its true light, such an objection will often be recognized by the prospect himself as the false generalization that it is. Since no person or company is perfect, it is easier for the prospect to forgive a single mistake when it is recognized as an isolated incident rather than thought of as typical of all the actions of the supplying company.

*Salesman.* Prospects may object to the particular salesman because of an isolated incident in the past as they will about a company but more often, because of the high turnover of sales personnel, the objection to a salesman personally is caused by a conflict of personalities. The salesman may be so young looking that the prospect refuses to take his suggestions seriously or the salesman may appear so old that the prospect becomes sarcastic when appraising the old-timer's advice. These and similar objections relate to the prospect's lack of confidence in the source of the sales message. In each case, the sales problem is to build the salesman's image into one of a friendly authority who is truly qualified to speak and advise on a specialized subject. This solution applies in extreme cases of personal bias or prejudice in which the prospect is so convinced by the knowledge and authority of the salesman that he can tell himself that the proposition was so good that he purchased the product in spite of the salesman. Abhorrent or distasteful though the prospect's personal prejudices may seem, the effective salesman is outwardly uncritical of them and is immediately concerned with making a profitable sale which will contribute to long-term profits for the supplier. Often such behavior on the part of the salesman will more effectively change the basic emotional attitude of the prospect than an overt challenge or cold logical argument might ever do. Young salesmen from minority groups often resent this direction which appears to make them subservient but maturity generally proves it is more effective in the long run. Therefore such intelligent behavior is of greater benefit both to the individual salesman and to his minority group.

*Acting Now.* Almost every salesman has met the problem of the prospect who agrees with every point in a sales presentation yet refuses to act now. He must consult with others or wait for certain other events to occur before he can take the recommended action. Since he agrees with the salesman in every other respect, it is difficult for the salesman to pursue the buyer seriously who is sidestepping the issue. The inexperienced salesman is tempted to accept such an objection at face value for fear of losing a good prospect who agrees with him. Buyers refer to this technique as the "kiss-off" and subsequent sales calls find these prospects too busy with new problems or changed conditions to reopen the original issue. The buyer remains a nice guy in the eyes of the salesman but he is no longer a good prospect. One-call closers use drastic techniques to call the bluff of such professional buyers but in a repeat call business, the salesman must be more diplomatic because the excuse may turn out to be a real objection. Proving the prospect's excuse to be false may be a temporary moral victory for the industrial salesman but it will boomerang if it so humiliates or irritates the prospect that he will never see the salesman on future visits.

Another variety of the common objection against acting now is the priority of desires which the prospect rates or ranks in his own mind. This was mentioned earlier in this chapter and simply calls for a greater selling effort to raise the one attitude or feeling to a superior or dominant position over the other nearly equal cross-pressures which demand attention.

*Reciprocity.* In periodic cycles, the problem of reciprocity or, "You buy from me and I will buy from you!" seems to become a large factor in the buying-selling relationship. In 1965 it was so dominant in many industries that this topic became primary in a top management seminar held for top business executives in New York.[2] Each case of reciprocity must be analyzed for its unique economic elements with an open mind about the actual sales and profit realized by the selling company as well as the total costs and benefits gained by the buying company. The best the two companies can hope for is to break even or exchange dollars. It hardly seems worth all the pressure and effort by top executives simply to break even when idle cash in the bank would earn at least a small profit. This oversimplification is not intended to denounce the practice of reciprocity but merely to awaken the ideas of creative salesmen who may meet this common objection. A careful analysis of the individual facts is mandatory before an effective appeal can be made and then the appeal most often should be directed to the top executives who create policy.

## CONSTRUCTIVE ATTITUDE TOWARD OBJECTIONS

Very few prospects will accept everything a salesman tells them without question or comment. If the prospect does not agree with the salesman, he can either cut short the interview and run away or he can object, argue, or otherwise resist the salesman. As noted in Chapter 6, when a prospect argues and objects, this indicates he is interested in the sales proposition and his inner stability has been upset enough to cause him to take some action to restore his balance. It is the salesman's purpose to interpret the objections correctly and, if possible, to turn them into reasons for buying. Such action will restore the customer's inner balance and peace of mind.

---

[2] As reported by Professor A. Shuchman of Columbia University Graduate School of Business, Spring, 1965.

If the prospect has been qualified correctly and really does have a want or need, the financial ability to acquire what he needs, and the willingness to spend rather than deny himself, then there should be no real objection that he is not interested in a proposition which will help him. Closely related to being qualified is the identity of the prospect and the purpose of the sales interview. As noted in Chapter 18, a number of people exert different influences on a sales proposition and it would be sheer folly to attempt to get the wrong person to issue a purchase order. A treasurer may not object to some product feature but to the total costs of a proposition while the ultimate user in the plant might object to both the costs and to certain product features. The effective salesman identifies the role of the buying influence and he is prepared to encourage the treasurer to accept the costs and to encourage the ultimate user to like and want the product features. If objections are interpreted correctly in the light of the part that the individual plays in the buying, the salesman's job in handling objections is made easier and this increases his ability to turn objections into reasons for buying.

Because objections are tangible evidence of interest they should be recognized by the salesman as opportunities to sell. Such an attitude will enhance the salesman's image in the prospect's eyes because the salesman can be positive, friendly, and legitimately encouraged by objections instead of exhibiting a negative or defeatist attitude. The constructive attitude enables the salesman to continue promoting friendliness between himself and the prospect and honestly to see the good points the prospect raises. The salesman can reserve his opinion when he has insufficient facts to go on and listen carefully for clues which indicate the buyer's preferences and biases. This information tells the effective salesman where and how the selling emphasis should be concentrated.

Objections should be encouraged and the prospect should be invited and sincerely welcomed to participate in a two-way conversation about the sales proposition. This gives the prospect a chance to express his own personality; a chance to bargain, if he so chooses; a chance to tell what points are confusing; a chance to answer his own questions; and, finally, a chance to help sell himself. In each case, the prospect and the salesman can continue in a friendly relationship going in the same direction with a true meeting of minds. This is the ideal situation as contrasted to that engendered by the direct frontal attack described in Chapter 9.

When a family or company is a legitimate prospect, objections from the right person are really buying signs which present golden opportunities to sell. A positive attitude which invites and welcomes prospect participation will aid the salesman and make it easy for the prospect to buy.

## PREPARATION NECESSARY TO ANSWER OBJECTIONS

Besides understanding why prospects object and developing a positive attitude toward objections, an effective salesman can prepare himself to handle many objections before the sales interview. From the experience of his company, his sales manager, and senior salesmen, a new salesman can learn of the most common objections against buying his particular products. More experienced salesmen learn directly from prospects and past experience in competitive situations. Prospects typically react in predictable ways to certain product features or strong points as well as to weak points. Certain companies will take great pains to stress points which will indirectly cast attention on the weak points of their competitors and play down the importance of their own weaknesses.

*Anticipate Objections.* Objections are likely to be encountered on price, product, service, company, the salesman himself, and against acting immediately. The experience of others can teach the salesman which objections to expect and in what form they are normally expressed as well as several alternate ways to handle such objections successfully. Before the interview, the salesman knows which objections are likely to be encountered but he cannot be sure which objections will be raised by a particular buyer. The effective salesman, while hoping the points will not be raised, can be prepared to answer any and all of these anticipated objections as they may occur later in a sales interview. This forethought enables the salesman to prepare for many contingencies which may or may not occur during the sales interview.

*Forestall Objections.* The direct experience of the salesman or the vicarious experience gained from other salesmen will tell the salesman certain features of the product or proposition are vulnerable. They may be complicated and difficult for the prospect to understand or they may be pet areas on which competitors like to pick. If such a problem is very common, the sales presentation can be broadened to explain fully the areas of difficulty in terms of benefits to the buyer. This preplanning will forestall such objections before they are ever stated by the prospect. For example, if one manufacturer offers his product line to a retailer allowing only a small markup to his nationally advertised "suggested retail price," it should be expected the retailer will object. The sales presentation of the manufacturer's representative should then include a message which explains that the policy of a low markup is intentionally designed to increase the rate of turnover, or retail sales, resulting in higher total profits for the retailer. Examples of test markets and other retailers' experience would tend to reinforce the creditability of this sales point.

*Skill in Fielding Objections.* Knowing what to say in reply to an objection or knowing what to demonstrate to clear up a misunderstanding is quite different from actually performing the act. Knowledge is not skill. The best books in the world on the techniques of riding a surfboard are of little help to the novice attempting to stand on his board under the curl of a 20 foot wave! Practice in applying static knowledge to moving, realistic situations is needed to develop any skill. After practice in training situations, the salesman must then practice on the firing line, in the customer's presence, to develop his skill. Each success as well as each failure should be analyzed continually to improve his effectiveness in handling objections.

## STRATEGY OF HANDLING OBJECTIONS

The basic purposes of a sales interview are to communicate a message, to increase awareness of a need or desire, and eventually to have the prospect convince himself that he should buy the proposition. The strategy or overall broad plan used to accomplish these purposes remains relatively constant when handling objections. Many objections are simply requests for additional information; hence the strategy is to communicate more effectively with this individual prospect than the general sales presentation and demonstration have permitted. Some objections are expressions of doubt about the creditability of either the message or the source of the message. The strategy remains constant because the overall selling plan is to build the highest possible confidence in the source of the sales message. The salesman's strategy in handling objections should be to increase his image as a friendly authority who is well qualified to speak and advise in his particular area. The strategy of building friendship can hardly be overstressed. Two businessmen are more apt to agree on the solution of a problem if they are both attempting to achieve the same objective.

It behooves the salesman to put himself in the prospect's position and to see the objection as the prospect does. The prospect has not had the product training of a new salesman or the firsthand experience of seeing the product in use for many years as older salesmen have. With the limited knowledge of the sales proposition which the prospect has, and of the thousands of facts that he does not know, what information is most relevant and important to his best interests? Being empathetic, the effective salesman can sense how the prospect feels and this in turn tells the salesman what information is lacking from his prospect's point of view. This strategy should have been employed before the call when the sales presentation was tailored for the individual prospect. Much additional knowledge is normally gained during the sales interview which can change original tentative plans. Objections are additional clues about this specific prospect and his needs as he is aware of them. The strategy remains the same throughout the handling of objections because the salesman's intent is to understand the prospect and to help satisfy his wants and needs.

All objections must be evaluated for their real meaning and for the degree of relevancy. For example, if a prospect voices an objection to a minor feature of the product and it is a realistic objection, the salesman can either attempt to enlighten and educate the prospect or he can lightly dismiss the feature as insignificant to the overall understanding of the proposition. His strategy should be based upon how important the minor feature appears to the prospect. Even if it is a minor product feature, if it is highly pertinent in the prospect's mind, he will not accept a light dismissal. This action would then serve to block all further communication and he would not receive or understand other points necessary to form a logical conclusion. On the other hand, if the prospect voices the same objection but indicates by word or manner that it is incidental to him, the salesman's strategy should be to continue with his broader point rather than appear supersensitive or dogmatic in challenging any criticism. The important thing about the degree of relevancy is that objections must be judged from the prospect's and not the salesman's point of view if effective communication channels are to be kept open.

Closely related to the problem of judging the degree of relevancy in objections is the timing of the answer. Early in a sales presentation, for example, the prospect might ask the price and then use this as an objection. If the salesman refuses to give the price at that point, it may block further communication and the reverse could be equally true. The strategy of handling such early objections is to maintain open communication channels. While it may seem the salesman is caught on both horns of a dilemma and is doomed if he does and doomed if he doesn't, there are techniques which will permit a light noncommittal but satisfactory treatment of the objection. Regardless of when it is completely answered, any objection which the customer voices should be acknowledged immediately either through word or gesture. Unfortunately, when his ideas, opinions, or comments are ignored, the prospect is apt to stop listening. Communication is a two-way street and the prospect should not have to exert himself unduly to get his message through to the salesman. This mistake can be costly and if a salesman chooses to ignore proven strategy, he should do so knowing the calculable risk he is taking. This is one gamble that very few effective salesmen are willing to take.

## TECHNIQUES USED TO HANDLE OBJECTIONS

Any list of specific techniques or effective methods used to handle objections can be dangerous and misleading when taken out of context. Each salesman is unique and quite different from all other salesmen and the same is true of each prospect. Each selling interview is different in some way from all other interviews because peoples' moods change, their needs and buying conditions change. A successful technique used one day to handle an objection may not be acceptable under similar conditions with the very same customer on a future sales call. The techniques suggested below are generalizations which must be tailored to fit the salesman, the prospect, and the particular occasion. They are intended to be a starting point for the effective salesman to develop into a personal tool to be honed by his own experiences.

*Agree and Counterattack.* This popular method of handling objections is often called the "yes—but" technique because the salesman agrees with the objection no matter what it is and then goes on to refute it. The salesman may admit one feature of his product is not equal to a competitor's model but neutralize the point or overwhelm it with a different feature which is exclusive to his product. In practice, salesmen use the following phrases:

"Yes, I'm glad you brought that up, Mr. Rightman, but you see . . . ."
"I understand how you feel, Mr. Rightman. On the other hand . . . ."
"Yes it does appear expensive, that's why you will want to know . . . ."
"I agree! I thought that too, at first, then I learned . . ."
"Yes, that's true but I would be remiss in my obligation to you if I did
    not explain why we do . . . ."

*Turn Objections into Sales Points.* This technique of handling objections is also known as "twisting the tale" or converting buying objections into buying reasons or motivations. It can be used to overcome an objection to starting a sales interview as well as throughout the presentation and is particularly effective in working into a closing technique. Common phrases used by salesmen include:

"Of course you are busy! That is exactly why I wanted to see you. . . ."
"Being overstocked won't help you make a profit and it may easily cost
    you future sales because you lack the latest styles. . . ."

"I'm glad you are not in the market now because you can calmly gather
     facts and study your needs without a lot of pressure. . . ."
"No one could afford it if that is all it would do but you also get . . . ."
"Yes, we do charge more because tests have proven . . . ."
"I don't want to sell anything today but I would like to give you some
     ideas for saving. . . ."
"Slow deliveries are relative, Mr. Rightman. How soon would you
     need . . . ."
"We have many sizes, that's true. What size do you need?"
"If it sounds like too much money to pay at one time, how would you like
     to pay for it?"

**Ask Why.**  Most adults are familiar with this technique as it is used
by children. Mother says they cannot go outside today and they ask why.
Her real reason or excuse may be because it is raining out and the child
asks why. Soon the discussion is on a tangent and the original objection is
forgotten. Carried to this extreme the technique can be maddening and it
is apt to boomerang against the salesman but used with discretion the
technique can be very effective. It is also effective in separating excuses
from real objections. For example:

"I have never heard that before, Mr. Rightman. Why don't you like . . . ."
"I don't understand, Mr. Rightman. Specifically, what is it about . . . ."
"That's strange. Why do you say . . . ."
"Apparently I have left something out because we don't seem to be talk-
     ing the same language. Why do you think . . . ."
"What is it that you don't like about . . . (price, product, and
     so on). . . ."

**Admit the Objection if Valid.**  There are many times when a prospect's
objection is both real and valid and it is most effective to praise the buyer
for his astuteness. In return he is apt to admit some sales points which he
might otherwise have argued against. It is often far better to concede on
minor points to win the sale. For example:

"Yes, my company does require a higher down payment than other sup-
     pliers. We have found this eliminates costly extras such as returns. . . ."
"Yes, our deliveries are running two weeks behind others. This tells you
     that other people have seen the superiority of . . . ."
"You are pretty sharp, Mr. Rightman; most buyers do not catch that point
     and in certain cases it could be important. Now, in your case. . . ."
"That's true, Mr. Rightman, our model does not have that desirable
     feature. But really, is that feature worth. . . ."

**Postpone the Answer.**  Some objections are voiced prematurely and if
answered directly will not carry the degree of conviction the answer should.

A trivial objection can be covered more conveniently later in a presentation or perhaps during a demonstration and it is more effective to avoid a direct clash early in the sales presentation. However the answer is postponed, the prospect should feel satisfied temporarily so that his mind will continue to receive the sales message. Some examples of postponing an answer might be:

"That's a good point, Mr. Rightman, and I will cover that in a moment."

"I'll show you that, Mr. Rightman, but first I would like to. . . ."

"What's the price? Well the range might be from . . . (low to high) . . . depending upon which model. For example, in this model. . . ."

"Before I quote firm prices, suppose you tell me . . . (size, quantity, and so on . . .)."

"At this point it appears that way but I haven't shown you. . . ."

*Deny the Objection.*  Perhaps the most dangerous technique for a new salesman to use is to deny the objection because any direct contradiction of the belief of a prospect is apt to close his mind completely. This technique must be handled diplomatically and the prospect must be left with the feeling that he was right in thinking as he did under the circumstances. If an objection is so large in importance to the buyer that it cannot be admitted or overlooked then the effective salesman must consider a direct denial but he must also provide the buyer with some face-saving grace.

"Some one has given you either false or misleading information, Mr. Rightman. You see, the complete facts are. . . ."

"Either you are kidding me, Mr. Rightman, or I left out. . . ."

"I'm sorry, Mr. Rightman. I didn't make myself clear on that point. You see, the way this works is . . . ."

"Of course, what you say is true under these conditions which you describe but if you will look at this another way you will see. . . ."

Price objections and objections to credit negotiations are highly specialized and are discussed more fully in Chapter 23. However, all objections are handled in basically the same way. The prospect objects because he sees the sales proposition from a different point of view from that of the salesman and he appraises the situation with vastly different knowledge. The salesman attempts to modify the prospect's outlook on the pertinent facts and to communicate to him all relevant information to make a favorable decision. Objections are normal and often indicate to the effective salesman that he is close to winning an order.

◆   ◆   ◆

## ANSWERING OBJECTIONS*

| QUESTIONS AND OBJECTIONS | ANSWERS |
|---|---|
| How much is it? | "Regular delivery to your home or office is only— 50¢ a week. . . . and for that you get . . . (review basic sales appeal.)" |
| How long do I have to take it? | "You can take it for as long as you like. Most of the men I talk with have me write it up for 12 months and they prefer it that way because then you have a chance to form your own judgment after a brief experience. The Journal is confident you'll renew . . . better than 80 percent of the annual subscribers do year after year." |
| Can I take it for less than 12 months? | "Yes sir, you can. It's more costly that way due to billing expense and the 12-month trial, besides being more economical, is better for you because, as you know, business is affected by seasonal changes and to make a good test of a service like The Journal's it's best to see how it performs under all conditions." |
| No time . . . I'm too busy. (Almost everybody makes this remark. Most of the time you can pass over it quickly.) | "Everybody's in the same boat these days, Mr. Wilson, that's why you'll like The Journal. It's made for the Busy man who has little time to read—6 minutes a day." |
| If no-time objection is made repeatedly or emphatically, say . . . | "That's just the reason I called, Mr. Wilson. The Wall Street Journal understands your problem and has done something about it. Busy men are headline readers and the busier a man is the better he likes The Journal. It's a paper to be CHECKED . . . the headlines tell the story. It gives you the FASTEST coverage of all the vital business news in one quick package, daily." |
| Let me think about it you can call back later. | "My only concern is that the way business is going nowadays, what's going to happen in the next few weeks will be very important to you. If there ever was a time to TEST The Journal, it is now." |
| My trade journals keep me informed. | "I'm sure they do. Most Journal readers usually subscribe to the trade journals for their particular industry, but The Wall Street Journal's main job, Mr. Wilson, is to give you a quick look at the TOTAL business picture. This protects you against |

---

* The above is reprinted with the kind permission of Dow Jones & Company, Inc., Community Sales Program, Circulation Field & Phone Sales Division, Princeton, N.J.

a surprise development in another industry that's liable to affect you. I know you'll agree one business more or less depends on another."

I read my local newspaper.

"It certainly is a fine newspaper and undoubtedly you receive benefits from reading it especially from the standpoint of local news coverage. However, much of the news and business information you receive in The Journal is not available from any other source." "News the average man never sees."

I tried it out before . . . it piled up and I didn't read it.

"That happens sometimes, Mr. Wilson. Perhaps I can be of some help to you."

"When you pick up your Journal, start under *What's News*. Quickly scan the Business and Finance column to see if anything important to your interests has happened in the last 24 hours. If you find something, turn to the inside pages for complete details."
"Next, bring yourself up-to-date quickly on general news which is capsuled for you in World-Wide column."
"Then look to the Special Report column which is designed for quick checking too. As you know, you get a different report each day. The Outlook on Monday, etc."
"Next, glance at the headlines in columns 1, 4 and 6 to see if any of the stories are of interest to you. And that's all there is to it. When you check The Journal like this, Mr. Wilson, they won't pile up on your desk. You'll get all the news that's important to you each day in less than 6 minutes."

Doesn't apply to my business.

"Most businessmen I talk with feel one business is more or less affected by another and The Journal gives you a penetrating look at the entire business community with very little effort. It's like having an Awareness Insurance Policy!"

Too many publications now.

"After you've had The Journal for a while, Mr. Wilson, you'll find yourself cutting down on other publications without sacrificing news and information that's vital to your business and personal needs. At the same time, you'll be cutting down on expenses, too."

I get all that information now through other sources.

"I know a man in your position wouldn't be without good sources of business information, but you may be getting conflicting reports from several different sources, quite often too late for you to take profitable action."
"The Wall Street Journal ORIGINATES most busi-

ness news. Every day the editors sift vital news from hundreds of different sources and present it to you in capsule form . . . like a telegram on your desk. It saves you time and assures you of prompt, reliable reporting all in one package."

**Not playing the Market.**

"Actually, Mr. Wilson, only four pages or so at the back of The Wall Street Journal are devoted to the stock market. The rest of the paper is just crammed full of other kinds of money-making information that you can apply to your business or personal affairs. The Journal is for everyone who earns a living in business, not just those who invest in the stock market."

**I travel too much.**

"Mr. Wilson, you're just the type of man The Journal's designed for. Thousands of our subscribers are active men like yourself who are out on the firing line bringing in business for their firms. I talked to a man who is away from his office all week and when he comes in on Friday he spends 15 to 30 minutes checking the front pages of the week's Journals to catch up on the news and make sure he hasn't missed anything important while he was away."

**My home office keeps me informed.**

"I'm sure they do. Many businessmen I talk with tell me that even though their companies keep them informed on developments within their industry, The Journal fills a need for general business news and information that is invaluable to their everyday PERSONAL activities. It can help you get ahead."

**Not interested.**

"Many men in your line of business tell me that The Journal is their 'bible.' Another feature they find useful is. . . ."

**I read the office copy or I read my neighbor's copy or I see it at the club.**
**(If you give this response in a friendly and chuckling manner it seldom fails to bring a laugh and often gets results.)**

"Well, fine, Mr. Wilson. I'm very glad it is available to you. You know, The Journal has no legal way to limit one copy to a reader. If it did The Journal certainly would have much greater circulation. Seriously, though, I'm confident you'd benefit more from your own personal copy. Secondhand news loses its value . . . why don't you let me make you a firsthand reader and put you down today for direct service?"

**Buys at newsstand occasionally.**

"Well, that certainly indicates you have more than a passing interest in The Journal. But why risk missing a copy when your newsstand is sold out, and why go to the trouble of picking it up when the postman will deliver it, rain or shine, right in your office . . . or in your home, if you'd prefer."

I got a special invitation from your firm for $5.00.

You must be one of the folks The Journal is really interested in having for a reader. I'm happy to say the annual subscription rate I'm recommending gives you the $5.00 rate all year long—it works this way—:

10 wks. for   5.00 = 50¢ per week
52 wks. for 26.00 = 50¢ per week

For areas where second day or later delivery is normal.

"Having the largest business newsgathering organization in the world, The Journal originates the vast majority of the business news. Even if The Journal reaches you the second day, most of the news will not be available as quickly from any other source."

# 21

## Understanding and Techniques to Obtain Buying Decisions

Obtaining a favorable buying decision is the ultimate objective of every sales presentation. The instant or point at which the prospect agrees to purchase the offering is known as the close. For some products, a close may be successful after a few minutes of the first interview simply on the power of suggestion. Much retail selling is based on a brief contact with the shopper and suggestion is most effective. "That hat makes you look so attractive, why not take it now?" Other products normally require a series of calls and the close may take several days, weeks, or even years. Selling computing machines to industry or institutions, for example, may require a two-year study before a formal offering can be prepared for each specific application. All the preparation, the preliminary study and brainwork before the legwork, the analysis of needs and how best to satisfy them, the actual sales presentation designed for an individual prospect, and the dramatized selling performance are all steps leading to the close.

Actual sales constitute the final yardstick by which most salesmen are measured. Their sales may be compared with last year's sales in the same area or last month's sales or against other salesmen on the same sales force. When the product is new, sales are compared against performance quotas set up by management. Sales are often broken down or analyzed by product line and by profitability to insure optimum effort by the sales force. However analyzed, it is the actual sales written that are the basis for evaluating the effectiveness of individual salesmen. A sales trainee is watched for the number and type of sales interviews he conducts, his competence in handling the sales presentation and answering objections, simply for evidence of sales potential and areas requiring possible further training. The acid test for salesmen is the total orders obtained. Closing the sale is their objective.

When and how often to close are two questions common to new salesmen. The ability to recognize closing signals and the opportunities to close comes from experience and intelligent observations of the prospect's reactions and comments. A close may be attempted at the beginning of a sales interview through the power of suggestion, particularly if the prospect appears to have a strong desire for the proposition. A close may be attempted early in the sales presentation if the prospect demonstrates sufficient knowledge, understanding, and desire. As illustrated in Chapter 20, on objections, a close is normally attempted after each objection is answered satisfactorily. A close is often attempted after a series of commitments or when the prospect appears impatient or impulsive. A close is always attempted after the first complete presentation by simply asking for the order. A close is attempted after a series of presentations during one interview and a close is attempted after several calls. Some salesmen are effective in closing a sale after the prospect has announced he has already decided to give an order to a competitor. When the buyer tells them how they lost the sale, they reopen the discussion and resell their product and again attempt to close it in their favor.

Selling is not a profession for the thin-skinned person who is defeated when he hears the first "no" or is easily frustrated when a prospect cannot seem to understand or appreciate the benefits of the proposition. In industrial selling, less than 20 percent of the salesmen call more than five times on prospects yet they write 75 percent of all of the orders. Stout-hearted salesmen try, try, and try again. When they have just about given up, effective salesmen try once more. As noted in Chapter 10, repetition with variation has a cumulative effect in persuading prospects to buy and this definitely applies to closing the sale.

## TRIAL CLOSE

A technique built into the basic sales presentation is the trial close, or asking for the order without risking a halt to the presentation. Normally, trial closes are attempted several times and in different forms during the presentation. For example, a salesman offering items in ten colors might narrow the choice of selection down to a choice of only two or three by helping the customer decide with less confusion. "Do you like the green one or would you prefer the brown?" If the customer picks one of the alternatives, the salesman moves directly into the close because the buyer has indicated he has decided favorably. On the other hand, if the buyer objects to picking a color at that point, the salesman can continue with his sales presentation naturally and smoothly. A trial close helps the salesman take the temperature of the prospect, or find out how strong the buyer's feelings may be at that point.

Seldom will a prospect simply say "no" when he indicates he is not ready to buy. Most prospects will give a reason or state an objection to substantiate the position they have taken. This gives the salesman the opportunity to discuss those points which are not clear and those points which seem to be of the greatest interest to the customer. The trial close helps the salesman place the emphasis where it is needed. As noted earlier, even a direct "no" can mean many things including:

No, I don't understand.
No, I'm not sure your price is right.
No, I'm not sure you can deliver as you promise.
No, I want more information.
No, I don't believe the benefits outweigh the cost.
No, I want more time to consider your proposition.

The important point is that a trial close can bring out what a prospect is thinking or reasons for his negative response. The salesman can and should continue with his presentation and be prepared to do so naturally without loss of poise or continuity of logic. A trial close is merely a test of the effectiveness of the presentation and the prospect's willingness to buy at that point. The results of the tests tell the salesman what he should do to make the message just right for a specific customer at that moment. Most trial closes are offerings of a choice of actions. The effective salesman always offers a choice between something and something else and never offers the choice between something and nothing. For example, if the salesman says, "Would you like these items delivered in a rush, or is our normal two-week delivery sufficient?" then he can continue the sales presentation no matter what answer the prospect gives. On the other hand, if the salesman asks, "Would you like these items delivered in a rush?", the prospect may reply, "No. I don't want them at all." It would then be difficult to continue the sales presentation naturally. Rather than risk a halt to the presentation, the choice should be between buying one alternative and buying another alternative rather than between buying and not buying.

## STRATEGY OF CLOSING

The close is likely to be successful only when the salesman has convinced the buyer that the purchase action is desirable. The buyer's attitude of conviction comes about when the salesman has planned his selling message and, during its delivery, adapts on the spot to the individual prospect. Part of the planning includes qualifying prospects. The salesman studies his prospect to determine if a legitimate need exists, to determine whether the prospect can afford the proposition, and to determine whether the prospect is willing to spend for things he needs rather than to deny himself. Planning his presentation for this prospect, the salesman learns what buying influentials are apt to become involved and how to contact each of them. He anticipates how he will change the emphasis of the selling message to appeal to each buying influential as his interest or viewpoint varies from the others. He develops a skill in dramatizing and conveying his sales message for each of the buying influentials. The effective salesman treats each buyer as an individual and lets the prospect talk freely while he listens and puts himself in the prospect's shoes. The salesman then knows which features of his proposition are apt to have the strongest appeal to the dominant buying motives of the particular prospect he is attempting to sell. Finally, the effective salesman recognizes that the close is an integral part of a well-planned procedure and is thoroughly prepared to close the order in a number of ways without undue pressure or risking an end to the sales interview prematurely.

## CONSTRUCTIVE ATTITUDE

New salesmen are often ill at ease when it comes to the critical moment of asking for the order. They may not have confidence in their presentation or demonstration and are afraid to have their worst fears confirmed by hearing a customer say "no." Rather than risk such a major catastrophe, they rationalize their way out of the interview by promising to bring more literature or other information on their next visit. While this behavior may seem natural from their point of view, it more often than not creates doubts in the prospect's mind which may not have existed before the salesman lost his nerve.

The fact of the matter is simple. The salesman, even a new man, has studied his product and selling proposition in great detail before going out to see prospects. The buyer who listens to the presentation and watches the demonstration is not nearly so well versed in this particular area as the new salesman. The buyer must depend upon the salesman for information upon which he can make an intelligent decision. If the prospect has a legitimate need or desire for such a product and will honestly benefit by purchasing it, then the salesman is truly helping the buyer to satisfy his needs. On the other hand, if the prospect is not qualified or has no legitimate need or cannot afford the product, then it is better to know this than to make many return calls only to find out at some future date that he is not qualified.

Effective salesmen maintain a positive attitude. They are searching for legitimate prospects whom they can help make an intelligent decision to satisfy their needs and desires. When they approach a new prospect, their attitude is one of intellectual curiosity. "*How* will this next prospect buy?" It is an assumed fact that he will buy if the product really will serve his needs. The effective salesman is performing an honest service for the prospect by bringing him information which will enable him to gain specific benefits. The sales problem is one of communication and persuasion but there is no question about whether the prospect will spend his money or not. If he does not buy from the new salesman, he may buy from a competitor. If he does not buy this product, he will spend his money for other products and other benefits. It is the salesman's responsibility to communicate effectively so the benefits of buying his product outweigh the benefits of either not buying or of buying someone else's product. The salesman who gives an honest presentation has a right to ask for the order, and buyers respect his sincerity when he does ask for the order.

## PREREQUISITES FOR SUCCESSFUL CLOSING

A salesman who has planned his strategy and maintains a positive attitude throughout his contacts with buying influentials needs only a few guidelines for a successful closing. While the sales interview is basically a two-way communication, it is important at the final stage for the salesman to maintain control of the direction of the interview. When the conversation begins to wander too far afield, the salesman must tactfully return the conversation to the sales story in a natural easy manner.

A second guide for successful closing is to allow the customer to set the pace. The salesman should vary the presentation to fit the reactions, the motives, and the basic personality or the current mood of each individual prospect. Each prospect may require different amounts of information to evaluate properly the selling proposition. The kind of information required and the speed with which it can be absorbed will vary with each prospect. To communicate the sales message effectively, the salesman must guide on the customer's reactions, both verbal and nonverbal, which indicate understanding and acceptance. Selective perception and retention of the sales message was covered earlier, in Chapter 8, and this is particularly applicable to successful closing.

A third guide for successful closing is to keep some selling points in reserve. An informed salesman knows literally thousands of facts about his selling proposition and it is impossible to attempt to tell a prospect everything about the product before asking for an order. This very definitely does not mean the salesman should withhold part of his presentation. In planning his strategy, the salesman elects to utilize certain benefits and technical product features to build a logical and interesting interview. He should fit this strategy to the unique situational conditions by adapting on the spot to meet the customer's needs. He should also be aware that in his initial selection of facts he had a wide range of information most of which was not used. With all this information still in reserve, the effective salesman knows he will still have something fresh to say when it is most likely to be effective.

A fourth guide for successful closing is most applicable to compulsive talkers because it seems so obvious to others: Give the customer an opportunity to buy. Don't monopolize the conversation. Be ready to close the sale when the customer is ready and then ask for the order. For example, suppose the customer asks, "Do you carry this in stock?" He is not requesting a long-winded discussion about the size of the supplier's inventory. An appropriate reply might be one of the following:

"Yes, we do have it in stock. When would you like it delivered?"
"No, we do not carry this in stock locally. It will have to come from our factory but if you order now I am sure you will have it installed in two weeks. Shall I put a rush through on your order?"

When a customer is ready to buy, he should be able to do so with a minimum of mental effort. The compulsive talker is more apt to talk himself out of the order at this point than to close successfully.

A fifth guide to successful closing is simply to sell the right item in the right amounts. Some salesmen become so elated when they get an approval from a customer that they literally pack their briefcase and run. To these men, the correct application does not matter, nor does the amount of merchandise. Unfortunately, merchandise returns are costly and attempting to resell a customer who has been treated unfairly is very difficult. The customer depends upon the salesman for expert advice in that field. He is legitimately entitled to the service. If, for example, a salesman representing a manufacturer of ladies' bathing suits were to offer his line to a retailer, he should recommend the logical styles, price range, colors, and sizes for that particular retailer. The order should fit the outlet so that the retailer could offer his trade maximum selection without undue risk of being overstocked. Too little stock will hurt the retailer because many customers will walk out without buying while too much stock will hurt the retailer by tying up his limited capital and forcing him eventually to sell below cost.

Closing a sale is important but the overall objective of the salesman should be his long-term contribution to profit. Repeat sales and customer referrals should be his objectives because they more than make up for quick orders which can boomerang. Each customer should know he is ordering the right item for his particular use and he is ordering the right quantity for optimum benefits. When this becomes an accomplished fact, he will be a loyal customer not easily switched by competitors and he will often refer other prospects to the salesman who has thus earned his confidence.

## TECHNIQUES FOR GETTING FAVORABLE ACTION

*Assume the Sale is Made.*   When a salesman establishes friendly relations with the prospect and they seem to have a meeting of the minds, assuming the sale is made is a natural and easy method of closing without pressure of any kind. Having discussed the prospect's needs and how the product will satisfy them, the salesman simply assumes the prospect wants to order now. "If I may use your phone, I'll call this in right now and arrange for the quick delivery you wanted." If the buyer does not object, the sale is closed. American businessmen have been exposed to this assumptive technique for so long that they either do not recognize it or, more likely, they accept it as standard practice. Every time the businessman buys a suit of clothes, the salesman says, "That jacket looks well on you, Mr. Rightman. Try on the trousers too and our tailor will make the necessary alterations to make it just right for you." If the businessman does not object, the sale is closed. The salesman assumes the sale is closed without actually asking for the order. The buyer goes along with the salesman's attitude and is relieved of the difficulty of making a decision. Buying is made easy and the customer is usually grateful.

*Build a Series of Acceptances from Minor to Major Points.*   This technique is analogous to building a pyramid in that small blocks of logic are put together to form the final master project. The salesman attempts to get agreement on the importance of each small benefit of his proposition as he goes along. The prospect agrees it is desirable and the product really will provide the promised benefit. In this form of close, agreement is built into the entire presentation and each minor decision of acceptance will reinforce the final major decision. When the prospect agrees all the way along, it makes it logical and easy to agree at the conclusion. This technique is common in selling consumer items in the home where the salesman can demonstrate each feature of his product on the personal items of the family. A vacuum cleaner, for example, will clean this living-room rug, which is very desirable. It will also shampoo this couch to make it look like new again which is also very desirable. It will also spray insecticides into this closet to protect your garments from damage by moths and that is very desirable protection. The health and comfort of the children are important and this wonderful machine will do much to reduce costly medical bills and discomforts of sick children. When such benefits are built into the sales presentation and the prospect agrees as the salesman goes along, the final decision to purchase the product is easy. Of course the prospect wants an attractive home that looks like new again. Of course he wants to make his furnishings last longer. Of course he wants his children to be healthy and happy. This product will help him realize these benefits so it is logical that he obtain it as soon as possible.

This technique is not confined to selling naïve consumers but is also frequently used in selling cold, practical businessmen. Stocks and bonds are sold in six-figure amounts using this closing technique. The series of minor acceptances of desirable benefits makes the major decision easy. Stocks and bonds may be purchased for possible profit, for tax advantages, as a hedge against inflation, or for a number of other reasons. The sales presentation is designed to gain acceptance of as many minor buying reasons as possible. The purpose of the investment may be to provide a college education for the children, a nest egg for retirement, a fund to start a new business, or many other things. Once such reasons and purposes are brought out in the interview, the prospect himself begins to close the sale. The major decision to invest a large sum is merely the logical conclusion.

*Summarize the Selling Points.* When a prospect appears to want the product but is hesitant, a good closing technique is to summarize the selling points. The salesman lists all the sound logical reasons for ordering and he puts the greatest emphasis on those benefits which seemed to have the greatest appeal for this prospect. This provides a brief and effective review of all the possible benefits which are of interest to the buyer.

A variation of the summary technique is the use of a "T" account or a two-column summation of buying against not buying, or buying product A against buying product B. This is the physical enumeration of the two-sided argument used in persuasion as developed in Chapter 10. The reasons for buying are summarized and the most appealing benefits for the particular prospect are emphasized strongly. The reasons for not buying are often limited to cost or financing the purchase. Clearly, to be successful,

the salesman must demonstrate that the benefits of buying heavily outweigh the benefits of not buying. The danger of using the "T" account
with an intelligent prospect is that it must be perfectly fair and honest or
else he will not agree with any conclusions. If a complete and honest two-
sided argument is used, it may actually come out so evenly balanced that
the buyer will be more reluctant to take action than before the test.
Clearly, this technique must be used with discretion but when the weight
is heavily in favor of buying it is very effective in persuasion.

**Get Decisions on Minor Points and Avoid Major Decisions.** Many
prospects are reluctant to make any major decisions even when it appears
to be in their best interest to do so. While this may be very frustrating to
the salesman, a slight change in technique will often be successful in
closing the sale. Once the salesman recognizes the problem he should
avoid requesting a major decision and instead attempt to close on a minor
point. Again, American tailors have conditioned most American men to
accept this technique. They do not ask the prospect if he wants to buy the
suit; they simply ask if he likes the pants with or without cuffs? While it
may be almost impossible for some men to decide on the purchase of a
suit, it is relatively easy for them to be quick and firm in their opinion of
whether their pants should have cuffs or not. Once the tailor marks them
accordingly, the sale is made and the buyer has not had to face the major
decision. In industrial selling, the same situation is handled by asking the
decision maker what he would want in the optional accessories to tailor the
product to suit his individual application. Major decisions are avoided and
attention is directed to minor decisions and the sale is then assumed closed
as in the assumptive technique.

**The Contingent Technique.** A technique used to get a hesitant buyer
to act is the contingent technique. The buying decision is changed from
the question of buy or not buy to a decision of, *if* something happens then
I will buy. The salesman restates his proposition so that the decision to buy
depends upon something else. For example, the salesman may state, "If I
can prove to your satisfaction that you will save 10 percent on labor
charges then you will want to order. Is that right?" If the customer answers
positively, the buying decision is then based upon the salesman's ability to
persuade the prospect that the savings will in fact be achieved. Obviously,
whatever benefits the salesman claims must be clearly proved. The point of
this technique is that it changes the viewpoint of the prospect from one of
hesitancy to one of positive action if a contingent event is proven.

In consumer selling, an insurance salesman will often use this closing
technique by emphasizing the importance of the insurance being a two-

party contract. The prospect may want insurance but the company may not want to accept it if he is a bad risk. "If you can pass the physical then you will want. . . ." The prospect changes his viewpoint from the question of wanting or not wanting insurance to one of buying insurance if he passes the physical.

In selling to retailers, the contingent method is used to line up exclusive outlets in each marketing area. The salesman presents his line with all the benefits that will accrue to the retailer that handles the merchandise and then uses the contingent technique to attempt to close the order. "If I can secure an exclusive outlet for your store, then you will want to start with an initial order of. . . ." Again, the prospect's point of view is changed from deciding whether or not to take on the new line to the question of whether the manufacturer will grant him an exclusive in his marketing area.

In industrial selling, the contingent technique usually revolves around the question of adapting the product features to serve a particular need of the prospect or the question of meeting unusual delivery requirements. "If my plant will modify this gizmo to suit your production line, then you will want delivery by. . . ." The attention is directed to the contingency and not to the question of buying or not buying. In each of the illustrations, the emphasis in selling is on the possibility of something which may or may not happen. The prospect agrees to buy only if the possibility becomes a reality.

*The Impending Event.* Closely related to the contingent technique is the impending event method of closing a sale. In this technique, the event will occur and if the buyer does not act now he will suffer a loss. He may lose money, health, comfort, convenience, or something else but he will definitely lose by postponement. There is no question about the event happening but only how much of a loss the prospect is willing to suffer. For example, a man wishing to trade in his old car for a new one may hesitate about ordering now. The salesman using the impending event technique will point out that the trade-in value of the old car will drop every month the buyer waits and he will have to pay that much more in cash to obtain his new auto. He may combine this with the contingent technique by explaining how expensive repairs may be necessary to keep the old car going while the prospect is hesitating.

In America as well as in most of the rest of the world in the late 1960s and 1970s inflation is apt to be a constant problem. Labor and production costs are rising and prices are apt to rise steadily for many lines of goods and services. The longer the prospect waits before placing his order, the higher the price is apt to be. Government taxes are often passed on to the consumer as part of his purchase price and the trend here is also upward. Impending events may include seasonal changes in the weather as used in selling air-conditioning units, heating plates, clothing, autos, and many similar consumer items. Accounting services are sold due to the impending tax deadlines. Gift items, including travel abroad, are sold due to the approach of June graduation dates. Grooming and medical products are sold due to the irreversible aging of people.

Life is full of changes and the creative salesman is able to develop good reasons which utilize the impending events to help close the sale of his products and services. Since such and such an event will occur if the prospect hesitates, now is the time to order to prevent losses of money, health, appearance, comfort, convenience, or something else. When used legitimately, this technique of closing is very effective.

*SRO Technique.* The standing room only technique is used to capitalize on a common human trait of wanting something that is a proven success. The Broadway show that is sold out in advance of a performance puts out a sign that reads "SRO" and more people than ever will try to get tickets. In selling, this technique is used when, for various reasons, the supply is limited. The successful introduction of Ford's Mustang sports car is a good example of this technique. Since initial public acceptance was in excess of production, a waiting list developed. Strangely enough, this encouraged other prospects to order sooner than they might have otherwise.

Many levels of selling utilize this technique, from consumer goods to those required by original equipment manufacturers. Whenever demand temporarily exceeds supply or there are only a few left in stock and it will take many weeks to replace the stock, this is prima-facie evidence of a shortage of a highly desirable product. For many prospects, this is sufficient reason to order. For other prospects, it is a contingent reason which contributes to their positive decision.

A variation of this SRO technique is utilized in selling the last few items of a commodity which cannot be reordered. For example, a housing development may be offered by a builder with a limited number of corner plots or a limited number with dock facilities in the rear. Once these plots are sold, that is the end of the builder's offering. If there are several prospects in the market, each is afraid the others will buy the few remaining choices and he will be left out. This impels many prospects into immediate buying action.

Industrial selling uses the SRO technique when closing out a line of products. For those customers that normally buy the discontinued line, the few remaining products become more desirable than previously and they do not want to be cut short. The items cannot be reordered at any price and they are offered on a "first-come first-served basis" until the supply is exhausted. With adequate promotional activity, a closeout need not be a losing proposition for the seller. The SRO technique can make it a highly profitable operation.

*Special Offer.* Many selling companies attempt to break into new markets with special introductory prices which are usually well below their standard price schedules. New products are often introduced as a special deal with the first item at full price and the second one for one cent more. A variation of this is the tie-in sale where the new product is offered for a nominal price with every purchase of a particular standard item. Such special offers are effective when the introductory promotion clearly limits the time the low prices will prevail. Selling to supermarkets and delicatessens frequently involves special offerings or "a deal" as it is known in the trade. For every order of ten cases of the new item, the supplier gives an extra case without charge. The initial supply may be offered at a special deal price with subsequent reorders at the normal wholesale price.

Unfortunately, special offerings are not limited to wholesale selling and professional buyers are well aware of this practice. Often they will screen out possible suppliers and narrow their choice down to two or three whom they consider equal. Then they state frankly and openly that they will give the order to the man with the lowest price. This leads to price cutting and price wars between would-be suppliers with progressively less and less salesmanship. When the smaller or weaker suppliers are finally driven out of that line of business, prices again tend to stabilize at the normal profit level.

Discounting from the established prices can be a dangerous practice because any one prospect will wait for a second or third discount which is still lower than the first one offered. Once discounting has begun, the prospect may withhold his order because he can never be sure that it will be the final or lowest price possible. If he orders at a given discount, he will always wonder if he made a mistake and bought before pushing the supplier to a better discount. Any new accounts which are obtained on a price appeal or discount basis are not apt to be loyal to the supplier and will quickly move to another supplier when his price is lower. Once a market has deteriorated to this stage, customer services become careless or nonexistent and the consumer ultimately suffers. Many large discount houses in the retail business have found the large volume which is essential for their profitable operations is possible only if they include more customer services than competitive discount houses. With each customer service added, costs go up and prices must also go up. The cycle is completed when the so-called discount house opens a new store in an exclusive part of town, offering the same quality merchandise, customer services, and prices as the neighboring prestige department store. The small, neighborhood, Mom-and-Pop type store is forced out of business.

When faced with such competitive situations in commercial or industrial selling, the effective salesman builds the benefits of owning his product higher than the benefits of owning the competitor's product. When he must either make his price more competitive or lose the business, he will make his special offer both logical and firm. For example, his offer will be on a limited number of items in the line because they are temporarily overstocked and must be sacrificed. The offer is good only as long as this temporary condition exists. Another common method of handling the discount problem is to educate the buyer to group his purchases either for many items from a single supplier or for his normal six months' requirement of many small orders into one large order. Tangible savings in ordering, shipping, and billing can then be passed on to the buyer on a legitimate basis. Quantity or volume price schedules are common to most industries and the terms are both firm and clearly understood by both buyer and seller. If the items are for resale, legal complications enter into this discount problem and will be covered in Chapter 22. However, the guiding line is that every account must be treated equally. If discounts are offered to one buyer which are below the offering to another, the selling company must be able to prove economies realized to justify lower prices to one and not the other.

Discounting or price wars are dangerous because customer loyalty fades, customer services are neglected or discontinued, the practices involved may be illegal, and the market becomes highly unstable. During the turmoil, desperate suppliers are forced to adopt a policy of "buyer beware" and both the consumer and the supplying industry suffer. Market stability is desirable both to protect the public and to maintain continuity of the flow of goods and services from producers to consumers at the lowest ultimate cost.

**Trial Order.** A common closing technique is the test case or trial order method. The doubtful prospect is urged to try the product for a given period to see if the claimed benefits really do materialize. This may be a free offer with all costs and risks taken by the supplier or it may be a money-back guarantee offer with the order shipped and billed in the normal manner. For example, a typewriter may be placed in a business office on demonstration with no billing whatsoever. After a two-week trial under regular office work conditions, the prospect either issues a purchase order and keeps the machine or he returns it to the supplier at no cost. A more expensive adding machine or calculator may be sold on a one-month trial money-back guarantee and the buyer need not prove there was anything wrong with the machine but simply state he was not satisfied with it.

When selling to retailers, manufacturers representatives often urge the prospect to try a small order of only part of their line priced and billed in the normal manner. If the merchandise sells well, the trial is a success for the store, but if it does not sell well the buyer has committed only a very small amount of his capital. Such offers may be combined with return privileges although this is usually reserved for the retailer who is willing to take on the full line in a complete range of colors, styles, and sizes. Clearly, return privileges must be limited to relatively stable items which can quickly be turned over in other outlets in the normal manner.

The trial order is a closing technique used to reduce the amount of risk which the buyer must take. He can use the product under conditions which he considers normal and give it a fair test. The supplier takes the risk in such cases, gambling that most trial offers will end up firm orders and any merchandise returned will be in usable condition so that it can be sold as a special or demonstrator model still priced above cost. Equipment that is offered for rent as well as for sale, with initial rent payments going toward the purchase price as an option, is another variation of the trial order. Large housing developments have been successfully promoted on this basis and much capital equipment for offices and factories is sold in this manner.

*Two-man Close.* As noted in the discussion of team selling (Chapter 16), a salesman can legitimately offer extra services of a staff of technical experts to aid the prospect to solve a problem. These extra members of the selling team help to close the sale indirectly and are often used as a condition contingent to the sale. If the experts can solve the prospect's problem, he will buy. A variation of team selling is the two-man close with the friendly salesman acting in total sympathy with the prospect and the sales manager or factory expert acting as the hard selling stranger. The salesman, acting as a true friend of the buyer, can voice doubts about his product which the prospect might not be willing to mention. The sales manager or factory expert must then answer the objection to the satisfaction of both the salesman and the prospect. This team effort is normally preplanned so that no questions will be embarrassing and the series of questions leads logically to placing an order. Two sharp minds are then pitted against the prospect. Too often this technique boomerangs because many people resent such high-pressure tactics. However, when handled with discretion and tact, it can be effective.

Another variation of the two-man close is the turnover technique or T.O. due to a personality conflict. This is very common in selling in a showroom that handles walk-in prospects. If the salesman that first handles the prospect cannot get along with him or for some reason does not seem to get his messages through to the buyer, he calls in another salesman under the pretext that the second man is more familiar with this type of problem or product. Clearly, this turnover technique, if it is to be effective, must be used while the prospect is still undecided. Just as buyers are predisposed to like certain types of personalities and dislike others, salesmen have the same fault. Salesmen are reluctant to admit they cannot get along with certain buyers; however, they would be well advised to utilize this turnover technique rather than risk losing an order. The method can also be used in outside selling in the same manner as long as the prospect is still undecided. If Mr. Rightman is considering the purchase of some equipment and the regular salesman is having this type of personality problem, he can suggest to the prospect that the supplier has a specialist in this product who will phone for an appointment. The specialist in this case is simply another salesman who is apt to get along well with Mr. Rightman. The prospect benefits by this technique because he can communicate more easily with the second man and the entire transaction becomes more pleasant.

**Negative Close.** Effective salesmen can close occasional orders by outwardly appearing not to want the prospect to order. This negative close works on prospects that are sensitive to sales pressure and it often works on prospects who are overly conscious of prestige symbols. When a salesman is well over quota or has had an exceptionally successful day, he is often more at ease with himself and with his prospects. He does not need that one extra sale that day so his manner relaxes and many buyers are grateful not to have to argue or fight with him. The salesman can take criticism of his product more gracefully because he has the necessary inner confidence founded upon success. He can sincerely joke with the buyer about the benefits claimed by his sales literature and become a much more pleasant individual. Such low-pressure selling, or the complete absence of pressure, is a welcome relief to some prospects and they are more apt to buy from this salesman than from the type they normally see. The salesman might say, for example, "I'd really like to spend more time discussing this with you, Mr. Rightman, but honestly I do have another appointment so if you don't mind I'll see you another time." Some prospects will react quickly, asking the salesman to stay longer.

A variation of the negative close is one called the snob appeal. The prospect is told he cannot afford the deluxe model and he reacts with proof of his financial ability instead of an objection about price. The negative close may be used to state the prospect probably could not understand or believe the prestige effect of owning the product but how some people really do get such enjoyment. Again, the prospect reacts by stating he positively does understand and believe the claim. The prospect reverses buying-selling roles and literally sells himself. Used on the proper occasion with an individual prospect, this technique is very effective. It is the complete opposite of high pressure and literally exerts negative pressure causing the prospect to sell himself while the salesman voices objections.

## HANDLING THE MECHANICS OF CLOSING THE SALE

Whatever technique is used to close the sale, the effective salesman handles the mechanics of writing up the order in a light easygoing manner which reassures the buyer he has made a wise decision. The buyer and seller are in complete agreement and the sale is assumed to be closed. For example, the salesman might say, "We want this order to be correct, Mr. Rightman, so just check over this list and I'll phone it in today." If the buyer normally issues a formal written purchase order, it is often wise to ask for a verbal OK so that the salesman can process the order faster and expedite delivery. The written confirmation can be mailed in later at the buyer's convenience. In each illustration, the salesman has assumed the order is firm and the delivery is his only concern. The buyer's attention is directed away from the formal mechanics of writing an order or signing a purchase order.

Many companies will not accept merchandise unless they have actually issued a purchase order and their purchase order number appears on the bill of lading. In such cases, the effective salesman still assumes the decision to buy has been settled and the buyer and seller are in full agreement. He simply asks for a purchase order number to put on his order. The buyer can then give him the next number in the series without waiting for all the details to be typed out when the secretary has time. The buyer need not sign anything because he still has the protection of being able to withhold the purchase order if he so desires. In many lines of business, a formal signature is necessary before any sales order will be processed. This often applies to consumer merchandise, to insurance and mutual fund sales, and to many industrial products. Whenever a product is modified or becomes special in some way, the supplier normally requires a signed order indicating either a noncancellation clause or a penalty clause. If the prospect must sign an order, it is still wise to treat it lightly and ask him to look over the offering and simply indicate his OK. This implies the buyer and seller are in perfect agreement and does not sound as cold and formal as a request for a signature. For example, "If you will OK these specifications, Mr. Rightman, I'll arrange delivery for next Tuesday." The salesman is not asking for a signed order but for approval of the terms they have already discussed and agreed upon.

## HANDLING THE PROSPECT THAT DOESN'T BUY

For many legitimate reasons, prospects often will not order and the salesman must accept their decisions. The disappointment for the salesman is great and the temptation is to blame the prospect for his stupidity or blindness rather than to admit the selling job was not all it could have been. If the salesman shows his disdain for the prospect, the latter will resent it and remember it in the future. If the salesman packs up abruptly he gives the impression that he could not care less about this individual prospect and is interested only in making a sale for his own benefit, not for the customer's benefit. Either action cancels out any respect and friendship the salesman may have created and makes future selling more difficult.

In industrial or commercial selling, the salesman attempts to learn from his mistakes and find out what errors of omission or commission he may have made which influenced the buying decision. The effective salesman maintains his friendship and mutual respect with the buyer thereby leaving the door open for future calls when he will want a friendly reception. The buyer appreciates the salesman who can take it like a man and will welcome him back in the future while avoiding the salesman who behaved in some childish manner. Effective salesmen are persistent and will call for several years on noncustomers waiting for their chance at success.

In door-to-door selling of consumer items, the same problem exists. If the salesman remains friendly it takes the pressure off the consumer and the salesman is more apt to get clues or leads to others in the neighborhood or friends and associates of the prospect. In this friendly manner, the salesman is able to get some return on his time already invested and the selling company is more apt to be welcomed back the next time it wants to cover the same territory.

When a prospect has considered several brands or several suppliers for his needs, clearly he cannot order from them all. When he makes his decision it is apt to be tentative and full of doubts. This is analogous to the man that decides to leave one job for employment on another. He is full of doubts and fears even after the decision has been made. The emotionally mature salesman will wish the lost prospect well and assure him that the salesman's company will always stand ready to help him in the future. When the new supplier falls down on delivery or service, the former prospect will wish he had purchased from the friendly salesman. He may then tell friends and business associates of his experience and this in turn will help influence their buying decisions. In commercial, industrial, and even consumer selling, buyers return to the market again and again. The patient salesman who can learn to be a good loser as well as a good winner can build his personal reputation over the years and his honesty and sincerity will ultimately insure his success.

## TERMINATING THE INTERVIEW

It probably cannot be said too often that when a buyer says "yes," the salesman should stop selling that product. If his product line lends itself to this, the salesman can easily increase the size of his order by adding on other items or accessories which are often purchased on impulse. The tailor writing up an order for a new suit will often sell shirts, socks, and ties. The file salesman will often add folders and index guides to his order. The auto salesman will often add seat covers, insurance, and other profitable services to his total order. This does not detract one iota from the principle of cease and desist once the buyer has said "yes" to the sale. The compulsive talker can easily become such a nuisance that the buyer will change his mind and cancel the order. The successful salesman concludes his presentation with delivery information and leaves on a friendly personal note.

Good manners are always impressive and it should not be necessary to remind any successful salesman to say thanks for the order. Good manners show the salesman really cares about the buyer and that he enjoyed dealing with him. When the prospect does not buy, the effective salesman will still thank him for spending so much time with him and for his interest in the product. In either case, the effective salesman will reassure the buyer that he is always ready and willing to serve him in the future and that he is as near to him as the telephone at his elbow on the desk.

◆  ◆  ◆

## ASKING FOR THE ORDER*

Many an order has been lost simply because it was never asked for. When selling The Wall Street Journal, you may miss a sale by not asking for the order often enough, or at the right time. Therefore, keep these guide-posts in mind:

1. Give your prospect a good, understandable sales presentation and ASK HIM TO BUY . . .
2. Tell your prospect what The Wall Street Journal will do for him, and ASK HIM TO BUY . . .
3. Show the prospect his need for The Wall Street Journal, how he will PROFIT by it, and ASK HIM TO BUY . . .
4. Be sure he understands what he is getting, and ASK HIM TO BUY . . . (Remember, if the prospect understands what he is buying, he will more readily make the purchase.)
5. Give the prospect an EXCUSE to make the purchase, and ASK HIM TO BUY!

---

* The above is reprinted with the kind permission of Dow Jones & Company, Inc., Community Sales Program, Circulation Field & Phone Sales Division, Princeton, N.J.

# 22

# Techniques to Handle Price, Discount, and Credit Problems

It requires considerable knowledge and understanding to explain why a product costs what it does and why it is worth that much to a prospect. By looking at the internal problems of pricing which confront the manufacturer or seller, one can gain a better understanding. Discounting practices are closely related to the initial pricing policy and credit problems are also related to the initial pricing decisions. The purpose of this chapter, accordingly, is to develop an awareness of some fundamental concepts that will be helpful to the salesman who must explain such policies.

## QUOTING AND JUSTIFYING PRICE

Specifically, what does a price represent to a buyer? The buyer must give up so many dollars to get a product or service. Clearly, he will not pay dollars to obtain five pounds of assorted nuts, bolts, and formed metal if he is in the market for a toaster. The product or service he wants must function to satisfy his needs. The product has certain features, physical attributes and components, a degree of quality in materials and workmanship, color and styling, and the like. It has a manufacturer's name and model number. The effective salesman combines these features to form a concept of benefits which the buyer or user will realize. A brand-name image is created enabling the prospect easily to picture himself owning and using the product.

Price also includes a choice of models and styles as well as delivery, possible installation, and instruction in the proper use of the product. It normally includes a guarantee which is an assurance of long life, trouble-free maintenance, and long-lasting satisfaction from any benefits claimed. The price further includes many customer services from expert advice in selecting the correct model all the way through to financing the cost of acquisition. Services included in the price might be professional advice on matters not related to the product, such as advertising or accounting procedures for a retailer. Price should include a reasonable profit for the seller, which assures the buyer of obtaining future service and attention which he expects.

Pricing is not simply a matter between the seller and the buyer. Generally there are many other people involved in any price decision. Price is simply one element in the total marketing mix and there are innumerable ways to vary the proportions of time and money spent on the product quality, customer services to be offered, distribution channels and their services, and various promotional activities. Within a selling company, various individuals and departments compete for their share of available time and money. The final outcome of this internal pressure is reflected in the pricing policy. The ultimate users, whether household consumers, industry, commerce, or government, influence price by their numbers, their location and their willingness to spend. Competitors selling the same or substitute products and services also influence the pricing policy because many buyers will shop or otherwise compare values offered. Potential rivals will affect pricing policy because while they do not make or handle the item now, if a high profit appears likely, they may decide to enter that market also. The choice of alternate channels through which the products must flow before reaching the ultimate user will also affect the final price. For each service expected from a reseller, some reasonable compensation must be provided. Those who supply the manufacturer with capital, raw materials, and labor will also influence the final price of products depending in part upon the shortage of supply and the anticipated overall profit picture. Finally, various government laws and administrative agencies will often influence pricing policy. Price legislation will be covered in greater length later in this chapter.

Clearly, prices are established at certain levels due to many independent but related factors rather than due to the simple cost plus profit concept. A justifiable compensation for effort was firmly established in the fourteenth century but this simple theory is not applicable in the twentieth century. Price today represents much more than the physical product and the effective salesman is fully aware of the various elements and extra benefits provided to his customers. His knowledge and understanding enable him to quote his price firmly and with complete confidence because he can justify the cost to the buyer.[1]

---

[1] For a complete discussion of the various elements of price determination see Alfred R. Oxenfeldt, *Pricing For Marketing Executives* (San Francisco: Wadsworth Publishing Co., Inc., 1961.)

## THE STRATEGY OF SELLING UP

A popular method of handling price is the strategy of selling from the minimum or lowest cost up to the higher deluxe price categories. The salesman attempts to gain acceptance of a given price for an economy model through the benefits which the buyer will receive and perhaps through favorable price comparisons. Intangibles are sold on the basis of minimum coverage or services offered in the same way. After the prospect indicates that these conditions appear acceptable to him the salesman introduces optional features and makes the benefits of owning them appear so attractive they outweigh the additional cost. For example, if the salesman gained the buyer's approval of an item for $130 originally, he would not have to justify selling the second item for $150 but only for $20 more than the buyer already indicated he was willing to pay. The salesman would then go on to the super deluxe model and sell only the $30 more than the middle model. In the deluxe model the buyer would get as standard equipment all the items they agreed he needed and wanted as worth the small extra charge, but in addition he would receive benefits, plus the prestige value of a product he feels is the best that money can buy. In this way, an item can be sold for $180 in a market where economy models are selling for only $130. This approach is particularly adaptable to men offering many items and models from the same source. The same strategy of using competitive items to illustrate his product features and customer benefits is employed by the salesmen who can offer only the top priced item. To obtain the minimum features, a customer would have to pay at least $130 from most competitors. If he desired these additional benefits, he would have to pay at least another $20. Finally, only his company or product has these extra features and services, for only $30 more. The total is $180 again and the customer gains whatever prestige value may be included because of the brand name or model.

## THE STRATEGY OF SELLING DOWN

Many effective salesmen find it more natural and comfortable to begin with the top of their line or the most complete service their company offers. Naturally, they attempt to justify the cost as being small in relation to all the benefits of owning or acquiring the product. Since all features and benefits will not have equally strong appeal or application for any two different buyers, the salesman attempts to portray all benefits and then to stress the areas which the prospect indicates appeal to him. When the buyer indicates a strong preference for certain features but disdain for others and is not willing to pay the premium price for the deluxe model, the salesman then offers a second model which includes the desired benefits but is less expensive because it does not include certain features. As long as the eliminated features were not important to the prospect or applicable to his situational needs, this is sound strategy. If the cost is still prohibitive, the salesman attempts to guide the prospect to narrow his preference for minimum features and benefits which are available in his economy model. In this final offering, the salesman emphasizes the utility value of his product and plays down the value of the expensive extras in the higher priced models which the prospect himself said he did not need or want.

When this strategy is used intentionally and with caution it can be very effective. However, there are dangers if the salesman is careless. Prices for the deluxe and middle priced offerings must still be justified and valid because after seeing the lower priced offering the prospect may decide the middle or top one really serves his needs best. The prospect should understand that all three offerings are the best of their kind for each price range and that to obtain certain benefits he is justified in paying that particular price.

## SELLING THE PRICE DIFFERENCE

Inexperienced salesmen in the common situation of finding their price considerably higher than their competitors' are often frightened. How can one company successfully sell an item for $200 when most or all competitors are asking only $150 for a similar item? Clearly, the extra $50 must provide extra benefits which are desirable to the buyer and the effective salesman will sell the price difference. In this illustration it is the same as selling up from one grade to a better grade within one line. The salesman knows the prospect must pay at least $150 for the lower grade and the sales job is to sell only $50 worth of additional benefits to the buyer, not $200 worth of benefits.

To sell the price difference, the effective salesman utilizes his tremendous knowledge of his own product and customer services, his competitors' weak points, and all possible benefits to the buyer. If the salesman is selling an expensive payroll system, for example, he must explain that his forms are rotary cut just like expensive bridge cards for easy handling and quick, precise top fingering which speeds posting and reduces clerical labor costs and expensive errors due to misfiling; that the card and paper stock have 50 percent rag content to stay white longer, to prevent yellowing with age which makes them difficult to read after many years; that the lines are printed in brown and green instead of black to eliminate costly errors due to the confusion of pencil or typewritten marks with the printed lines. Each product feature is interpreted for the prospect into language which he can easily understand and believe. The prospect must understand that he will actually save more money in the use of the more expensive product than the relatively little price difference the salesman is asking for his superior product.

The reverse of selling a high priced item is equally true but is more often ignored by the salesman. If a salesman offers a low priced item, too often he feels the savings in purchase price will more than offset any advantages the higher priced item may offer. He may speak disparagingly of the extra features others offer and base his entire presentation on the economy of acquisition. If he claims his item is fully equal to the high priced item, the prospect becomes suspicious and wary of the offer. Other salesmen can then sow the seeds of doubt, which the prospect is predisposed to believe. Selling a low priced item is very similar to the technique of selling down. The effective salesman attempts to learn which product features and user benefits are most important to the prospect and which ones the prospect considers superfluous for his use. The salesman then carefully explains how his company has eliminated those costly extras without sacrificing any quality or user benefits in the areas which the prospect considers important. These economies of design, production, materials, packaging, or distribution are then passed along to the buyer in an honest attempt to increase sales voulme. The benefits of buying the product he offers then appear well in excess of the low price he asks while the extra cost of competitors' so-called deluxe features no longer appear of value. Clearly, it is much more difficult to sell an inferior product legitimately but it can be done effectively and honestly by using the technique of selling down.

Most buyers like a bargain and want to reduce their cost of acquiring goods and services but it is a rare person who will openly admit that he knowingly purchased an inferior product. The salesman should do the rationalizing or mental reasoning for the prospect to justify his buying the lowest priced item. As noted earlier, any product, including U.S. space vehicles, can be made better with the expenditure of enough time and money. The salesman must justify his price in terms of realistic benefits to the buyer. A company may offer many inferior products side by side with superior products and label them good, better, and best quality. If honest descriptions and advice are conveyed to the prospect, the cheaper or inferior models serve a legitimate purpose. Many prospects desire only temporary use of a product, for example, a post hole digger. Once their fence is up, they do not care if the tool lasts another 25 years or not. Young children will often grow out of a party dress or Sunday school suit long before it can wear out.

Clearly, different prospects will have very unique and personal requirements to fill their needs as well as differing attitudes about extra benefits and prestige values. An effective salesman will draw out the prospect and listen carefully for clues about his needs and his methods of judging competitive products. There is a real market for a broad price range and quality range of products and the effective salesman can honestly sell either extreme to the right prospects.

## PRICES AND PROFITS

Throughout these chapters, it has been stressed that the effective salesman has as his goal the long-term contribution to profits. Many manufacturers as well as retailers have certain loss leaders or items priced below cost to attract customers, and suppliers carry convenience items which are sold at or near the break-even point simply to discourage old customers from shopping and thereby becoming exposed to competitors. Most suppliers have certain items which yield a higher profit than other items in their line. Some companies will spend the bulk of their advertising budget promoting a few items and expect their salesmen to sell the entire line on the basis of the brand name. Whatever pricing policy the supplier elects, clearly he cannot stay in business very long without a profit. The salesman cannot be paid commissions or salary if the selling price does no more than cover the cost of making and distributing the merchandise. Dollar sales volume, enormous though it may be, means little until it is converted into profit. On the other hand, a quick profitable order due to high pressure or misleading claims that eventually harms the buyer and loses a customer or hurts the seller's company image is equally bad business. Effective salesmen realize a sale must be mutually beneficial to both buyer and seller before an order placer becomes a steady profitable customer.

This does not mean that suppliers always insist on a profit. For example, in promoting a new product or attempting to open new markets, a supplier might be willing to lose money for several years due to high selling costs and low sales volume. He would take this calculated risk if he felt the odds were in his favor to succeed eventually and gain more than the whole operation cost. As noted earlier, he might offer his products at near cost to gain an inroad into the competitors' market share. They might react by offering the same low price deals to keep the newcomer out of their market. In these cases, the salesmen cannot be held responsible for the profit results during the short-term period.

Another apparent exception to the profit rule occurs when a supplier has too much capital tied up in finished goods. A warehouse full of merchandise will not pay creditors and a time arises when top management must decide to sacrifice the profit in order to convert this asset back into cash. At this time, the effective salesman is expected to unload large quantities of goods quickly in a market that may already be weak or unstable due to overproduction. The very life or existence of the company may depend upon his success even when there is no hope of a profit and the objective is to minimize the loss.

Almost all cases of pricing an entire line below cost occur in an unstable market under conditions which are temporary. The objective remains constant and an effective salesman realizes his long-term contribution to profit is a major key to the success of his company. Should the company go into bankruptcy, then creditors lose, suppliers lose, old customers are at least inconvenienced if not losers, and many people are out of jobs. Society in general loses employed taxpayers and producing tax property and is burdened with more unemployed people which others must support through their taxes. While such temporary selling assignments might be distasteful to the individual salesman, he carries this huge responsibility on his shoulders. His dealings with customers should remain fair and honest if he is to save the company from disaster and not merely to postpone it.

## PRICE LEGISLATION

In many highly competitive lines of business, salesmen are offering specials and buyers are shopping for bargains. These conditions lead to frequent negotiations for special terms regarding advertising allowances, special brokerage allowances, trade and cash discounts, quantity discounts, and fair-trade prices. This can, and often does, lead to unfair trade practices. Legal complications most frequently arise when a market situation becomes unstable and production exceeds demand. Forced sales are often a desperate attempt to survive. Producers with high operating costs or poor capitalization are the first to suffer in an unstable market and they quickly meet competitive pricing policies. Even the old established, well-financed companies are caught in price negotiations and they often are forced to meet the competitive challenge in order to maintain their positions of industry leadership.

When some buyers are charged more than others for the same items in the same quantities, public anger is aroused and some legislators speak out demanding protection of the public welfare. State laws change as pressures by local industry, labor, and an injured public demand. An effective salesman covering several states, for example, must keep himself fully informed regarding what pricing and discount practices are legal in his area as well as any changes in the local laws which may affect his method of operation. While only a small portion of all goods marketed is protected from destructive price cutting, some 60 percent of the states have passed their own Unfair Trade Practice acts. These laws vary from state to state but generally prohibit retail price cutting below 6 percent above the supplier's invoice price. Such laws are generally designed to protect the small retailer from unscrupulous chain stores which might otherwise lower their prices temporarily to force the little ones out of business. The consuming public is not protected by such legislation and large discount stores, buying in volume, can often circumvent the intent of these laws.

All but a few states permit resale price-maintenance contracts between manufacturers and distributors to protect trademarked or branded merchandise from injurious and uneconomical practices. Fair-trade laws generally provide that the vendor not resell the product at less than a minimum price set by the manufacturer. Such agreements are difficult and often costly to maintain and many firms with well-advertised brand names have given up this form of price control.

Federal legislation on unfair pricing and trade practices began in the last quarter of the nineteenth century after big businesses had abused their responsibilities to the public. The Sherman Antitrust Act of 1890 is still utilized to prohibit all agreements and combinations in restraint of trade or to monopolize any part of interstate or foreign commerce. The Clayton Act of 1914 outlawed price discrimination in interstate commerce by prohibiting one firm from buying the capital stock of its competitors, by outlawing interlocking directorates which may tend to lessen competition, and by prohibiting various forms of price discrimination.

Most federal control in this field today is exercised by the Federal Trade Commission which was created by Congress in 1914 to guard against illegitimate competitive methods between business firms. The Wheeler-Lea Act of 1938 broadened the powers of the FTC to issue a complaint without proving injury to a competitor thereby shifting the burden of proof to the company accused of unfair trade practices and it also provided penalties for violations. The FTC has condemned many practices including:

1. The giving of premiums to retail clerks with the purpose of getting them to sell one company's products at the expense of a competitor's.
2. Making false, deceptive, or disparaging statements about a competitor or his products.
3. Representing as new products those which are rebuilt, secondhand, or "seconds."
4. Using bribery or espionage to learn the trade secrets of competitors.
5. Making false, misleading, or deceptive claims about services which accompany the purchase of a product.
6. Making false or misleading claims regarding the financing and interest charges involved in installment sales.
7. Requiring a customer to buy one product which he does not want in order to get another which he really wants.
8. Misleading the customer into thinking he is getting a bargain, a reduced price, or some sort of free deal when such is not the case.
9. Giving extra discounts or advertising allowances to customers if they will not handle competing products.

The most basic federal statute affecting competitive pricing is the Robinson-Patman Act of 1936 which forbids price discrimination generally. Subsequent court decisions have described illegal discrimination as the giving an unjustified special price or discount concession or special service to some customers and not to others. To justify a special price the seller must be able to prove that the price differentials are the result of differences in the cost of manufacture, sales, or distribution; the result of changes in the quality or nature of the product or market conditions; or the result of an attempt to meet equally low prices of competitors. While the Robinson-Patman Act applies to interstate commerce, most states have passed similar laws to cover interstate sales.

Today, government powers are so strong and litigation so costly, the trend is for business to file a brief of intended actions with the government regarding anything that borders on antitrust action. The government can then issue a restraining order if it does not approve and no great loss is incurred. The lack of such an order does not constitute approval, however, and the government may later review the action and issue a complaint.

These antitrust laws are complicated and controversial and interpretations by the courts and the Federal Trade Commission have caused much doubt in business circles. The effective salesman will pay strict attention to his company's advice as to how specific legislation affects his selling methods and to subsequent information on any changes which apply in his area. Since his actions are company actions, the salesman has a great responsibility in pricing within the legal limits established by his management.

## NEGOTIATING DISCOUNTS

There are many legitimate discounts allowed today to different buyers on the basis of the functions which they perform. The wholesaler is expected to buy in volume, warehouse, and sell to retailers. The retailer is expected to stock and display the merchandise. Financial discounts are offered to encourage prompt payment in credit sales. Quantity discounts are normally offered when savings are achieved from handling large scale orders. Special marketing and promotional discounts are offered to "early order" placers in seasonal business; to a group of independent buyers for pooling their orders into one large order; to push or promote a new product line in a particular area. These discounts may take the form of special freight allowances, free deals such as an extra case for every ten ordered, bonuses, premiums, and cooperative advertising allowances.

An effective salesman can give his customers a clear explanation of any discount which his company offers. Allowances must be offered on proportionately equal terms to all competing buyers not only to steer clear of legal complications but also to enhance the long-term contribution to profits. Even if the action is legal, if a competing buyer feels he was unfairly treated or misunderstands the discount terms he may be reluctant to order again in the future. On the other hand, many professional buyers today realize any reduction in price is apt to be accompanied by a loss of something in either product, service, or attention he would otherwise get. Professional buyers are very suspicious of discounts offered for no apparent reason and to be effective salesmen must explain their offering in terms which the buyer clearly understands and can accept.

One of the basic functions of a salesman is to provide creative ideas and suggestions to the buyer. Both buyer and seller should be on the same team, interested in cutting total costs and not simply cutting the purchase price. As noted earlier, a given price includes certain services and guarantees which may be very different from a similar product with different services and guarantee. The salesman should operate on the premise that his total product offering is different from that of anyone else and has more value and benefits to the buyer than his competitor's total offering.

Once a price is quoted to a prospect, the salesman must justify that price. Should he change to a lower price, he acknowledges the product was not worth the original asking price and the prospect is apt to think the product is not worth the second price either. This can spiral downward to eliminate profit, which hurts the salesman, and to force a reduction in services, which hurts the buyer. Any discount allowance or special offering must be made on a justified, logical, and firm basis. The prospect should feel he is being treated fairly and equally with all other buyers and is being offered proportionate savings. If he later learns this was not true, the sale may have been made but the customer will be lost. A dissatisfied buyer can quickly create many other complaints which are costly to handle and also hurt the seller's reputation.

## CREDIT SALES AND MARKET SHARE

Most salesmen would have an extremely difficult job if they were limited to prospects with adequate cash to pay in full for their goods or services. Credit has enabled American business to expand to its present enormous size and has brought the American standard of living to its all-time high with no limit in sight. Today men in credit and in selling must work closely together because business conditions change so quickly and radically. A sale one day may be profitable and the next day it may mean a loss. Credit and selling should both contribute their knowledge of customers in order to increase sales, lower costs, and keep losses to a minimum. Making a decision when some facts are missing can be extremely difficult and making a credit decision in such cases can be dangerous.

Salesmen and credit men should combine their efforts to determine the management, marketing, and financial objectives of the companies to whom they sell. In modern business, the credit people and the sales people are cooperative members of the same team with common objectives and common goals. Both groups have as their ultimate goal the long-term contribution to profit and their proximate goals are to reduce uncertainty in decision making, increase sales, lower costs, and keep losses to a minimum. To increase its share of the market, a supplier should use its credit policy with optimum efficiency as one of the several components of its marketing mix just as it would use advertising, product quality; and all the others.

## CREDIT AND PROFIT

An enthusiastic salesman occasionally will persuade people to order goods or services which they cannot afford. Often this will involve selling a line of merchandise for resale which seems to be a good money-maker for the retailer. Before the manufacturer's bill is due, the retailer should sell the entire line and have more than enough cash to meet this obligation. Unfortunately, the line may not move in one particular store due, for example, to a local strike or local abnormal weather conditions. If things really do work out as desired and the line sells as well as expected, the merchant may use his receipts to pay off an older debt, hoping that future receipts from other items will repay the current obligation. The salesman's immediate concern is to write up a profitable order which is priced fairly and will show a normal return on the merchandise or service. If the retailer's credit goes bad and several months later the amount is taken out of "Accounts Receivable" and transferred into "Loss for Bad Debts," it is not directly related to the representative's ability as a salesman. In many companies, the salesman is paid to sell and the credit manager is paid to reduce or prevent bad debt losses and seemingly the twain shall never meet. More and more successful companies today are relating bad debt losses to unscrupulous or poor salesmanship.

If an industry normally operates on 36 percent gross profit and a net profit before taxes of 6 percent, a loss for bad debts of only $500 does not mean the salesman must get a replacement order of $500 to offset this loss. It means he must sell an order of $3,000 to yield a net profit of $500 which will equal the loss. The $500 sale which went bad and the good $3,000 order will then balance out to zero profit and eliminate the loss. If this type of sales washout or break-even order is repeated by the same salesman, it is a good indication that the salesman is either pushing too hard or is neglecting to prospect honestly in order to screen out those who do not have the ability to finance their purchases realistically.

## CREDIT POLICY AND CREDIT INFORMATION

Normally a company's credit policy is determined by the industry in which it operates and by the market segment which it seeks. To be competitive, the sales company must offer selling terms which are comparable in its industry, such as net thirty days or 2 percent discount if paid within 10 days, otherwise the full amount is due in 30 days (2/10/30). Whatever credit policy a sales company maintains, it can be tightened or relaxed as the situation warrants in relation to increased sales and profits. For example, customers who have a poor credit reputation or are known to take extra long in paying their obligations may be required to pay part cash in advance, to pay cash on delivery, or to sign a credit instrument indicating the title to the goods remains with the supplier until they are paid in full. On the other hand, the same credit risk might be anxiously accepted on 2/10/60 terms by another selling company which was in a strong cash position but is sorely in need of production orders. Whatever the basic credit policy of a firm, its salesmen should understand not only what the policy is but why it is that way and not another way. If they know why their company has tight or relaxed credit, they can solicit their accounts accordingly and can be positive in their explanations to customers. If the salesmen do not understand why the policy is as it is, they are apt to argue frequently with their own credit people to get orders accepted and in the field they are apt to give only a halfhearted defense of it when with their prospects.

When a customer gives his check for merchandise received, he is not paying cash but in effect gives the supplier his authorization to collect the cash from his bank. The time delay in the normal clearing of checks makes it possible for the customer to use or even resell the merchandise before the supplier actually receives his cash payment. If the check was drawn against insufficient funds it is returned to the supplier who deposited it in his bank. In the meantime, the merchandise has already been used or resold and the customer still owes the entire amount. For this reason many auto dealers, for example, insist on receiving a certified check before delivering a new car. Such a check is certified by the customer's bank as being valid or legitimate and his bank immediately posts his account accordingly and guarantees that check. Occasionally a customer will offer a postdated check to cover his purchases because he is temporarily short of cash. A postdated check is a regular personal or business check which is dated days, weeks, or even months ahead and the supplier cannot deposit it until that date arrives. This method of payment is considered undesirable by most buyers and sellers alike although it is common in many industries. It helps facilitate sales which could not be made otherwise and it helps the customer without alarming his other creditors. If the account is well known and trusted by the selling company, they may elect to do business in this manner as an extra, even though unusual, customer service.

Promissory notes are often used as payment for capital goods and each note is signed individually by the buyer with payment due in regular equal installments over many months or several years. As each payment is received, one cancelled note is returned to the buyer. Such notes normally include interest and the transaction is legally filed in the county clerk's office so that other interested parties can be made aware of the existence of the long-term debt. Such notes may be based on the reputation of the individual signing them, on one or more cosigners, or they may be based upon a secured sale. A secured sale—for example, a conditional sales contract—normally gives the supplier complete title or ownership of the goods until the supplier is fully paid. In the event the customer fails to complete his payments, the supplier can physically take back the goods.

Whatever the industry, the salesman should be thoroughly familiar with his own company's selling terms and its current credit policy in relation to his competitors and he should understand why they are so constituted. In most industries he need not be familiar with the accounting procedures required to interpret financial statements, such as a balance sheet or a profit and loss statement. This normally is the realm of the credit manager. The salesman can contribute a wealth of information to aid the credit manager make an intelligent decision. This area is often neglected by selling companies that are reluctant to allow marketing personnel to intrude into the credit domain.

Credit, when stripped of all its complicated legal language, is simply man's faith in man. A supplier gives his goods or services to a customer in the belief the customer will pay in full as agreed. Since credit is founded upon faith in men, this is the area in which the salesman in the field, in contact with the customer, can and should be most helpful to his team workers in the credit department. Cold figures do not tell the complete credit story because it is the people behind the figures that must be judged and trusted.

To determine the credit risk, the salesman should judge the management of the prospect's business and its method of operating. The competence of management is based upon their age and experience in this and related fields as well as on their general background. Such historical information is easily obtained after the salesman has established friendly relations with his prospect. Everyone is interested in his own progress and most people are flattered to be asked to tell of their experiences. A young businessman is apt to be proud of his early success and will often point out how early in life a family business or college course provided him with vicarious experience which shortened his route to his present position. From a credit standpoint, it is important to know from what source he obtained his starting capital. Heavy initial borrowing may indicate the young man is simply a front for someone else who has a very different credit reputation. On the other hand, the older businessman is more often proud of his direct experience in the many phases of his business and is pleased to tell an interested salesman of his life journey in the school of hard knocks.

The method of operating a business is often highly indicative of management's competence and can be a good key to opening the credit risk dilemma. The method of operating includes such things as lines of merchandise carried, price range, and market sought; the location of the business in relation to the type of customers sought; the size of the operation both physically and by number of employees; and the maintenance and appearance of the stock and facilities. Finally, describing the method of operation should include some indication of the difference or uniqueness of this particular business as compared to its typical competitors.

Industrial and commercial salesmen quickly become oriented to their customers' type of business and can see minor differences in policy and methods of operating which the untrained eye might easily miss. In the normal process of selling, they attempt to learn about their prospects both as individual personalities and as companies with specific problems and needs. Much of this information is not available when a credit manager attempts to appraise a credit risk. The cold statistics of a balance sheet or a profit and loss statement can be interpreted much more accurately when the antecedents of the principles and the specific method of operation are known.

Old customers often change key personnel and methods of operating. Reputations of individuals as well as reputations of companies can change, some quickly and others gradually over a period of years. An effective salesman keeps abreast of the changes taking place in his market, chases down competitive rumors, and observes operations directly. If a customer serves a population which is dominated by one large industry, then labor conditions and the profit picture of that industry become important bits of information bearing on the credit of the customer. Normally a credit manager back in the home office has no awareness of such changes and the effective salesman will so advise him.

Many established selling companies maintain complete credit files on each customer and prospect for their area. Such information can be most helpful to the salesman before he makes his first contact. If the information is scant or completely lacking he then knows what will be needed to offer normal credit terms. By the same token, if information on file indicates a poor financial or moral risk, then the salesman can decide whether it would be better to spend his time elsewhere or to offer his services on a COD basis only.

As noted earlier in Chapter 17, on prospecting, Dun and Bradstreet, Inc., has recognized the obvious tie between credit risk and marketing information. They publish several directories listing companies of a certain size with considerable credit and sales information about each one. In addition they offer custom services which provide selective data on specified industrial code numbers in prescribed marketing areas. Confidential credit reports on individual companies are also available and normally include the detailed information on antecedents of the principals, the capitalization and form of business organization, the method of operation, and considerable financial data which is analyzed for the credit manager. The cost of such information must be related to the number of credit problems being faced as well as to the marketing value of increasing profitable sales to unknown prospects.

## SALESMAN'S EVALUATION OF CREDIT

As valuable as any commercial data may be, common sense is required in analyzing any credit information and one must always be aware of the time element. Since business conditions can change radically in a short time, the salesman in the field is the one logical person to flag or signal an order for a new credit check when indications of change are evident. A few companies place the ultimate credit responsibility directly upon the salesman and he makes the decisions regarding how much credit and on what selling terms their merchandise is offered to a particular customer. Clearly, these salesmen should have been taught to interpret financial information, a detailed and technical subject beyond the scope of this text. There are many excellent textbooks in that field for those interested in further pursuit of such knowledge. For most commercial and industrial salesmen, final credit evaluation is best left in the capable hands of the credit department but an open exchange of information between the salesmen and the credit people can be highly beneficial. With complete up-to-date customer information, prospecting and selling become easier, credit sales help increase a company's share of the market, losses due to bad debts are reduced, and long-term profits are increased. In modern American business, credit and selling are two complementary elements in the total marketing policy.

◆   ◆   ◆

## MORSE SALES REPRESENTATIVES AND SERVICE ENGINEERS ARE READY TO HELP*

Morse sales representatives are cutting tool experts who are called upon daily to recommend optimum tools and methods of cutting and drilling materials as diverse as soft plastics and special-alloy steels.

* The above is reprinted with the kind permission of E. I. duPont de Nemours & Company, a division of Universal American Corporation, New Bedford, Massachusetts.

Backstopping the sales staff is the Morse Sales Service Engineering department. Under the direction of Edward Rolnick, six trained engineers, specialized in problems of metal cutting, are in the field to lend assistance.

When a customer's problem is so complex that design engineering is required for its solution, the sales rerepsentative immediately recognizes the situation. He then can call on Morse's staff of metal-working engineers to tackle the problem.

The Morse organization's concern with the problems of its customers, and its willingness to provide services beyond merely supplying a complete line of quality cutting tools, has kept Morse among the leaders in its industry for a hundred years.

Morse has technical knowledge and experience gained over this period, plus continuing research and experimental programs which add to their store of technology. It then follows that the Morse organization probably has the answers to any metal cutting problems.

"In fact," says Ed Rolnick, "Morse has answers to problems which haven't been invented yet. Lockheed, for example, had a drilling problem; Morse engineers immediately recognized the basic nature of the problem; the laws of physics and mathematics were applied and presto! the answer."

"In short," Mr. Rolnick said, "our job at Morse is to provide tools which will create empty space where there once was material—in the shortest time, at the least cost, and with the most accurate results."

"All cutting tool problems, therefore, are just variations of the one problem we have been working on for a century. We continue to experiment with new techniques to cut new metals—and to improve methods of cutting standard metals."

Among the types of experiments cited by Mr. Rolnick was the test procedure used to determine the optimum tools and methods to cut new metals. When a new alloy is developed, it is often first sent to the Morse plant in various forms —sheet, plate, bar stock, etc.

Morse engineers will work the metal and recommend, for example, the proper tool material and geometry to drill the new alloy in its various forms. When the metal is marketed, there is no need for manufacturers to experiment. . . .

Morse has the answer!

# 23

# Cultivating Customers and Building Goodwill

Despite cynical essays which seem to be popular today, customers are sensible and not easily swayed when it matters. They are spurred on by success to higher levels of aspiration and they can become vindictive when fooled by the supplier. It is not the producer who alone decides what is to be produced, who is to produce it, when it is to be produced, in what quantities, and at what price. Economists hold that the consumer, with his economic life-and-death power of the purse, is king. Actually our economy is consumer oriented rather than consumer directed and the economic action is really an interaction between many factors in our society. The consumer is king insofar as his discretionary power permits him to buy or postpone purchases and this does have a tremendous influence on business cycles. With such sovereign power the consumer waves his magic wand, the almighty buck, and business courts him for special favors and their own security.[1] Such wooing of the customers is known in business as cultivating customers and building goodwill.

## THE NATURE OF GOODWILL AND ITS EFFECT

When the first order is placed with a supplier of goods or services it is most often a tentative action and it is viewed as a trial or test of the seller's claims. The buyer is temporarily changing his behavior either from no action or from obtaining his goods through a different supplier. He has moved from a familiar and friendly supplier into an area of doubt, uncertainty, and unknown danger. He has stopped buying from his old supplier

---

[1] For this argument against John Kenneth Galbraith and Vance Packard, see George Katona, *The Mass Consumption Society*. (New York: McGraw-Hill Book Co., Inc., 1965), p. 343.

and this may involve hurting old business friends. He has stopped being loyal to a once friendly supplier but does not have the security of pleasant experience with the new supplier. Inside, the buyer may be filled with doubt, fear, and anxiety.

The new supplier, clearly, must perform almost perfectly at this point in order to assure the buyer that his decision to change was wise and will be rewarding. All promises and claims of benefits should be fulfilled beyond the buyer's expectations. Because of this initial superservice and the high original selling cost to obtain the order, many suppliers actually lose money on the first order. They are willing and eager to do so because follow-up orders will make the account increase in importance and as these orders continue to mount, the initial selling and service cost will dwindle into insignificance.

Gradually the buyer's tentative behavior involves less and less conscious thought. His initial doubts and fears fade away and gradually they seem to have been foolish because the rewards justify the actions. The new supplier is proved reliable, trustworthy, and pleasant so the buyer can feel assured and relaxed in this area and turn his attention to other problems. His buying behavior becomes habitual or practically automatic as the new friendship replaces the old. A new customer has been developed and goodwill established. The salesman's responsibility now is to continue to provide good service so that the buyer will not readily reopen this issue and so that any competitive challenges will be expensive for the would-be supplier as well as very discouraging to his salesmen.

Repeat sales to the same account are common in commercial and industrial selling; however, the same psychology applies even when repeat sales cannot be expected very soon, if ever. Satisfied customers make the best salesmen because they enjoy pointing out the benefits they have gained and encourage their friends and business associates to buy from the same salesman. An important customer may well become the center of influence and provide leads to many other sales. In selling home improvements such as aluminum siding, for example, one job well done can lead to others in the same area. Conversely, a dissatisfied buyer can cause so much trouble that sales in that neighborhood become difficult if not impossible. Insurance, stocks and bonds, advertising, accounting, legal, and similar intangible services are sold initially on a casual or temporary buyer-seller relationship which effective salesmen cultivate over the years into a continuing client-adviser relationship.

There is another dimension to goodwill and that is the salesman's responsibilities to a broader population than just his customers. He is accountable to society in general. As noted in the previous chapter, if the salesman does not operate in an efficient, ethical, and socially desirable manner his consistent refusal or failure to perform in the proper fashion will result in society's restricting or entirely withdrawing his freedom of operation. Most of the political limitations placed upon sales activities through the years have been the result of the salesman's failure to recognize and live up to his social responsibilities.

If a salesman misrepresents a product or tries to use high pressure selling techniques, any ill-will incurred is reflected on his firm. If he eats his meals in cheap and dirty restaurants and sleeps in run-down rooming houses, the public sees these activities and it becomes the basis for their judgment of the concern. It the salesman drinks too much in public, is loud or uncouth, or generally conducts himself in an unbecoming manner, he is creating an unfavorable image of the company in the minds of those who observe his behavior. It reflects on the company's standards for hiring, or lack of control. On the other hand, a salesman who is sincere and honest in his dealings with customers and who conducts himself off the job with equal dignity reflects credit on his firm. The supplier is appraised by the public in the light of the impression left by the visiting salesman; hence anything the salesman can do to develop a socially desirable sales operation will do much toward perpetuating the company's public image and goodwill.

The value of goodwill may range from a few thousand dollars to many millions of dollars in a large company. It is an intangible asset because it represents the value of the feelings or attitudes that customers, prospects, and the general public have toward the company and its products. This attitude is subject to change depending upon the reaction of the public to changes in company products and policies. When buyers are satisfied and place more trust and confidence in the company, the value of goodwill increases. When highly competitive products are offered to a prospect with similar services, prices, and effective salesmen, the buyer prefers to buy from the company he likes best.

Since all companies attempt to build goodwill, they are competing for customer and public preference or favor. In any selling, the Roman saying, *quid pro quo*, is applicable—something given for something received. The public in general and customers in particular will give their favorable opinion to those salesmen who provide an honest evaluation of product, legitimate customer services especially beyond the initial offering, and sincere attention to their needs and interests. If the salesman wants goodwill he must give these extras freely and in good measure calculated to make his company outstanding. Paying lip service to the concept of customer-oriented selling is not enough to cultivate customers and build goodwill. Performance over extended periods of time is required to build customer loyalty, repeat orders, referrals, and long-term profits. This is a practical application of the law of cause and effect. The salesman must observe the results of all the little things he can do for his customers because, while he may not be able to predetermine the effects of a little thing, he should know that every action of his will bring a chain of reactions from customers, prospects, and the general public.

## WHEN TO CULTIVATE CUSTOMERS

Cultivating customers is normally an active process in their presence and a passive process when they are absent but both are positive processes. The salesman who offers and performs services while with customers but then complains in their absence is neither sincere nor effective. A salesman who complains about customers that abuse his services or one who brags about wooing a customer and "putting over a fast one" may quickly learn the order placer is no longer a customer. It is impossible to turn sincerity on and off as one would a faucet. Even an actor onstage, if he is effective, is apt to live the same part offstage. Whenever an individual honestly believes he is serving a responsible function in society he lives the role in all parts of his life. His behavior pattern becomes established and he conducts himself with dignity and propriety, building a personal reputation as a fine man.

In the United States everyone has the democratic responsibility to enter into civic affairs to better our society. Some may choose to raise funds for charitable purposes, others engage in school activities, attack slum conditions or juvenile delinquency problems. Volunteers are needed by the Boy Scouts, Girl Scouts, Little League, and many similar programs to help the young. A salesman is especially responsible for active participation in such affairs. A good salesman is a leader of men and activities because he is an effective communicator and persuader. People often look to him for service and guidance and he should willingly accept his responsibility for spearheading community projects. Not only does he gain respect and build his reputation locally, he gains an inner peace of mind and personal satisfaction which is reflected in his dealings with customers thousands of miles away.

Another major responsibility of the salesman is to determine what his market or customers want and then to supply products and services to satisfy those wants. Customers have their own specialties and problems

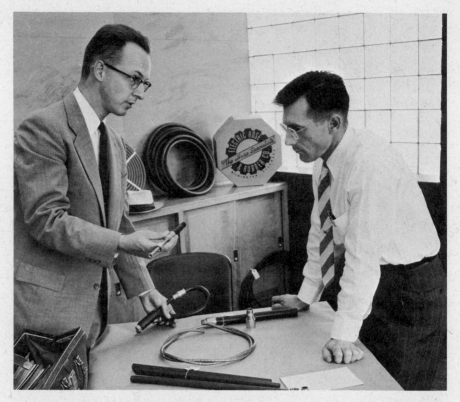

*Courtesy: E. I. du Pont de Nemours Co., Wilmington, Del.*

**FIG. 16. A salesman explains his product to a customer.**

and will not spend their resources inventing new products for the supplier. The demand may be unrecognized or not considered pressing by the customer until a new product appears to fulfill the need. Many new products introduced since World War II, which people seemed to get along without very well, are now considered more than convenience items and almost necessities. Air conditioning, television, frozen foods, and new packaging materials were all successful because unsatisfied demands were discovered by responsible salesmen and their companies. If private industry ignores the market demand, other institutions, such as government agencies, may take over such functions by default. An effective salesman is aware of his responsibility to feed back useful marketing information to his research and development department to better serve his customers.

Cultivating customers is a regular full-time responsibility of salesmen and is most often seen in the actual selling processes of prospecting, demonstrating, answering objections, and closing the sale. When attempting to earn the first order, the salesman's actions will influence subsequent reactions by the prospect. Benefits claimed and promises made during the sales presentation will be sought at a later date. The salesman's behavior during his initial or early contacts will be judged as representative of the supplier. Anything devious, underhanded, high pressure, or frankly dishonest will boomerang sooner or later at the supplier's expense. After the initial sale is made and the order is placed, the salesman should provide complete information and guidance on the care and optimum use of the product or service. When the buyer is satisfied with the performance of his purchase but the salesman recognizes it is not operating at the best level for this application, the salesman who wants to build goodwill for his company and a good personal reputation will take the time and effort to show how to get satisfactory use of the product. Handing a customer a booklet of instruction and running on to the next prospect is hardly providing information or service. Effective salesmen realize that if the buyer does not understand how to get optimum use from the product or does not understand how preventative maintenance should be performed, the salesman will later be vulnerable to complaints and competitive challenges. Merchandise returns, expensive service calls, and detrimental word-of-mouth communications can be reduced if not entirely eliminated by the salesman who takes time after the sale to insure correct application, use, and maintenance of his products.

Perhaps the most neglected time for cultivating customers occurs when an order is lost. The salesman is naturally disappointed and is tempted to move on quickly to new prospects. Showing disappointment—or worse, resentment—of the buyer's action can only create a bad impression and reflect on the supplier. It speaks eloquently of the salesman's desire to be friendly only on the condition that he is favored with the order; hence he does not really care about the buyer's welfare. On the other hand, the salesman who can be a good loser, a perfect gentleman at all times, will generally be welcome again in the future. Since the buyer's action in purchasing from a diffrent supplier is often tentative and full of doubts, this puts the unsuccessful salesman in an excellent position for future orders. If he continues to be helpful and sincerely serves the account, the slightest slip in product value, customer service, or attention by the first successful salesman will send the account back into the market for an alternate supplier. The salesman who has continued to show interest in the buyer's welfare, even after losing an order, will be the next logical choice. In commercial and industrial selling, this technique can succeed when the day seems lost. It requires patience, self-confidence, and a good amount of faith in man's integrity. Contrary to the cynical expressions about nice guys always finishing last, the man who really believes in serving his customers may not always win the order but he is always near the top and ready to take over the account if the short-term winner falters in any way.

## METHODS OF CULTIVATING CUSTOMERS
## AND BUILDING GOODWILL

If one uses empathy and puts himself in the buyer's shoes it is quickly apparent that he wants prompt, courteous service and to be treated fairly and honestly. Buyers rarely judge a supplier by the latter's office or plant workers because in the normal course of business he does not see these people. The sales representative is the individual frequently blamed for any errors or inefficiencies on the part of office, production, and distribution personnel. If the product does not function properly or an invoice is made out incorrectly, the sales representative must face the angry customer and pacify him. It is the manner in which the salesman handles such difficult situations that can determine whether or not the customer will remain loyal or seek another supplier.

Having analyzed his accounts and classified them according to call frequency, the effective salesman reduces the chances of neglecting some accounts and becoming something of a pest to other accounts. While he may intend to perform extra services for his accounts, the best intentions in the world do not forgive a salesman who demands more of the buyer's time than is justified by the situation. Too much of a good thing can be as sickening as too much of a bad thing and it is wise to remember customers have limitations on their time, energies, and attention span.

Customer services beyond those normally offered with the product include creative ideas and suggestions or help in all the business areas which interest the customer. These would include advertising, promotional literature, point-of-purchase displays, floor planning for flow of store traffic or office work flow, pricing, stocking, and inventory controls, accounting procedures, increasing sales through training of the customer's sales personnel, reducing expenses, increasing profits, analyzing markets, and isolating important segments which the customer seems best able to cultivate. The customer is normally confined to his own place of business while the salesman visits many similar businesses and can keep abreast of new and interesting developments. Many manufacturers and large suppliers have facilities and personnel for administrative assistance which would otherwise be too costly for the small retailer. Often this information is available in the field to customers who seek it and the sales representative can offer this extra service when it applies. Other suppliers have a staff of experts who make regular field visits to help their customers in many management areas which are not directly related to selling the supplier's line. While no one expects the salesman to be an expert in all phases of his customers' business, he can be alert to recognize problem areas and intelligently discuss topics beyond his immediate product area. As the salesman utilizes the extra services of his company he gains knowledge and firsthand experience, gradually becoming an expert in his own right.

Another method of cultivating customers is to keep in touch with them between regular calls. A few extra telephone calls each day will enable the salesman to keep up to date on customer problems and show sincere interest in their business without taking a lot of time. Frequently, minor sources of irritation can be discovered and quickly corrected before they grow out of proportion and become complaints. Occasionally fill-in orders can be obtained which will carry the customer over until the salesman's regular visit. These small orders may not show more profit for the sales time and shipping costs involved but the sincere effort is greatly appreciated by the customer.

A number of companies require their salesmen to compile a mailing list which is then used for congratulatory messages such as birthday greetings, anniversary greetings, Christmas, New Year's, and the like. The supplier then automates the mailing with preprinted cards bearing the company name and the salesman simply signs each card. While few people are apt to be offended by such mail, it does seem too artificial and commercial to be appreciated as a friendly gesture. A mass mailing technique is not designed to substitute for a personal method of building goodwill. Any such greetings to be really appreciated should have the personal element featured. A personal handwritten note, omitting the company name would be a better way to congratulate an individual. Often mailings of a personal nature are used to precede a sales visit but are self-defeating because the customer quickly recognizes the so-called personal message as simply a commercial prospecting device. A phone call to wish a customer a happy birthday, for example, might serve the same purpose and appear more spontaneous and less of a cold, calculated sales maneuver. If the salesman actually cultivates his customers as friends, it usually pays dividends.

One of the most common and effective ways to cultivate customers is getting to know many individuals in their companies. This would include as many of the buying influentials as possible such as the order placer, the specifier, the information gatherer, the advisor, the user, the kibitzer, the decision maker, and the vetoer. It would also include nonbuying employees that might receive merchandise, unpack it, and move it to the stockroom or to the point of use. It might include secretaries, accounting clerks, and engineers. The salesman should attempt to become friendly and acceptable in all phases of his customer's business. This will increase the chances of his goods being handled more carefully and reduce minor complaints and petty annoyances. In time some of these people will be promoted to positions which may influence buying and even the office boy may one day become president. It is just as easy to be sincere and polite to everyone as it is to ignore people and hurt their feelings. The salesman cannot tell the potentialities of these people and his only safe course is to treat everyone courteously, wisely, and even flatteringly.

The most lasting method of cultivating customers is by building a personal reputation as the kind of person they like to have visit. To make a good impression on customers the salesman should be well groomed in a conservative manner acceptable to the customer and he should know his product, its applications, and how they fit his customer's business. The salesman should be a friendly authority who can state facts to support his business theories and claims of benefits. By observing the physical environment of the customer, his personal dress and manner, the salesman can often recognize clues which indicate areas of personal interest. Everyone has a deep-rooted desire to be appreciated and to feel important. Trophies, pictures, lapel pins, and other symbols of past achievements indicate areas of personal interest. Good human relations are built on making the other fellow feel important and doing it openly and honestly. Everyone likes a compliment when it is earned even when modesty causes them to underplay their personal accomplishments. Friendship can be built on such personal notes which are beyond the immediate business at hand. Friendship also requires an uncritical attitude in listening. One is not blind to the faults of a customer but the effective salesman does not criticize or assume a superior attitude. He takes the man as he really is with his good and bad points. With such an understanding, the salesman can appreciate how the customer will feel in a given situation and can avoid areas which he knows will upset the customer.

The personal reputation of a salesman is in direct relationship to his sincerity and his willingness to take a personal interest in his customers. The salesman should speak well of other customers and of his competitors, being very careful to maintain all confidential information. A man who reveals confidential information implies he will reveal all such information and he soon cuts himself off from any personal communications. Reputations are built on honesty, dependability, consideration, and courteous behavior. When the salesman can offer friendly advice and be helpful in areas beyond his normal selling responsibilities, he is building his personal reputation which reflects credit on his company. Customers like to do business with people they know and in whom they have confidence. It pays dividends to get to know each customer as an individual and adapt to him so the salesman is the kind of person with whom he likes to do business.

In some selling fields, entertaining is the normal and accepted practice while in other fields it is not expected and may be in poor taste to offer. Even when entertainment is customary, salesmen have limited expense accounts and limited time which prohibits entertaining all customers and prospects. Discretion must be used to determine which accounts should be cultivated by entertaining so that no one feels slighted because he was overlooked. Many times an offer to go to lunch or dinner is refused but the thought is appreciated.

The trend today is away from expensive entertainment and toward using the lunch hour as extra time to conduct business in a friendly atmosphere. Buyers do not want to feel obligated to the salesman and will often pick up the check on alternate dates. Such an arrangement is ideal because the two men can get to know each other in a social setting which is relaxed and totally voluntary. Each party is there because he wants to be there and enjoys the company of the other. When evening entertainment is expected, as at conventions and visits to distant cities, it is wise to find out what kind of entertainment is acceptable and desirable to the customer. Tickets to an expensive Broadway musical show might be ideal for one customer while another customer might prefer a quiet evening playing cards with old business friends. The amount of money spent is not nearly as important to customers as the thoughtful selection of entertainment for the particular customer and the careful attention to little details that make for a pleasant evening. Regardless of government tax regulations the salesman would be wise to avoid talk of business unless and until it is initiated by the customer. Such entertainment is designed to build personal friendship and goodwill but is not generally used to get immediate business. No one in business wants to feel he was bribed and a sincere salesman will not use entertainment to impose an obligation on the customer.

## HANDLING COMPLAINTS AND BUILDING GOODWILL

Inexperienced salesmen often fear a customer complaint and look upon it as an unfortunate part of their selling responsibilities. On the other hand, confident salesmen recognize a complaint as an opportunity to be of service to the customer, prove their sincerity, and earn the customer's confidence. This is literally a golden chance to build personal reputation and goodwill for the supplier. Effective salesmen realize that complaints will be made and they are inevitable but these men know enough about their business operations to handle complaints as a normal part of their selling job.

Once a complaint is evident, whether voiced or not by the customer, the salesman should immediately preinvestigate to determine whatever facts he can establish from his company's records. For the inexperienced salesman this may mean gathering all possible information internally and discussing the problem with senior salesmen or the sales manager. Perhaps alternate solutions or procedures may be suggested depending upon additional information later obtained from the customer. If the trouble lies entirely within the supplier, it would be well to have action initiated to correct the fault before seeing the irate customer. When the salesman makes his initial visit he will be prepared with a full explanation and be able to state in detail what steps have already been taken to correct the error. Such planning will forestall further ire. When he visits the customer, the situation is similar to handling an objection during a sales presentation but it is often supercharged with emotion. The customer feels injured or insulted and regardless of where the fault lies he is apt to vent his anger on the sales representative.

The salesman's immediate objective is to create an atmosphere of calm logic with the salesman completely on the side of the customer in demanding fair treatment for him. The effective salesman agrees that the customer has every right to complain and be angry if the facts are as he sees them. The customer is encouraged to talk about his understanding of what was to be expected—in delivery, product performance, product application, price and terms of sale, payment or credit policy, guarantee and return privileges. If the salesman listens attentively without interrupting with critical comments, some complaints will resolve themselves because they were simply bids for attention. At other times the mere voicing of a complaint in detail has the effect of catharsis. Having spoken and brought the problem out into the open to be examined, the customer himself may no longer see it as the "hidden monster inside" and it may now even appear trivial to him.

If the complaint is not resolved by simply talking things over and clearing up misunderstandings then the salesman should attempt to get all the facts from the customer's point of view without emotional overtones. Perhaps the merchandise did arrive on time but was poorly marked and stayed on the receiving platform longer than usual. The product may have been defective or it may have been misapplied. Errors can and do occur in pricing and billing. Policies are misinterpreted and credit decisions can be unfair. The important element at this point is to transfer the blame from the individual representative to an unfortunate but natural human error. The salesman then acts as the customer's agent to fight his battle and correct the situation. The buyer and seller are going the same way and are again personal friends with mutual respect and confidence restored.

Once the facts are clear, in that errors or faults can be assigned to specific areas, the alternate solutions become obvious and the probable results of various actions can be evaluated. It is generally a wise policy to give the customer the benefit of any doubt, particularly when the supplier shared in causing the error or misunderstanding. When it is clearly the fault of the customer it is often good policy to concede on minor points giving the customer a face-saving out so that he in turn will concede the major point. Any adjustment policy must be interpreted in the light of the individual circumstances and pleasing the customer should be the guiding principle. An occasional adjustment in favor of the customer even when he is at fault may be good business in the long run. Few customers will attempt to abuse such a policy and they are quickly recognized. Perhaps the supplier is better off without these few accounts.

The key to handling customer complaints is to make the customer feel he was fairly treated and is a very important person in the eyes of the supplier. The final decision should be prompt and should be handled entirely by the one salesman. Nothing is more irritating to the customer than to be bounced from one department or individual to another before getting a decision. Delayed decisions, even when favorable to the customer, will leave an unpleasant impression of the supplier.

Finally, in handling customer complaints, it is imperative that the salesman follow through on any promises made. If the customer is promised delivery or a refund it should be handled with special priority and not in the usual due course of events, which may have caused the problem in the beginning. If a replacement product or special services were offered, they should be supplied promptly and the salesman should accompany or follow up delivery to insure complete satisfaction. Much advertising and sales literature is written about guarantees and a policy of customer satisfaction because the supplier backs his products but it is the salesman in the field making the personal contacts who bears the brunt of any complaints and is able to turn them into opportunities for performance which ultimately builds goodwill.

## SELECTING CUSTOMERS FOR CULTIVATING

Goodwill seldom is built on a single sales call and normally a long period of time is necessary to build it. One good deed may help but most people like to know a salesman well before they will put complete confidence in him or his company. Time is the most precious commodity an effective salesman has and he must spend it wisely to achieve the greatest satisfaction. His energy and money are also relatively limited but they can be renewed periodically. Once time is spent, the past cannot be changed regardless of all the wishing and hindsight in the world. If months or years are spent cultivating one account, it cannot be spent cultivating another account. The salesman should select customers for cultivating only after rigorous thinking and deliberation. Long-term plans require patience and considerable seemingly unproductive effort.

Customer selection begins with identifying the market segments which the supplier is particularly adept at servicing due to his facilities, geography, finances, unique product features, or some other strength. Once a group of customer targets is isolated, the salesman should analyze and classify each account as to its potential and his chances of getting their business. Finally, the salesman should analyze his own personal strengths and weaknesses to determine with which accounts he will best fit. Part of this self-analysis may include a plan for self-development to become more expert in his customer's line of business.

This type of long-term planning can only succeed as it focuses on long-term contribution to profits, which in the larger sense means communicating with and persuading people to become customers. The salesman should view his company and his actual and potential customers as engaged in equal relationships for personal satisfaction in dealings, mutually profitable operations, and growth. Specific accounts selected for long-term cultivation should show signs of all three elements if the time invested is to be ultimately rewarding. In this context, the effective salesman will regard himself not as working for his employer but for his customer—to help the customer achieve greater satisfaction, greater profits, and greater growth. This is enlightened self-interest.

As noted throughout this text, the salesman is in a unique position in the total marketing plan. He usually is the only company representative who has personal contact with the customer and, in fact, he *is* the company to the customer. That personal contact is the basis for building goodwill and customer loyalty. As long as the selling involves the personal element, advertising and other promotional methods of building goodwill must continue to be of secondary importance to the customer.

◆   ◆   ◆

## THE CUSTOMER IS THE BOSS*

*He buys on the basis of quality, service and price, and his decisions set the course for all industry*

The audience Du Pont salesmen must please are officers, buyers, and purchasing agents of the 75,000 enterprises to which Du Pont sells. They represent the bosses of the American economy. As customers, they decide whether a product shall be ignored or hailed, whether a company shall fade or grow large, whether a new development shall be accepted or sent back for further work, or abandoned.

Like all customers, they base their decisions on quality, service and price, and buy from the salesman who offers the best combination of all three. The job of selection is a difficult one, for the products and services offered are many and varied, and the competition among those seeking orders is today greater than ever before.

In plastics, as an example, the buyer can buy from Du Pont or any of 18 major competitors. In anti-freezes, Du Pont's competitors total 245; in explosives, 16; in sulfuric acid, 20. And in the paint field the customer may choose any of 1200 brands.

Du Pont customers represent every geographic section and every size of venture. They range from a one-man auto refinish shop to Chrysler, Ford, and General Motors; from Bethlehem and U.S. Steel to a five-man metal-coating shop founded with the product and the know-how Du Pont provided.

Some customers have bought from Du Pont for generations. Others are new. But old or new, large or small, they present the same challenge to the salesman. He must help them produce a product that will earn greater rewards, and win them new customers.

Those who speak glibly of industry's "power" often fail to see that the real power in the American economy lies in the customers' hands. Their voice governs the research programs, production schedules, and sales of industry.

---

* The above is reprinted with the kind permission of E. I. duPont de Nemours & Company, Inc., Wilmington, Delaware.

# PART V

# Developing the Marketing
# Manager's Viewpoint

# 24

# Why Irrational and Misleading Persuasion Attempts Boomerang

Some salesmen seem to live in perpetual hope that infallible means will be developed whereby one man can control another's behavior. Some selfishly see the possibility of advantage for themselves in gaining control over their fellow men. There is something very plausible in the concept that if we understand another person's unconscious motives, then we can appeal in such a way that we can get him to do something without his knowing why he did it. He ought to be powerless to resist. As appealing as this concept may be to some salesmen, it is equally frightening to some consumers. Recent experiments in psychology and some of the publicity given to its more sensational applications—such as hidden persuaders, brainwashing, subliminal advertising, and motivation research in marketing—have strengthened the public's fears of being manipulated to the advantage of someone else. Such fears on the part of the consumer and such hopes on the part of the seller are based on ignorance of the causal relations between the persuaders and the persuaded.[1]

There can be no serious doubt that the social science fields have developed and refined many effective techniques of persuasion. This has benefited the fields of human relations, education, and communication, to name but a few. After the scarcities created by World War II were eliminated and production began to exceed consumer demand, buyers became more particular in their choice of goods and services. Marketing executives could not persuade consumers to buy more goods or inferior goods with their old promotional methods and were forced to seek something new. The psychologists had some of the answers then and they are

---

[1] For an excellent discourse on this theme, see Raymond A. Bauer, "Limits of Persuasion," *Harvard Business Review*, Vol. 36, No. 5, pp. 105–10.

DEVELOPING THE MARKETING MANAGER'S VIEWPOINT

DEVELOPING THE MARKETING MANAGER'S VIEWPOINT

steadily developing more. None of this knowledge, however, enables marketing people to effect more persuasion. This apparent paradox exists because the increased knowledge benefits not only the persuader but the consumer as well. As the marketers become more sophisticated, so do the people to be persuaded. Manipulation and persuasion have become more difficult, not less difficult. Each new psychological finding or theory is well publicized in the daily papers as well as in professional trade journals and by the time business and industry apply the new knowledge to their marketing policy, the public is not the same as it was during the experiment. The published results of the experiment also educate the public and resistance to persuasion and manipulation increases. As long as new developments and knowledge are shared by the would-be manipulators and their intended victims there is no danger that society is on the verge of being able to establish complete control over human behavior to the extent that the victims of this control do not have a chance to resist it because they do not realize it is there.

A study of the methods which people use in choosing or making a buying decision, as covered in Chapter 5, leads inevitably to the conclusion that some problems are solved one way and some another. There is perhaps no normal adult who does not employ, at least occasionally, each of the methods described previously. Under certain conditions one uses one method and under different conditions he will use others. One varies from day to day and from moment to moment in his susceptibility to logic and his susceptibility to suggestion. In deciding certain classes of questions one does not feel satisfied until he has deliberated; in other instances he feels no such need for deliberation but responds quickly to appropriate suggestions. Persons and classes of society differ also in the extent to which they use the different methods of deciding questions. Furthermore, some salesmen are trained experts in presenting logical arguments while others are most successful when avoiding logic and depending upon suggestion. To influence men effectively is no simple task. Some men seem naturally gifted with this power and are able to accomplish as much intuitively as are other men after much study devoted to the subject. The men with such talents as well as those less generously endowed may increase their skill in persuading men by proceeding scientifically at their task. Both groups should look at the tools of irrational and misleading persuasion to see how they are normally used and why they often backfire.[2]

---

[2] See Roger Brown, *Words and Things* (New York: The Free Press of Glencoe, 1958, particularly chap. ix, "Persuasion, Expression, and Propaganda."

## ECONOMIC DETERMINISM VERSUS PROPAGANDISTIC
## MANIPULATION

The term "propaganda," because of its various meanings in popular usage, is difficult to employ exactly in a discussion. It is often used to indicate either an underhand campaign to influence people or the spreading of falsehoods and misrepresentations. In this analysis its connotation is restricted to the management of collective attitudes by the manipulation of words, phrases, gestures, and the speaker's manner. Under this definition the propagandist becomes one who endeavors to manage collective attitudes, whatever his motive. He may attempt to present the cause of a company that pursues selfish gain in such a light that the cause will be acceptable to the general public or he may be promoting an unselfish project such as slum clearance that unquestionably is in agreement with the general welfare. He may shade the truth, suppress matters of negative value, and emphasize those of positive value. Thus considered, propaganda is neither moral nor immoral but simply amoral.

The theory of propaganda presupposes a method of influencing attitudes that is different from the process of deliberation or reasoning. The decision of the buyer becomes a choice between competing propagandists and this may turn out to be no decision at all, for the victory may belong to the more skillful symbol manipulator without relating to the buyer's needs. There is an assumption that, within limits, the collective attitudes of humans may be managed by the manipulation of symbols to which men have been conditioned to respond in a predictable way. The manipulator uses existing attitudes and group prejudices to intensify the attitude favorable to his purpose, to reverse the attitudes hostile to it, and to attract the indifferent, or at the worst, to prevent them from assuming a hostile bent. If he can associate his goal with an element of the tradition of the group, he is likely to succeed. Something of the same notions are impilcit in the concept of stereotypes. Words evoke certain pictures in our minds and propaganda technique involves the selection and use of words that will create the desired pictures.

An apparent conflict may exist between the theory of propaganda and the theory that buying behavior may be determined by some external condition, such as economic need. Between extreme formulations of the two doctrines a conflict exists, yet a line of reconciliation may be pointed out. It would be absurd to say that an adroit manipulator of symbols could influence mass buying in certain ways under certain conditions. When buyers want high quality regardless of the price the advocate of economy in pricing may make little headway. But when the time is ripe for reducing all costs including acquisition costs, the salesman with the keener perception of the expectations of the buyers and with the better judgment of the sorts of symbol appeal to make may wield the greater influence. And, unfortunately for the reputation of professional selling, it can be shown that the skilled propagandist in marketing may induce buyers to follow, within limits, a course of action contrary to their interests, or to what would be expected from the application of a doctrine such as economic determinism—or any similar theory of behavior.

Marketing studies have shown that buyers and consumers in general can be readily grouped into different information levels by their knowledge of a given area. Knowledge is the fundamental defense against irrational persuasion attempts. The chief effect of greater information is to make the well-informed group more sensitive to the implications of events or points of view to their own self-interest. Such studies also indicate that information tends to be generalized so that persons who are well informed in one area tend to have the same opinions as persons well informed in other areas. The opinions of the well informed and the uninformed can be affected in the same direction—to like a product, for example—and appeals to special interest groups can produce the opposite effect by dividing the groups more sharply. In marketing, a prestige item may lose its appeal to wealthy prospects if it becomes a common sight in lower-class neighborhoods.

People do buy many things for noneconomic reasons but their behavior can be very conscious and logical. They are aware, for example, of the value of prestige, status, self-esteem, and buying something simply because it makes their mood more pleasant. Some people have come to accept these as proper buying motives while others still resist these appeals. In addition, there are some unconscious motives which a buyer is not aware of and would not acknowledge consciously to himself even if they were called to his attention. Current motivation research studies have noted many connotations which various products acquire. For example, in the United States tea is reputed to be a feminine beverage while coffee has a definite masculine overtone.[3] Many male tea drinkers would not agree with this, especially if they were accused of being feminine. There is a reason for certain motives remaining unconscious. If the individual consciously acknowledged to himself the existence of such motives, he would suffer

---

[3] See Ernest Dichter, *Handbook of Consumer Motivations* (New York: McGraw-Hill Book Co., Inc., 1965).

intolerable personal doubts and fears. Appeals to such unconscious motives can easily boomerang. Many people respond negatively to subliminal or hidden persuaders even in some instances where it may be in their own interest. Buyers resist anyone telling them what's good for them and their resistance to persuasion has increased if it has not preceded improvements in the marketing techniques of persuasion.

## IRRATIONAL PERSUASION

At the beginning of World War II, American fear of being manipulated by propaganda grew to the point that an Institute for Propaganda Analysis[4] was founded and their findings published and distributed to schools and libraries for high-school teaching. This extensive study provides natural guidelines for a marketing analysis of the rhetorical devices of irrational persuasion. The institute classified the characteristics of propaganda to include: name-calling; glittering generality; transfer; testimonial; plain folks; card stacking; and bandwagon.

Actually very few people need to be taught that devices of this kind are sometimes used in an unscrupulous effort to make people do what is not in their own best interests. From childhood on, natural exposure to other people causes one to work at propaganda detection and by adulthood he is pretty good at it. Separating propaganda from good advice and useful information involves perceiving or understanding the motives and knowledgeability of the source of the message. The effectiveness of irrational persuasion attempts is limited by the buyer's lifetime experience of treating speech and all behavior as revealing of the salesman's character.

1. *Name-calling.*—Name-calling involves the repetition of "the big lie" in the belief that if a falsehood is repeated often enough and exaggerated out of proportion, some people will believe there must be at least some element of truth behind it. Hitler used this device in his attempt to destroy the Jews in Germany. The big lie was that Jews controlled all the money in Germany and were parasites who contributed nothing to that society. Any minority can be attacked by name-calling techniques and some people who because of ignorance or personal greed are predisposed to harbor racial antipathies will tend to believe the propaganda. If a manufacturer enters a new field, other manufacturers' representatives are apt to use the name-

---

[4] Bruce Lannes Smith, "Propaganda Analysis and The Science of Democracy," *Public Opinion Quarterly*, Vol. 5, 1941, pp. 250–59. For a guide to the extensive literature on propaganda, see B. L. Smith, H. D. Lasswell, and R. D. Casey, *Propaganda Communication, and Public Opinion: A Comprehensive Reference Guide* (Princeton, N.J.: Princeton University Press, 1946).

calling technique, claiming the newcomer does not know the business and is turning out inferior products attempting to gain quick profits and then leave that industry. If enough salesmen call on the same prospect and each voices this same big lie over and over, the prospect may begin to have serious doubts about the new manufacturer. Such collusion in restraint of trade is illegal but even if it were not, the new manufacturer is not at the mercy of such irrational attacks. He also has a propaganda machine in the form of advertising and this together with his own personal sales force can counterbalance competitive efforts. In addition, the buyer is generally suspicious of any claims made by one salesman against another and the name-calling efforts may boomerang, causing the buyer to investigate the product which seems to have frightened all the competition. Their very efforts may drive him to the doorstep of the new manufacturer.

2. *Glittering Generality.*—This device is widely used by most salesmen who do not know their product as well as they should. They paint a beautiful picture of all the benefits of owning their product but gloss over the details which should justify such claims. Their offering to the retailer will sell like hot cakes and return fabulous profits. Their offering to the commercial or industral business will increase production and reduce costs well beyond anything on the market. As the prospect well knows, their products will produce tremendous benefits. The trap in this device is intended to be the timidity of the prospect which prevents him from admitting that he does not know how something will be accomplished. The buyer will not wish to expose himself to possible ridicule because he does not know something he apparently should know or because he is not intelligent enough to understand the salesman's explanation. This use of suggestion is intended to focus the prospect's attention on the glittering rewards of buying and to avoid his deliberate thought processes which require that logical reasoning precede buying action. This is the device used to "part the fool from his money" in most confidence swindles and in selling it is used to make conversation without really communicating anything. There are not many businessmen who will tolerate such sales tactics and there are even fewer who will be fooled by them. If the salesman does not know his product the buyer can hardly place much confidence in his advice and suggestions. If the salesman's attitude implies the prospect is uninformed or of low intelligence there can be no mutual respect, confidence, or satisfaction in being together. While the glittering generality may occasionally work in mass communications, where an audience can be carried away by an eloquent speaker who really says very little, this device is much more apt to boomerang in personal selling

situations where the listener can interrupt the salesman and demand clarity and more specific information.

3. *Testimonial and Transfer.*—The technique of testimonial—the doctors who prefer one brand of cigarette to others or the unsolicited letter from an insured praising the quick and generous settlement of his fire insurance claim—is used to lend credibility to a claim. The implication of the one letter is that all claims are settled quickly and generously. Transfer, on the other hand, involves a product endorsement by a famous personality such as the World Series baseball player who has grown strong by eating certain breakfast foods or the busy executives who keep abreast of the times by reading certain magazines or newspapers. The implication of transfer techniques such as these is that if the prospect does the same things, some of the glamour of the famous people will rub off or be transferred to him.

These two techniques are often combined so that a famous personality is used to give an endorsement to a particular product or service. In social psychology the two devices are combined and treated as one under the heading of "prestige and suggestion." In the early days of radio, prestige suggestion seemed to be an invariably effective device. Evaluations of literary productions were influenced by supposed authorship; judgments of beauty in paintings were influenced by the prestige of the supposed artist; and acceptance of extreme statements depended on the respect of the audience for the presumed author of the statement. In those early days the use of a name of high prestige seemed to compel approval regardless of the merits of the product.

Due to the overuse as well as the obvious abuse of this device, audiences have become more sophisticated and are suspicious of most prestige suggestions as being simply paid endorsements. Recent studies have shown that changing the supposed authorship of a buying claim will not work with people who are well informed about the attitudes of the persons whose names are used. The information possessed by the prospect sets definite limits on the effects that can be achieved by prestige suggestion. The suggestion must be probable to be seriously considered rather than ridiculed. Clearly, the President of the United States is not likely to endorse the products of an office furniture manufacturer, for example, so a more subtle technique is used by picturing the president leaning on a particular file talking to a famous cabinet member. The Madison Avenue group is now promoting this concept as "tie-in advertising," which features one product as the obvious paid commercial message while another product is subtly used in the background. For example, a manufacturer of women's wear might have his name on the advertisement but his pretty models are shown around an automobile which can be easily recognized by prospects who are then expected to associate that particular make of auto with pretty girls. Such tie-in ads are, of course, reciprocal over the contract period. The suitability of the endorsement also determines the limits of the effect in many cases. If a product is designed for use by small business, it would be difficult to apply endorsements by the largest industrial giants of America. Athletes known in the gossip columns for their nocturnal activities can hardly be expected to lend authority to temperance campaigns.

4. *Plain Folks.*—This device of irrational persuasion is the opposite of prestige suggestion because it attempts to bypass or avoid logic with an emotional appeal in which the seller is identified as a nice plain fellow just like the prospect. If one or two large manufacturers dominate an industry, the small supplier attempts to paint the others as being enormous, cold, and impersonal corporate machines while he is a regular guy working hard for an honest living just like the prospect. He admits his limitations and faults and attempts to have the prospect identify with him in sympathy against the machine. The legitimacy of this technique is questioned when the prospect is asked not to consider the merits of the product offering or the selfish motives of the salesman but rather to avoid all logic and act on suggestion alone. Many people want to help the little man in a fight and this technique may have some appeal to such people. However, when a prospect is asked to pay his hard-earned cash for a product, he is much more apt to consider rationally its value and the degree of bias in the sales presentation.

This technique can also boomerang with prospects who want to be associated with a successful salesman and a successful product. To these prospects, success connotes public acceptance, true product value, the esteem of associates, and reduced doubt for the buyer. The plain folks technique serves in these cases only to call the prospect's attention to the seller's lack of success and to drive buyers into the arms of their competitors.

5. *Card Stacking.*—This technique involves arguing unfairly in favor of an idea by leaving out arguments on the other side. In selling it is most commonly used by those suppliers of the lowest priced merchandise. They stress the low cost of acquisition and attempt to have the prospect avoid consideration of the quality of the product or its possible operating or maintenance costs. In the psychology of communications this device is known as a one-sided argument and it has proven effective for some men with less than a high-school education and some men who were initially

inclined to believe in the paramount importance of the low cost of acquisition. This small group is upset mentally by a two-sided argument which serves more to confuse than to convince.

A two-sided sales presentation invites the use of logic or rational consideration and is more effective with high-school graduates and with those who initially opposed the idea presented. For example, if a low priced chair will last half as long as a high priced chair but can be economically replaced three times during the life span of the expensive chair, the advantage of changing style or color more often at no increase in the total expenditure may be a sound logical reason for choosing the lower priced item. There are dangers in a two-sided sales presentation. First, it must be complete for all salient points or the prospect will recognize omissions and attach undue emphasis on what was omitted and why it was omitted. Second, if the two-sided sales presentation is complete and unbiased, it may leave the prospect more in doubt than ever and reluctant to buy anything.

However unscrupulous the salesman, it will be difficult for him to know whether or not to stack the cards. Prospects are heterogeneous in respect to education and it would be awkward to ask each prospect if he had graduated from high school before giving a sales presentation. In addition, there would be no way to discover how much informal education the buyer may have had. Another problem the salesman must face is the decision of which cards should be straight and which cards should be slanted or biased for each individual prospect. Card stacking as an attempt to avoid logical thought appears to have more traps for the salesman than for the prospect.

6. *Bandwagon.*—The bandwagon technique attempts to convince a prospect that everyone believes in one product or is buying only one brand and that it behooves the prospect to go along with the others. In a sales situation, this device is normally used to guide the prospect to select one particular item or group of products from the entire line offered by the salesman. For example, the salesman might suggest a certain initial stock because every single one of his successful retailers did the same and they all realized very quick profits. An optional but higher priced engine is offered in a new sports car, for example, and every single buyer has recognized the added value and ordered it. The salesman subtly suggests the prospect would be wise to take this engine and conform with the group without further thought or consideration.

Will the prospect continue to insist on what he wants or will his judgment conform to that of the group? Experiments have shown that in some cases there are more conformists than independents. However, the success of this technique depends upon a number of things. If, for instance, there is but one other buyer known to the prospect who makes the same judgments as the prospect the latter is far more likely to persist in his independent selection. The effectiveness of the bandwagon pressures is contingent on the purchase involved, the size of the purported majority against the prospect, and the personal character of the prospect. Experiments suggest that a bandwagon will be likely to work when the individual stands alone in his selection and has no way to judge or appraise the real situation. Since conditions of this sort are almost impossible to establish in a selling situation, the salesman using the bandwagon effect may be suspected of high pressure selling and cause the prospect to withdraw from an unpleasant situation and take his business elsewhere. If the bandwagon technique is tried with prospects who like to be different from their associates, it will also boomerang.

7. *Trustworthiness Depends on Expressive Meanings.*—From analyzing these techniques one whould like to conclude that when people are well informed an irrational or misleading persuasive effort can only succeed when it is truly advantageous to the prospect. Unfortunately, this is not a valid conclusion. Some well-informed people are fooled and occasionally can be persuaded to do things which are contrary to their own best interests.

A message will be believed, a recommendation to buy will be persuasive, to the degree that the salesman presenting the message is thought to be trustworthy. For a salesman to be considered trustworthy he must be either disinterested personally in the sale—have absolutely nothing to gain or lose by it—or he must be devoted to the welfare of the prospect as his own enlightened self-interest would dictate, for he cannot gain unless the buyer also gains. In addition, the salesman must be knowledgeable or an authority in his field. To the degree that the salesman is *believed* to have these qualities the sales presentation will be effective. All the conditions and contingencies governing the effectiveness of irrational and misleading persuasive efforts can be summarized by saying that a biased sales presentation will be effective to the degree that the bias is not detected. When the bias is observed the salesman is considered interested primarily in his own gain without regard for the prospect, the sales message is identified as irrational, and the prospect is not persuaded.

Such tactics are not limited to selling and politics. Everyone uses these devices at one time or another in his personal life. For example, the wife needs a mink coat because all of the girls in her club have mink coats. The teen-ager must stay out until midnight because everyone in the sophomore class is allowed to stay out until midnight. Normal people consciously use and are exposed to such tactics and become good analysts of these techniques from early childhood. It seems highly naïve to assume such underhanded tricks put a prospect at the mercy of unscrupulous salesmen. Prospects are a tough audience and any salesman who attempts to persuade them to act in his interests rather than in their own will have a difficult time. He can expect such efforts to boomerang more often than not and this will reflect on his personal reputation and the reputation of his employer as well. The loss of one's job and personal reputation is a horrible price to pay for a few shady sales.

As Harold J. Leavitt has written, "In a long-term relationship, when A knows he must go on living or working with B *after* he tried to change B's behavior, he may proceed with caution no matter what his personal ethics. His own dependency on the others in the relationship serves as a built-in governor on his influence techniques, even if his conscience doesn't."[5]

## PERSUASION MONOPOLY

In business the nearest thing to a persuasion monopoly occurs when a customer has purchased so many units which must match, intermember, or otherwise remain standard that it behooves him to remain loyal to his supplier. He cannot economically change suppliers because he would have to discard all previous purchases and buy everything new. This may occur, for example, in the type of machines used on a production line, the office and showroom furniture and fixtures, or in data-processing equipment. The account standardizes on one brand and is committed to it at least for the length of the product's normal life-span.

As long as the customer believes he is committed to this type of policy he will not see competitive salesmen or be interested in reading the advertisements and promotional literature that he might be exposed to during the normal course of business events. He will neither perceive nor retain information contrary to his beliefs. Ideally, to be effective the supplier must be perceived by his customer as one who is more knowledgeable and expert in this field than the customer but completely identical in interests with the customer. Unfortunately, it is always possible that the customer will find out the supplier has goals of his own which are in

---

[5] Reprinted from *Managerial Psychology* by Harold J. Leavitt by permission of The University of Chicago Press (1st Phoenix ed., Chicago: University of Chicago Press, 1962), p. 113.

conflict with those of the customer. In the persuasion monopoly, since the supplier is the only one providing information, the principal dangers lie with the expressive behavior of the supplier himself and with the course of events. If the products break down, for example, the supplier will be categorized as a selfish manipulator and his future presentations will be recognized as biased and not to be trusted. Under such ideal conditions as a monopoly of exposures, there is still danger in using irrational and misleading persuasion techniques. Once the steady customer's suspicions are aroused, the monopoly of exposure is broken and competitors can quickly show the customer ways out of his dilemma resulting from standardization.

## PERSUASION COMPETITION WITH A MOST FAVORED SOURCE

In this situation a number of different suppliers attempt to persuade a customer to buy from all of them at the same time. One supplier is the most favored source because he is believed to have the same interests as the customer. The sales message of the friendly supplier is viewed as an honest presentation of facts while competitors' sales talks are considered biased. If the supplier continues to operate with a policy of mutual satisfaction, profit, and growth for both himself and for his customer, he will remain the most favored supplier. However, customers will often like some of the policies of competitors and some of the individual competing salesmen. Since the sales messages of the favorite supplier are considered fair and honest while the others are irrational or misleading, the first problem of a competitor is to get his true message heard. The customer will not willingly expose himself to a misleading sales talk. One technique is to combine the sales message with something else which the customer normally will select, such as a business or professional convention or a public service piece of promotional literature. The most effective way is through direct personal contact by the sales representative. Friendly persistence and patience will often succeed in gaining exposure.

After the sales message reaches the customer the problem is to cause it to be recognized as trustworthy rather than biased. There are many customers whose brand loyalty is not too strong to begin with and they will consider the possibility that the competing salesman has their interests at heart. One method of gaining creditability is to utilize an endorsement by a disinterested party, for instance, by Good Housekeeping Magazine, Consumers Union, the American Dental Association, other trade associations, or an independent research or testing laboratory. If such an endorsement is suspected of having been purchased—for example, in exchange for heavy advertising in the endorsing publication—it can easily be unmasked and is apt to boomerang.

As an alternative to such methods, the competing salesman can attempt to discredit the favored supplier and replace him by pointing out selfish or biased claims of this favored supplier. This is a dangerous practice because it may be taken as an indirect criticism of the buyer's judgment and he will feel compelled to defend it. A more practical method would be to establish gradually a reputation for truth and service and then wait for events such as product or service breakdowns to cause a split between the customer and his most favored source. Once again it can be seen the irrational persuader is very limited in what he can accomplish.

## PERSUASION COMPETITION WITH NO FAVORED SOURCE

In the most common selling situation, a prospect feels a need for a general type of product and is then aware of the persuasive efforts of a number of suppliers, all of which are known to have self-interests. A large number of suppliers urge the prospect to take mutually exclusive actions. The prospect has already decided to buy but now must select from among equally biased suppliers. Here the principle of repetition is primary in persuasion. Frequent exposure to the brand name, the supplier, or the friendly but persistent salesman increases the chances of selecting that supplier without further conscious reasoning. The repetition serves to simplify the buyer's selection but does not influence his attitude toward the various products offered and will not build customer loyalty.

In a competitive sales situation with no favored source the effective salesman who investigates the prospect and his wants and needs will attempt to provide an honest solution through his product and services. He will earn more initial orders and build more loyal customers than the salesman using the so-called shortcuts of irrational and misleading persuasion.

## CONCLUSION

To be fair, it should be acknowledged that there are bound to be situations where irrational appeals to the emotions rather than logical appeals to reason can be employed effectively and without harm to either the customers or the supplier. For example, after a complete sales presentation has moved a prospect from unawareness to conviction using the problem-solving approach it remains to cause him to act. An appeal to emotion at this point is apt to be very effective. A second concluding point is that most illustrations of irrational and misleading persuasion were in situations where the salesman was soliciting new customers whereas in reality the bulk of selling consists of calling on old customers. Nevertheless, here too most of the observations made in this chapter apply since the task of keeping old customers loyal and increasing the size of their orders is still selling. As a matter of fact, it is this field that lends itself best to honest and logical selling methods.

# 25

# Effective Attitudes and Work Habits of Successful Salesmen

Many experienced marketing managers hold the firm opinion that the salesman who knows *why* communication and persuasion work will be more successful than the salesman who knows *how*, assuming they each work steadily. Since one of the greatest advantages of personal selling lies in the ability of the salesman to adapt, adjust, or alter the sales message to suit an individual prospect, it follows that the man who knows why things work when they do can more easily adapt to changing conditions, strange situations, and new people. The salesman who understands why his company seeks a particular market segment and why his company has established particular policies such as pricing and credit terms can more easily appreciate and agree with company goals and cooperate to achieve them. Proper sales attitudes are based upon complete information from the marketing department, which has the salesman's individual success as its primary objective. Once proper attitudes are established, guidance in daily activities becomes more acceptable and productive work habits can be developed with minimum confusion or resistance. With effective attitudes and work habits, salesmen and marketing management can cooperate and go in the same direction to achieve the greatest individual and joint success while making the organization a pleasant and satisfying place to work.

## THE VALUE OF SALESMANSHIP TO THE MANUFACTURER OR SUPPLIER

During the early period of American industrial development many rugged individualists did their own inventing, producing, and selling of their products. As volume grew, specialists in each category were hired to perform these functions. In either case, future success or failure of the entire business was measured by profitable sales. The ultimate sale is the incentive for the discovery of new raw materials, better production processes, more efficient layout of plant and office, the reduction of costs throughout. It is the incentive for people to invest their money in the enterprise. Today even the toughest of union officials recognizes the basic fact of business life, that if there is no sale there is no job. Sales create a need for capital, for raw materials, for production facilities, for production workers, for office equipment and workers, for marketing and distribution facilities and people.

Our economy is a huge dynamic social phenomenon that is continually growing larger. As the population grows in geometric proportions, more and more people demand a higher standard of living. They want more products, higher product quality, extra services and conveniences in acquiring, transporting, and storing. The government is assuming greater social responsibility, particularly in the fields of health, education, and welfare and this requires tremendous financing. Supporting taxes are derived from business profits and earned personal income, which in the larger sense are derived from profitable sales. Meeting this ever increasing demand and in turn contributing to further demand, American industry is expanding and more and more businesses are being created.

The economy has been forced into a distribution or marketing age by mass demand and the mass production of industry. The problem today is one of getting the goods and services to the markets in an economical way. This places increased responsibility upon the shoulders of the salesman as well as increases the number of salespeople required. Effective salesmen who can move more goods and services to people who can honestly benefit by their use are in demand in every phase of business. For sales to remain profitable, the selling must be efficient and relatively inexpensive for the services performed. All the evidence indicates that the demand for salesmen who can meet this criteria will be increasing continually during the next 25 years.

## THE SERVICE CONCEPT TO BUYERS

Buyers are people with needs, wants, desires, and problems which require solutions. An effective salesman obtains a great deal of personal satisfaction from knowing that his customers are better off for having purchased from him. He is there to serve the customer in the latter's best interest. Nor does his job end once the order is obtained. Effective salesmen realize the difference between an order placer and a loyal customer and they willingly work as hard, if not harder, to serve their new accounts.

There are many buyers who do not—as a matter of strong principle—exercise their full bargaining power because they want to establish a long-term relationship with a seller that is not based exclusively on raw bargaining power. They seem to feel that if they pay as little as possible the seller will not value their business highly and will treat them less well in ways that matter much more than their possible savings.

After the initial purchase has been delivered, for example, an effective salesman will often inspect the product to make certain it is operating properly; that the customer's personnel know how to operate it for optimum benefits; that the product satisfactorily solves the customer's problem. Buyers do not purchase products as such but rather they buy combinations of benefits which include the product, service, and convenience of location. If they do not receive expected services from one supplier, they will seek other suppliers.

The effective salesman is an expert in his field and he knows more about his products and customer services and the problems they will solve than any other person. This knowledge function is of vital importance in communicating information and building buyer confidence in the salesman. The effective salesman considers himself a consultant to his customers whenever they have technical problems. If this customer service were not available to the buyer, he would have to hire a consultant with expert knowledge. Eliminating the salesman would not lower the customer's total costs and it might increase them since such technical assistance is often considerably higher. This function of communicating expert information and advice to customers by itself is enough to justify fully the effective salesman's existence. This single function can often save the customer more than the total distribution cost which he will pay.

## INTRODUCE INNOVATION TO MARKETS

Earlier it was noted that customers have neither the time nor the interest to develop new products for a supplier, yet consumers continually demand product and service improvements and a higher standard of living. Business has responded to this demand with more products and innovations than the market is able to accept. Each new product, researched and developed by a manufacturer, requires a marketing decision upon which millions of dollars may be risked. Unfortunately, more new products and innovations fail than succeed. Business is ready and able to produce new products but is willing to do so only when the odds of acceptance are favorable. The decision to go or not to go is not made easily.

The salesman normally is the only person in his company with direct personal contact with prospects and customers and the necessary training and experience to recognize areas of interest to his company. He has the responsibility for recognizing customer problems, wants, or desires and for communicating this information back to his management. This type of grass roots market research can be organized and developed to yield much more pertinent and valid information than the more expensive professional market research services of ivory tower psychologists or marketing consultants. The value of good research cannot be seriously questioned in aiding marketing management to reduce the uncertainty of new product acceptance. This market research function alone can often justify the cost of maintaining a sales force.

What does the customer gain from a sales force in regard to innovation? The life cycle of many products is growing shorter and shorter with many companies planning completely new product offerings every five to ten years. For example, in the drug industry advances in new products repeatedly make older ones obsolete. In many fields automation is rapidly changing the entire production and paper flow processes. The problem in most fields today is not one of developing new products and services but rather of keeping informed and abreast of the availability of the latest developments. The doctor depends upon the drug salesmen to keep him abreast of new drugs and their uses. The business executive depends upon the machine salesmen to keep up to date on cost reduction systems and equipment. The engineer depends upon the tool and machine salesmen to bring new products and services to his attention. Most people cannot by themselves possibly keep informed about all the innovations affecting their professional fields. They must rely on the salesmen in their field to provide accurate and current information on many new developments. Without salesmen, their own time would be used to gather such information or they would have to hire enough assistants to do the same job for them. Because people have neither the time nor the interest to seek out information on new developments continually, without salesmen the entire process of innovating would be slowed down to the detriment of the customer and the general public as well.

## FACILITATE THE CONSUMPTION PROCESS

There are many reasons why people put off buying things they need, things they want, things they would enjoy. Simple inertia and unawareness are probably the two main reasons which prevent people from buying who could normally afford to do so. If goods and services are not purchased in sufficient volume, the entire production and distribution processes slow down and all economic activity tends to spiral downward. The reverse is equally true and increased consumption gives a rise to the entire economy. The federal income tax reduction of 1964 was intended to stimulate the economy by providing higher disposable income to consumers. It resulted in higher spending, increased business profits, more employment, and, finally, greater revenue for the federal government.

The effective salesman stimulates the consumption process by reducing the inertia some people have and making others aware of the benefits they are missing. The effective salesman will also interest prospects in new goals or objectives for themselves which they might not set if left alone to be content with their existing situation. Many appeals to pride, prestige, and self-image will cause people to improve themselves or their enjoyment of life by doing things they would not otherwise attempt. Not only does the salesman's persuasive effort stimulate demand but in most cases he makes it easier or more convenient for people to buy what they want. The advantages of personal selling over other components in the marketing mix were illustrated in the first chapter and they generally apply to stimulating market demand. This is the underlying function of all salesmen and when done effectively it not only serves the self-interest of the salesman and his company but also the interest of the customer and it benefits our entire society as well. Effective salesmen provide a service which is essential to our economy.

## SELF-DEVELOPMENT

While some successful salesmen are content to know how to sell and to realize a steady comfortable income, the future belongs to those salesmen who are willing to prepare for better things. These men keep their sights high enough to avoid total preoccupation with sales and acquire a substantial understanding of the other phases of business activities. The effective salesman, by the very nature of his job, is forced to acquire a broad perspective on the entire operation of his firm. He is continually faced with problems involving the raw materials which his company uses, the production processes and limitations, the financial and credit policies, the research and development activities, and most of the supporting personnel. In addition, the effective salesman has extensive contact with the top level management of his customers' firms and can easily learn what is being done outside his own organization. He is in a position to observe successful businesses and personalities directly, to analyze and formulate plans which can improve his company and himself.

Because of his broad experience, the intelligent salesman can formulate general theories or laws of marketing which can be applied to specific business problems in many industries. He is not tied to one company or even one industry because the principles of selling, public relations, and working with people in general are common to all business. The technical specialist is apt to become more proficient in one narrow field limited to his own industry or his own company while the salesman can become broader and of greater potential for higher openings in his own company and others outside of his industry. Most management jobs require increasing skill in human relations activities and conceptual skills in appraising a number of ideas and divergent factors simultaneously. The salesman who is willing to develop these skills is in an excellent, almost unique, position to apply his abilities as they grow.

An effective salesman realizes he can never achieve perfection and must continually improve himself. He reads as much as five times more than other adults and particularly studies human behavior through psychology and sociology. He learns all he can about new products in his field, new applications of old products, and new solutions to his customers' problems. More and more firms require a college education as a prerequisite for sales managers and the trend is to upgrade the minimum educational specifications. The effective salesman will complete his formal education to maximize his chances of future success. He is a leader of men who continually improves his ability to command the confidence of those he leads through their self-interests, his own technical ability, and his fair treatment of people.

More and more top business executives have been promoted up through the sales department. In two recent studies, for example, more top executives had previously had major line sales experience than had previously had legal, financial, production, engineering, or other experience.[1] The combination of broad perspective, personality, and performance seems to lend itself to the talents of the effective salesman. His upper limit appears to be only his own sight or aspirations and his willingness to work for his goal through self-development and good work habits in his daily activities.

## ORGANIZING SALES WORK

People are judged by what they say, which indicates their attitudes, as well as by what they do and salesmen in particular are judged by the work

---

[1] See the comments of J. Philip Smith of Charles Pfizer & Co. regarding what sales offers to effective salesmen in, "Selling's Talent Shortage: How to Find 1,000,000 Good Salesmen," *Printer's Ink*, March 27, 1959, p. 21.

habits they exhibit. Until a man shows he can manage himself as a salesman, few firms are willing to risk letting him try management. The trend in sales management today is to adopt a scientific approach to planning and controlling the efforts of salesmen. More and more firms are making a job analysis to determine specifically what their salesmen really do. Some sales jobs are to sell while others are to service. Some technical selling jobs are really analytical exercises in solving customer's problems. Some sales jobs include the function of collection while others include considerable public relations work. One sales job may involve missionary or promotional activities while another consists primarily of maintaining and servicing dealer's inventory. Manufacturers' sales representatives often have the responsibility to train their dealers' salesmen in sales techniques. The selling job can contain many basic functions beyond direct selling and a detailed job analysis is necessary in order to know what is to be organized.

*Courtesy: Sperry & Hutchinson Company, N.Y.*

**FIG. 17. Window display sign is put up by a salesman for a stamp company.**

Another tool sales managers are now using is the difficulty analysis which determines how hard the various responsibilities are to accomplish and how much emphasis should be placed on training and preparing their salesmen for each phase of the selling job. For example, this analysis might indicate required skills should include persuasion and mechanical adeptness in product demonstration rather than analytical and memorization skills. The difficulty analysis provides insight to the critical activities which the salesman must perform to permit the myriad details of selling to operate in his favor. This information is essential if sales training and self-development are to be effective.

The third tool being used by sales management is the time and duty analysis which determines the motions and amount of time spent on each duty. Management tries to improve the ratios to increase selling time and then set standards for the entire sales force. This analysis permits the establishment of standards of performance with minimum goals set for the salesmen. It would include the minimum number of working hours to achieve given results. It would be broken down further into the number of daily calls to be made, the number of product demonstrations, window displays, nonbuying contacts with influentials to be made, and the like. Sales themselves would be broken down into product categories with certain minimum goals for dollar volume, gross profit, and number of units. An effective salesman should become familiar with these sales management tools because many companies either do not use them or do not explain or enforce them. If management defaults on this responsibility, the effective salesman will employ these tools to improve himself.

## TIME AND ENERGY CONTROL

Time and energy control consists of three basic functions: analyzing the territory, record keeping, and scheduling activities by route and mode of travel. Each of these functions will operate differently for different product lines, different types of customers being solicited, and different geographic areas. However, there are certain basic principles which apply to all selling activities.

Many companies that have initiated selling cost studies have found that as much as 20 percent of their orders do not produce any profit and in fact cause a loss when the salesman's time and expenses, inside administrative costs, delivery, packing, warehousing, and billing are included. Every territory should be analyzed to determine which accounts can buy in quantities sufficient for the seller to operate profitability. For the individual salesman, this means classifying his accounts by size or potential and relating this to the number of calls which will achieve the business desired. For example, the largest accounts might be classified in category A which requires weekly visits. Category B might require 24 visits per year and others might be monthly, bimonthly, quarterly, or only semiannually. By summarizing the total number of calls required to cover all accounts as classified, the salesman can then divide by the number of working days per year and determine the minimum number of calls per day which he should average to adequately cover the accounts exactly as management wants. This should also indicate the amount of time remaining each day to develop new business and cultivate long range customers. It is vital that the salesman not use this extra time seeing buyers who may be friendly but who cannot buy more. Putting in a long day calling on small accounts or those that are nearly saturated with the product is not the same as working efficiently for fewer hours. Classifying accounts will help the salesman determine the optimum number of calls for each account and the remaining time should be utilized locating new sources of business or working on a large customer's problem where the ultimate loyalty justifies the time and effort.

Record keeping should be a tool for more effective selling and not a policing device. Each account card should have the vital statistics and historical record of the personnel and buying activities of the account. However, it must also include a follow-up system to be of value to the salesman. This follow-up system should indicate the date of the previous call, the purpose of the last call, and the results of that call with a specific follow-up date and new objective. Some firms have follow-up forms which provide a simple checking of applicable boxes with a minimum of writing. These are then filed by follow-up date and each week the salesman can see in advance where he should be as well as quickly review each account he will visit.

It is at this point the salesman will be able to preplan his call schedule and activities for the immediate future. By reviewing the data in the follow-up system he can determine what action he wants to take when visiting each account, such as gathering special information, planting new ideas, closing an old quotation, or whatever, and how he will go about this action. Knowing what he wants to do, he will be able to determine which buying influence is apt to be most receptive to and effective for his purpose. Then, if the nature of the business lends itself to such a procedure, he can telephone ahead to establish firm appointments which will reduce his waiting time. This is the point in planning which determines his route and mode of travel. His objective is to conserve his selling time and minimize his total expenses, which is quite different from calling on every customer in a given area regardless of potential and traveling by the cheapest method.

## VALUE OF SELLING TIME

Based on 244 working days of eight hours each, a salesman earning $5,000 a year is paid $2.56 an hour. A salesman earning $10,000 earns $5.12 while the salesman earning $20,000 is paid $10.25 an hour. Studies have shown, on the average, salesmen actually spend 20 to 33 percent of their time in face-to-face conversation with their customers and prospects. Therefore, even the best, most persuasive salesmen can benefit by controlling and reducing their nonselling time. Time spent traveling cannot be avoided, of course, but by preplanning the route and mode of travel the salesman can reduce wasted time and motion. Waiting time in customers' offices can be reduced somewhat by making appointments ahead and it can be used to write reports, plan future calls, observe, and learn additional information pertinent to the current call. Many magazines found in reception areas are addressed to individuals in the firm and provide some clue to their interests and attitudes.

Some salesmen race all day long trying to see as many accounts as possible and they are impatient and frustrated when they must wait to see a buyer. Their poor mood is almost impossible to hide from the buyer and tends to negate whatever good they may hope to accomplish. In the evening they spend several hours trying to recall events of the day and completing their records. Contrast this with the salesman who plans a reasonable work load for each day and uses his waiting time to fill out his records while the details of the previous call are still fresh in his mind and, if time permits, adding to his knowledge of the individuals he may visit then or in the future. His mood is relaxed and his approach to the buying influential will be friendly and will carry something of interest to that particular party. And, not incidentally, his evening will be pleasant, permitting him to relax and be refreshed for the next morning.

In some industries, providing special services to customers can account for a large part of the time spent during the day. The effective salesman will be alert to the danger of spending disproportionate time on nonprofitable or small accounts. Where heavy service is the expected and normal thing, the salesman should utilize his supporting personnel in the home office to provide special literature and information requested by the smaller accounts. One never knows when the small account will become a large account and it always pays to be courteous and fair with all accounts. That little extra service will often pay big dividends. However, the time spent should be used with discretion. Little accounts are painfully aware of their small size and do not often request much of the salesman's time. When he can be personally helpful, he would be wise to do so.

Coffee breaks, lunchtime, and dinner time can often be spent with prospects and customers to mutual advantage. However, such time should be relaxing and pleasant. If the salesman must work at being nice and guarding his every word in the customer's presence, perhaps this time would be better spent alone. As noted earlier in this chapter, it is very normal for salesmen on the road to build true and lasting friendships with their customers and this is an excellent way both to relax and to build long-term customer loyalty. The situation should be natural and mutually satisfying to both the customer and the salesman.

Spare time during the day traveling on a public conveyance and in the evening is best spent relaxing to be refreshed for the next challenge. Many salesmen who have higher goals in life will use some of their spare time in self-improvement. This would include learning of competitive products, practices, and problem-solving techniques; studying changing conditions in the market and within the customer's industry, and reading sales literature. It also goes well beyond sales information, however, because an effective salesman is well informed on many topics and activities throughout the nation and the world. He develops interests in hobbies, sports, politics, and civic responsibilities. He becomes an interesting person whom people like to be with and to give their business.

## ORGANIZING AND SYSTEMATIZING A SALES DAY

Organizing sales work should begin with an analysis of long-term goals and objectives followed by a realistic appraisal of the various market segments and specific accounts to be selected as targets. Having classified each account by potential and the frequency of calls per year and established the minimum number of calls per day required to cover the territory, the salesman must then decide specifically where he will go monthly, weekly, and on each particular day. This involves combining the processes of account classification, record analysis, planning, and routing.

For purposes of illustration, assume a machine tool salesman has been assigned 300 selected accounts in upstate New York and his management has already classified them according to potential. If 25 of these accounts are large enough to be visited monthly and are located in four or five different industrial areas, the salesman plans his call route in a circular pattern to return to the first large account approximately one month after his first call on them. Clearly, the 275 remaining accounts cannot be visited equally so they must also be broken down into groups which justify visits every two months, quarterly, semiannually, or annually. Each of these groups is then fitted into the basic calling route. If 18 Class II accounts, or bimonthly calls, are required in the Syracuse area for a total of 128 calls per year, then once each month when going through this area the salesman should see a group of 9 different accounts. The smaller accounts are fitted into the schedule in the same manner, so they are visited no more nor less than management desires. Naturally, as conditions change, accounts can be reclassified for either more or less frequent visits.

Having scheduled eight days' work in the Syracuse area, the salesman then will review the previous history of each account he is to visit, particularly with regard to the purpose and results of the previous call. He will then decide what the purpose or objective will be for each account and then he will decide what individual should be seen. Equipped with this information the salesman can review his sales presentations or approaches as he anticipates each situation and equip his briefcase with the materials that will be logical for these particular calls. Finally, he will make the visits on his schedule for each day and utilize his remaining time to solicit new accounts or to cultivate customers that had previously been selected for that purpose.

After each call, the salesman notes his experience with each prospect and the prospect's reaction to his suggestions. At that point, while all the details are still fresh in his mind, he makes a notation of how to follow up on that account on his next visit and what additional information he may need or what customer service he can perform on his next visit. Frequently there will be some interesting literature or other information which can be mailed to the customer between calls and the effective salesman will send a request to his home office for their assistance. Occasionally letters can be used to thank the prospect for his time and to place certain facts and figures in written form for his future reference and comparison. For many people the written word carries more authority than the spoken word and a letter repeating a product offering which spells out the details of the customer services will be more convincing than the sales talk. Any orders received during the visit should normally be acknowledged by the home office together with delivery information and confirmation of prices and credit terms. If there is any doubt in the customer's mind, he should not be expected to wait a month or more to ask the salesman but rather should communicate immediately with a predetermined individual in the home office for confirmation or clarity. These are a few of the nonselling details which are part of the salesman's responsibility and which help to build loyal customers over the years. Reports to the home office regarding market intelligence information, market surveys, activities reports, call reports, and sales orders are most easily compiled during the day while the salesman is waiting to see the next customer. Evenings at strange motels are normally spent relaxing and in self-improvement activities such as reading or studying marketing data from the home office.

With this full-time itinerary, it is not surprising to find the salesman on the road honestly looking forward to a luncheon or dinner engagement with a customer he enjoys. He does not have to feign sincerity or friendliness with customers because he really does enjoy being with them. Such accounts often become the regular steady buyers who provide the total job satisfaction that is essential to effective salesmanship.

## CONCLUSION

An effective salesman has tremendous confidence in his knowledge of the products he sells and his ability to solve customer problems. He is aware of his value both to the customer and to his own company, including its employees and suppliers. Aware that he is serving society in general, he can confidently talk with any man about the values of selling and its contribution to the standard of living, increasing employment, and returning a reasonable profit to stockholders or other owners of a business who risk their capital. By this daily behavior and his work habits he quickly shows his willingness to serve others, his ability to lead, and his ability to perform a task independently. Such effective men are rare and are often promoted rapidly into management, which in turn provides additional openings for other new salesmen. Work habits are the acid test of all the theory on selling the exhibit the true character of the individual under some of the most trying and tempting conditions possible. It requires a man of strong character and dedication to perform steadily and effectively. Lesser men will yield to normal human temptations and quickly fade under this pressure, tending to visit only friendly accounts and to skip the problems and difficult people. It is no wonder that effective salesmen are highly sought by suppliers, are well paid, and are quickly promoted to more responsible positions.

◆ ◆ ◆

## WORKING EFFECTIVELY IN THE FIELD*

The degree of success you experience in selling will depend largely on how you manage your time. If you plan your work wisely, work efficiently and make the most of every minute, other things being equal, you will be in a top income bracket. Everything you do should be directed toward the goal of making a maximum number of interviews and sales, for maximum income.

*Use of Map*

Whether your territory is a postal zone in a large metropolitan city, an entire city, or an area that includes a number of small towns, having a map of your territory will help you work systematically. The map is the basic starting point for efficient operation in the field. Marking this map, coloring the streets worked as you work them, and inserting dates on the map to govern your timing for reworking an area, will enable you to get the most sales out of each area.

With the map as your guide, begin to work your territory systematically street by street, taking each street in order, working up one side of the street and down the other, opening every business door. In the office buildings, start at the top floor and work down to the first floor, calling on every office.

*Save Office Buildings*

It is almost always best to start your coverage of a city or small town on the outskirts and work your way into the main business section where you ultimately cover the office buildings.

Of course, this procedure is flexible. There are times when you will find it desirable because of inclement weather to interrupt your coverage of the outlying districts and work one of the office buildings. For example, a salesman working in a large metropolitan city that experiences severe seasonal weather changes should save the office buildings for the rainy season or the winter snows.

*Working Smaller Towns*

In working the smaller towns under 5,000 population, it is usually best to start making your calls the moment you encounter a place of business on the highway into town. When you reach the center of town, or main street, call on the bank or Chamber of Commerce, if there is one, and ask questions as to the location of the business establishments in town.

Another advantage of talking to one of the prominent citizens upon your arrival in town is that you can obtain names of some of the leading business-

---

* The above are reprinted with the kind permission of Dow Jones & Company, Inc., Community Sales Program, Circulation Field & Phone Sales Division, Princeton, N.J.

men and establish a contact with a well-known person in the event you should want to use the man's name as a reference. However, be sure to tell your acquaintance that you may have one of the townspeople call him as a reference or for a testimonial about one of The Dow Jones Publications.

If you live in a town away from a large metropolitan city and your territory is a portion of the state embracing many small towns, the best method of covering the area is to use your home city as a base and fan out to a radius of about 50 miles in all directions until you have covered the section you outlined for yourself. After you have completed this much of your territory, it is generally best to select another key town, preferably a county seat about 100 to 150 miles away from your home base, where you can establish headquarters and work a radius of 50 miles again in the same fanning style you worked from your home city. This method is most successful and avoids traveling the same routes over and over again.

*Start the Day Right*

A good objective in the morning is to be in front of your first prospect at the start of the business day, which is between 8 and 9 A.M., depending on the nature of the territory in which you are working. In the downtown areas, the starting time is usually 9 A.M., but even there some offices are open at 8:30 A.M. In the outlying districts, some manufacturing plants are open as early as 8 A.M. Try not to allow any personal matters or travel time to interfere with your starting or to interrupt your day in the field. By being in front of your first prospect at the very start of the business day, you can have your first sale by 10 A.M. This is a sound goal for high earnings.

*Read Your Paper*

Each morning, before making your first call, obtain your current issue of The Journal and spend about fifteen minutes reading the headlines and scanning the contents of the paper so that you can quickly spot the main features and also take advantage of any item in the news that may have application to a particular business situation.

*Keep Selling Tools Neat & Clean*

Folding your sample publication inward, covering over the top of the front page will protect it. Ragged edges, dirt and rumpled pages detract from the impression and concentration you want the prospect to have as you point out its unique features.

*Call-Backs*

An important factor in the conservation of time is the manner in which you handle your call-backs. To begin with, you should call back only on those people you did not talk to. If you've given your sales presentation to the prospect and he cannot, or will not, make up his mind about The Journal, a call back later is no guarantee of a sale. If the party you want to see is not in, find out as nearly as possible the time he will return; make careful note of the name, location and time of call-back on a 3" by 5" card and then make your call-back at the appointed hour. Of course, as you work your territory and accumulate call-backs it becomes impractical at times to interrupt your regular work to make the call-back because of the amount of time involved. The objective in working call-backs is to work them as quickly as possible. Do not discount the value of calling back on people who are out on your first call. More often than not, these men who are most responsive to our story because they are active, busy men and can appreciate the value of the service we have to offer.

*Lunch Time*

It is important to take your break for lunch just as everyone else does. You burn up energy in a morning in the field and a little wholesome food and an hour's rest can help you store up more fuel for the afternoon's work. As far as the proper time is concerned, "When in Rome, do as the Romans do." In the small towns you may find all the businessmen at the Rotary or Kiwanis luncheon at 12 o'clock. You will acquire the feel of people's habits as you work the area. Another thing to remember is that sales are frequently made in a relaxed conversation with businessmen you may happen to meet at the lunch table or over the coffee cup.

*One More Call*

An objective during the day is to have at least 20 interviews. Under normal conditions, you will probably have to make 30 calls to get the 20 interviews. From the 20 interviews, you will make 3 to 5 sales. As the afternoon wears on, making one more call will often pay dividends when you need an order. A lot of businessmen work past five o'clock. Some of them are "leveling off" about that time after a hard day's work and are in a mood to have a conversation about an interesting topic like The Wall Street Journal. Many sales have been made between 5 and 6 o'clock.


◆  ◆  ◆


## WORKING EFFECTIVELY ON THE PHONE*

Your work habits for high income vary little from those in the field. The same basic presentation, energy, enthusiasm and planning . . . but here your voice should capture the prospect instead of a catchy headline. So, tell him about a story in clearer detail and listen for his reaction so you can understandably express the products value to him. As you can't walk in on a prospect you must find ways to locate people to speak with. From the following sources you should be able to find fifty people a day to call.—"Leads *are* the Lifeblood of sales."

*Local Newspapers*—Personnel notes on the business pages; men promoted, transferred to your city, honored; stories about business firms in your area indicating growth, favorable progress; names of business, political and professional men in the general news section; mentions in the Society pages; firms that advertise in the classified section; firms involved in real estate and industrial property transactions; all types of business and service advertisers throughout the paper.

*Chambers of Commerce*—Lists of industrial plants in the city (usually a

* The above is reprinted with the kind permission of Dow Jones & Company, Inc., Community Sales Program, Circulation Field & Phone Sales Division, Princeton, N.J.

yearly compilation); weekly and monthly bulletins (new members, new companies, other mentions).

*Classified Phone Directory*—Select a group of names in a business related to a story in the current issue of The Wall Street Journal, Barron's or The National Observer.

*Membership lists*—Trade associations; clubs (athletic, country, etc.); other organizations and groups.

*Trade Publications*—Personnel and news notes; advertisers.

When to Call

Remember, when you approach a prospect at the wrong time, nothing you can say will bring a favorable response. Timing is, therefore, of the utmost importance.

Shown below are some general guides to assist you in selecting the time to place your call. Coupled with your own good judgment, the list below should prove helpful in making sales.

Chemists and engineers—between 4 and 5 P.M.

Clergymen—any time after Tuesday.

Contractors and builders—before 9 A.M. or after 5 P.M.

Dentists—before 9:30 A.M.

Druggist—between 1 and 3 P.M.

Lawyers—between 11 A.M. and 2 P.M.

Physicians and surgeons—between 9 A.M. and 11 A.M.

                   "   1 P.M. and 3 P.M.

some        "   7 P.M. and 9 P.M.

Professors and school teachers at home—between 7:30 P.M. and 9 P.M.

Public accountants—any time, but keep in mind that January 15 through April 15 is a very busy period for them.

Publishers and printers—after 3 P.M.

Retail butchers and grocers—before 9 A.M. and between 1 P.M. and 2:30 P.M.

◆    ◆    ◆

## SALESMEN CREATE A MASS MARKET*

*They carry the fruits of large-volume, low-cost production to the heart of every American family*

America's material abundance is a triumph of creative salesmanship. The productive genius that developed the nation's resources gained meaning only because its fruits were distributed widely. It was salesmen who spurred development of the mass market to support mass production. By creating the sales volume that made large-scale, low-cost output feasible salesmen established the broad base of our national well-being. Other nations are rich in resources, but none has equaled the U.S. in its ability to organize production and distribution to benefit all. In Europe, for instance, industrialists long held that success lay in restricting production, and making a high profit on each item sold.

---

* The above is reprinted with the kind permission of E. I. du Pont de Nemours & Company, Inc., Wilmington, Delaware.

Early in U.S. history, American business pioneers adopted another philosophy. They reasoned that mass production, with a small profit on each unit, held far brighter prospects for them and for everyone else. The success of the idea hinged upon their ability to create new markets and expand old ones enough to justify volume production.

It was here that salesmen made their principal contribution. They popularized the products of science and invention, and foresaw the day when luxuries would become commonplace. To Elias Howe's conception of the sewing machine, for example, Isaac Singer brought the idea of putting them in homes all over the world. To the work of earlier motor car builders, Henry Ford added the idea of building cars at a price all could afford. Such contributions are essential, for without them, an invention might remain a laboratory curiosity, or, at best, its price would be high, its market narrow. New products can be mass produced only as sales develop a market for them. Prices can fall only when a booming demand makes possible efficient mass production.

# 26

# The Future of Personal Selling and Effective Salesmen

The trend toward want-satisfaction, problem-solving and depth selling will continue in the future. Customer-oriented sales presentations will generally dominate in most industries and effective salesmen will become known as good listeners just as they were once known as fast talkers. They will become stimulators of buying action by awakening interests and desires which were dormant in the mind of the buyer and they will, with discretion, cause the prospects sufficient inner conflict to take buying action they would not have taken otherwise. The behavior of prospects will not remain static in the future nor will competition behave as it does today. Rapid change seems most likely to occur in the immediate future.

## THE FUTURE OF MARKETING[1]

It is estimated that by 1980 over 50 percent of many an industry's profits will come from things not even known today. Some sales jobs will be completely transformed in this period but it would be dangerous to project the market for any particular product or sales job. Change will affect buying practices and future customer demands.

The United States is embarked upon its greatest period of expansion in industry and government. It is estimated that by 1975 the population will approximate 235 million people. These additional millions will have to be fed, clothed, and educated and they will also demand all the necessities and luxuries in goods and services that are associated with the American standard of living.

Together with the population explosion, economists forecast a gain in

[1] See "An Economic Forecast for 1975," Standard & Poor's Corporation, 1965.

415

real personal income over and above inflation of 50 percent. Average family purchasing power should be around $9,500 as contrasted with $6,480 in 1965. In just 15 short years the United States will be 30 percent larger in consumers who are 50 percent richer in purchasing power.

In the 20 years from 1941 to 1961, the United States spent an estimated $42 billion on research and development. In the following four years, through 1965, another $42 billion more was spent. During the next 15 years, American business and government plan to spend over $250 billion more! There should be many new products, entire new industries, and as yet unforeseen services. Unemployment is expected to decline. In other words, economists in both government and industry forecast that more people will be making more money and enjoying a higher level of disposable income.

Industrial production is expected to almost double its 1960 capacity of $112 billion annually to nearly $225 billion by 1975. In this process there are apt to be some temporary conditions where capacity exceeds demand. For example, new plants and equipment are generally built in anticipation of increased markets. Periodically such industries as steel, paper, autos, appliances, and soft goods operate well under 100 percent of rated capacity. Research and development are capable of turning out more new products and services than consumers are ready to accept. Clearly, it is the responsibility of marketing specialists to increase demand and continue the upward spiral historic in the American standard of living.

When temporary conditions of overproduction arise, history has shown a decrease in prices, unprofitable operations, more bankruptcy, and fewer jobs. Much of the sleeping population of the world is now awakening and is in dire need of many products and services. Some industries have realized the fallacy of dumping surplus goods on the American market and creating economic havoc. They are now cultivating foreign markets in an attempt to maintain a healthy, stable domestic price structure. New emerging countries which lack the wealth of the United States welcome such commodities and services at bargain prices. It stimulates their growth and economy and, in turn, they will be able to purchase more goods at competitive world prices, which will tend to stabilize. International marketing is becoming as glamorous as research and development. In this field of international trade, the basic concepts of the customer's predisposition, selective perception, selective retention, and selective recall are highly significant.[2] While beyond the scope of this text, international selling would be a fascinating study.

---

[2] See Peter Bart, "Advertising: Tips on What Foreigners Like," *New York Times*, January 2, 1964, p. 42.

## THE FUTURE OF PERSONAL SELLING

What can be predicted for sales in the future? An increase in self-service is one major trend that will continue in consumer fields and spread to new areas of business and industry. Indeed, data processing of industrial pur-

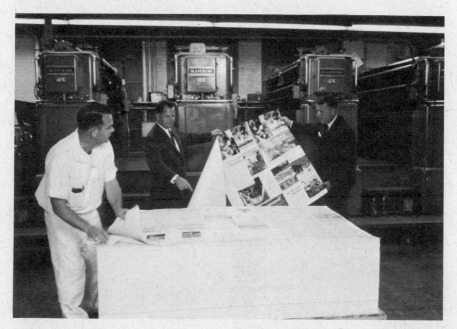

*Courtesy: Marketing Dept., Westvaco, N.Y.*

**FIG. 18. Paper company salesmen assist a printer in starting up a special job.**

chase orders has already begun to replace the old order taker for many routine order situations. This, together with the forecasted affluent society of 1980, may cause worn-out or defective products to be inexpensive enough to be thrown away rather than returned for expensive repairs. Another trend already apparent is the vertical integration of companies, with one supplier controlling his product from the raw material through various conversion operations to the retailing of a finished product to the ultimate consumer.

An affluent society will demand more deluxe models and more optional accessories as an integral part of the standard models. The auto industry and the home appliance industry have already felt this demand and it will probably spread to many other fields. Even textbooks may become entertaining as well as educational! Customers will demand greater speed of delivery, more convenient warehousing, and more technical advisory services.

As noted earlier, the trend in business and industrial purchasing is toward the formal techniques of value analysis. This means the salesman of tomorrow will become more of an executive with complete mastery of product knowledge and applications, manufacturing processes and limitations, cost accounting procedures, and the techniques of dealing with more sophisticated buying committees. Such qualified sales executives will be in great demand and their cost will be high. This in turn will cause many suppliers to seek large accounts that they are best staffed and equipped to handle. Segmenting the market will become a highly mathematical science demanding more computer programmers who are market oriented. The small supplier will survive only if he specializes in areas the larger ones cannot handle due to economics or individual talents.

Since there will be fewer small orders, the trend toward team selling is apt to increase. The coordinator of this team, the sales executive, will have to be an effective communicator and persuader to understand and lead people in the marketing effort. Indeed, such personal selling is apt to become transformed into marketing management. The salesman of tomorrow will be more intelligent, industrious, and creative than ever before and he will be well trained in problem analysis, decision making, and performing effectively before groups of sophisticated buyers. He will have to learn entirely new products and industries as rapidly as they appear. His techniques for communicating and persuading will have to be updated constantly to keep up with his ever changing audiences.

## NEEDED RESEARCH

The various social studies, cited as research fundamental to the concepts explored in this text, were selected partially because of their acceptance by authorities in the various disciplines. Since truth is never really known, conclusions must always be tentative. Further research may confirm accepted concepts or deny their validity. Undoubtedly much refinement will occur in future research to clarify some of the apparent contradictions. Social psychology seems to lend itself most directly to marketing efforts although other disciplines can also contribute greatly. Political scientists have long compiled facts and figures relating to mass behavior as have sociologists and anthropologists. Psychological studies of individual behavior have yielded many case histories from which useful generalizations can be made. The new techniques and equipment available in statistical analysis make it increasingly more feasible to study existing data which heretofore was either too voluminous for the human mind to comprehend or too costly a process.

Practical selling problems are multidimensional and a simple set of rules is as inadequate as the concepts of a single discipline. Hopefully, future research will provide findings to enable the salesman to perform his role more effectively and to predict, within an ever decreasing margin of error, the effects of his decisions and actions.

## NEUROPHYSIOLOGY

Occasionally in sales literature one reads of an author's personal experience in recognizing buying signals in a prospect's movements or various body postures. These signals might include, for example, the forward thrusting of the jaw, the absentminded rubbing of an ear, a slight rising of the voice, or the widening of the eyes. A prospect's leaning forward is supposed to indicate interest while one sitting back relaxed is not emotionally involved. Similar signals are often found in books of instructions for magicians who do card tricks. For example, the identity of a card a subject is thinking about supposedly can be selected by watching his pupils enlarge when the card is turned up. Since there is little or no agreement on such buying signals, this area was intentionally omitted from this text. However, future research might very well produce valuable information for selling.

Physical movements controlled by the parasympathetic nervous system such as the dilation and constriction of the pupil of the eye are due to changes in light intensity. However, pupil size is also governed by the sympathetic nervous system in response to strong emotional states. One interesting experiment on eye pupil size reveals that the pupil really does constrict when viewing certain aversive stimuli while it opens or dilates in the case of interesting or pleasant pictures. Tentative conclusions of these experiments strongly suggest that pupillary changes reflect ongoing activity in the brain and so indicate favorable and unfavorable attitude much more accurately than verbal response.[3] Experiments are being conducted on such diverse attitudes as political preference, racial attitudes, taste in foods, music appreciation, responses to packages, products, and advertising on television. Measurement of attitude change promises to be the most interesting aspect of these studies. Such communications research in the labora-

---

[3] For a well-written description of the eye pupil response to changes in attitude as well as the experiments being conducted, see Eckhard H. Hess, "Attitude and Pupil Size," *Scientific American*, Vol. 212, No. 4, April, 1965.

tory by psychologists and physiologists may soon yield significant data applicable to the field of sales.

Dealing with business people requires a new combination of knowledge and a broader approach to sales problems. Sales educators can and should borrow the findings, the methods, and insights of other disciplines. Salesmen are not dealing with a group of willing students under college laboratory conditions but with more senior citizens in business who have earned their positions of decision and command. Immediate feedback is available if one is bold enough to apply theory and to conduct experiments in the cold hard reality of the business world.

## MARKETING'S RESPONSIBILITY FOR LEADERSHIP

The marketing mix—including such factors as marketing research, development of new and improved products, competitive pricing, efficient distribution and service, advertising, sales promotion, and personal selling—must be accountable for a company's success or failure in the future. As this becomes the condition, more and more top executive positions will be filled by men with a well-rounded marketing background. Captains of team selling should fill more and more of the top corporate jobs.

Personal selling is the broadest function of the marketing mix and often touches directly on all other phases. Working directly with the customers, the salesman feeds back information to the market research and product development people. It is the salesman in the field who is first aware of the effect of pricing and distribution policies of his employer and of competitors. Sales executives can judge most accurately the effects of advertising and sales promotion campaigns. Effective salesmen will become the key executives in many industries and the entire profession will be upgraded. Through attention to their public relations image, sales executives will cause society to become more aware of the actual work of a salesman and how he does serve society in both social and economic ways. The sales profession will become quite honest through self-policing and the blacklisting of undesirables. As professional salesmen gain higher prestige, better recruits will apply and there will be fewer and fewer misfits.

Salesmanship needs to become a social science, a specialized study of human behavior with increased knowledge of the psychology of persuasion, the psychology of communications, and the psychology of making business decisions. Due to increased training, salesmen should become more mature and more responsible. While many top salesmen today are extremely customer oriented in the sense that their customer is always right, the future mature salesmen will realize an equal responsibility to earn a profit for their own company and for the stockholders, and to provide steady jobs for the factory workers, the office staff, and the distribution people. Salesmen will become more sophisticated and discretion will be revered equally with honesty. With an increased sensitivity to people's needs in both their personal and organizational roles, salesmen will be permitted a greater flexibility of presentation methods.

## TRAINING OF SALESMEN IN THE FUTURE

As salesmanship becomes more of a social science, recruitment will be done fundamentally on the college campus. Sales applicants will have some education in psychology, English, sociology, anthropology, economics, statistics, accounting, history, and geography. Upon this broad base additional courses in business administration will be highly desirable. Company training will become a full-time top management job and the director will have the full cooperation of the entire organization. When the president of a corporation talks on company history, purposes, and objectives, the sales trainees will believe what is said. When the plant engineer talks on his assigned topic, the men will understand the problems and practical limitations of their facilities. When the sales manager gives a selling demonstration, the men will be persuaded to believe in their own product. The professional training director will most often be an experienced college instructor with knowledge, understanding, and sympathy for business. He will teach such areas as the psychology of persuasion and communications as they apply to a particular company. He may often ghostwrite, or at least outline, much of the material he wants company experts, including the president, to cover. Company training will be a continuous process which intentionally covers appropriate knowledge, skills, attitudes, and work habits.

## REWARDS FOR RESPONSIBLE SALESMEN

Professional salesmen will begin to rise in social prestige as they have already risen in economic position. Society will become more aware of the economic value of salesmen; of the high educational requirements; of the new and firm moral standards; of the increasing role of leadership that salesmen will play in American business; of the direct personal service and problem solving salesmen do for the buyer.

America started with great natural resources, little or no capital, and a handful of men. An agricultural economy was natural and encouraged the country's growth and development. Wars stimulated productive capacity and increased capital wealth to exploit further this country's great natural resources. With the growth of industry, more and more people could leave farming for relatively higher wages and suburban living. The population boomed and the United States became a seller's market for all the wonderful new products and services developed through scientific discoveries and applications—things such as petroleum, electricity, the automobile, the airplane, radio, and television. Throughout this amazing growth of the United States, the great natural resources enabled America to remain the breadbasket of the world but, due to mechanization, fewer and fewer men are required on the farms. Now productive capacity in most fields has exceeded normal buying demands and automation of factories and offices is well underway. Americans have more leisure time and a higher standard of living than ever before in the country's history. Exploration of space has begun and by-products have already opened new fields of science and production.

Are Americans to become fat and lazy with leisure? Can the United States decline, as so many great nations have in history, into an immoral, irresponsible, greedy, and self-indulgent people with neither ambition nor pride? Not as long as there are effective and responsible salesmen who can and do create personal dissatisfaction and cause people to want more goods and services which will truly benefit them. Not as long as responsible salesmen continue to encourage people to raise their levels of aspiration and personal goals in life. These men will be the future leaders who will motivate the masses to self-improvement.

Another war or threat of war could stimulate the economy. However, with the atomic and neurological weapons already perfected, the entire world would, of course, lose more than any survivor could possibly gain. One alternative way to stimulate the economy is an effective marketing program to further increase the standard of living in the United States and throughout the world. This can and should be done by private enterprise without undue taxation and without expensive foreign aid programs.

The modern Yankee trader is the marketing specialist who is ready, willing, and able to assume direction of American industry and move more goods and services to people throughout the world who can honestly benefit by their use. These are the few bright, ambitious, and well-trained salesmen of today who will become the leaders of tomorrow. Good luck and God speed!

# SELECTED REFERENCES

# CHAPTER 1

ALEXANDER, RALPH S., AND COMMITTEE ON DEFINITIONS OF THE AMERICAN MARKETING ASSOCIATION. *Marketing Definitions.* Chicago: American Marketing Association, 1960.

BORTON, WILLIAM M. "Respectability for Marketing?" *Journal of Marketing* (October, 1959), pp. 47–50.

BURSK, EDWARD C., CLARK, DONALD T., AND HIDY, RALPH W. (eds.). *The World of Business*, Vol. I. New York: Simon and Schuster, 1962. This collection of business writings projects a sense of the long and intensive history of business and the way business is intertwined with the other strands of society.

BUSKIRK, RICHARD H. *Principles of Marketing: The Management View.* New York: Holt, Rinehart and Winston, Inc., 1966. Emphasis is on the problems faced by the marketing manager when making decisions concerning markets, products, prices, channels, promotions, and basic marketing strategy.

*Dupont: The Autobiography of an American Enterprise.* New York: Charles Scribner's Sons, 1952.

GREIF, EDWIN CHARLES. *Modern Salesmanship: Principles and Problems*, chap. i. Englewood Cliffs, N.J.: Prentice-Hall, Inc., 1958.

HAGLER, JAMES A. "How are Marketers Meeting the Import Challenge?" *Harvard Business Review* (September–October, 1960), pp. 107–14.

HALBERT, MICHAEL H. *The Meaning and Sources of Marketing Theory.* Marketing Science Institute Series. New York: McGraw-Hill Book Co., Inc., 1965. The author explores the relationship between theoretical and substantive material and examines in considerable detail the implications of marketing actually becoming a science.

HEAD, G. W. "What Does Automation Mean to the Marketing Man?" *Journal of Marketing* (April, 1960), pp. 35–37.

HOWARD, JOHN A. *Marketing Management, Analysis and Planning.* Rev. ed. Homewood, Illinois: Richard D. Irwin, Inc., 1963. For the student with business experience or a background of courses in economics and accounting and statistics. Essentially an economic view of marketing.

JONASSEN, CHRISTEN T. "Contributions of Sociology to Marketing," *Journal of Marketing* (October, 1959), pp. 29–35.

KATONA, GEORGE. *The Powerful Consumer.* New York: McGraw-Hill Book Co., Inc., 1960.

KEEZER, DEXTER MERRIAM. *New Forces in American Business.* New York: McGraw-Hill Book Co., Inc., 1959.

LOHSE, CHARLES F. *Creative Selling.* New York: Charles Scribner's Sons, 1960.

MCCARTHY, E. JEROME. *Basic Marketing. A Managerial Approach.* Rev. ed. Homewood, Ill.: Richard D. Irwin, Inc., 1964. Marketing strategy and designing a marketing mix are stressed to give the reader a broad and necessary understanding of marketing problems.

MELOAN, TAYLOR W., AND RATHMELL, JOHN M. *Selling: Its Broader Dimensions.* New York: MacMillan Co., 1960.

MOULTON, HAROLD G. *America's Wealth—the Last Hundred Years—the Next*. Washington, D.C.: Brookings Institution, 1952.

NYSTROM, P. H. (ed.). *Marketing Handbook*, sec. 18. New York: The Ronald Press Co., 1948.

OXENFELDT, ALFRED R. *Pricing For Marketing Executives*. San Francisco: Wadsworth Publishing Co., Inc., 1961.

PEDERSON, C. A., AND WRIGHT, M. D. *Salesmanship: Principles and Methods*, chap. i. 4th ed. Homewood, Ill.: Richard D. Irwin, Inc., 1966.

RANDALL, CLARENCE B. *A Creed for Free Enterprise*. Boston: Little, Brown & Co., 1952.

RUSSELL, FREDERIC A., AND BEACH, FRANK H. *Textbook of Salesmanship*, chap. ii. New York: McGraw-Hill Book Co., Inc., 1959.

SKINNER, B. F. " 'Superstition' in the Pigeon," *Journal of Experimental Psychology*. Vol. 38 (1948), pp. 168–72.

SMITH, WENDELL R., CASCINO, ANTHONY E., AND LAZER, WILLIAM. "Innovations in Marketing Management," *Business Horizons*, Vol. II, No. 3, pp. 52–67.

TIBBEL, JOHN. "What's the Status of Mathematical Marketing?" *Sales Management* (July 1, 1960), p. 25.

TOSDAL, H. R. *Selling in Our Economy*. Homewood, Ill.: Richard D. Irwin, Inc., 1957.

# CHAPTER 2

BENGE, EUGENE J. "What Traits and Work Habits Characterize Successful Salesmen?" *Sales Management* (July 15, 1956), pp. 54–56.

BRIDGMAN, C. S. ET AL. " 'Salesman Helped by Bringing Out Jobs' 'Critical Incidents,' " *Personnel Journal* (April, 1958), pp. 411–14.

CANFIELD, BERTRAND R. *Salesmanship, Practices and Problems*, pp. 7–21. New York: McGraw-Hill Book Co., Inc., 1958.

CASH, HAROLD C., AND CRISSY, DR. W. J. E. "When Salesmen Ask 'What Books Should I Read?' " *Sales Management* (April 5, 1957), pp. 94–96.

DAROFF, J. "Your Underdeveloped Selling Asset (Salesman's Wardrobe)," *Sales Management* (December 6, 1957), pp. 62–68.

DARTNELL CORPORATION, *Compensation of Salesmen*. Chicago: Dartnell Corporation, 1959.

FRANCISCO, L. MERCER. "How Can You Get Salesmen to Sell Today?" *Sales Management* (September 5, 1957), pp. 62–68.

GREENWALT, CRAWFORD H. *The Uncommon Man*. New York: McGraw-Hill Book Co., Inc., 1959.

GREIF, EDWIN CHARLES. *Modern Salesmanship Principles and Problems*, pp. 3–43. Englewood Cliffs, N.J.: Prentice-Hall, Inc., 1958.

GROSS, ALFRED. *Salesmanship*, pp. 3–11. New York: Ronald Press Co., 1959.

KATZ, ROBERT L. "Skills of an Effective Administrator," *Harvard Business Review* (January–February, 1955).

MAYER, DAVID AND GREENBERG, HERBERT M. "What Makes A Good Salesman," *Harvard Business Review* (July–August, 1964), pp. 119–25.

McMURRY, ROBERT N. "The Mystique of Super-Salesmanship," *Harvard Business Review* (March–April, 1961), pp. 113–22.

MORSE, LEON. "The Sound of a Different Drummer." *Dun's Review and Modern Industry*, August, 1963.

PEDERSON, C. A., AND WRIGHT, M. D. *Salesmanship: Principles and Methods*, chap. ii–iii. 4th ed. Homewood, Ill.: Richard D. Irwin, Inc., 1966.

RICE, JOHN H. "How Your Men Can Find Courage," *Sales Management* (March 6, 1959), pp. 89–91.

"Sales or Production: Which Is Best Background for a Top Executive," *Industrial Marketing* (January, 1953), pp. 52–57.

SALISBURY, PHILIP. "Notes from The Editor's Side Pocket. 'Questions Without Answers,'" *Sales Management* (May 7, 1965), p. 90.

STANTON, WILLIAM J., AND BUSKIRK, RICHARD H. *Management of the Sales Force*, pp. 117–31. Homewood, Ill.: Richard D. Irwin, Inc., 1964.

TOBIN, W. J. "What Makes a Man a Successful Salesman?" *Sales Management* (October 2, 1959), pp. 121–24.

U.S. DEPARTMENT OF LABOR. *Occupational Outlook Handbook*, pp. 239–52. Washington, D.C.: U.S. Government Printing Office, 1959.

WHYTE, WILLIAM H. *The Organization Man*. New York: Simon and Schuster, 1956.

WILSON, R. S. *Salesmanship as a Profession*. Akron, Ohio: Goodyear Tire and Rubber Company, 1958.

# CHAPTER 3

BLUM, MILTON L. *Industrial Psychology and Its Social Foundations*. Rev. ed. New York: Harper & Brothers, 1956.

CRUISE, K. A. "Salesman's Biggest Weakness (Failure to Analyze Unique Requirements of Customer)," *Purchasing* (September 29, 1958), p. 67.

EDITORS OF *Grey Matter*, "What Buyers Expect from Salesmen," *Sales Management* (April 17, 1959), pp. 96–98.

EISELEY, LOREN. "Introduction," *Epic of Man*, by eds. of Time, *Life*, Inc. p. 308. New York: Time, Inc., 1961.

FREUD, ANNA. *The Ego And The Mechanisms of Defense*. Trans. CECIL BAINES. New York: International Universities Press, Inc., 1946.

FREUD, SIGMUND. *The Problem of Anxiety*. New York: W. W. Norton & Co., 1936.

GATES, JAMES, AND MILLER, HAROLD. *Personal Adjustment to Business*. New York: Prentice-Hall, Inc., 1960.

HENRY, W. E. "The Business Executive: The Psychodynamics of a Social Role," *American Journal of Sociology*, Vol. 54 (1949), pp. 286–91.

HORNEY, KAREN. *Our Inner Conflicts*. New York: W. W. Norton & Co., 1945.

JENKINS, THOMAS N. "The Neutral Theory of Personality: New Evidence and a Review of the Argument," *Transactions of the New York Academy of Sciences*, Vol. 17 (1955), pp. 315–30.

LEAVITT, HAROLD J. *Managerial Psychology*. 1st Phoenix ed. Chicago: University of Chicago Press, 1962.

LEVITT, THEODORE. "Marketing Myopia," *Harvard Business Review* (July–August, 1960), pp. 45–56.

NICHOLS, RALPH G., AND STEVENS, LEONARD. *Are You Listening?* New York: McGraw-Hill Book Co., Inc., 1957.

OXENFELDT, ALFRED R. *Executive Action in Marketing*. San Francisco: Wadsworth Publishing Co., Inc., 1966.

SCHULTZ, WHITT N. "25 Techniques to Help You Learn to Be More Creative," *Sales Management* (July 19, 1957), pp. 34–35.

SHAFFER, LAURANCE FREDERIC, AND SHOBEN, EDWARD JOSEPH, JR. *The Psychology of Adjustment*. 2d ed. Boston: Houghton Mifflin Company, 1956.

SHOBEN, EDWARD J. "Toward a Concept of the Normal Personality," *American Psychologist*, Vol. 12 (1957), pp. 183–89.

TOBIN, W. J. "Good Selling Is Good Communications," *Sales Management* (May 17, 1957).

## CHAPTER 4

BERNSTEIN, JACK. "Changing Language of the Sales Call," *Sales Management* (May 1, 1959), pp. 44–47.

BRITT, STEUART H. *The Spenders*. New York: McGraw-Hill Book Co., Inc., 1960.

CANFIELD, BERTRAND R. *Salesmanship, Practices and Problems*, pp. 356–77. New York: McGraw-Hill Book Co., Inc., 1958.

CERAMI, CHARLES A. "How to Sell Against Imports," *Sales Management* (June 17, 1960), pp. 33–35.

DAHL, ROBERT A., HAIRE, MASON, AND LAZARSFELD, PAUL F. *Social Science Research on Business: Product and Potential*. New York: Columbia University Press, 1959.

FERBER, ROBERT. "Our Changing Consumer Market," *Business Horizons* (Spring, 1958), pp. 49–66.

GENTILE, JOSEPH. *Some Do's and Don'ts of Selling as One Buyer Sees Them*. New York: Dun & Bradstreet, Inc., 1955. 27 pp.

GREIF, EDWIN CHARLES. *Modern Salesmanship. Principles and Problems*, pp. 101–17. Englewood Cliffs, N.J.: Prentice-Hall, Inc., 1958.

CROSS, ALFRED. *Salesmanship. Principles and Practices of Professional Selling*, chaps. ii, iii, and iv. New York: The Ronald Press Co., 1959.

HEGARTY, ED. J. "Casing Your Competition," *American Salesman* (May, 1958), p. 44.

KATONA, GEORGE. *The Powerful Consumer*. New York: McGraw-Hill Book Co., Inc., 1960.

LESLY, PHILIP. "The New Consumer Who Thinks for Himself," *Sales Management* (March 18, 1960), pp. 33, 130–32.

RESEARCH DEPARTMENT, CURTIS PUBLISHING Co., *Market for Office Machines*, September 14, 1959.

PEDERSON, C. A., AND WRIGHT, M. D. *Salesmanship: Principles and Methods*, chaps. v and vi. 4th ed. Homewood, Ill.: Richard D. Irwin, Inc., 1966.

REEDER, CHARLES B. "How Population Composition Affects Economic Growth," *Business Horizons*, Vol. III, No. 4 (Winter, 1960), pp. 54–61.

"Rapid-Fire Introduction of New Drugs Requires Special Skills of Detail Men," *Printers' Ink* (June 20, 1958), pp. 64–65.

"24-Point Checklist: What Every Salesman Should Know About His Customers," *Printers' Ink* (January 9, 1959), p. 40.

U.S. NEWS & WORLD REPORT. *How Business Buys*. Washington, D.C.: United States News Publishing Corp., 1957. 144 pp.

"Why Every Sale Must Have Two Parts," *Sales Management* (March 15, 1957), p. 88.

WOLFF, JANET. "New Directions in Marketing: Answering Woman's Hunger For Information," *Sales Management* (November 10, 1959), pp. 22–36.

# CHAPTER 5

ADAMS, F. GERARD. "Consumer Attitudes, Buying Plans, and Purchases of Durable Goods: A Principal Components, Time Series Approach," *Review of Economics and Statistics* (November, 1964), pp. 347–55.

BIRREN, FAHER. "Colors That Sell: How Can You Find Them?" *Sales Management* (June 6, 1958), pp. 38–44.

BOWER, JOSEPH L. "The Role of Conflict in Economic Decision-Making Groups: Some Empirical Results," *Quarterly Journal of Economics* (May, 1965), pp. 263–77.

BURCK, GILBERT. "What Makes Women Buy?" *Fortune* (August, 1956).

CHESKIN, LOUIS. *Why People Buy*. New York: Liveright Publishing Corp., 1959.

COLLAZZO, CHARLES J. *Consumer Attitudes and Frustrations in Shopping*. Publication of the Retail Research Institute of the National Retail Merchants Association, 1964.

COX, REAVIS, ALDERSON, WROE, AND SHAPIRO, STANLEY J. *Theory in Marketing: Second Series*. Homewood, Illinois: Richard D. Irwin, Inc., 1964.

COX, DONALD F., AND BAUER, RAYMOND A. "Self Confidence and Persuasibility in Women," *Public Opinion Quarterly* (Fall, 1964), pp. 453–66.

DAHL, ROBERT A., HAIRE, MASON, AND LAZARSFELD, PAUL F. *Social Science*

*Research on Business: Product and Potential,* pp. 108–23. New York: Columbia University Press, 1959.

DUNTON, LOREN. *How To Sell To Women.* New York: McGraw-Hill Book Co., Inc., 1965.

EDIN, MARGARET. "A Puzzle for Appliance Retailers: What Makes Today's Woman Buy?" *Merchandising Week* (May 10, 1965), pp. 11–14.

ELLIS, MARY JANE. "Spending Patterns Over the Life Cycle." Presented at 42d *Annual Agricultural Outlook Conference,* Consumer and Food Economics Research Division, U.S.D.A., Washington, D.C. November 17, 1964.

FURST, SIDNEY, AND SHERMAN, MILTON (eds.). *Business Decisions That Changed Our Lives.* New York: Random House, Inc., 1964.

HOLLOWAY, ROBERT J., AND HANCOCK, ROBERT S. *The Environment of Marketing Behavior: Selections from the Literature.* New York: John Wiley & Sons, Inc., 1964.

JUSTER, F. THOMAS. *Anticipations and Purchases: An Analysis of Consumer Behavior.* Princeton, N.J.: Princeton University Press, 1964.

KATONA, GEORGE. *The Mass Consumption Society.* New York: McGraw-Hill Book Co., Inc., 1964.

KATZ, ELIHU, AND LAZARSFELD, PAUL F. *Personal Influence: The Part Played by People in the Flow of Mass Communications.* Glencoe, Illinois: The Free Press, 1955.

MCNEAL, JAMES U. *Dimensions of Consumer Behavior.* New York: Appleton-Century-Crofts, 1965.

OTTESON, SCHUYLER F. "Sizing Up Customers: Are You Selling to Strangers?" *Merchandising Week* (January 25, 1965), p. 103.

OXENFELDT, ALFRED R. *Marketing Practices in the T.V. Set Industry.* New York: Columbia University Press, 1964.

PACKARD, VANCE. *The Hidden Persuaders.* New York: David McKay Co., Inc., 1957.

PESSEMIER, EDGAR A. "A New Way to Determine Buying Decisions," *Journal of Marketing* (October, 1959), pp. 41–46.

"Psychology: A Behavioral Reinterpretation," *Proceedings of the American Philosophical Society,* Vol. 108, No. 6 (December, 1964), pp. 451–85.

SAMPSON, RICHARD T. "Sense and Sensitivity in Pricing," *Harvard Business Review* (November–December, 1964), pp. 99–105.

"Where Experts Are Worlds Apart," *Business Week* (November 7, 1964), pp. 74–78.

# CHAPTER 6

CANNON, W. B. *The Wisdom of the Body.* Rev. ed. New York: W. W. Norton & Co., 1939.

DICHTER, ERNEST. "How to Tailor Your Selling to the Individual Prospect," *American Salesman* (January, 1959), p. 36.

HENRY, W. E. "The Business Executive: The Psychodynamics of a Social Role," *American Journal of Sociology*, Vol. 54 (1949), pp. 286–91.

HORNEY, KAREN. *Neurosis and Human Growth*. New York: W. W. Norton & Co., 1950.

JAMES, WILLIAM. *Pragmatism*. New York: Longmans, Green, 1907.

JENKINS, THOMAS N. "The Neutral Theory of Personality: New Evidence and a Review of the Argument," *Transactions of the New York Academy of Sciences*, Vol. 17 (1955), pp. 315–30.

JUNG, CARL G. *Psychological Types*. New York: Harcourt, Brace, 1923.

KATZ, ELIHU, AND LAZARSFELD, PAUL F. *Personal Influence: The Part Played by People in the Flow of Mass Communications*. Glencoe, Illinois: The Free Press, 1955.

LANDIS, CARNEY, AND BOLLES, M. MARJORIE. *Textbook of Abnormal Psychology*, chaps. i–iv. New York: Macmillan Company, 1947.

LEAVITT, HAROLD J. *Managerial Psychology*. 1st Phoenix ed. Chicago: University of Chicago Press, 1962.

MARTINEAU, PIERRE, "Social Classes and Spending Behavior," *Journal of Marketing* (October, 1958), pp. 121–30.

PACKARD, VANCE. *The Status Seekers*. New York: David McKay Co., Inc., 1959.

SHAFFER, LAURANCE F., AND SHOBEN, EDWARD J., JR. *The Psychology of Adjustment*. 2d ed. Boston: Houghton Mifflin Company, 1956.

SHAW, F. J., AND ORT, R. S., *Personal Adjustment in the American Culture*. New York: Harper & Bros., 1953.

SHOBEN, EDWARD J. "Toward a Concept of the Normal Personality," *American Psychologist*, Vol. 12 (1957), pp. 183–89.

STAGNER, R. "Homeostasis as a Unifying Concept in Personality Theory," *Psychological Review*, Vol. 58 (1951), pp. 5–17.

WARNER, W. LLOYD, AND LUNT, PAUL. *The Social Life of a Modern Community*. New Haven: Yale University Press, 1950.

WHITING, J. W. M., AND CHILD, I. L. *Child Training and Personality*. New Haven: Yale University Press, 1953.

## CHAPTER 7

BAUER, RAYMOND A. "Limits of Persuasion," *Harvard Business Review*, Vol. 36, No. 5 (1958), pp. 105–10.

BETTGER, FRANK. *How I Raised Myself from Failure to Success in Selling*. Englewood Cliffs, N.J.: Prentice-Hall, Inc., 1949.

BLAKE, ROBERT R., AND RAMSEY, GLEN V. *Perception: Approach to Personality*. New York: Ronald Press, 1951.

CANNELL, CHARLES F., AND MACDONALD, JAMES C. "The Impact of Health News on Attitudes and Behavior," *Journalism Quarterly*, Vol. XXXIII (1956), pp. 315–23.

Dorwin, Cartwright. "Some Principles of Mass Persuasion: Selected Findings of Research on the Sale of United States War Bonds," *Human Relations*, Vol. II (1949), pp. 253–67.

Eriksen, C. W. "The Case for Perceptual Defense," *Psychological Review*, Vol. LXI (May, 1954).

Hovland, Carl I., Janis, Irving L., and Kelley, Harold H. *Communication and Persuasion*. New Haven: Yale University Press, 1953.

Hovland, Carl I., and Weiss, W. "The Influence of Source Credibility on Communication Effectiveness," *Public Opinion Quarterly*, Vol. XV (1951), pp. 635–50.

Ittleson, W. H. *The Ames Demonstrations in Perception*. Princeton, N.J.: Princeton University Press, 1952.

Kahn, George N. "The 10 Biggest Mistakes Salesmen Make," *Sales Management*, booklet reprinted from a series of articles (1962).

Lazarsfeld, Paul. "The Effects of Radio on Public Opinion," *Print, Radio, and Film in a Democracy* (ed. Douglas Waples). Chicago: University of Chicago Press, 1942.

Lazarsfeld, Paul F., Berelson, Bernard, and Gaudet, Hazel. *The People's Choice*. New York: Columbia University Press, 1948.

Leavitt, Harold J. *Managerial Psychology*. 1st Phoenix ed. Chicago: University of Chicago Press, 1962.

Lee, Irving. *How to Talk with People*. New York: Harper & Bros., 1952.

Maier, Norman R. F. *Principles of Human Relations*. New York: John Wiley & Sons, 1952.

Powell, Frederic A. "Open- and Closed-Mindedness and the Ability to Differentiate Source and Message," *Journal of Abnormal and Social Psychology* (July, 1962), pp. 61–64.

Roth, Charles B. *How to Make $25,000 a Year Selling*. Englewood Cliffs, N.J.: Prentice-Hall, Inc., 1953.

Smith, G. H. *Motivation Research in Advertising and Marketing*. New York: McGraw-Hill Book Co., Inc., 1954.

Star, Shirley A., and Hughes, Helen McGill. "Report of an Educational Campaign: The Cincinnati Plan for the United Nations," *American Journal of Sociology*, Vol. LV (1950), pp. 389–400.

Stein, Karl H. "Disease and Cigarettes—A Consumer Opinion Study," *Business and Society* (Autumn, 1964), pp. 32–37.

Waples, Douglas, Berelson, Bernard, and Bradshaw, Franklyn R. *What Reading Does to People*. Chicago: University of Chicago Press, 1940.

## CHAPTER 8

Allport, Gordon, and Postman, Leo, J. "The Basic Psychology of Rumor," *Transactions of the New York Academy of Sciences*, Vol. VIII, Series II (1945), pp. 61–81.

Asch, S. E. *Social Psychology*. Englewood Cliffs, N.J.: Prentice-Hall, Inc., 1952.

Bettelheim, B., and Janowitz, M. "Reactions to Fascist Propaganda: A Pilot Study," *Public Opinion Quarterly*, Vol. XIV (1950), pp. 53–60.

Blake, Robert R., and Ramsey, Glen V. *Perception: Approach to Personality*. New York: Ronald Press, Inc., 1951.

Bruner, Jerome S., and Goodman, Cecile C. "Value and Need as Organizing Factors in Perception," *Journal of Abnormal and Social Psychology*, Vol. XLII (1947), pp. 33–44.

Cannell, Charles F., and MacDonald, James C. "The Impact of Health News on Attitudes and Behavior," *Journalism Quarterly*, Vol. XXXIII (1956), pp. 315–23.

Cherry, Colin. *On Human Communication*. New York: John Wiley and Sons, Inc., 1957.

Cooper, E., and Jahoda, M. "The Evasion of Propaganda," *Journal of Psychology*, Vol. XXIII (1947), pp. 15–25.

Decker, Frederic C. "Publisher's View," *Printers' Ink*, September 10, 1965.

Eriksen, C. W. "The Case for Perceptual Defense," *Psychological Review*, Vol. LXI, May, 1954.

Henry, W. E. "The Business Executive: The Psychodynamics of a Social Role," *American Journal of Sociology*, Vol. LIV (January, 1949).

Hymann, Herbert H., and Sheatsley, Paul B. "Some Reasons Why Information Campaigns Fail," *Public Opinion Quarterly*, Vol. XI (1947), pp. 412–23.

Ittleson, W. H. *The Ames Demonstrations in Perception*. Princeton, N.J.: Princeton University Press, 1952.

Jacobson, E. "Electrophysiology of Mental Activities," *American Journal of Psychology*, Vol. 44 (1932), pp. 677–94.

Janis, I. L., and Feshback, S. "Effects of Fear-Arousing Communications," *Journal of Abnormal and Social Psychology*, Vol. XLVIII (1953), pp. 78–92.

——— and Milholland, H. C. "The Influence of Threat Appeals on Selective Learning of the Content of a Persuasive Appeal," *Journal of Psychology*, Vol. XXXVII (1954), pp. 75–80.

——— and Terwillinger, Robert F. "An Experimental Study of Psychological Resistances to Fear Arousing Communications," *Journal of Abnormal and Social Psychology* (December, 1962), pp. 403–10.

Kendall, P. L., and Wolf, K. M. *The Personification of Prejudice as a Device in Educational Propaganda*. New York: Bureau of Applied Social Research, Columbia University, 1946.

Levine, Jerome M., and Murphy, Gardner. "The Learning and Forgetting of Controversial Material," *Journal of Abnormal and Social Psychology*, Vol. XXXVIII (1943), pp. 507–17.

Nirenberg, Jesse S. "How to Reach Minds—and Hearts—When You Talk to People," *Sales Management*, December 19, 1958, p. 33.

SHERIF, MUZAFER. *The Psychology of Social Norms.* New York: Harper & Bros., 1936.

WARNER, W., AND ABBEGGLEN, J. C. *Big Business Leaders in America.* New York: Harper & Bros., 1955.

WHEELER, ELMER. *Sizzlemanship.* Englewood Cliffs, N.J.: Prentice-Hall, Inc., 1937.

———— *Tested Sentences That Sell.* Englewood Cliffs, N.J.: Prentice-Hall, Inc., 1937.

WIENER, NORBERT. *Cybernetics.* Cambridge, Mass.: Technology Press, 1948.

———— *The Human Use of Human Beings.* Garden City, N.Y.: Doubleday & Co., Inc., 1954.

# CHAPTER 9

COLEMAN, JAMES, KATZ, ELIHU, AND MENZEL, HERBERT. *Doctors and New Drugs.* Glencoe, Illinois: The Free Press [forthcoming].

COX, DONALD F., AND BAUER, RAYMOND A. "Self Confidence and Persuasibility in Women," *Public Opinion Quarterly* (Fall, 1964), pp. 453–66.

JANIS, IRVING L. "Personality Correlates of Susceptibility to Persuasion," *Journal of Personality,* Vol. XXII (1954), pp. 504–18.

———— ET AL. *Personality and Persuasibility,* p. 237. New Haven: Yale University Press, 1959.

KATZ, DANIEL. "The Functional Approach to the Study of Attitudes," *Public Opinion Quarterly* (1960), 24 (2), pp. 163–204.

KATZ, ELIHU, AND LAZARSFELD, PAUL F. *Personal Influence: The Part Played by People in the Flow of Mass Communications.* Glencoe, Illinois: The Free Press, 1955.

KELLEY, HAROLD H. "Salience of Membership and Resistance to Change of Group Anchored Attitudes," *Human Relations,* Vol. VIII (1958), pp. 275–89.

———— AND VOLKART, EDMUND H. "The Resistance to Change of Group Anchored Attitudes," *American Sociological Review,* Vol. XVII (1952), pp. 453–65.

KELMAN, HERBERT C. "Attitude Change as a Function of Response Restriction," *Human Relations,* Vol. VI (1953), pp. 185–214.

KING, B. T., AND JANIS, IRVING L. "Comparison of the Effectiveness of Improvised versus Non-Improvised Role-Playing in Producing Opinion Changes," *Communications and Persuasion* (ed. CARL I. HOVLAND, IRVING L. JANIS, AND HAROLD H. KELLEY), New Haven: Yale University Press, 1953.

KRACAUER, SIEGFRIED, AND BERKMAN, PAUL L. *Satellite Mentality.* New York: Frederick A. Praeger, Inc., 1956.

LAZARSFELD, PAUL F., BERELSON, BERNARD, AND GAUDET, HAZEL. *The People's Choice.* New York: Columbia University Press, 1948.

LEVENTHAL, HOWARD H., AND PERLOE, SIDNEY I. "A Relationship Between

Self-Esteem and Persuasibility," *Journal of Abnormal and Social Psychology* (May, 1962), pp. 385–88.

SHILS, EDWARD A., AND JANOWITZ, MORRIS. "Cohesion and Disintegration in the Wehrmacht in World War II," *Public Opinion Quarterly*, Vol. XII (1948), pp. 280–315.

WAPLES, DOUGLAS, BERELSON, BERNARD, AND BRADSHAW, FRANKLYN R. *What Reading Does to People.* Chicago: University of Chicago Press, 1940.

ZIMMERMAN, CLAIRE, AND BAUER, RAYMOND A. "The Effect of an Audience Upon What Is Remembered," *Public Opinion Quarterly*, Vol. XX (1956), pp. 238–48.

# CHAPTER 10

ANNIS, A. D., AND MEIER, N. C. "The Induction of Opinion through Suggestions by Means of Planted Content," *Journal of Social Psychology*, Vol. V (1934), pp. 65–81.

ASCH, S. E. *Social Psychology.* Englewood Cliffs, N.J.: Prentice-Hall, Inc., 1952.

CANNELL, CHARLES F., AND MACDONALD, JAMES C. "The Impact of Health News on Attitudes and Behavior," *Journalism Quarterly*, Vol. XXXIII (1956), pp. 315–23.

CARTWRIGHT, DORWIN, "Some Principles of Mass Persuasion: Selected Findings of Research on the Sale of United States War Bonds," *Human Relations*, Vol. II (1949), pp. 253–67.

COFFIN, THOMAS E. *The Hofstra Study: A Measure of the Sales Effectiveness of Television Advertising.* New York: NBC Research Division, 1950.

————"Television's Effects on Leisure Time Activities," *Journal of Applied Psychology*, Vol. XXXII (1948), pp. 550–58.

HOVLAND, CARL I. ET AL. *The Order of Presentation in Persuasion.* New Haven: Yale University Press, 1957.

———— JANIS, IRVING L., AND KELLEY, HAROLD H. *Communications and Persuasion.* New Haven: Yale University Press, 1953.

———— LUMSDAINE, ARTHUR A., AND SHEFFIELD, FRED D. "Studies in Social Psychology in World War II," *Experiments on Mass Communication*, Vol. III. Princeton, N.J.: Princeton University Press, 1949.

JANIS, IRVING L., AND FESHBACH, S. "Effects of Fear-Arousing Communications," *Journal of Abnormal and Social Psychology*, Vol. XLVIII (1953), pp. 78–92.

KATZ, ELIHU, AND LAZARSFELD, PAUL F. *Personal Influence: The Part Played by People in the Flow of Mass Communications.* Glencoe, Illinois: The Free Press, 1955.

KELMAN, HERBERT C., AND HOVLAND, CARL I. "Reinstatement of the Communicator in Delayed Measurement of Opinion Change," *Journal of Abnormal and Social Psychology*, Vol. XLVIII (1953), pp. 327–35.

LAZARSFELD, PAUL F., BERELSON, BERNARD, AND GAUDET, HAZEL. *The People's Choice*. New York: Columbia University Press, 1948.

——— AND MERTON, ROBERT K. "Mass Communication, Popular Taste and Organized Social Action," *The Communication of Ideas* (ed. L. BRYSON). New York: Harper & Bros., 1948.

LEWIS, HELEN B. "Studies in the Principles of Judgments and Attitudes: IV. The Operation of Prestige Suggestion," *Journal of Social Psychology*, Vol. 14 (1941), pp. 229–56.

LUMSDAINE, ARTHUR A., AND JANIS, IRVING L. "Resistance to 'Counter Propaganda' Produced by One-Sided and Two-Sided 'Propaganda' Presentations," *Public Opinion Quarterly*, Vol. XVII (1953), pp. 311–18.

MANDELL, WALLACE, AND HOVLAND, CARL I. "Is There a Law of Primacy in Persuasion?" *American Psychologist*, Vol. VII (1952), p. 538.

PETERSON, RUTH C., AND THURSTONE, L. L. *Motion Pictures and the Social Attitudes of Children*. New York: Macmillan Co., 1933.

PREVETTE, EARL. *The Power of Creative Selling*. Englewood Cliffs, N.J.: Prentice-Hall, Inc., 1954.

THOMPSON, JOSEPH W. "A Strategy of Selling," *Salesmanship: Modern Viewpoints on Personal Communication* (ed. STEVEN J. SHAW AND JOSEPH W. THOMPSON). New York: Holt, Rinehart and Winston, Inc., 1960.

# CHAPTER 11

BETTGER, FRANK. *How I Raised Myself from Failure to Success in Selling*. Englewood Cliffs, N.J.: Prentice-Hall, Inc., 1949.

CANFIELD, B. R. *Salesmanship; Practices and Problems*, chap. v. 3rd ed. New York: McGraw-Hill Book Co., Inc., 1958.

"Doctor's Orders: Sell Me in a Hurry," *Sales Management* (December 6, 1957), pp. 99–100.

GREIF, EDWIN CHARLES. *Modern Salesmanship; Principles and Problems*, chaps. viii, xi, xiv. Englewood Cliffs, N.J.: Prentice-Hall, Inc., 1958.

GROSS, ALFRED. *Salesmanship*, pp. 141–67. New York: Ronald Press Co., 1959.

HICKERSON, J. M. "Successful Sales Techniques," *Harvard Business Review* (September–October, 1952), pp. 33–46.

HUSBAND, RICHARD W. *The Psychology of Successful Selling*, pp. 133–68. New York: Harper & Bros., 1953.

KIRKPATRICK, CHARLES ATKINSON. *Salesmanship; Helping Prospects Buy*, chaps. xi and xiii. Cincinnati: South-Western Publishing Co., 1956.

PAVLOV, I. P. *Conditioned Reflexes*. Trans. G. V. ANREP. London: Oxford University Press, 1927.

——— *Conditioned Reflexes and Psychiatry*. Trans. by W. H. GANTT. New York: International Publishers, 1941.

PEDERSON, C. A., AND WRIGHT, M. D. *Salesmanship: Principles and Methods*, chap. xi. 4th ed. Homewood, Illinois: Richard D. Irwin, Inc., 1966.

PREVETTE, EARL. *The Power of Creative Selling.* Englewood Cliffs, N.J.: Prentice-Hall, Inc., 1954.

RUSSELL, FREDERIC A., AND BEACH, FRANK H. *Textbook of Salesmanship,* chaps. x–xii. New York: McGraw-Hill Book Co., Inc., 1959.

SCHLAIN, BERT. *Big League Salesmanship.* Copyright by National Sales Executives, Inc. Englewood Cliffs, N.J.: Prentice-Hall, Inc., 1955.

"So You Think You Can't Sell Big Ticket Items On One Call?" *Sales Management,* September 20, 1957, pp. 58–60.

STRONG, EDWARD K., JR. *Psychological Aspects of Business.* New York: McGraw-Hill Book Co., Inc. 1938.

WHEELER, ELMER. *How to Sell Yourself to Others.* Englewood Cliffs, N.J.: Prentice-Hall, Inc. 1954.

——— *Sizzlemanship.* Englewood Cliffs, N.J.: Prentice-Hall, Inc., 1937.

——— *Tested Sentences That Sell.* Englewood Cliffs, N.J.: Prentice-Hall, Inc., 1937.

——— *The Wealth Within You.* Englewood Cliffs, N.J.: Prentice-Hall, Inc., 1955.

# CHAPTER 12

BETTGER, FRANK. *How I Raised Myself from Failure to Success in Selling.* Englewood Cliffs, N.J.: Prentice-Hall, Inc., 1949.

CANFIELD, B. R. *Salesmanship: Practices and Problems,* chap. vii. 3rd ed. New York: McGraw-Hill Book Co., Inc., 1958.

GROSS, ALFRED. *Salesmanship,* chaps. x–xiii. New York: Ronald Press Company, 1959.

HAGARTY, EDWARD J. "How You Can Make Your Own Visual Presentation," *American Salesman* (August, 1958), p. 38.

HAYAKAWA, S. I. "How Words Change Our Lives," *Saturday Evening Post* (December 27, 1958), pp. 22, 72–74.

IVEY, P. W., AND HORVATH, W. *Successful Salesmanship,* chap. xv. 3d ed. Englewood Cliffs, N.J.: Prentice-Hall, Inc., 1953.

KIRKPATRICK, C. A. *Salesmanship: Helping Prospects Buy,* pp. 343–57. 2d ed. Cincinnati: South-Western Publishing Co., Inc., 1956.

KITSON, W. D. *The Mind of the Buyer.* New York: Macmillan Co., 1940.

LEWIS, C. W. (ed.). *Essentials of Selling,* chap. vii. 2d ed. Englewood Cliffs, N.J.: Prentice-Hall Inc., 1952.

McMURRAY, ROBERT N. "How to Win or Lose Sales at the Point of Purchase," *Journal of Marketing* (July, 1959), pp. 41–49.

——— "The Mystique of Super-Salesmanship," *Harvard Business Review* (March–April, 1961), pp. 113–22.

PEDERSON, C. A., AND WRIGHT, M. D. *Salesmanship: Principles and Methods,* chap. xi. 4th ed. Homewood, Illinois: Richard D. Irwin, Inc., 1966.

ROTH, C. B. *Professional Salesmanship,* chap. xii. New York: McGraw-Hill Book Co., Inc., 1949.

RUSSELL, F. A., AND BEACH F. H. *Textbook of Salesmanship,* chaps. x–xii. 5th ed. New York: McGraw-Hill Book Co., Inc., 1955.

SCHLAIN, BERT. *Big League Salesmanship.* Copyright by National Sales Executives, Inc. Englewood Cliffs, N.J.: Prentice-Hall, Inc., 1955.

STRONG, EDWARD K., JR. *Psychological Aspects of Business.* New York: McGraw-Hill Book Co., Inc., 1938.

WHITING, P. H. *The 5 Great Rules of Selling,* chaps. v, vii, and xii. Rev. ed. New York: McGraw-Hill Book Co., Inc., 1957.

WILSON, JOHN M. *Open the Mind and Close the Sale,* pp. 102–59. New York: McGraw-Hill Book Co., Inc., 1953.

# CHAPTER 13

BETTGER, FRANK. *How I Raised Myself from Failure to Success in Selling.* Englewood Cliffs, N.J.: Prentice-Hall, Inc., 1949.

BORDIN, EDWARD S. *Psychological Counseling.* New York: Appleton-Century-Crofts, Inc., 1955.

BLUM, MILTON L. *Industrial Psychology and Its Social Foundations.* Rev. ed. New York: Harper & Bros., 1956.

CANFIELD, B. R. *Salesmanship: Practices and Problems,* chaps. v–viii. 3rd ed. New York: McGraw-Hill Book Co., Inc., 1958.

DICHTER, ERNEST. "What the Older Man Wants When He Buys," *American Salesman* (August, 1958), p. 82.

GREIF, EDWIN CHARLES. *Modern Salesmanship: Principles and Problems,* chaps. viii, xi, xiv. Englewood Cliffs, N.J.: Prentice-Hall, Inc., 1958.

GROSS, ALFRED. *Salesmanship,* chaps. x–xv. New York: Ronald Press Co., 1959.

KIRKPATRICK, CHARLES ATKINSON. *Salesmanship: Helping Prospects Buy,* chaps. xi–xiii. Cincinnati: South-Western Publishing Co., 1956.

LEE, IRVING. *How to Talk with People.* New York: Harper & Bros., 1952.

MENNINGER, KARL. *Theory of Psychoanalytic Technique.* New York: Basic Books, Inc., 1958; Science Editions, Inc., 1961. Menninger Clinic Monograph Series.

NICHOLS, RALPH E., AND STEVENS, LEONARD A. *Are You Listening.* New York: McGraw-Hill Book Co., Inc., 1957.

NIRENBERG, JESSE S. "How to Reach Minds—and Hearts—When You Talk to People," *Sales Management* (December 19, 1958), p. 33.

PEDERSON, C. A., AND WRIGHT, M. D. *Salesmanship: Principles and Methods,* chap. xi 4th ed. Homewood, Illinois: Richard D. Irwin, Inc., 1966.

RIESMAN, DAVID, AND BENNEY, MARK. "Asking and Answering," *Journal of Business* (October, 1956).

RORSCHACH, H. *Psychodiagnostics.* 2d ed. Berne, Switzerland: Verlag Hans Huber, 1942.

RUSSELL, F. A., AND BEACH, F. H. *Textbook of Salesmanship,* chaps. x–xii. 5th ed. New York: McGraw-Hill Book Co., Inc., 1955.

SMITH, G. H. *Motivation Research in Advertising and Marketing.* New York: McGraw-Hill Book Co., Inc., 1954.

SNYDER, WILLIAM U. "An Investigation of the Nature of Non-directive Psychotherapy," *Journal of General Psychology,* Vol. 33 (1945), pp. 193–224.

SULLIVAN, HARRY S. *The Psychiatric Interview.* New York: W. W. Norton & Co., 1954.

"What Will PA's Demand This Year?" *Sales Management* (February 3, 1961), p. 37.

WHYTE, WILLIAM H., JR. *Is Anybody Listening?* New York: Simon and Schuster, 1952.

WILSON, JOHN M. *Open the Mind and Close the Sale,* pp. 102–59. New York: McGraw-Hill Book Co., Inc., 1953.

# CHAPTER 14

ALEXANDER, R. S., CROSS, J. S., AND CUNNINGHAM, R. M. *Industrial Marketing.* Homewood, Illinois: Richard D. Irwin, Inc., 1956.

ALJIAN, GEORGE W. (ed.). *Purchasing Handbook,* sec. 11. New York: McGraw-Hill Book Company, Inc., 1958.

ARCHER, STEPHEN H. "The Structure of Management Decision Theory," *Journal of the Academy of Management* (December, 1964), pp. 269–87.

BORTON, WILLIAM M. "What's Wrong With the Way We're Selling Sales Careers to Collegians," *Sales Management Magazine* (March 15, 1957).

BURSK, EDWARD C. "Low-Pressure Selling," *Harvard Business Review,* Vol. 25, No. 2 (1947), pp. 227–42.

EASTON, WILLIAM H. "Creative Thinking and How to Develop It," *Mechanical Engineering* (August, 1946).

FOUNTAIN, R. E. *The Importance of Value Analysis.* American Management Association, New York, 1956.

FOWLKES, JACK K. "The Vendor's Role in Value Analysis," *Midwest Purchasing Agent* (August, 1958).

HODNETT, EDWARD. *The Art of Problem Solving.* New York: Harper & Bros., 1955.

KEPNER, CHARLES H., AND TREGOE, BENJAMIN B. *The Rational Manager: A Systematic Approach to Problem Solving and Decision Making,* p. 275. New York: McGraw-Hill Book Co., Inc., 1965.

LEHRER, ROBERT N. *Work Simplification: Creative Thinking about Work Problems.* Englewood Cliffs, N.J.: Prentice-Hall, Inc., 1957.

LEWIS, RONELLO B. "The Role of Accounting in Decision Making," *Accounting Review* (January, 1956).

LOEWY, RAYMOND. *Never Leave Well Enough Alone.* New York: Simon and Schuster, Inc., 1951.

MILES, LAWRENCE D. *Techniques of Value Analysis and Engineering.* New York: McGraw-Hill Book Co., Inc., 1961.

MILLER, S. "How to Get the Most from Value Analysis," *Harvard Business Review* (January–February, 1955).

MORSE, LEON. "The Sound of a Different Drummer," *Dun's Review and Modern Industry* (August, 1963), p. 26.

MORSE, MORTON F., AND HASEMAN, WILBUR C. "Direct Costing and Decision Making," *Accounting Review* (April, 1957).

OSBORN, ALEX. *Applied Imagination.* New York: Charles Scribner's Sons, 1953.

OXENFELDT, ALFRED R., AND WATKINS, MYRON W. *Make or Buy.* McGraw-Hill Consultant Reports. New York: McGraw-Hill Book Co., Inc., 1956.

STAUNTON, J. DONALD. "I Didn't Raise My Boy to Be a Salesman!" *Management Review*, American Management Association, Inc. (March 1958), p. 9.

VANDEWATER, JOHN. "RCA's New Concepts in Value Buying," *Purchasing* (May 18, 1964).

WASSON, CHESTER R. *Research Analysis for Marketing Decision*, pp. 278. New York: Appleton-Century-Crofts, 1965.

YAHRAES, RICHARD A. "Can Saleswoman Teach Men about Selling?" *American Salesman* (May, 1959), p. 50.

# CHAPTER 15

BERLE, A. A. "The Impact of the Corporation on Classical Economic Theory," *Quarterly Journal of Economics* (February, 1965), pp. 25–40.

BONJEAN, CHARLES M. "Class, Status, and Power Reputation," *Sociology and Social Review* (October, 1964), pp. 69–75.

BURSK, EDWARD C. "Low-Pressure Selling," *Harvard Business Review*, Vol. 25, No. 2 (1947), pp. 227–42.

CHERRY, COLIN. *On Human Communications.* New York: John Wiley & Sons, Inc., 1957.

DOTY, R. A., AND WALD, R. "The Top Executive: A First-Hand Profile," *Harvard Business Review* (July–August, 1954).

HENRY, W. E. "The Business Executive: The Psychodynamics of a Social Role," *American Journal of Sociology*, Vol. LIV (January, 1949).

LEAVITT, HAROLD J. *Managerial Psychology*, p. 327. Chicago: University of Chicago Press, 1958.

MALTZ, MAXWELL. *The Magic Power of Self Image Psychology*, p. 216. Englewood Cliffs, N.J.: Prentice-Hall, Inc., 1964.

McNEAL, JAMES U. *Dimensions of Consumer Behavior*, p. 310. New York: Appleton-Century-Crofts, 1965.

MORSE, LEON. "How to Create a Salesman," *Dun's Review and Modern Industry* (December, 1963), p. 46.

——— "The Sound of a Different Drummer," *Dun's Review and Modern Industry* (August, 1963), p. 26.

MURRAY, THOMAS J. "Systems Selling: Industrial Marketing's New Tool," *Dun's Review and Modern Industry* (October, 1964), p. 51.

OSBORN, ALES. *Your Creative Power.* New York: Charles Scribner's Sons, 1951.

PLUNKETT, JAMES G., VOGL, A. J., AND DAIGNAULT, PHYLLIS. "Union Carbide: Marketer on the Move," *Sales Management* (November 10, 1964), pp. 21–66.

SMITH, G. H. *Motivation Research in Advertising and Marketing.* New York: McGraw-Hill Book Co., Inc., 1954.

THOMPSON, JOSEPH W. "A Strategy of Selling," *Salesmanship. Modern Viewpoints on Personal Communication* (eds. STEVEN J. SHAW AND JOSEPH W. THOMPSON). New York: Holt, Rinehart and Winston, 1960.

VON FANGE, EUGENE. *Professional Creativity.* Englewood Cliffs, N.J.: Prentice-Hall, Inc., 1959.

WARNER, W., AND ABBEGGLEN, J. C. *Big Business Leaders in America.* New York: Harper & Bros., 1955.

## CHAPTER 16

ADLER, LEE. "Phasing Research Into the Marketing Plan," *Harvard Business Review*, Vol. XXXVIII (May, 1960), pp. 113–22.

BALES, R. F. "How People Interact in Conferences," *Scientific American*, Vol. CXCII (March, 1955).

BAVELAS, ALEX. "Communication Patterns in Task Oriented Groups," in LASSWELL, H., AND LERNER, D., *The Policy Sciences.* Stanford, California: Stanford University Press, 1951.

BOWER, JOSEPH L. "The Role of Conflict in Economic Decision-Making Groups: Some Empirical Results," *Journal of Economics* (May, 1965), pp. 263–77.

CHASE, STUART. *Roads to Agreement.* New York: Harper & Bros., 1951.

CARTWRIGHT, D., AND ZANDER, A. (eds.). *Group Dynamics.* Evanston, Illinois: Row, Peterson and Company, 1953.

DAVIS, ROBERT TYRRELL. *Performance and Development of Field Sales Managers.* Boston: Division of Research, Graduate School of Business Administration, Harvard University, 1957.

GARDNER, BURLEIGH B., AND MOORE, DAVID G. *Human Relations in Industry.* Homewood, Illinois: Richard D. Irwin, Inc., 1955.

GLANZER, M., AND GLASER, R. *Techniques for the Study of Team Structure and Behavior*, Part II. Pittsburgh: American Institute for Research, 1957.

HARE, A. PAUL, BALES, R. F., AND BORGATTA, E. F. (eds.). *Small Groups.* New York: Alfred A. Knopf, 1955.

HENRY, W. E. "The Business Executive: The Psychodynamics of a Social Role," *American Journal of Sociology*, Vol. 54 (1949), pp. 286–91.

HOMANS, GEORGE C. *The Human Group*. New York: Harcourt, Brace & Co., 1950.

LEABITT, HAROLD J. *Managerial Psychology*, p. 327. Chicago: The University of Chicago Press, 1958.

LOMBARD, GEORGE F. F. *Behavior in a Selling Group: A Case Study of Interpersonal Relations in a Department Store*. Boston: Harvard Business School, Division of Research, 1955.

LORSH, JAY W., AND LAWRENCE, PAUL R. "Organizing for Product Innovation," *Harvard Business Review* (January–February, 1965), pp. 109–22.

MORSE, LEON, "The Sound of a Different Drummer," *Dun's Review and Modern Industry* (August, 1963), p. 26.

MURRAY, THOMAS J. "New Man in Selling," *Dun's Review and Modern Industry* (February, 1965), pp. 38–40.

RIESMAN, DAVID ET AL. *The Lonely Crowd*. New Haven: Yale University Press, 1950.

ROETHLISBERGER, F. J. *Human Relations for Management*. New York: Harper & Bros., 1956.

SHARTLE, CARROLL L. *Executive Performance and Leadership*. New York: Prentice-Hall, Inc., 1956.

TEAD, ORDWAY. *The Art of Leadership*. New York: McGraw-Hill Book Co., Inc., 1945.

ZALEZNIK, A. *Worker Satisfaction and Development: A Case Study of Work and Social Behavior in a Factory Group*. Boston: Harvard Business School, Division of Research, 1956.

# CHAPTER 17

ASPLEY, JOHN CAMERON (ed.). *The Dartnell Sales Promotion Handbook*, p. 1053. Chicago: Dartnell Corp., 1964.

BURY, CHARLES. "Tips on Telephone Techniques That Build Sales and Good Will," *Sales Management* (March 15, 1957), pp. 120–22.

DIX, ARTHUR H. "Measuring Ad Impact with Mail Surveys," *Industrial Marketing* (March, 1965), pp. 61–63.

"Experts Advise Salesmen on How to Use the Telephone to Increase Their Sales," *Printers' Ink* (December 20, 1957), p. 30.

GARRETT, WILLIAM A. *Phonemanship*, p. 301. New York: Farrar, Straus, & Cudahy, 1959.

GREGORY, C. V. "What Do You Do With Inquiries?" *Sales Management* (October 3, 1958), p. 123.

HODGSON, RICHARD S. (ed.). *The Dartnell Direct Mail and Mail Order Handbook*, p. 1092. Chicago: Dartnell Corp., 1964.

"How Mail Helps Print Ads Sell," *Printers' Ink* (March 17, 1961), pp. 50–51.

Hoyt, Homer. "Recent Distortions of the Classical Models of Urban Structure," *Land Economics* (May, 1964), pp. 198–212.

Kirkpatrick, C. A. *Advertising*, pp. 384–404. Cincinnati: South-Western Publishing Company, 1959.

Mauheim, Ferd. *Business Letters That Turn Inquiries Into Sales*. Englewood Cliffs, N.J.: Prentice-Hall, Inc., 1957.

Mayer, Edward N., Jr. *How to Make More Money With Your Direct Mail*. New York: Printers' Ink Publishing Co., Inc., 1953.

"Media Spotlight on Major Appliances," *Merchandising Week* (June 14, 1965), pp. 13–16.

Murray, Bruce W. "Test Market by Mail and Save," *Media/scope* (September, 1964), pp. 105–8.

"Seven Ways to Build Sales With A Telephone," *Management Methods* (October, 1958), pp. 57–60.

"Telephone Selling Comes to Industry," *Industrial Marketing* (November, 1956), pp. 44–46.

"Who's for Mail Order?" *Economist* (March 27, 1965), pp. 1406–7.

"A Portfolio of Award-Winning Sales Letters," *Portfolio of 1965 Selling Plans*, sec. 4, pp. 140–55. New York: Sales Management, Inc., 1965.

# CHAPTER 18

Aspley, J. C. *Getting Better Interviews*. Chicago: Dartnell Corp., 1947.

Bettger, Frank. *How I Raised Myself from Failure to Success in Selling*, chaps. 25–27. Englewood Cliffs, N.J.: Prentice-Hall, Inc., 1949.

Breen, G. E., Thompson, R. B., and West, Harry. *Effective Selling*, pp. 68–75. New York: Harper & Bros., 1950.

Canfield, Bertrand R. *Salesmanship Practices and Problems*, chaps. 2, 4, and 7. New York: McGraw-Hill Book Co., Inc., 1958.

Greif, Edwin Charles. *Modern Salesmanship Principles and Problems*, chaps. 9 and 10. Englewood Cliffs, N.J.: Prentice-Hall, Inc., 1958.

Gross, Alfred. *Salesmanship*, chaps. 7–9. New York: Ronald Press Co., 1959.

Husband, R. W. *The Psychology of Successful Selling*. New York: Harper & Bros., 1953.

Hummel, Francis E. "Pinpointing Prospects for Industrial Sales, *Journal of Marketing* (July, 1960), pp. 26–31.

Lapp, C. L. *Successful Selling Strategies*. New York: McGraw-Hill Book Co., Inc., 1957.

Lewis, C. W. (ed.). *Essentials of Selling*, chap. 3. 2d ed. Englewood Cliffs, N.J.: Prentice-Hall, Inc., 1952.

Letterman, E. G. *Personal Power Through Creative Selling*, Part II. New York: Harper & Bros., 1955.

Pederson, C. A., and Wright, M. D. *Salesmanship: Principles and Methods*, chap. xi. 4th ed. Homewood, Illinois: Richard D. Irwin, Inc., 1966.

ROTH, CHARLES B. *How to Find and Qualify Prospects and Get Interviews.* New York: Prentice-Hall, Inc., 1954.

RUSSELL, FREDERIC A., BEACH, FRANK H., AND BUSKIRK, RICHARD H. *Textbook of Salesmanship.* 7th ed. New York: McGraw-Hill Book Co., Inc., 1963.

SAWYER, HOWARD G. "Your Best Prospects: Your Present Customers!" *Sales Management* (September 18, 1959), p. 82.

———— "Sighting the 20% That Buy 80%," *Sales Management* (April 15, 1960), pp. 123–26.

SHAW, S. J., AND THOMPSON, J. W. (eds.). *Salesmanship: Modern Viewpoints on Personal Communication.* New York: Holt, Rinehart and Winston, 1960.

"64% of Industrial Calls Are On the Wrong Men," *Sales Management* (February 6, 1959), pp. 53–56.

WHITING, PERCY H. *The Five Great Problems of Salesmen and How to Solve Them,* p. 291. New York: McGraw-Hill Book Co., Inc., 1964.

# CHAPTER 19

"Audio-Visual Selling Devices," *Printers' Ink* (August 23, 1957), pp. 384–85.

"Back Up Your Salesmen With Experts," *Sales Management* (April 1, 1960), pp. 83–84.

BETTGER, FRANK. *How I Raised Myself from Failure to Success in Selling,* chaps. 14–19. Englewood Cliffs, N.J.: Prentice-Hall, Inc., 1949.

BLACK, VIRGINIA, BLACK AND PERCY. "Why Flip Charts Flop," *Sales Management* (September 20, 1957), pp. 144–46.

CORTRIGHT, RUPERT L., AND HINDS, GEORGE L. *Creative Discussion,* pp. 89–103. New York: Macmillan Co., 1959.

CURREY, N. S. "Show Them With Visual Aids," *American Business* (December, 1958), pp. 18–20.

DE JEON, JEAN. "In Defense of Flip Charts," *Sales Management* (December 6, 1957), pp. 93–94.

DUNCAN, JOHN E. "Should You Illustrate Your Talks?" *Sales Management* (June 7, 1957), pp. 52–56.

GROSS ALFRED. *Salesmanship,* chap. 13. New York: Ronald Press Co., 1959.

HEGARTY, ED. J. *Get the Prospect to Help You Sell.* New York: McGraw-Hill Book Co., Inc., 1959.

"How Sound-Slides Help Sell Mutual Funds," *Salesweek* (October 31, 1960), pp. 18–19.

"Industrial Sales Call—By Hi Fi," *Sales Management* (April 21, 1961), pp. 119–20.

KIRKPATRICK, CHARLES A. *Salesmanship,* chap. 14. Cincinnati: South-Western Publishing Co., 1956.

O'NEILL, J. R. "Why Visualize at All?" *Sales Management* (September 19, 1958), p. 33.

PEDERSON, CARLTON A., AND WRIGHT, MILBURN D. *Salesmanship Principles and Methods*, chap. 12. 4th ed. Homewood, Illinois: Richard D. Irwin, Inc., 1966.

POWERS, DAVID GUY. "The Sales Psychology Behind Demonstrations," *American Salesman* (March, 1959), p. 90.

WHITING, PERCY H. *The Five Great Problems of Salesmen and How to Solve Them*, p. 291. New York: McGraw-Hill Book Co., Inc., 1964.

WILLIAMS, M. C. "Say It With Pictures (on 35-mm. slides)," *Sales Management* (March 20, 1959), pp. 121–25.

# CHAPTER 20

ARNOLD, RAY H. *How to Overcome Objections in Selling Real Estate.* Englewood Cliffs, N.J.: Prentice-Hall, Inc., 1955.

BOWER, DANIEL. "Everybody Seems Grumpy These Days," *American Salesman* (July, 1958), p. 81.

CALDWELL, E. B. "Have You Tried Selling Profits?" *Sales Management* (August 21, 1959), pp. 52–53.

CANFIELD, BERTRAND R. *Salesmanship: Practices and Problems*, chap. x. New York: McGraw-Hill Book Co., Inc., 1958.

GREIF, EDWIN CHARLES. *Modern Salesmanship*, chap. xii. Englewood Cliffs, N.J.: Prentice-Hall, Inc., 1958.

GROSS, ALFRED. *Salesmanship*, chap. 14. New York: Ronald Press Co., 1959.

HEGARTY, ED. J. *Get the Prospect to Help You Sell.* New York: McGraw-Hill Book Co., Inc., 1959.

KIRKPATRICK, C. A. *Salesmanship: Helping Prospects Buy*, chap. 15. 2d ed. Cincinnati: South-Western Publishing Co., Inc., 1956.

LAPP, C. L. *Successful Selling Strategies.* New York: McGraw-Hill Book Co., Inc., 1957.

LEWIS, C. W. (ed.). *Essentials of Selling*, chap. 8. 2d ed. Englewood Cliffs, N.J.: Prentice-Hall, Inc., 1952.

PEDERSON, C. A., AND WRIGHT, M. D. *Salesmanship: Principles and Methods*, chap. 13. 4th ed. Homewood, Illinois: Richard D. Irwin, Inc., 1966.

POLLOCK, T. "How to Sell the Prospect Who Wants to Think It Over," *Management Methods* (May, 1959), pp. 44–46.

"Prospect Won't Buy? Try Leasing," *Salesweek* (August 8, 1960), pp. 23–24.

"Reciprocity," *Sales Management* (May 20, 1960), pp. 40–44.

ROSENBLOOM, IRVING J. "What's Your Prospect Afraid Of?" *Sales Management* (May 3, 1957), pp. 54–58.

ROTH, C. B. *Professional Salesmanship*, chap. 15. New York: McGraw-Hill Book Co., Inc., 1949.

RUSSELL, FREDERIC A., AND BEACH, FRANK HERMAN. *Textbook of Salesmanship*, chaps. 13–14. 7th ed. New York: McGraw-Hill Book Co., Inc., 1963.

SORBY, E. CARL. "Help People Overcome Obstacles to Buying," *American Salesman* (July, 1958), p. 81.

WHITING, PERCY H. *The Five Great Problems of Salesmen and How to Solve Them*, Part I, p. 291. New York: McGraw-Hill Book Co., Inc., 1964.

# CHAPTER 21

ARNOLD, RAY. *How to Close in Selling Homes*. New York: Prentice-Hall, Inc., 1953.

ASPLEY, JOHN CAMERON (ed.). *The Dartnell Sales Promotion Handbook*. 4th ed. Chicago: Dartnell Corp., 1964.

BERMAN, EDWARD. *Successful Low Pressure Salesmanship*. Englewood Cliffs, N.J.: Prentice-Hall, Inc., 1957.

BREEN, G. E., THOMPSON, R. B., AND WEST, HARRY. *Effective Selling*, chap. ix. New York: Harper & Bros., 1950.

BRUEGGEMANN, E. "Close That Sale," *Office Appliances* (January, 1958), p. 29.

CANFIELD, BERTRAND R. *Salesmanship: Practices and Problems*, chap. xi. New York: McGraw-Hill Book Co., Inc., 1958.

GREIF, EDWIN CHARLES. *Modern Salesmanship*, pp. 303–19. Englewood Cliffs, N.J.: Prentice-Hall, Inc., 1958.

GROSS, ALFRED. *Salesmanship*, chap. xv. New York: Ronald Press Co., 1959.

IVEY, P. W., AND HORVATH, W. *Successful Salesmanship*, chap. xxvi. 3rd ed. Englewood Cliffs, N.J.: Prentice-Hall, Inc., 1953.

KIRKPATRICK, CHARLES A. *Salesmanship*, chap. xvi. Cincinnati: South-Western Publishing Co., 1956.

LEWIS, E. W. (ed.). *Essentials of Selling*, chap. ix. 2d ed. Englewood Cliffs, N.J.: Prentice-Hall, Inc., 1952.

MINNICK, WAYNE C. *The Art of Persuasion*, Boston: Houghton Mifflin Co., 1957.

MOOCK, H. G. "There Is a Knack to Closing a Sale," *American Business* (August, 1957), p. 17.

PEDERSON, C. A., AND WRIGHT, M. D. *Salesmanship: Principles and Methods*, chap. 14. 4th ed. Homewood, Illinois: Richard D. Irwin, Inc., 1966.

POLLOCK, T. "How to Ask for an Order and Get It," *Management Methods* (December, 1959), pp. 51–53.

ROTH, C. B. *Professional Salesmanship*, chap. xvi. New York: McGraw-Hill Book Co., Inc., 1949.

——— *Secrets of Closing Sales*. Englewood Cliffs, N.J.: Prentice-Hall, Inc., 1940.

RUSSELL, FREDERIC A., AND BEACH, FRANK HERMAN. *Textbook of Salesmanship*, pp. 303–19. Englewood Cliffs, N.J.: Prentice-Hall, Inc., 1958.

TRALINS, ROBERT S. *How to Be a Power Closer in Selling*, p. 227. Englewood Cliffs, N.J.: Prentice-Hall, Inc., 1960.

WHITING, PERCY H. *The Five Great Problems of Salesmen and How to Solve Them*, p. 291. New York: McGraw-Hill Book Co., Inc., 1964.

WILSON, JOHN M. *Open the Mind and Close the Sale*. New York: McGraw-Hill Book Co., Inc., 1953.

# CHAPTER 22

ANGLIN, F. W. "Cues for Salesmen Confronted with Prospects' Poor Credit," *Sales Management* (October 19, 1956), pp. 62–64.

ASPLEY, JOHN CAMERON (ed.). *The Dartnell Sales Promotion Handbook*. 4th ed. Chicago: Dartnell Corp., 1964.

BENNETT, C. E. "How to Sell Higher Prices—At a Profit," *Sales Management* (April 19, 1957), pp. 78–80.

CALDWELL, E. B. "Have You Tried Selling Profits?" *Sales Management* (August 21, 1959), pp. 52–53.

CANFIELD, BERTRAND R. *Salesmanship, Practices and Problems*, pp. 378–417. New York: McGraw-Hill Book Co., Inc., 1958.

COLE, ROBERT H., AND HANCOCK, ROBERT S. *Consumer and Commercial Credit Management*, pp. 183–360. Homewood, Illinois: Richard D. Irwin, Inc., 1960.

GREIF, EDWIN CHARLES. *Modern Salesmanship: Principles and Problems*, pp. 63–71. Englewood Cliffs, N.J.: Prentice-Hall, Inc., 1958.

HEGARTY, EDWARD J. (ed.). *Your Price Is Too High*. Chicago: The Dartnell Corp., 1960.

"How to Fight Price-Cutting," *Sales Management* (February 17, 1961), pp. 40–41.

"Is Your Credit Man a Member of Your Sales Team?" *Sales Management* (January 18, 1957), pp. 42–46.

KINTNER, EARL K. *An Antitrust Primer*, p. 316. New York: Macmillan Co., 1964.

OXENFELDT, ALFRED R. *Pricing for Marketing Executives*. San Francisco: Wadsworth Publishing Co., Inc., 1961.

PEDERSON, C. A., AND WRIGHT, M. D. *Salesmanship: Principles and Methods*, chap. 7. 4th ed. Homewood, Illinois: Richard D. Irwin, Inc., 1966.

PHILLIPS, CHARLES F., AND DUNCAN, DELBERT J. *Marketing: Principles and Methods*, pp. 682–757. Rev. ed. Homewood, Illinois: Richard D. Irwin, Inc., 1960.

POLLOCK, T. "How to Convince the Prospect That Your Price Is Right," *Management Methods* (June, 1959), pp. 42–44.

ROBBINS, W. DAVID. "A Marketing Appraisal of the Robinson-Patman Act," *Journal of Marketing* (July, 1959), pp. 15–21.

ROTH, C. B. *Finding the Prospect and Getting the Interview*, chap. vi. Englewood Cliffs, N.J.: Prentice-Hall, Inc., 1946.

Wood, Joseph L. *Better Sales Through Credit*, p. 163. New York: Vantage Press, Inc., 1954.

# CHAPTER 23

Aspley, John Cameron. *The Dartnell Sales Promotion Handbook*, p. 1053. 4th ed. Chicago: Dartnell Corp., 1964.

Bender, James F. "Little Things Are the Hallmark of the Great Salesman," *Sales Management* (March 6, 1959), pp. 46–50.

"Business Gifts and Awards for Christmas and All the Year, *Sales Management* (September 10, 1960).

Canfield, Bertrand R. *Salesmanship: Practices and Problems*, pp. 519–63. New York: McGraw-Hill Book Co., Inc., 1958.

Cumming, James C. "Some Plain Talk About the Cooperative Advertising Mess," *Sales Management* (March 25, 1957), pp. 56–58.

"Easy Way to Analyze Industrial Sales," *Portfolio of 1965* Selling Plans, pp. 158–60. New York: Sales Management, Inc. 1964.

Gross, Alfred. *Sales Promotion*. New York: Ronald Press Co., 1961.

Hodgson, Richard S. (ed.). *The Dartnell Direct Mail and Mail Order Handbook*, p. 1092. Chicago: Dartnell Corp., 1964.

"How to Get Retailers to Use Your P-O-P Displays," *Sales Management* (March 4, 1960), pp. 93–100.

Kirkpatrick, Charles A. *Salesmanship*, pp. 505–52. Cincinnati: South-Western Publishing Co., 1956.

Lewis, C. W. (ed.). *Essentials of Selling*, chaps. 15–17. 2d ed. Englewood Cliffs, N.J.: Prentice-Hall, Inc., 1952.

Nystrom, P. H. (ed.). *Marketing Handbook*, chap. xii. New York: Ronald Press Co., 1948.

Pederson, C. A., and Wright, M. D. *Salesmanship: Principles and Methods*, chap. 15. 4th ed. Homewood, Illinois: Richard D. Irwin, Inc., 1966.

*Printers' Ink* (Editors and Contributors). *Sales Promotion Idea Book*. New York: Funk & Wagnalls Co., 1950.

"Service: The Secret to Sales Success," *Salesweek* (August 22, 1960), pp. 23–24.

Simmons, Harry. *Successful Sales Promotion*. Englewood Cliffs, N.J.: Prentice-Hall, Inc., 1950.

Turner, Howard M., Jr. *Sales Promotion That Gets Results*. New York: McGraw-Hill Book Co., Inc. 1959.

Weiss, E. B. "Message to Salesmen About Retail Ad Tie-ups," *Advertising Age* (October 12, 1959), p. 97.

Whiting, Percy H. *The Five Great Problems of Salesmen And How To Solve Them*, p. 291. New York: McGraw-Hill Book Co., Inc., 1964.

Wilson, Aubrey. "What Is Your Company's Image?" *Manager* (November, 1964), pp. 40–41.

# CHAPTER 24

Asch, S. E. *Social Psychology*. New York: Prentice-Hall, Inc., 1952.

Bauer, Raymond A. "Limits of Persuasion," *Harvard Business Review*, Vol. 36, No. 5, pp. 105–110.

Berelson, Bernard, Lazarsfeld, Paul F., and McPhee, William N. *Voting: A Study of Opinion Formation in a Presidential Campaign*. Chicago: University of Chicago Press, 1954.

Brown, Roger. *Words and Things*, p. 398. New York: The Free Press of Glencoe, 1958.

Coffin, T. E. *The Hofstra Study: A Measure of the Sales Effectiveness of Television Advertising*. New York: NBC Research Division, 1950.

Doob, L. "Goebbels' Principles of Propaganda," *Public Opinion Quarterly*, Vol. 14 (1950), pp. 419–42.

Herz, M. F. "Some Psychological Lessons from Leaflet Propaganda in World War II," *Public Opinion Quarterly*, Vol 13: (1949), pp. 471–86.

Hovland, C. I., Lumsdaine, A. A., and Sheffield, F. D. *Experiments on Mass Communication*, Vol. III. Princeton, N.J.: Princeton University Press, 1949.

Hyman, H. H., and Sheatsley, P. B. "Some Reasons Why Information Campaigns Fail," *Public Opinion Quarterly*, Vol. 11 (1947), pp. 412–23.

Kris, E., and Speier, H. *German Radio Propaganda: Report on Home Broadcasts During the War*. London: Oxford University Press, 1944.

Lazarsfeld, P. F., and Kendall, Patricia L. *Radio Listening in America*. New York: Prentice-Hall, Inc., 1948.

Lazarsfeld, Paul F., Berelson, Bernard, and Gaudet, Hazel. *The People's Choice*. New York: Columbia University Press, 1948.

Leavitt, Harold J. *Managerial Psychology*, p. 327. 1st Phoenix ed. Chicago: University of Chicago Press, 1962.

Lee, A. M. *How to Understand Propaganda*. New York: Rinehart, 1952.

Lewis, Helen B. "Studies in the Principles of Judgments and Attitudes: IV. The Operation of Prestige Suggestion," *Journal of Social Psychology*, Vol. 14 (1941), pp. 229–56.

Merton, R. K., assisted by Marjorie Fiske and Alberta Curtis. *Mass Persuasion*. New York: Harper & Bros., 1946.

Phifer, Gregg. "Propaganda and Critical Listening," *Journal of Communication* (May, 1953).

Reik, Theodor. *Listening with the Third Ear*. New York: Farrar, Straus & Co., 1949.

Rogers, Carl R., and Roethlisberger, R. J. "Barriers and Gateways to Communication," *Harvard Business Review*, Vol. xxx (July–August, 1952).

Schank, R. L., and Goodman, Charles. "Reactions to Propaganda on Both Sides of a Controversial Issue," *Public Opinion Quarterly*, Vol. III (1939), 107–12.

SHERIF, M. "An Experimental Study of Stereotypes," *Journal of Abnormal and Social Psychology*, Vol. 7 (1935), pp. 386–402.

SMITH, BRUCE LANNES. "Propaganda Analysis and the Science of Democracy," *Public Opinion Quarterly*, Vol. 5 (1941), pp. 250–59.

LASSWELL, H. D., AND CASEY, R. D. *Propaganda, Communication, and Public Opinion: A Comprehensive Reference Guide.* Princeton, N.J.: Princeton University Press, 1946.

# CHAPTER 25

BARRINGTON, ARTHUR R. "How to Help Your Salesmen Plan Their Travels Better," *Portfolio of 1965 Selling Plans*, p. 160. New York: Sales Management, Inc., 1964.

BERMAN, EDWARD. *Successful Low Pressure Salesmanship.* Englewood Cliffs, N.J.: Prentice-Hall, Inc., 1957.

CANFIELD, BERTRAND R. *Salesmanship: Practices and Problems*, chap. 13. New York: McGraw-Hill Book Co., Inc., 1958.

CASWELL, W. CAMERON. "Marketing Effectiveness and Sales Supervision," *California Management Review* (Fall, 1964), pp. 39–44.

CHEIT, EARL F. "Why Managers Cultivate Social Responsibility," *California Management Review* (Fall, 1964), pp. 3–22.

"The Complete Guide to Cutting Field Selling Costs," *Sales Management* (January 6, 1961), p. 37.

COX, REAVIS; in association with GOODMAN, CHARLES S., AND FICHANDLER, THOMAS C., *Distribution in a High-Level Economy*, p. 331. Englewood Cliffs, N.J.: Prentice-Hall, Inc., 1965.

DEVOE, J. *Effective Self-Management in Selling*, Englewood Cliffs, N.J.: Prentice-Hall, Inc., 1956.

DOOR, WILLIAM C. "The 'Sales Acres' Approach to Managing Sales Territories," *Portfolio of 1965 Selling Plans*, p. 166. New York: Sales Management, Inc., 1964.

GROSS, ALFRED. *Salesmanship*, chap. 20. New York: Ronald Press Co., 1959.

HEGARTY, EDWARD J. *Get the Prospect to Help You Sell.* New York: McGraw-Hill Book Co., Inc., 1959.

HAMILTON, HERBERT A., JR. "70% of Industrial Sales Calls Are Ineffective and Worthless," *Sales Management* (April 5, 1957), pp. 82–87.

HIMLER, LEONARD E. " 'R.S.V.P.': A Formula for Maintaining Happy and Productive Salesmen," *Portfolio of 1965 Selling Plans*, p. 128. New York: Sales Management, Inc., 1964.

KATZ, H. *How to Make the Most of Your Sales Territory.* Englewood Cliffs, N.J.: Prentice-Hall, Inc., 1957.

LOEN, RAYMOND O. "How Do You Build 'Want-to' Attitudes in Salesmen?" *Portfolio of 1965 Selling Plans*, p. 136. New York: Sales Management, Inc., 1964.

Nevis, Edwin C. "What Makes Your Salesmen Sell?" *Portfolio of 1965 Selling Plans*. New York: Sales Management, Inc., 1964, pp. 123–28.

Pederson, C. A., and Wright, M. D. *Salesmanship: Principles and Methods*, chap. 18. 4th ed. Homewood, Illinois: Richard D. Irwin, Inc., 1966.

Russell, Frederic A., and Beach, Frank H. *Textbook of Salesmanship*, chap. 18. New York: McGraw-Hill Book Co., Inc., 1959.

Semlow, Walter J. "How Many Salesmen Do You Need?" *Harvard Business Review* (May–June, 1959), pp. 126–32.

"Sighting the 20% That Buy 80%," *Portfolio of 1965 Selling Plans*, pp. 156–58. New York: Sales Management, Inc., 1964.

Stanton, William J., and Buskirk, Richard H. *Management of the Sales Force*, chaps. 17–19. Rev. ed. Homewood, Illinois: Richard D. Irwin, 1964.

Whiting, Percy H. *The Five Great Problems of Salesmen And How To Solve Them*. New York: McGraw-Hill Book Co., Inc., 1964, Part I.

# CHAPTER 26

Adams, Velma. "The Forgotten Sales Manager," *Dun's Review and Modern Industry* (March, 1965), pp. 45–46.

———— "The Rise of the Trade Relations Director," *Dun's Review and Modern Industry* (December, 1964), pp. 35–36.

Backman, Jules. "How Your Competition Will Change," *Nation's Business* (February, 1965), pp. 38–39.

Burck, Gilbert. "Will the Computer Outwit Man?" *Fortune* (October, 1964), pp. 120–21, 162 ff.

"Color as a Merchandising Tool," *Chain Store Age* (March, 1965), pp. E26–29.

Cyert, Richard M., and Dill, William R. "The Future of Business Education," *Journal of Business* (July, 1964), pp. 221–37.

Ellis, Mary Jane. "Spending Patterns Over the Life Cycle," *42nd Annual Agricultural Outlook Conference*. Consumer and Food Economics Research Division, U.S. Dept. of Agriculture. Washington, D.C., November 17, 1964.

Ferrell, Robert W. *Customer-Oriented Planning*, p. 253. New York: American Management Association, 1964.

Hess, Eckhard H. "Attitude and Pupil Size," *Scientific American* (April, 1965), pp. 46–54.

Johnson, Arno H. "Background of Progress and Planning," *The International Advertiser* (September, 1964), pp. 14–16, 22.

Kahn, George N., and Shuchman, Abraham. "Specialize Your Salesmen!" *Harvard Business Review* (January–February, 1961), pp. 90–98.

Katona, George. *The Mass Consumption Society*, p. 343. New York: McGraw-Hill Book Co., Inc., 1964.

Kepner, Charles H., and Tregoe, Benjamin B. *The Rational Manager: A*

*Systematic Approach to Problem Solving and Decision Making*, p. 275. New York: McGraw-Hill Book Co., Inc., 1965.

KRAMER, ROLAND L. *International Marketing*, p. 651. 2d ed. Cincinnati: South-Western Publishing Co., 1964.

LESSING, LAWRENCE. "Synthetics Ride Hell-Bent for Leather," *Fortune* (November, 1964), pp. 172–75, 180 ff.

MALTZ, MAXWELL. *The Magic Power of Self Image Psychology*, p. 216. Englewood Cliffs, N.J.: Prentice-Hall, Inc., 1964.

MILES, LAWRENCE D. Techniques of Value Analysis and Engineering, p. 267. New York: McGraw-Hill Book Co., Inc., 1961.

"The New Breed of Salesman—Not Like Willy," Spotlight On Business, *Newsweek* (October 5, 1964), pp. 94–99.

NICHOLS, RALPH G., AND STEVENS, LEONARD A. *Are You Listening?* p. 235. New York: McGraw-Hill Book Co., Inc., 1957.

"Participation: Key to Profits Abroad," *Business Abroad and Export Trade* (September 7, 1964), pp. 28–30.

"Preview of Your Markets in '75," *Nation's Business* (November, 1964), pp. 66–88.

ROPER, ELMO. "Advertising in the 1970's," *Saturday Review* (February 13, 1965), pp. 74–75.

ROSEN, GERALD R. "Is There a New Economy?" *Dun's Review and Modern Industry* (June, 1965), pp. 38–41, 71 ff.

SOMMERS, ALBERT T. "The Economic Environment of the Middle Sixties," *Conference Board Record* (September, 1964).

TAYLOR, THAYER C. "Fewer Salesmen, Bigger Paychecks," *Sales Management* (January 1, 1965).

TOFFLER, ALVIN. *The Culture Consumers: A Study of Art and Affluence in America*, p. 263. New York: St. Martin's Press, 1964.

WELLES, JOHN G., AND WATERMAN, ROBERT H., JR. "Space Technology: Pay-Off from Spin-Off," *Harvard Business Review* (July–August, 1964), pp. 106–118.

# QUESTIONS AND PROBLEMS

# CHAPTER I

1. Which component of the marketing mix is most important? Explain.
2. Is it possible for a company to market its products without any personal selling? Under what conditions might this be so?
3. "Advertising is a less expensive, faster, and easier way to reach a mass market and should be substituted for personal salesmen." Discuss the implications of this statement.
4. "We make the best product man has devised so the product should easily sell itself." Discuss the ideas behind this concept.
5. "Personal salesmen are parasitic and an economic waste because they do not produce or create anything." Evaluate this criticism.
6. "The customer in our economy historically has exercised the freedom of choice to accept or reject products and services according to his needs or desires." Should personal selling be permitted to influence his choice? Why?
7. Do you believe "the customer is always right?" What qualifications, if any, would you put on your own concept of selling?
8. Is it wise to make people dissatisfied with their present status or standard of living? Explain.
9. What can advertising accomplish better than personal selling? How?
10. How do utility companies market their services? What is their product, in the broad sense?
11. "The needs and wants of modern economic man are virtually insatiable. Two-thirds of the world's population is in dire need of the basic necessities of life." If this is true, what function can salesmen serve?
12. Critics of business frequently charge that business is selfishly motivated for higher and higher profit without heed to public benefit. What is your reaction?
13. What have psychologists and sociologists contributed to marketing that might be applicable for personal selling?
14. Do you believe it is possible for vending machines and "talking computers" to eliminate personal selling? Where are they apt to make their greatest inroads?
15. How can personal selling help meet the challenge of imported goods?
16. How do consumers decide on filling their needs? Do you think the same way?
17. Have economic conditions changed in the past 50 years to effect the difficulty of personal selling? How?
18. How has research and development affected selling since World War II?
19. Are new auto models every year good for the people of the United States? Discuss your views.
20. Should drug companies be permitted to make a profit on such essential items as polio vaccine? Explain your views.

21. What alternates to personal selling might a supplier consider to market his goods? Evaluate the alternatives for marketing office furniture.

22. What is the basic difference between reliability and validity as applied to the relating of one's own experiences?

23. How can the art of selling be made more of a social science?

24. Is customer loyalty reliable? Give illustrations of your viewpoint.

25. Are businessmen heading toward a profession or are they simply satisfying their own selfish desires?

# CHAPTER 2

1. What qualifications are likely to be found in experienced salesmen that a new salesman is not apt to have?
2. How might the basic qualifications for selling the same product vary from manufacturer's representative to wholesaler to retailer? Illustrate with a product with which you are familiar.
3. Does applying for a job differ from selling a service to an executive in a business? Illustrate.
4. Frequently qualifications required by sales managers for new applicants screen out some better men. What requirements seem too high? Why?
5. Does success in other occupations indicate a similarity of qualifications with success in selling?
6. Changing economic conditions influence sales volume for many industries. How will economic conditions influence industrial salesmen in the next decade?
7. Compare the qualifications you think are desirable for a job selling corrugated paper boxes to food packers as opposed to a job selling proprietary drugs to a drugstore.
8. What requirements would you set for men to sell a highly complex scientific computer? Explain.
9. Can the average man learn to sell industrial products? In what areas would he be strongest and in what areas would he be weakest?
10. Do you believe an effective salesman is really a "loner" or a lone wolf? Explain.
11. What areas of the selling job appeal to you the most and what areas seem most distasteful?
12. How can an effective salesman use his talents and skills to help improve his community?
13. Prepare a list of your qualifications as they would seem most attractive to a wholesaler of hardware.
14. Cut out a newspaper ad for "Salesman Wanted" and discuss the listed requirements in relation to what you think the actual job duties would include.
15. Compare two newspaper ads, one for a salesman and one for any office job in relation to requirements and compensation.
16. Describe a sales job which relies primarily upon communication of facts as contrasted to one which relies primarily upon persuasion.
17. How can the skills of an effective salesman aid in his promotion to greater responsibility in management of his company?
18. What college courses seem to be of the most benefit to a career in sales? Explain.
19. How might a college course in salesmanship aid in the self-development of an individual in nonselling occupations?

20. How does one acquire a proper attitude about selling? Illustrate using a specific product.

21. What selling jobs would women be better suited for than men? Why?

22. How might job qualifications differ between selling a product such as a photocopy machine and selling an intangible such as accounting services?

23. Give an illustration of how several different geographic locations might vary the job qualifications for selling the same product.

24. Compare the advantages and disadvantages of a young person in sales as contrasted to an older person in sales.

25. How can a sales applicant determine the actual time, duties, and difficulties of a position outside of the company which is recruiting?

# CHAPTER 3

1. What sales practices have you experienced recently which you felt were offensive or unfair? Explain how this might or might not apply to all salesmen.

2. Many salesmen and consumers still think of a sale as a battle between the buyer and the seller. Is a salesman justified in arguing or verbally fighting with a prospect? Explain.

3. Is it wise for a community to pass ordinances prohibiting soliciting or the sale of merchandise on a door-to-door basis? Explain.

4. In your personal experience, what have the successful salesmen done to earn your trust and confidence? How might this apply to all salesmen?

5. What services might an electric or water company supply to the consumer beyond the physical product?

6. From your personal experience, give an illustration of a courteous listener who completely misunderstood a speaker because the listener was impatient to speak.

7. Illustrate how a receptionist might communicate an unfavorable impression of a visitor to her boss without saying anything that would offend the visitor.

8. List the areas of interest which a salesman and a prospect might genuinely share, excluding the immediate sales proposition.

9. Describe a situation which seems to indicate a psychological fit between two people meeting for the first time. How would you account for their intuitive behavior?

10. Compare a situation in which a hostile prospect is permitted to talk first with a situation in which the salesman attempts to dominate the entire interview.

11. Show how a husband and wife might have honest differences of opinion about buying a new auto which they both agree they need and can afford.

12. Describe a recent argument or difference of opinion you experienced where you later modified or changed your opinion because you subsequently realized the validity of the other fellow's point of view.

13. How can parents attempt to persuade their grade-school children to eat a balanced diet?

14. Illustrate the types of interesting information a dress manufacturer's representative might bring to a retailer beyond the actual selling proposition.

15. Beyond the product application, how can a salesman exhibit sincere interest in the welfare of his prospect? Illustrate with a retail product and an industrial product.

16. What factors do you consider when judging how much of an authority a speaker may be the first one or two times you hear him talk?

17. Illustrate how you might indicate understanding of a speaker's point of view without committing yourself to either agreement or disagreement with his position.

459

18. List at least five things which you have in common with one particular friend and the same number of different things which you have in common with another particular friend. Might this indicate you are insincere?

19. What wants or needs do you think a particular friend has, the satisfaction of which will help him succeed in life? Is he aware of the exact same needs and wants?

20. Illustrate how a person may be blind to his own best interests or to additional ways to solve a personal problem.

21. Illustrate how apparently illogical behavior can be consistent with an individual's personal goal in life.

22. Describe a situation in which a salesman views a problem from the customer's position which is not in accord with his own position.

23. How would you attempt to deal with an individual who is outspokenly prejudiced against your nationality?

24. List, in order of importance, the things which you consider related to building a mature attitude.

25. Illustrate how a young man may be more mature than another ten years his senior.

# CHAPTER 4

1. Visit a local typewriter dealer and ask to see a number of competing brands of portables. Ask about the advantages and disadvantages of each model. How much of the salesmen's product knowledge influenced your opinion and in what manner?

2. What products can you identify that are suffering from indirect competition due to new materials or technological changes in other industries?

3. Illustrate your reactions to a situation when a salesman belittles the competitive brand which you mentioned you were considering.

4. In what ways can a visit to the salesman's own plant be both more or less educational to him than a good company manual or brochure?

5. Describe sources of product information that would be available to you and keep your knowledge current if you were selling office systems.

6. Assume a friend wants to buy your portable radio and he incorrectly assumes it is covered with expensive leather. How can you correct his misunderstanding and still maintain his buying interest?

7. Assume that you are attempting to sell a complicated display stand to a retailer. It is too large to demonstrate and because of telescoping features, it is a difficult idea to explain. How would you attempt to communicate this concept to the prospect?

8. Select a foreign sport or activity which is neither popular nor generally understood in the United States. Assume you want your listener to join you in watching or participating in the activity. Describe how you would communicate this new idea to the listener.

9. Select a product or service with which you are familiar and list the points you would communicate (1) to a prospect very well versed in that area, and (2) to a prospect suddenly aware of his need but with little or no background in that area.

10. Illustrate how two experienced buyers for a trucking firm might have different technical questions for a tire salesman.

11. Illustrate how an inferior camera might be a better buy than an expensive, well-made, fine camera. Illustrate the reverse.

12. List a number of specific ways the phrase "saves money" might be applied to owning a new tape recorder.

13. What limits of a mutual fund should the stock salesman communicate to his prospects? Explain your reasoning.

14. Illustrate how a young packaging salesman can be more of an authority in his specialty field than many of the prospects upon which he will call.

15. What can customers teach the steel shelving salesman to make him more of an authority in his field?

16. What type of marketing information would be of importance to a sales manager thousands of miles away from the salesman in the field?

17. Describe a situation where two printers might honestly and logically evaluate the performance of your printing paper and arrive at entirely different conclusions.

18. What additional information other than price might a buyer consider when analyzing two product offerings which seemed reasonably equal in quality for his purposes?

19. What might be included in analyzing the total cost of a business truck for comparative purposes?

20. What information would you consider essential to make an intelligent buying decision regarding a fire extinguisher for your residence? What additional information might be of interest, although not essential?

21. What factors would be of interest to you as an industrial purchasing agent when considering a new supplier of chemicals if your old supplier went out of business?

22. How does the brand name influence prospects for color television sets? What might the salesman point out about the manufacturer that would influence the prospect's decision?

23. What extra services can a manufacturer of children's wear offer to retailers that handle his line of goods?

24. When should a salesman inform his existing customers of the numerous services his company offers?

25. Select a product with which you are familiar and locate several published articles on the industry trends which will be of interest to customers and prospects. Explain.

# CHAPTER 5

1. Under what conditions is a person most apt to investigate thoroughly, even exhaustively, a proposition before he makes his buying decision?

2. Describe an experience you have had where problem solving dictated your choice of which product to buy.

3. Illustrate how a buyer might gradually learn about various products in one industry and settle down to choosing one line habitually without much conscious thought.

4. Describe your feelings regarding the choice of a restaurant for a special date in a city in which you are a stranger.

5. What products are you personally most apt to buy on impulse and how do you explain such choices?

6. In your experience, what products or services that you have purchased have been chosen primarily by group norms or other person's opinions? Explain.

7. What hidden motives do you think cause some people to buy illicit or forbidden products and services?

8. Illustrate a situation where pure chance might explain your choice of a product or service.

9. How can envy or the respect of others be used to motivate a college student to greater effort?

10. Describe a situation where a businessman's pride might motivate him to invest huge sums of money for nonprofit achievements.

11. Show how a desire to be recognized as an intelligent person can motivate a person to volunteer his services to a charitable organization.

12. Under what conditions is a person most apt to follow recognized leaders in their choice of products or services?

13. Illustrate how the consulting services of college professors can utilize the alleviation of fear as a motivational device to obtain a contract from an industrial concern.

14. Illustrate your choice of motivational appeals to convert an investment in overstocked inventory of water pumps back into usable cash.

15. How would you use the desire to dominate others as a motivational device when selling a forklift truck to a warehouse manager?

16. Illustrate how an appeal can be made to an economic motive for one prospect while an appeal to personal pleasure can be made to a second prospect when selling an accounting service to a businessman.

17. How could you relate the improved glamour of using cosmetics to dollar gains when selling to a man who is office manager?

18. How could you relate a speech course to dollar gains when selling to a charter boat captain?

19. Illustrate how an expensive advertisement in a newspaper might produce greater returns than a less expensive ad in the same paper.

20. What convenience features appeal to you when you are considering the purchase of a radio-phonograph set?

21. What satisfactions would you expect to derive from ownership of a new boat?

22. Show how the sale of cameras could be promoted in ten or more different departments of an exclusive department store.

23. Illustrate how dependability might be of interest to a prospect considering the purchase of a plain wood pencil.

24. Select a product or service with which you are familiar and list ten or more inherent features or built-in qualities. Opposite that list indicate what benefit this would provide to the owner or user of the product or service.

25. Illustrate the difference between buying motives and the basis for making a selection.

# CHAPTER 6

1. Show how three products are acceptable in one part of the United States but not in other parts. Indicate for each product whether this is for physical needs, economic needs, due to habitual buying behavior, or to some other influence.

2. If you planned to establish a set of retail outlets for ski equipment, what marketing information would you desire and where would you obtain the data?

3. How do you think a child being raised as a member of a middle-class family would view his social mobility in later years? How would this vary if he were raised as part of an upper-class family?

4. Illustrate how the effects of social class on individual members of a group vary with: freedom of emotional expression; immediate gratification of needs and wants *vs.* delayed gratification; the types of crime more apt to be committed.

5. How can the furnishings of a person's residence reflect some of his feelings and ambitions in life? Illustrate.

6. Illustrate how mobility can sometimes indicate some of an individual's desires or aspirations in life.

7. Describe the market segment which is sought by two competing businesses and the image each store attempts to create to attract its customer targets.

8. Select a successful businessman whom you know and show how his personality is different from that of another businessman.

9. From your experience select an attitude or opinion which you hold or believe and describe how earlier experiences in life helped to build this belief.

10. Show how it can be very misleading to stereotype an individual businessman because of one outstanding character trait.

11. Describe a successful businessman of your acquaintance and show how he tends to react to certain trying situations in a consistent manner.

12. What do the words "extrovert" and "introvert" mean to you when someone uses them to describe a salesman?

13. How can a person's attitude about sickness indicate something of his earlier learning experiences. Illustrate with a sales situation to predict his behavior.

14. What contradictory feelings or desires does a young man in college have about writing to his parents asking them for money?

15. Do you believe a man past 40 years of age can learn a more tolerant attitude to replace a bias he may hold? Discuss and illustrate.

16. Illustrate what feedback you would look for and expect when selling an executive self-development program to a young man in a junior executive position in business. What information about his background would you like to have and why?

17. Show how packaging materials can help to solve a buyer's desire to become a senior executive yet remain consistent with his organizational role of being an efficient buyer.

18. What immediate circumstances might cause a businessman to be more receptive toward a salesman? Less receptive?

19. Describe a situation which illustrates how the ideas and attitudes a prospect already has will predispose him to behave in a predictable manner toward a new salesman.

20. From what sources can a salesman learn about the predisposition of a particular businessman before he makes his first visit to see the man?

21. List four questions you might ask logically, naturally, and in a friendly way which would be apt to solicit the kind of personal information you seek when with a new prospect.

22. What physical objects in an executive office might tell you something about the nature or personality of the individual? Explain.

23. What jewelry worn by a prospect would be of particular interest to a salesman and how could he use this to obtain additional information about the prospect's predisposition?

24. Discuss the various methods which you might use to get a prospect to disclose his predisposition to you as a salesman.

25. In general terms illustrate how knowledge about a particular prospect's predisposition can be utilized in planning a sales presentation.

# CHAPTER 7

1. Assume you are selling lubricants to industry and represent a small distributor. Describe the buyer and indicate how you would make your request to see him compatible with his predisposition.

2. From your experience, illustrate how someone attempted to persuade you without gaining your trust or confidence in him.

3. Take a poll or survey among your friends and associates asking for the title or the author of the report on smoking and its association with cancer. Compare the results of the responses by smokers *vs.* the responses of nonsmokers.

4. In what trade magazines might you place advertisements to gain selective exposure to each of the following groups:

   1. petroleum engineers
   2. teen-age girls
   3. college professors
   4. retailers of women's wear
   5. packaging designers
   6. corporation presidents?

5. What promises can a salesman offer to justify the time for an interview he is requesting? Illustrate, using a specific product. *Chapter 7 Sell the idea of the interview*

6. What kind of guest speaker is most appealing to you? Are you apt to expose yourself willingly to the opposite type of guest speaker? Explain.

7. Illustrate how a salesman of athletic equipment to colleges might build the athletic director's trust and confidence in the salesman.

8. When a prospect is aware of his need for heating equipment how can the salesman make himself personally believable?

9. In professional football games it is often said the lucky breaks go to the better team that plays hard and forces fumbles and dropped punts. How might this compare to the lucky salesman who always seems to be in the right place at the right time?

10. It has been stated that about 20 percent of the doctors in the Columbus, Ohio, area prescribe about 50 percent of all drugs sold and another 20 percent of the doctors prescribe about 30 percent of the drugs. If you were a detail man selling for a drug company in this area, how might you use the principle of reverse-order prospecting?

11. How can a lucky salesman making three calls per day outsell another salesman making eight to ten calls per day if they have similar experience and similar market potential?

12. When a prospect has a problem and calls in several competing salesmen, what might influence his original selection of the many possible concerns to call?

13. How can a salesman discover a prospect's problem if the prospect himself is not aware of any problem? Illustrate, using a product with which you are familiar.

14. Assume you were selling office calculating machines and your sales audit showed the prospect did not need either replacements or additional machines. Outline your report to him and indicate separately how this report might be a contribution to either immediate or future sales.

15. How can a salesman keep his customers and prospects up to date on their own competitors without violating confidences?

16. Do intelligent businessmen always resist the persuasion attempts of salesmen? Explain and illustrate.

17. "You can fool all of the people some of the time. You can fool some of the people all of the time. But you can't fool all of the people all of the time." How does this philosophy compare with your own regarding the limits of persuasion? Explain.

18. Select a product or service with which you are familiar and compile a list of possible sources of new prospects.

19. Assume you had a list of "suspected" prospective industrial accounts who might use tapered roller bearings in their production machinery. Show how you might learn the identity of the specific individual you should contact.

20. What approach might you use in contacting a list of former customers who are no longer active accounts with your company but now buy from your competitors?

# CHAPTER 8

1. Observe an audience of a televised athletic event such as the World Series, a professional football game, or a boxing match. When there is a close play or decision by a referee notice how violently the audience reacts. One person may agree while another disagrees. Explain this behavior in terms of selective perception.

2. Illustrate how a listener's thoughts on a different subject can easily change the meaning of the speaker's message so that what is perceived by the listener is quite different from what was intended by the speaker.

3. Illustrate several things that might interfere with the verbal transmission of a message.

4. What can a communicator do to overcome noise or other interference to enable his audience to receive a more accurate message?

5. Give two illustrations of business facts being interpreted quite differently by two individuals because of their feelings and emotions rather than economic differences.

6. From your personal experiences illustrate how a threat can interfere with a message so as to distort or completely negate the speaker's intent.

7. How can language or code noise interfere with the transmission of a message? Illustrate.

8. Illustrate how message context can change when passed from Mr. A to Mr. F if the communication must proceed through Mr. B, to Mr. C, to Mr. D before Mr. F hears it.

9. Is it possible for a listener to be so afraid of a speaker that he doesn't hear a message accurately? Illustrate.

10. What advantages can you see in presenting a message in a one-way direction? Illustrate, using a public speaker, a college lecturer, a salesman.

11. What disadvantages can you see in presenting a message in a two-way direction? Again illustrate, using a public meeting, a college seminar, and a sales situation.

12. Illustrate how a salesman might utilize knowledge of a discrepancy between what a prospect is doing and what he would like to be doing.

13. Illustrate how you might handle a situation in which the prospect seemed to have a mental block to any further communications.

14. Most college students experience little difficulty in learning one group of subjects and on the other hand considerable difficulty in learning another group of subjects. Show how this might be caused by the student's attitudes and beliefs before he is exposed to either group.

15. Why do you remember certain books or parts of them yet quickly forget other books completely?

# CHAPTER 9

1. People often have contradictory desires. From your experience, illustrate this concept and show how you resolved the dilemma in a particular situation.

2. If an attack is directed toward a more central part of an individual's self-concept such as his honesty, he is more likely to exhibit defense mechanisms than if attacked in an area where he is not overly concerned, such as his inability to play tennis. Discuss this concept.

3. Illustrate how additional knowledge of a topic caused you to modify or change completely your opinion of that topic.

4. How might adjustment to changing situations or new people cause a young adult to see his own behavior change as in his own best interest? Illustrate.

5. From your own experience show how an individual seemed suddenly to become more expressive and critical of another person because he sensed personal gain.

6. Do you think salesmen should avoid areas of deep ego involvement when talking to prospects? Explain.

7. Using a product or service with which you are familiar, show how opinion changed by revaluing by the same standards, because of one of the four causes of conversion.

8. Using a product or service with which you are familiar, show how opinion changed by new expectations or new standards of evaluating because of one of the four causes of conversion.

9. How might a salesman divert the aggressive behavior of a prospect so that he could maintain an open two-way channel of communication? Illustrate.

10. How might a salesman gain additional interviews with a prospect who seems very interested but claims he does not want to think about that problem now? Illustrate.

11. From your experience, illustrate how you once investigated several products which might serve your needs, decided on one, and have since purchased it again and again with less and less conscious thought.

12. Illustrate how your defenses against persuasion were aroused due to a direct criticism or attack on your beliefs by an aggressive salesperson.

13. Illustrate how a salesman can avoid direct contradictions of a prospect's errors in judgment yet communicate his message in terms acceptable to the prospect.

14. Show how a relatively minor or insignificant attitude can be raised to dominate all others in a particular situation.

15. Do you believe some people are easier for you to persuade than others? Explain in terms of their behavior as well as your own.

16. How do political candidates with approximately the same qualifications for office attempt to gain the voters' favorable opinion? Illustrate with national elections.

17. How can an industrial salesman be persistent yet perfectly acceptable to a prospect in a highly competitive situation? Illustrate.

18. Give an instance in which primary groups influenced your decision to purchase a particular product or service.

19. Illustrate how primary groups can prevent a person from taking an action he might otherwise have taken.

20. Show how a person's life can suddenly become unattractive in his own eyes and cause him to look for new attitudes.

21. Conduct an experiment with a friend who has expressed a *negative* opinion on a particular subject. Try to get him to help you build a *positive* argument on the subject for presentation to a class. Observe his subsequent attitude for modification or change and report the results.

22. Show how a salesman might get a prospect to assume the role of the salesman and favorably demonstrate the product.

# CHAPTER 10

1. Evaluate the human traits of someone you know well. List those combinations which seem to be opposites, such as industry and laziness. Explain the apparent contradiction.

2. Ask two of your friends to evaluate a third party independently and ask the third party to evaluate himself. Compare and explain the discrepancies

3. How might you help a person who has a problem if he does not want your help?

4. What attitude do you think is most responsible in a salesman about to entertain an important prospect? Explain.

5. What is your feeling regarding arguing and bargaining over price when making a purchase? Can you justify the opposite feelings other people may have?

6. When people attempt to change your behavior, apparently for your own benefit, how do you feel? Illustrate.

7. How can a salesman effectively persuade a prospect if he feels the prospect is an obnoxious person? Explain.

8. Describe several situations which show a speaker revealing something about himself that he did not intend to reveal.

9. From a current newspaper or magazine editorial, select a positive statement that is charged with emotion. Quote it to several people but vary the supposed source, attributing the editorial first to a highly conservative and respected newspaper and then to a highly radical or yellow journal type of publication. Report their actions.

10. Describe situations in which you would use a two-sided presentation in selling cosmetics and sundries.

11. Give a one-sided argument to a friend and try to get him to agree in front of several other friends. Then try to persuade him to accept the opposite point of view and report the results in terms of the difficulties you encounter.

12. Present a completely impartial two-sided argument about a good novel you have read recently and ask your audience to indicate those who agree and those who disagree with your opinion. Explain the divergences and particularly why some have no opinion.

13. How would you determine the choice of a one- or two-sided sales presentation when selling air-conditioning equipment to an office manager?

14. Illustrate how fear might prevent the sale of life insurance and how many insurance salesmen attempt to avoid this mental block by their prospects.

15. What consumer products do you purchase because you like their radio or television commercials? Explain how the message motivates you to buy the product.

16. What consumer products do you purchase even though you dislike their radio or television commercials? Why?

17. Illustrate how ambiguity can aid in persuading a friend to go with you to a sporting event he had not planned to attend.

18. Listen to a favorite musical theme and count the number of times small portions repeat. Report the results in terms of repetition and repetition with variations affecting your original opinion.

19. Illustrate how a chemical salesman might use existing attitudes of an industrial prospect to motivate him to change his formula rather than stay with the old tried and proven chemicals.

20. How might a water softener salesman appeal to existing attitudes of a prospect who had not thought about such a product before?

# CHAPTER 11

1. When a clerk in an appliance store recites a brief memorized talk explaining the benefits of a television set, do you resent his presentation? Discuss briefly.

2. Why do you think doctors and college professors buy from salesmen using a canned talk?

3. How would you feel if the safe salesman discussed in this chapter picked up your mail and records as he started to leave? Why?

4. What products seem to be best suited to the stimulus-response method of sales presentation? Discuss in terms of the market and repeat call situations.

5. What tips off the audience to a canned talk when it is given professionally, with enthusiasm and conviction? Explain.

6. Discuss the advantages of a memorized sales presentation to the *prospect*.

7. How would you go about testing the effectiveness of different canned talks if you were the national sales manager of a company selling office machines?

8. What factors seem to help the salesman using a canned or planned talk when he works on a referral basis?

9. A disadvantage of a memorized sales talk seems to be its basic product orientation rather than customer orientation. Using a product with which you are familiar, show how this might be true.

10. Boredom is a problem with many salesmen who give the same memorized talk to every prospect. Compare this to the problem of an actor in a show that runs for 50 weeks on Broadway.

11. Do you think most consumers respond alike to various sales stimulants? Compare their behavior with that of professional people and with the behavior of industrial buyers.

12. Can a salesman so dominate a conversation that he literally forces a chain of thought in the listener's mind? Justify your answer.

# CHAPTER 12

1. In what way does formula selling seem to be an improvement over stimulus-response selling? Explain.

2. How might a man selling safes adapt his memorized talk, illustrated in Chapter 11, to the formula method? Outline the mental steps and the phrases he might use.

3. Using the AIDA formula, show how a salesman of industrial lubricants might prepare his sales presentation.

4. Select a product with which you are familiar and prepare an outline showing buying motivations and how you would utilize the formula method to solicit buying action.

5. Illustrate how you might vary your presentation on three successive calls to the same prospect, using the formula method on each of the calls.

6. Compare the AIDA formula with the six C's and Bert Schlain's formula. What similarities and differences do you recognize?

7. Illustrate how the concept of refractory phase is utilized both in education and in formula selling.

8. Show a friend a picture which has a considerable amount of written copy and talk to him while he reads. Then ask him questions about what he read and about what you said. Report the results.

9. In what way might formula selling be less effective than a memorized sales talk? Illustrate.

10. Using a product or service with which you are familiar, show how you might *justify* claims of benefits in order to build conviction in the mind of a prospect.

11. Illustrate the concept of formula selling by applying it to a sport or game which you enjoy.

12. Experiment using several friends to test the validity of the concepts of "You have got to tell 'em"; "You have got to show 'em to sell 'em"; "Get 'em to tell you!" Report the results in terms of speed of communications and audience acceptance of the message.

13. Many companies hire twice the number of sales trainees as the number of job openings in the belief that survival of the fittest will produce the best salesmen. Does this approach seem logical to you? Explain your answer.

14. Illustrate how you might get a prospect to believe you were a completely unbiased authority or else acting unselfishly in his behalf.

## EXERCISE

Conduct Leavitt's communication experiment at the end of Chapter 11, but change the geometric figures into three-dimensional objects. Add a third step to the experiment by using visual aids.

# CHAPTER 13

1. Construct four questions that cannot be answered with a "yes" or "no" or a very short answer relating to the need or use of a product with which you are familiar.

2. Construct four questions that will reflect the prospect's statements but elicit further details or additional information from him.

3. Construct four questions that will gain an honest statement of opinion rather than an answer influenced by the question. These questions should not be leading but open-ended.

4. Construct four questions that are indirect. Show the information you would like and the indirect question you would use to gain this information without revealing your own motives.

5. Experiment with a friend using the want-satisfaction strategy. Get him to discuss his ambitions and goals in life and afterward attempt to persuade him to take a course in public speaking to further his career. Report the results.

6. Illustrate how a businessman's needs or wants might be used to motivate him to purchase a new office building the same size as his existing building.

7. Do you think helping a man satisfy his inner wants and thereby change his buying behavior is manipulating him? Discuss your answer.

8. From your experience, show how the emotional needs and wants of a particular older person might be utilized by a salesman using the want-satisfaction strategy.

9. What emotional needs and wants might a young adult have that could be used to motivate a buying action? Illustrate your answer.

10. What emotional needs and wants might a 40-year-old professional purchasing agent have that might be used to motivate a change in his buying habits? Illustrate.

11. Illustrate how guilt feelings can cause a desire for self-punishment in a college situation, a criminal action, and, finally, in a business situation.

12. From your experience, illustrate several contradictory wants in one person at the same time. How is such a conflict resolved?

13. Show how a businessman could have an emotional want or need and not be aware of it. If the salesman simply stated this need, would the businessman be apt to accept it?

14. What organizational role do you think a corporate treasurer or comptroller might play in a pending purchase of computing machines?

15. Construct several questions which might elicit information about the aims and aspirations for the future which a businessman might have.

16. Look over the Foreign Flag Airlines article and answer the following:
    a. As sales manager, what strengths and weaknesses do you see?
    b. Do you feel the summarized presentation on the want-satisfaction method would be more effective for a new salesman? Explain your reasoning.
    c. How might you dramatize the advantages of using a particular airline?

# CHAPTER 14

1. Customers are direct and indirect. Direct customers are those to whom the business sells its product or service. Indirect customers are all others in the channel of distribution down to and including the ultimate consumer of the good. The smart producer looks beyond his direct customers. Show how this concept could be of aid to a salesman for a nylon manufacturer.

2. Robert W. Ferrell (in his *Customer-Oriented Planning* [American Management Association, N.Y.], p. 254) asserts that a corporation can only succeed as it focuses on profits—which, in a larger sense, means on sales, which, in a still larger sense, means on customers. The salesman must view his company and his actual and potential customers as engaged in mutual satisfaction, mutual profit—mutual growth. How does this concept compare with that of a salesman using the problem-solving method?

3. Show how the problem-solving sales method could be used to sell aluminum castings to an original equipment manufacturer of auto wheel drums.

4. Selling chemicals which are identical by definition can be extremely difficult. What can a salesman do to aid his customers and become a most favored supplier?

5. Show how value analysis might help a salesman perform a customer service to a manufacturer that is growing significantly in volume.

6. What results might be expected from having a buyer or value analyst visit the vendor's manufacturing facilities?

7. When a prospective customer specifies a special size, special thread, weight, and so on, what can the salesman do to help the buyer and himself in the long run?

8. Show how it might be advantageous to buy preplated or prepainted components for a manufacturer.

9. How might a salesman convince a customer to make a long-range commitment on certain basic parts other than a possible price advantage?

10. What advantages might accrue to a manufacturer of electric ovens if he switched from self-tapping screws to the use of rivets in final assembly?

11. Manufacturing and engineering personnel occasionally specify production tools on the basis of their technical aspects and neglect the commercial aspects. Show how a salesman using value analysis might earn the buyer's respect and gain an order.

12. Show how comparative information on buying and leasing equipment could be utilized to sell machine tools, lift trucks, and so forth to a manufacturer.

13. Show how a salesman might provide a genuine service through a study of material handling in a plant.

14. What priorities would you place on the amount and location of storage of parts and components used in manufacturing?

15. How might you use two-way radio and industrial television to expedite materials handling?

16. If a salesman wished to use the problem-solving method to review the

possibilities of containerization, palletization, and unitization as transportation cost-cutters, where might he obtain expert help in these areas?

17. What advantages can you list for alternate packaging materials—wood, metal, plastic, wire, strapping, corrugated boxes, bags?

18. What shortcuts might be possible to reduce paper work and effort in buying items for maintenance, repair, and operating supplies.

19. Read the article on Great Company Filters and answer these questions.

    1. As a sales trainee for this company, what part of this material do you feel would be most helpful? Explain.

    2. How might you dramatize the product or system if your presentation were made to a vice-president who was not oriented to a technical presentation?

    3. How do you feel prospects will react to Mr. Mason's comments about competition? Illustrate.

# CHAPTER 15

1. Show how the various selling strategies from a memorized talk through problem solving could be planned into a single presentation selling a new line of candy to a drug and variety store.
2. Illustrate a strategy which combines stimulus-response with problem solving in attempting to sell office furniture to an office manager.
3. How might a mutual fund salesman plan a combined strategy to sell his service to a man who was a foreman in a factory?
4. What combination of sales strategies might be successful in selling a line of women's knitted bathing suits to a department store in midwinter?
5. What factors in the psychology of persuasion might apply to a value analysis engineer considering the purchase of a new type of conveyor for a packaging plant?
6. Under what conditions do you think quoting a single firm price would be better than bargaining or negotiating a final price?
7. How might the depth method of selling be used by a management consultant firm which is geared to one-call closing?
8. Can telling a half-truth be more effective in building a long-term relationship with a customer than being completely honest? Illustrate your answer.
9. Hunches and guesses in judging prospects are giving way to careful quantification and logical evaluation. What types of information would you want to make an intelligent appraisal of a prospect for corrugated boxes?
10. Flexibility, energy, and creativity are said to be tomorrow's salesman's best assets. How might these attributes be related to the depth selling strategy?
11. Re-read Holly Merritt and Company and answer these questions.
    a) Do you feel the totally professional attitude is justified in this case? How might the presentation be made warmer but still maintain the necessary authority?
    b) What appears to be the main strength of this sales strategy and where might its weakness lie?
    c) Outline the progressive steps which were designed to lead to the sale as used in the presentation of the "findings" by Mr. Bayer.

# CHAPTER 16

1. It has been predicted that by 1980 distribution channels in many lines will be as different from today's as the modern supermarket is from the old-time general store. How might this affect team buying and team selling?

2. In routine buying situations the use of computers is likely to become commonplace, with a customer simply dropping a card into his data-processing machine which communicates instantly with the vendor's machine. What function will tomorrow's salesman serve under such conditions?

3. The cost of processing a single order in some industries encourages buyers to deal with as few suppliers as possible and to analyze their economic order quantity (E.O.Q.) If this trend continues, how will it affect tomorrow's salesman and what can he do to prepare himself better?

4. The trend toward sales specialization is already evident in many industries, with separate sales staffs for retailers, wholesalers, chains, supermarkets, governments, industrials, and so forth. How can trade associations help provide useful knowledge for the new specialty salesman?

5. Select a product or service with which you are familiar and predict how it will be produced or changed in ten years and what implications these changes may have for selling it.

6. How would you prepare to present a sales proposition of new transformers to the RCA value analysis team described early in this chapter?

7. What products or services do you think would be best sold through a team effort rather than an individual salesman?

8. When an experienced sales manager accompanies a young salesman and takes over to close the sale, could this be considered team selling? What similarities and differences do you recognize?

9. It was stated that it is often more effective to select men who are good salesmen and teach them the new technicalities than it is to teach technicians to become good salesmen. How do you feel about the validity of this statement?

10. Outline the various duties or functions which might be assigned to the different team members selling the freight transportation facilities of an international airline.

11. How might team selling be utilized to sell a custom-built prefabricated steel building for a manufacturing facility?

12. Credit insurance against the losses due to bad accounts receivable is normally sold to a committee of members of top management. Would this be an area for team selling? Explain.

13. New schools are being constructed throughout the country today and many school boards decide in committee what furniture and equipment shall be purchased. Illustrate how you would present your proposal to furnish such equipment to a school board.

14. A hospital often has a professional administrator to investigate requirements and issue purchase orders. However, a group of doctors may make

the buying decisions. Show how you might present a proposal to furnish new x-ray equipment to such a team of buyers.

15. How might packaging machinery, materials, and services be sold by a team effort on the part of a supplier?

# CHAPTER 17

1. Using the classified telephone directory of your community, select a line of business and construct two letters soliciting these accounts for an appointment for a personal sales visit. Vary the letters only in your choice of appeals.

2. If a vendor wishes to hold his share of an expanding market, what might be wrong with adding salesmen in proportion to the expanding market?

3. Interview five sales managers to learn their opinions on the amount of face-to-face time their salesmen spend with prospect decision makers. Report the results.

4. What disadvantages can you see to having an inside salesman supporting an outside salesman? Explain.

5. Telephone a friend while looking at yourself in the mirror. Attempt to smile most of the time and see if your friend comments on the pleasant tone of your voice. Report the results.

6. Construct a model, or matrix, showing results you might expect from a test mailing to three similar communities with two different messages using the split sample technique.

7. Compose a letter designed not to sell but to solicit inquiries for a home air-conditioning unit.

8. Where might you obtain a list of likely prospects for industrial water softener equipment?

9. Illustrate how a person might deny himself a product even though he was aware of the need and had the funds necessary to pay for it.

10. Show how a person might need a product but not be aware of his need. Would this person be a prospect? Explain.

11. Compose a brief telephone appeal to be used to invite a selected list of noncustomers to visit an automobile showroom when new models are to be introduced.

12. In soliciting an executive appointment by telephone, what element of news might you use when attempting to sell corrugated boxes?

13. Do you believe the use of the telephone to solicit sales appointments is an invasion of privacy? What do you feel should be done to reduce unethical practices regarding telephone selling?

14. Count the number of pieces of mail your family receives in one week. What percentage of the total was impersonal printed sales appeals?

15. Collect several envelopes which your family received illustrating an appeal to open and read the message rather than toss it out unopened. Describe the appeal.

# CHAPTER 18

1. Select a recent purchase of a novel, record, or article of clothing and analyze the various information or incidents which influenced you to buy in general and to select the one item in particular.

2. Ask members of your family about the various buying influences of a recent family purchase of a major appliance. Report as many attitudes as possible which influenced the final selection.

3. When a boy purchases cigarettes for his father, what buying influence does he play? Explain.

4. Select a product with which you are familiar which could be sold to business or industry and show how various executives could influence the buying decision.

5. What might a salesman say to a cold prospect in business or industry to gain information which he would use on subsequent visits?

6. During an interview how could you discover problems or needs of a prospective customer of new boiler equipment for a large building?

7. Assume a prospect has a need for a floor cleaning and maintenance service but is not aware of this need. How might the salesman create awareness without offending the prospect?

8. What legitimate service could a representative of a tire company offer to an owner of a gas station other than services directly related to the sale of tires?

9. How might advertising suggestions be offered by a camera salesman to benefit the owner of a drug store?

10. If you were selling adding machines to businessmen and one asked your advice on which brand of delivery truck he should buy, how would you handle the situation?

11. If you were the advertising manager for a company and a space salesman went over your head to sell a top executive, how would you treat this man in the future? What could he have done to maintain your goodwill before he went over your head?

12. Construct your opening remarks to gain friendly interest and mutual respect when selling a product with which you are familiar.

13. How might a token gift be used to gain acceptance to a busy executive when attempting to sell office furniture?

14. Assume you were the aircraft salesman illustrated in this chapter and had gained the support of the vice-president in charge of sales. What would you plan for dealing with the corporate treasurer?

# CHAPTER 19

1. How might you dramatize a sales presentation for accounting services to a small businessman?
2. How would you present a filing system such as the Dewey Decimal System to a business librarian to dramatize its presentation?
3. Flip charts have been used effectively to dramatize sales presentation but some buyers resent their use. When buyers resist the use of such visual aids what is apt to be their reasoning and how can the salesman alleviate their resistance?
4. What advantages and disadvantages can you visualize of using cartoon film strips to sell technical products to a technically trained specialist?
5. If a prospect picks up a sales portfolio early in the presentation and begins to leaf through the pages, apparently ignoring the salesman, what might the salesman do to increase his chances of making a sale?
6. What might you use to demonstrate and dramatize a new sales analysis service?
7. During a visual presentation to a professional buyer, a second man enters and observes noncommittally. How would you handle the situation? What would be your objective?
8. What personality factors do you notice when first meeting someone in a business situation? How might these apply to a salesman?
9. When one person in a group tends to monopolize a conversation, light a match and stare at it as long as it will stay lit. Report the reaction of the members, particularly of the dominant speaker.
10. How can visual aids be used to sell steel bars for use in manufacturing other products? Illustrate.
11. Of the various audio and visual aids with which you are familiar, describe the one that has the most appeal for you and tell why.
12. Illustrate how a salesman with only a pencil and paper can create visual aids on the spot to help persuade his prospect.
13. What products would best lend themselves to models or miniatures for demonstration purposes?
14. What is it about an advertisement appearing in a technical journal that lends creditability or prestige to the product?
15. List five products other than food which might be dramatized by their distinct odor. Describe how this could be used in sales.
16. List five products other than food which might be associated with another product or service and dramatized by their distinct taste. Explain how the mental association could be made.
17. Show how a physical demonstration of a product might change mild awareness to firm conviction in the mind of a prospective customer.
18. If audiovisual presentations are so effective, why don't sales companies send their salesmen out with a prepackaged sound film in many industries? What disadvantages can you visualize?

19. How might you get a reluctant professional buyer to participate in a physical demonstration of your product?

20. From your experience, illustrate how you or another changed a buying decision to a decision to wait a while longer when waiting for firm prices or other information from a vendor.

# CHAPTER 20

1. It has been stated the only objection that cannot be answered is the unknown or hidden objection. Show how you might encourage a prospect to state his real reason for not buying through the use of indirect and reflective questions.

2. How might you handle the buyer who objects to your proposition because he is satisfied with his existing source of supply?

3. What negative factors exist in a prospect's mind before the salesman makes his first call? What can the salesman plan to do to reduce this resistance?

4. Some sales strategies attempt to anticipate and answer all possible objections in the sales presentations before they are voiced by the prospect. Other strategies encourage the prospect to raise objections so the salesman can effectively deal with them. Which strategy do you prefer? Show the advantages and disadvantages of both.

5. Salesmen have been advised to acknowledge the apparent soundness of the prospect's point of view in dealing with objections. In other words, agree as far as possible with his thinking before providing an answer. Make a list of phrases which might be used to begin the answer to various objections.

6. How might you handle the prospect who states he likes your proposition and will buy but not now? What is the hidden objection built into this typical objection?

7. In what areas are reciprocal buying agreements weakest, assuming they are legal and voluntarily entered into?

8. Many manufacturers are integrating their market program to include direct ownership of retail outlets while still maintaining wholesale and distributor agents. A sales representative frequently is faced with the objection that his company is in direct competition with the prospect. How would you handle this objection?

9. A vendor who is new in a field can expect objections based upon his lack of experience. What might the sales representatives do to offset this objection?

10. If a prospect says he likes the sales proposition but he does not have the authority to purchase, what should the salesman do? Suppose this is the situation but the prospect does *not* admit he has no authority. How would this change the sales strategy?

11. If a prospect obviously intends to heckle a salesman to get out of seriously considering the proposition, what can the salesman do?

12. Suppose, on the first call, a purchasing agent begins the interview with an aggressive blast against the vendor and that industry in general about its pricing structure. What should the salesman do? What might he say?

13. How can a salesman determine a prospect's attitude regarding his desire to bargain on price or his wanting a single firm price?

14. Much industrial and business capital equipment is offered for sale or alternately for lease. List both the advantages and disadvantages of each of these methods of acquisition.

15. If a qualified prospect states in a firm manner that he is not ready to make a decision now, what might the salesman do to keep an open channel of communication?

16. Price objections can take a variety of forms and are often used simply to dismiss a persistent salesman. What strategy can a salesman employ to handle price objections?

17. While most sales propositions for competitive products seem relatively equal, what can the individual salesman do to make his proposition stand out above the competitor's?

18. Show how a salesman can draw a prospect out to state and answer his own objections so the salesman need not risk contradicting or arguing with the prospect.

19. When a prospect objects to dealing with a relatively young salesman, what can the latter do to earn the prospect's trust?

20. Illustrate the effect of cross-pressures causing a prospect to postpone purchasing something he needs and wants. What can the salesman do to encourage a buying decision?

# CHAPTER 21

1. Assume you were trying to sell paper to a printer who is dissatisfied with his present supplier. The close seems at hand since you are in agreement and he is about ready to sign the order. But then he says, "It seems logical but I had better check with some of my friends." How would you handle the situation?

2. Illustrate how you might attempt to close a sale in the first few minutes of a presentation, in the middle of a presentation, at the end after answering an objection, and finally after receiving two refusals.

3. Give five phrases which might be used as a trial close when attempting to sell a fleet of trucks to an interstate carrier.

4. How can a salesman permit the prospect to talk freely when the salesman senses the time to close may slip by and be lost?

5. Obtaining a buying decision implies more than the phrase "close an order." Discuss the implications and differences as you view them.

6. In your opinion does a new salesman, fresh from training, know more about his specialty than the average buyer he will meet? Explain.

7. Can a salesman help a legitimate prospect make an intelligent decision to satisfy his desires if the salesman is compensated on a commission basis? Explain your viewpoint.

8. When a prospect seems to be slow and deliberate in coming to a decision, what should the salesman do to increase his choices for a favorable decision?

9. A sales presentation is normally based upon those points considered most important for a particular prospect. Illustrate how this strategy permits additional selling points to be kept in reserve for the close without weakening the basic presentation.

10. Illustrate the assumptive closing technique in selling a product with which you are familiar.

11. Show how the summary closing technique might boomerang when selling a cola vending machine service to the manager of a company-owned cafeteria.

12. How might a close on a minor point be achieved by a salesman representing a machine-tool manufacturer?

13. Select a product with which you are familiar and illustrate how a contingent close might be effective.

14. Check the "Sales Help Wanted" advertisements in the newspapers and select one which asks for a strong closer. What do you think the employer is looking for in salesmen? Explain.

15. The standing room only closing technique is very similar to the political bandwagon technique. What types of products or services might lend themselves to this technique and what ones would not?

16. How do you react when a salesman, refusing to accept your turndown of his product, offers you a second price considerably lower than his first asking price? Describe your attitude.

17. Discount stores seem to be increasing in importance in America. What advantages and disadvantages can you visualize if this phenomenon continues?

18. If you were exposed to a two-man close with one salesman acting in your behalf and the other acting as a forceful enthusiastic agent of the vendor, how would you react? Describe your attitude.

19. Using a product with which you are familiar, show how you might use a negative close or snob appeal to obtain a favorable buying decision.

20. If an industrial buyer gave you his verbal permission and his order number, stating that his written confirmation would follow, what would you do when you got back to your office and found a message to cancel his order?

# CHAPTER 22

1. Illustrate how two competitive offerings of smoking pipes to a retail tobacco shop might differ even though their price structure was the same.

2. What would you expect from the vendor and manufacturer of a portable typewriter beyond the physical product itself?

3. Assume part of the profits from your product are invested in research and development. How might this apparent extra cost be justified to a prospect? Illustrate.

4. Various advertising and sales promotional campaigns are very expensive and this cost is included in the selling price. How might this extra cost be justified to a prospect? Illustrate.

5. What disadvantages might be inherent in a simple cost plus profit formula for setting prices in a retail store?

6. Illustrate how you might sell up to a super deluxe model if you represented a manufacturer of a complete line of business machines such as calculators

7. Show how you might use the strategy of selling down without making it difficult to subsequently go back up to the highest priced model. Illustrate.

8. Assume you were representing a manufacturer of earthmoving equipment and attempting to sell a construction contractor. If your equipment were priced at $17,000 while most competitors' models were priced around $15,000, how would you handle the situation? Illustrate.

9. List the reasons you think a low priced inferior quality product might better serve a buyer than a well-built but more expensive product.

10. Under what conditions might a vendor be willing to suffer a loss in pricing his product below cost?

11. To emphasize profit, some vendors compensate their sales representatives on a percentage of net profit. What problems might arise if a competitor started a price war?

12. Do you think there is too much government control over marketing policies? Justify your opinion.

13. How would you explain an "early order" discount to satisfy a buyer who waited too long to take advantage of it?

14. What dangers or disadvantages can you visualize which might occur if, as a buyer, you forced a vendor to discount his selling price to the point of breaking even?

15. How might the consuming public be hurt as a result of a price war between a number of competing companies?

16. What should govern the credit acceptance of an order by a new account? Explain.

17. Illustrate how the credit department and the salesman can operate to each other's mutual benefit.

18. Select an industry or trade which interests you and investigate the credit terms they offer to their customers. Note the variation and explain the probable credit policies behind such differences.

19. Do you believe a salesman should be held responsible for making the final decision on credit? Justify your opinion.

20. If a prospect cannot afford to pay cash for the things he needs in business, what other sources of financial assistance can he obtain other than credit from the vendor?

21. What changes might occur to a business which could move it from a good credit risk to a bad risk in a very short time? Would a credit manager in a distant home office be aware of such changes?

22. How might the credit files in the home office of a supplier aid a salesman assigned to a new territory?

# CHAPTER 23

1. In the depression days of the 1930s some economists held that the consumer was king. In the early 1960s some sociologists and psychologists portrayed the consumer as an idiot who could easily be misled. What do you think of the consumer today and how does business relate itself to such an opinion?

2. From your experience buying merchandise in a new store or in a strange community, show how your initial behavior might have been tentative and full of doubts. What caused you to return or, as the case may be, to stay away in the future?

3. Do you think it is fair to judge an employer by the after-hours behavior of his sales representatives? Discuss your opinions.

4. Large corporations often value their goodwill in the millions of dollars yet they do not show this on their annual financial statements. Beyond the fact that goodwill is an intangible asset, what might cause these companies to withhold setting a dollar evaluation on goodwill? Explain.

5. Do you believe *quid pro quo*—something given for something received—is limited in its application to just a commercial selling situation? Illustrate your opinion.

6. How might a person's activities outside of his job reflect in his day-to-day business behavior with other people?

7. If a manufacturer has a research and development department or a new product development manager, what is apt to be their attitude regarding a new salesman who constantly submits ideas or customer requests for changes?

8. Since selling time is precious, do you think it it is wise to show a customer how to get greater use from the product particularly if he does not ask for such help? Explain.

9. Do you know a person who is a poor loser in cards or sports? How do others react when he suggests they play together? Relate this to the maturing process observed in teen-agers.

10. Assume you were selling advertising space for a large national magazine. What nonbuying accounts might you select for long-range cultivation? Explain the reasons for your choice.

11. Small fill-in orders received between the salesman's regular visits are often a nuisance and unprofitable to the supplier. What purpose does it serve to fill such orders and how might the salesman improve such a situation?

12. How might a corporate public relations staff serve the distant salesman out in the field to build goodwill with his customers and prospective customers?

13. If you disagree with a friend's attitude or prejudice about a minority group, do you think you can change his ideas by arguing? How might you broaden his outlook over a period of several years?

14. Do you believe entertaining customers imposes an unfair obligation on the buyer? What would be your objective in using entertainment?

15. Assume a customer phones you voicing a complaint. Show how you might use this situation to sell more merchandise in the future.

16. How might a salesman diplomatically reduce or eliminate a customer's abuse of services such as return privileges?

# CHAPTER 24

1. What products do you purchase with little or no deliberation? Might you change brands simply because a friend suggested it? Discuss the implications in terms of propaganda *vs.* economics.

2. Illustrate how a product promoted for its prestige value to the owner can lose its appeal if it becomes too common.

3. One authority notes that buying life insurance or taking out a loan is often considered to be proof of adulthood and masculinity by the individual himself. Do you think a direct appeal to such motives would be apt to boomerang? Discuss your opinion.

4. How do you react when someone begins to tell you what is good for you, assuming you did not ask for his opinion?

5. List the outstanding characteristics of an important student or professor whom you have not seen. How many of these attributes did you list because you have heard them many times? Discuss the validity of such opinions.

6. Consider your high school days and list several shortcomings of your school's big rival as you believed they were when still in high school. Show how this might relate to the name-calling propaganda technique.

7. Ask a friend to attempt to sell a novel to you which he has not read. Report his use of glittering generalities and rewards and his avoidance of logic.

8. Collect five advertisements which illustrate direct testimonial and five which illustrate transfer. Compare the effectiveness of the two techniques.

9. Collect five advertisements which clearly promote one product and more subtly show a second product in a favorable association. Show all five ads to a friend and then ask him to name the five different sponsors. Discuss his reaction to the five hidden tie-in sponsors.

10. Analyze the copy in a few advertisements or "canned" sales presentations in the light of the general discussion of propaganda in this chapter.

11. Discuss the problem of choice and emphasis among media in the conduct of a marketing campaign.

12. Illustrate how the technique of "plain folks" might be used successfully by a small manufacturer of automobiles.

13. Assume you were selling imported glass to a retail glazier. What facts might you intentionally withhold from the prospect in an attempt to stack the cards in your favor? What reaction would you expect?

14. Analyze the copy in a few advertisements which use the "bandwagon" technique to persuade consumers to buy. Report your findings.

15. Political campaigns often use many of the propaganda techniques discussed in this chapter and politicians do get elected. Why do well-informed people vote for a candidate who uses irrational or misleading persuasion techniques?

16. A persuasion monopoly by a private company can exist in a given community for such services as telephone, electricity, and water. How do such utility companies handle their corporate image? Illustrate.

17. Assume a prospect is satisfied with his existing supplier. Show how a competitor might utilize the principles of persuasion competition against a most favored source.

18. How might you use irrational or misleading persuasion techniques in selling without harm to either the customers or the vendor?

19. Do you believe the various propaganda techniques discussed in this chapter would work better on old existing accounts? Explain.

# CHAPTER 25

1. Efficiency and economy have long been stressed in production facilities while marketing has been left to those who practice an art. List the various functions of marketing and attempt to cite studies which measure its effectiveness.

2. How would you justify the sales costs or commissions paid on an expensive accounting machine to an irate customer?

3. Investigate the buying policy of a large corporation and report how they handle the fact that they have tremendous bargaining power over suppliers.

4. When a customer forces the vendor to lower his price, what is the customer apt to lose while he gains a lower acquisition cost?

5. What services can food suppliers offer to help supermarkets and grocery stores increase their profits?

6. Do you believe an effective salesman can discover customer needs for new or improved products before the customer himself is aware of such needs? Illustrate.

7. How much time and effort do you think it would take a doctor to learn of the new medical products and new developments every month in this specialty field if he had no contact with salesmen? How would this apply in another field of selling? Illustrate.

8. Many products today are considered, if not necessities, basic to a new home. Show how these products 20 years ago had to be sold through expensive communications and personal persuasion.

9. Illustrate how inertia has prevented you from making a purchase of something which you needed and could afford.

10. What would you like to do to improve yourself or your enjoyment of life that could not have been possible ten or fifteen years ago? Show how this helps to justify marketing costs.

11. It has been said, a specialist is one who learns more and more about less and less until he knows all about—nothing! How might this apply to the salesman who learns more and more about selling?

12. Why are effective salesmen more apt to become top executives than equally effective men in other phases of business?

13. Select a sales field with which you are familiar and construct a job analysis to determine what the salesmen really do. Relate the job specifications to an applicant.

14. Assume you were representing a chemical company selling to paper mills in the southeastern states and had 120 accounts. How would you control your time and energy to optimize your coverage of these accounts.

15. Before calling on industrial prospects you will want to select information in several areas. What general variables should be considered before making the sales call?

16. If seven personal sales interviews per day is a realistic full day's work, would

it be wise for an ambitious salesman to try to average nine such visits a day? Discuss your reasons.

17. For many people the written word carries more authority than the spoken word. What justification can you cite for this attiude?

18. What dangers are inherent in feigning friendliness with customers in social situations?

19. If you were a sales manager in the home office of a national company, how would you judge the different salesmen in the field? List the criteria you might use.

20. An effective salesman serves his customers yet is expected to be a leader and to work independently. Explain this apparent paradox.

# Index

*This book has been set in 10 point Electra
with Cursive, leaded 3 points, and 9 point
Electra, leaded 2 points. Chapter numbers are
in 24 point Lydian Arabic; chapter titles are
in 18 point Lydian Bold. The size of the type
page is 27 by 45 picas.*